# Banking in India

# Banking in India

M.S. Shetty

ATLANTIC
PUBLISHERS & DISTRIBUTORS (P) LTD

Published by
**ATLANTIC**
**PUBLISHERS & DISTRIBUTORS (P) LTD**
7/22, Ansari Road, Darya Ganj,
New Delhi-110002
Phones : +91-11-40775252, 23273880, 23275880, 23280451
Fax : +91-11-23285873
Web : www.atlanticbooks.com
E-mail : orders@atlanticbooks.com

Branch Office
5, Nallathambi Street, Wallajah Road,
Chennai-600002
Phones : +91-44-64611085, 32413319
E-mail : chennai@atlanticbooks.com



ISBN: 978-81-269-1817-1



Printed in India at Glorious Printers, A-13, D.S.I.D.C.,
Jhilmil Industrial Area, Delhi-110095

# Preface

Banking in India in the modern sense originated towards the end of the 18th century. The first banks were Bank of Hindustan and The General Bank of India, which started in 1770 and 1786 respectively, but both are now defunct. The still existing oldest bank in India is State Bank of India. India's Partition in 1947 after Independence adversely impacted the economies of Punjab and West Bengal, paralyzing banking activities for months. India's Independence also marked the end of a regime of the laissez-faire for the Indian banking. The Government of India initiated measures to play an active role in the economic life of the nation, and the industrial policy resolution ushered in by the Government in 1948 envisaged a mixed economy. This resulted into greater involvement of the state in different segments of the economy including banking and finance.

Several steps were taken by the Government to regulate banking in India. The Reserve Bank of India, India's central banking authority, was established in April 1935 but was nationalized on 1 January 1949. The Banking Regulation Act, 1949 was enacted which empowered the RBI "to regulate, control, and inspect the banks in India". The Act also provided that no new bank or branch of an existing bank could be opened without a license from the RBI, and no two banks could have common directors. Despite the provisions, control and regulations of RBI, banks in India except State Bank of India continued to be owned and operated by private persons. By the 1960s, the Indian banking industry had become an important tool to facilitate the development of Indian economy.

An ordinance was issued in 1969 and 14 large commercial banks were nationalized. These banks contained 85 per cent of bank deposits in the country. Six more commercial banks were nationalized in 1980. The stated reason for the nationalization was to give the Government more control of credit delivery. With this second phase of nationalization, the Government of India controlled around 91 per cent of the banking business of India. Later on, in the year 1993, the Government merged New Bank of India with Punjab National Bank. It was the only merger between nationalized banks and resulted in the reduction of the number of nationalized banks from 20 to 19. After this, until the 1990s, the nationalized banks grew at a pace of around 4 per cent, closer to the average growth rate of the Indian economy.

In the early 1990s, under its policy of privatization and liberalization, the Government issued licenses to some private banks. These came to be known as new generation tech-savvy banks, and included Global Trust Bank (the first of such new generation banks), which later amalgamated with Oriental Bank of Commerce, UTI Bank (now renamed Axis Bank), ICICI Bank and HDFC Bank. This move, along with the rapid growth in the economy of India, revitalized the banking sector in India, which has seen rapid growth with strong contribution from all the three sectors of banks, namely government banks, private banks and foreign banks.

The new policies that are obtaining in banks in India have discarded much of what may be called traditional style of functioning. There are extended hours of work and public dealing in the banks these days. Through the CBS system, a group of networked branches provide core banking services to the customers. The new developments have ushered in a modern outlook and tech-savvy methods of working in the banks. All this has led to the retail boom in India. People have not just demanded more from their banks but also received more.

Banking in India is now fairly mature in terms of product range and reach. Even the rural areas are covered in the network of banking in India—mostly through public sector banks. In terms of quality of assets and capital adequacy, Indian banks are considered to have clean, strong and transparent balance sheets as compared to banks in other economies in the region. The RBI is an autonomous body, with minimal pressure from the Government. The stated policy of the apex bank on the Indian rupee is to manage volatility but without any fixed exchange rate.

With the growth in the Indian economy expected to be strong in future, particularly in its services sector, the demand for banking services, especially retail banking, mortgages and investment services will remain strong. We may also expect mergers and acquisitions, takeovers, and asset sales. In March 2006, the RBI allowed Warburg Pincus to increase its stake in Kotak Mahindra Bank to 10 per cent. This was the first time an investor was allowed to hold more than 5 per cent in a private sector bank since the RBI announced norms in 2005 that any stake exceeding 5 per cent in the private sector banks would need to be vetted by them.

The IT revolution has had a great impact in the Indian banking system. The use of computers has introduced online banking in India. The use of the modern innovations and computerization of the banking sector of India have increased after the economic liberalization of 1991 as the country's banking sector has been exposed to the world's market. The Indian banks were finding it difficult to compete with the international banks in terms of the customer service without the use of the information technology and computers. The new policy has focused on computerization of branches and increasing connectivity among branches through computers. There is Electronic Funds Transfer (EFT) system, with the BANKNET communications network as its carrier. MICR clearing system is also in place. It is being extended to all branches of all banks with more than 100 branches. The new Private Sector banks in India have the largest numbers of ATMs followed by off-site ATMs belonging to SBI and then by new private banks, nationalized banks and foreign banks.

The book provides a history of banking in India, from the origin of money and banking to the present scenario of technology-driven services. The aspects related directly and indirectly to banking have been studied. Banks in India from the 18th century, different types of banks in India, bank credit, banker-customer relationship, foreign exchange business, non-performing assets, financial sector reforms, risk management, Basel Accord, rupee convertibility, technology developments in India, social responsibility of banks and Right to Information Act (RTI) are the major topics taken up in this book. A peep into the future of banking in India has also been given.

Banking is a vast subject and is perpetually evolving with the introduction of new policies and systems. It is not practicable to put everything in detail in a book. Each subject demands volumes of books to analyze it properly. For the student of banking and the staff working in banks, concise information on various aspects is more useful. That is what this book aims to provide.

Topics like NPA, risk management, Basel Accord, KYC guidelines are for the understanding the implications they have on banking. Topics like cheques, clearing systems, deposit accounts, current accounts, equitable mortgage and advances are for understanding the basics of banking.

The book will be useful for the students of banking, bank staff and those preparing for competitive examinations. To those who wish to learn about banking in India, it will provide for a richly rewarding and inculcating reading.

**M.S. Shetty**

# Acknowledgements

My years of service with the bank from 1971 to 2010 were a long journey and I saw major changes happening in banking in the country. The evolution of banking always interested me, as I was a keen learner. This book is an attempt to record all the major issues and events of banking as they took place.

History of Indian banking is interesting though not much research has gone into it. In compiling the facts, the major support is from RBI's recorded history on Indian banking and its evolution. I am indebted to the apex bank for using its database. I also acknowledge with thanks all the banks in the country, all Indian financial institutions from whose records/sites I have gathered useful information about those banks and also other topics on banking.

My endeavour is to create a short history of Indian banking. For this purpose, I have tried to collect information from many sources like RBI, SBI, *The Cambridge Economic History of India*, Volume 2 (by Dharma Kumar, Tapan Raychaudhuri and Meghnad Desai); *The History of British India: A Chronology* (by John F. Riddick); *An Economic History of India: From Pre-Colonial Times to 1991* (by Dietmar Rothermund); *Modern Banking in India* (by S.K. Muranjan), and Wikipedia. I hereby acknowledge these sources and thank the authorities and authors.

This book is not exhaustive and the statistics and data are used for highlighting the importance of the topic and making it more authentic.

I again thank all the banks and authorities whose websites I have visited and borrowed the contents from there to make this book rich with facts.

**M.S. Shetty**

# Contents

# Origin of Money and Banking

# 1

## Origin of Money

Money in simple terms means cash. Money represents the purchasing power stored by people who hold cash with them. We all know that Government of India (GOI) through Reserve Bank of India (RBI) prints the currency notes and also mints the coins which are then put into circulation for use by public. In fact, RBI is entrusted with the responsibility of managing the same on behalf of the Government of India.

Origin of money is as old as the civilization of nations in the world. Money in the form of coins was in use from time immemorable. India was one leading country in coinage. It was believed that coins were in use in India almost six hundred years BC. It is also known that many kings in the past issued silver or gold coins with inscriptions, which were in use.

Ancient India, is one of the earliest issuers of coins in the world (circa 6th century BC), along with the Chinese *wen* and Lydian *staters*. The origin of the word "rupee" is found in the word rūp or rūpā, which means "silver" in many Indo-Aryan languages such as Hindi. The Sanskrit word rupyakam means coin of silver. The derivative word Rūpaya was used to denote the coin introduced by Sher Shah Suri during his reign from 1540 to 1545 CE. The original Rūpaya was a silver coin weighing 175 *grains* troy (about 11.34 grams). The coin has been used since then, even during the times of British India.

Formerly the rupee was divided into 16 *annas*, 64 paise, or 192 *pies*. (*Source*: Wikipedia)

In modern era, after the arrival of the British in the country, the recorded history reveals that in the year 1672, the Governor of Bombay, Mr. Gerald Aunger established the first British mint in India. At first only Copper and Tin coins were made. Use of silver began in 1675 and the same year the mint began the production of Indian rupee. In 1775, Govt. directed that all Indian coinage be made at Calcutta mint in order to seek a level of standardization. It was also known that Indian cowrie shells were in use as small denomination coins and in 1787, Warren Hastings, John Princep and Mr. Ross combined to mint and introduced the copper pice as a replacement to cowrie shells for small financial transactions. In 1835, East India Company introduced the company's rupee as the uniform currency in British India.

Immediately after independence, the British coinage was continued. The Monetary System remained unchanged at one rupee consisting of 64 *pice*, or 192 *pies*.

The 1955 Indian Coinage (Amendment) Act that came into force with effect from 1 April 1957 introduced a "Decimal series". The rupee was now divided into 100 'paisa' instead of 16 *annas* or 64 pice.

Legal currency of the country is rupee—originally is a silver coin. Government of India (GOI) issued one-rupee notes later during wartime as silver became short in supply. It is the legal currency and along with the coins, rupees form the actual currency of the country. They are legal tender and nobody can refuse accepting it in discharge of monetary obligation by anyone. Besides this, RBI also issues bank notes in the denomination of 2, 5, 10, 20, 50, 100, 500, and 1000-rupee notes. Currency notes in denomination of 5000 and 10000 were also issued earlier which were subsequently demonetized in the year 1978.

Use of Paper currency/bank notes in the country also has a long history. The British Agency Houses who acted as banks in the initial period starting from 1767 were reported to have issued bank notes. The first bank to issue bank notes was the bank of Hindustan started in 1770 by an Agency House. Few other banks of that period also issued bank notes. This function was then taken over by three presidency banks (bank of Bengal, bank of Bombay and bank of Madras) started in 1806, 1840 and 1843 who issued bank notes. It is also known that State Bank of Hyderabad (1941) issued its currency–Osmania Sikka, in pre-independence period.

Paper Currency Act was passed in the year 1861 and the Govt. took over the note printing from the presidency banks. Thereafter this function was transferred to RBI after its formation. At present Issue Dept. of RBI is managing it. The coins are issued as per provisions of Coinage Act passed in the year 1906.

Bank notes issued by RBI contain a promise to pay the amount. In fact, RBI issues these as bearer promissory notes. For this reason, no other individual or company can issue any bill of exchange, hundi, promissory note payable to bearer on demand (section 31 of RBI Act, 1934). Others can only issue order promissory notes. Bearer promissory note assumes the status of cash and hence the prohibition to issue it, by other than the central bank of the country. Section 26 of RBI Act, 1934 prescribes banknotes as legal tender and that it carries the guarantee of the central government. Hence the word 'promise to pay' appearing on the bank notes has no special meaning and nobody can invoke the promise as bank note itself is the legal tender. The word 'promise to pay' is in fact is the past legacy of bank notes when it started originally as a promissory note and hence contained a promise by the bank issuing it.

RBI maintains sufficient currency in its currency chests. These chests are also attached to banks who on behalf of RBI manage the same. It is like a currency godown. However, the difference is that the currency notes lying in the chests are not valid money till such time they are taken out of the chest and put to circulation. These godowns are maintained to ensure that currency notes are available at every part of the country as per demand.

As per law, notes can be printed to the extent the Issue Deptt. is holding eligible assets against such issue. However replacements of old notes can be done by the dept. Historically the reserves against the notes issues was in the form of gold to maximum extent and other eligible securities to some extent. Now the gold reserve has become smaller in proportion to other eligible securities.

RBI regularly publishes the currency statistics, which gives the total currency in circulation and is with the public. This is called cash with public. The statistics also gives Money Stock or Broad Money or M3, which includes demand deposits with banks, term deposits with banks, and some other deposits with RBI.

## Origin of Banking

Money enabled everyone to earn and save their labour in the form of money, which they can use later. Money represents value stored for future use by the owner. If he keeps it with himself, the purchasing power of that money is blocked and cannot be used by anyone else. However, when the money is lent to someone, may be on certain condition, then the purchasing power of the money is put to use immediately by that someone and the original owner still has a promise and security to get back his money when he actually needs it.

Thus, it became obvious that some sort of pooling of money saved by owners and bringing it back to circulation can spur the economic activity. The problem is how to make the owners to agree for the arrangement of pooling. They will have to be amply assured of the arrangement as otherwise they will not have faith to handover their money.

Then the indigenous bankers came on the scene who are the forerunners of present day financial system. They provided services like safe keeping of the money, transfer of money from one place to another and lastly giving loans either on security or otherwise.

### *Origin of Banking in the World*

Banking activity was recorded from all the ancient civilisations like Mesopotamia, Greece, Rome, India, China, etc. Banking is as old as civilisation itself and existed in some form or other in all the above mentioned civilisations. It is learnt that the banking activity in Mesopotamia and Greece were started by temples. Records prove existence of banking in 18th century BC in Babylon.

During medieval time, banking was present in Europe, in all countries, mostly controlled by moneylenders and was mostly family owned business.

Organised banks in way made their appearances in Europe in 14th century onwards.

Banca Monte dei Paschi di Siena S.p.A. (MPS) is the oldest surviving bank in the world. Founded in 1472 by the Magistrate of the city-state of Siena, Italy, as a Mount of Piety, it has been operating ever since. Today it consists of approximately 3 thousand branches, 33 thousand employees and 4.5 million customers in Italy, as well as branches and businesses abroad.

### *Origin of Banking in India*

"Globally, the story of banking has much in common, as it evolved with the moneylenders accepting deposits and issuing receipts in their place. According to the Central Banking Enquiry Committee (1931), money lending activity in India could be traced back to the Vedic period, i.e., 2000 to 1400 BC. The existence of professional banking in India could be traced to the 500 BC. Kautilya's *Arthashastra*, dating back to 400 BC contained references to creditors, lenders and lending rates. Banking was fairly varied and catered to the credit needs of the trade, commerce, agriculture as well as individuals in the economy. Mr. W.E. Preston, member, Royal Commission on Indian Currency and Finance set up in 1926, observed "...it may be accepted that a system of banking that was eminently suited to India's then requirements was in force in that country many centuries before the science of banking became an accomplished fact in England". An extensive network of Indian banking houses existed in the country connecting all cities/towns that were of commercial importance. They had their own inland bills of exchange or hundis which were the major forms of transactions between Indian bankers and their trans-regional connections. Banking practices in force in India were vastly different from the European counterparts. The dishonoring of hundis was a rare occurrence. Most banking worked on mutual trust, confidence and without securities and facilities that were considered essential by British bankers. Northcote Cooke observed "...the fact that Europeans are not the originators of banking in this country does not strike us with surprise". Banking regulation also had a rich tradition and evolved along with banking in India. In fact, the classic *Arthashastra* also had norms for banks going into liquidation. If anyone became bankrupt, debts owed to the State had priority over other creditors (Leeladhar, 2007").

(*Source:* RBI—Evolution of Banking in India)

Banking business is not a new concept in Indian society. There were indigenous bankers in every part of the country. There were Shroffs, Sahukars, Mahajans and other moneylenders. Even Jewelers also acted as pawn brokers and provided loans against gold ornaments. In villages, there were Sahukars whose business is to provide loans even to poor farmers. Zamindars at many places, also acted like moneylenders. However, there was exploitation to some extent as these people charged usurious interest rates and many a time cheated illiterates out of their valuable assets including land. Practice of Bonded labour was also prevalent, wherein for repaying the loan taken, the borrower had to work for lender, sometimes for the whole life, and in some cases the bond extended to the heirs who also remained as bonded labour.

Mostly these indigenous bankers of different hues lent their own money and few accepted deposits from others for using it for this purpose. Wealthy businessmen also acted as lenders some time, in many places. We were told that there were such wealthy businessmen and sometimes even the kings borrowed from them.

When the business and society felt the need for financial services like transfer of money from one place to another, a new breed of bankers came on the scene, who provided this service. These bankers operated from many centres or had associates at different centres and provided remittance facility. Mostly they issued promissory notes popularly called as hundies for this purpose, which were honoured by their office or associates. This was in great use and these bankers created good reputation for themselves. Businessmen started using their facilities. This type of bankers existed in places like Bengal, Uttar Pradesh, and Gujarat, which were important centres for trade and commerce. There are many who are functioning even today and have developed their business on the very lines of a modern day bank.

Banking activities were in the hands of indigenous bankers. They played an important role and in the process, they became financial intermediaries. The definition of banking took shape as acceptor of deposits for the purpose lending it and maintaining the trust of the depositors by returning their money when demanded by them.

This basic definition of banking still holds good, with some additional functions by the modern day banks. Banks maintain accounts for both depositors and borrowers wherein the balance is maintained on daily basis in the books of the bank. Once money is deposited or loan taken, the physical cash is converted into a book entry by the bank. This book entry and the account becomes primary and original record for the depositors and borrowers.

In India, during the Mauryan period (from 321 to 185 BC), a commercial instrument called 'adesha' was in use, which was an order on a banker desiring him to pay the money of the note to a third person, which corresponds to the definition of a cheque.

Cheque is a written order to the bank/banker to pay specified amount and debit it to customers account. Later, cheques were made as an instrument, which can be acted upon by the bank without insisting for the presence of account holder, as bank knew the signature of its customer. Further, the cheques were modified to suit other requirement like—it can be a bearer cheque in which case the bank need not ask for identity of the person receiving the payment. It can be made payable to order, in which case bank is bound to identify the payee before making payment.

Trade and commerce extensively used cheques, to settle payments and because of their regular usage, many practices in handling cheques by banks came into existence. Subsequently Negotiable Instruments Act 1881 enacted by the Government gave legal sanctity to these practices of the banks. Many countries in the world enacted negotiable instruments acts around the same time.

# Banks in India from 18th Century

2

## Banks in India—18th Century

Banks in organised sector made appearances in the country only in the later part of the 18th century. Before this the banking scene was dominated by indigenous bankers and after British occupation, by agency houses who also acted as banks.

### *Indigenous Bankers*

Before the banks in joint-stock sectors came into picture, trade and commerce was mostly dependent on the indigenous bankers for their banking requirements. History tells us about existence of many such bankers. Notable amongst them were Muslim moneylenders of Trichinopally district in Tamil Nadu, Chettiars of Tamil Nadu, Jagat Sheths of Bengal, the Shahs of Patna, Arjunji Nathji of Surat, and Gopaldas of Benares. These indigenous bankers were big time bankers, had good reputations and were known in most part of the country. It is recorded that even the East India Company in the initial years, used the services of these indigenous bankers. It is part of banking history that in the year 1782, East India Company announced that the House of Gopaldas would replace Jagat Sheth as Govt. of Bengal banker.

These indigenous bankers were reported to be wealthy and influential and had their branches and associates at many centres. It is reported that they have been lending to traders and farmers. They were reported to have financed kings and later East India Company. Many of them acted as bankers to governments and their network was used by the princely states for collection of revenues and tax. Besides taking deposits and lending, they were also involved in minting coins. These bankers extensively used Hundies as an instrument for transferring money.

Few of the big and important indigenous bankers known were as under:

### House of Jagat Sheth

- House of Jagat Sheth was started in the earlier part of 18th century and was in business for many generations. It is believed that House of Jagat Sheth financed the English leading to the fall of Nawab Siraj-Ud-Daulah in Bengal in 1757. It is said that House of Jagat Sheth had its monopoly of the mint, currency business and banking sectors of Bengal, Bihar and Orissa for over 100 years between the 18th and 19th centuries. The house had served as the East India Company's official banker for years. The Jagat Sheth House was the most influential bank at a time when there was no formal or regular banking in the subcontinent. They had their merchant and loan offices in Dhaka, Calcutta (now Kolkata) and Murshidabad. These loan offices extended their lending activities to rural areas and gave short-, medium- and long-term credit at a 40-50% rate of interest.

(*Source:* Banking on the page of history: Asiatic Society seminar: focuses on how the sector went from strength to strength by Sajjadur Rahman published on 2010-02-19.)

### House of Gopal Das

- House of Gopal Das was a contemporary banker to House of Jagat Sheth, which also had good reputation. It also acted as banker to government of Bengal for some time. The Gopaldas Manohardas family was founded sometime in the seventeenth century in northern India. It provided credit and currency exchange services to its clients. The clients of the business included local landowners and the East

India Company. The business was based in Benares and it had branches in 52 cities throughout India.

### *Arunji Nathji*

- Arunji Nathji founded the family business of 'Travadis' in the early eighteenth century at Surat. Arunji Nathji had access to the Mughal court and started his business career as a moneylender. He was succeeded by his son Shrikrishna who successfully established a family network throughout India. Shrikrishna maintained a cordial relationship with the British provided them with capital during their military campaigns in India. Before his death in 1822, Shrikrishna appointed his adopted grandson Mani Kisan Dube as head of the business, which created a crisis of succession and eventually led to the collapse of the business.

### *The Jhaveris*

- The Jhaveris settled in the region of Gujarat became big time bankers during the last quarter of the sixteenth century under the leadership of Shantidas Jhaveri and by the early seventeenth century they had amassed an enviable fortune. The family established close relations with the Mughal court and served them in two capacities as jewellers and moneylenders. The Jhaveris used their wealth and connections with the Mughal court to acquire political influence in Gujarat and were able to remain in business until the early nineteenth century.

(*Source:* The divergence of the economic fortunes of Hindus and Muslims in British India: A Comparative Institutional Analysis by Anantdeep Singh.)

### *The Chettiars of Tamil Nadu*

- The Chettiars, a community in the state of Tamil Nadu, started out as salt traders and moneylenders in the seventeenth century and evolved into a full-fledged banking system by the nineteenth century. Their banking system extended from South India to Burma, Malaya, Ceylon (now Sri Lanka) and parts of China.

Their activity spread to these regions as the British got control of these countries in the early nineteenth century. The Chettiars as bankers lasted till around 1930. They were an important source of credit in the countries where they did business, and were widely acknowledged as instrumental to the economic development of various industries.

(*Source*: Workings of a Nineteenth Century Indigenous Banking System: A Case in Support of Free Banking by Malavika Nair.)

### *Agency Houses*

In the beginning during British rule, the 'Agency Houses' established mainly for trading purposes also acted as banks. The first Agency House was Forbes & Co. started by John Forbes in the year 1767 in Bombay. Later it was merged with Parry & Co. of Madras and Palmer & Co. of Calcutta. The first Agency House in Calcutta was opened in 1768, named M/s Kelr. Reed and Cator. In the year 1770, two more agency houses were opened at Calcutta: M/s Croftes and Johnson and M/s Paxton and Cockerel. These two Agency Houses undertook deposit banking and issue of paper money along with other business. By the year 1800, Calcutta had about 50 agency houses, Bombay had 17 and Madras had 10. Many of these Agency Houses acted like banks or created banks to accept deposits and give loans. Some of them have reported to have financed the East India Company and were also issuing paper money. However, all of them perished with time.

One of the leading agency house which also functioned as bank in Madras presidency was Arbuthnot & Co.

- George Arbuthnot a Scot, arrived in Madras in 1800 and joined the firm of Francis Latour & Co. established in 1777. Other partner was Jon de Monte, a Portuguese from Pondicherry. In 1810, the firm was named Arbuthnot, de Monte & Co. and in 1821 after the death of Jon de Monte it became Arbuthnot & Co. It continued in business of banking for more than 100 years under the control of founder's family before it collapsed in 1906.

- Prior to its collapse, Arbuthnot & Co. employed over 11,000 people, had 7,000 creditors and £1,000,000 in liabilities. Arbuthnot & Co. had two partners at the time of its failure, namely Sir George Gough Arbuthnot and J.M. Young. The firm had entered into an arrangement with Patrick Macfadyen who operated P. Macfadyen & Co., which was effectively Arbuthnot's London branch. It is said that both firms invested in daring enterprises, such as searching for gold in the Nilgiris and Anamalais, investing in American railway projects, new South African goldfields, and in the plantation crops of the West Indies, and other ventures.

(*Source:* "The Fall of Arbuthnot & Co." by Rangaswamy Srinivasan.)

### *Joint Stock Banks in 18th Century*

The western variety of joint stock banking was brought to India by the English Agency houses of Calcutta and Bombay. However the first known bank of a joint stock variety was Bank of Bombay, established in 1720 in Bombay. The bank was said to have started by the government, which provided capital of ₹ one lakh and the bank was placed under the immediate direction of the Governor and two members of Council. It collapsed subsequently in the year 1770. It appears that the government paid the dues of the bank on its failure. (*Source*: Modern Banking in India by S.K. Muranjan-Sydenham College, 1st August 1940.)

Next earliest bank established in the country, was The Bank of Hindustan, in 1770, started by an Agency House named Alexander & Co. at Calcutta and functioned as a commercial bank. It remained functional for more than 50 years. It was closed subsequently in 1832. This bank also issued bank notes.

Warren Hastings (later Governor General) established the General Bank of Bengal and Behar in 1773 but it was short-lived and closed in 1775.

The Bengal Bank was established in 1784 and it also functioned for few years and closed in 1791. Both these banks also issued bank notes.

The General Bank of India, which started in 1786, by Europeans associated with East India Company, was a joint stock bank opened in the country. It also issued bank notes. However, the bank did not last long and was closed in the year 1791.

The Carnatic Bank was started in the year 1788 and the British Bank of Madras in the year 1795 in Madras province. Both these banks along with another two banks were amalgamated in the year 1843 to form Bank of Madras, which became a presidency bank later.

Hence, though banks in organized sector came into existence in the later part of 18th century only two of them survived. The earliest banks in the history of Indian banking which survived is the Carnatic Bank opened in 1788, the British Bank of Madras opened in 1795 which were merged to become Bank of Madras in 1843. Bank of Calcutta opened in 1806 is another of the earliest banks. (Hence, State Bank of India's origin can be traced to these three banks.)

It is difficult to collect information on banks that existed during 18th and 19th century as not much information is available. It can be presumed that many banks existed mostly started by the British in the country, which were closed subsequently. There was no control on banks and banking laws did not exist. Joint stock banks were started under the provisions of companies act then prevailing. Until 1860, the joint stock banks were with unlimited liability as the law permitting joint stock banks with limited liability came into force in the year 1860.

### Banks in India During 19th Century

According to recorded history, banking business in this century was dominated by three presidency banks which survived and other banks started by British Agency Houses. Some of them were successful but did not survive for long.

Private Joint stock banks came into existence after 1860 when principle of limited liability was permitted by the law.

In the beginning of the century, banking was in the hands of Agency Houses and indigenous bankers. It appears that the Agency Houses started failing between the year 1820 to 1835. In the year 1830, a major Agency House, Palmer & Co. went bankrupt. Within next four years, some others like Scott & Co., Alexander & Co. and Mackintosh & Co. failed. Many other Agency Houses also closed creating a void in banking scene. This was the time when the Govt. established presidency banks.

### *Presidency Banks*

The Government wanted a treasury to take care of its funds and hence the British started few banks. The first bank was Bank of Calcutta in 1806, which became Bank of Bengal in the year 1809. Then Bank of Bombay came in 1840 (*) and Bank of Madras in 1843 [**], all three were established under charters from the British East India Company. These were the banks which were started as joint stock companies, that survived. In the year 1876, the Presidency Banks Act was passed and these three banks were called the 'Presidency Banks' and were permitted to issue their own bank notes and manage Govt. accounts. Later on, in the year 1921, these three banks were merged and Imperial Bank of India, which is the forerunner of State Bank of India, came into existence.

* (Bank of Bombay came into problems due to speculative business and closed in 1868 and the same year the New Bank of Bombay was created.)

** [The Bank of Madras was formed in 1843 as a joint stock company with a capital of ₹ 3 million by the amalgamation of Madras Bank (1806), Carnatic Bank (1788), the British Bank of Madras (1795), and the Asiatic Bank (1804).]

The authority to issue bank notes was subsequently withdrawn in the year 1861 when Govt passed Paper Currency Act of 1861 and the function of issuing notes was taken over by the Govt. itself. However, this function was managed by these presidency banks.

Banking business conducted by the three presidency banks as chronicled by SBI is as below:

"The business of the banks was initially confined to discounting of bills of exchange or other negotiable private securities, keeping cash accounts and receiving deposits and issuing and circulating cash notes. Loans were restricted to ₹ one lakh and the period of accommodation confined to three months only. The security for such loans was public securities, commonly called Company's Paper, bullion, treasure, plate, jewels, or goods 'not of a perishable nature' and no interest could be charged beyond a rate of twelve per cent. Loans against goods like opium, indigo, salt woollens, cotton, cotton piece goods, mule twist and silk goods were also granted but such finance by way of cash credits gained momentum only from the third decade of the nineteenth century. All commodities, including tea, sugar and jute, which began to be financed later, were either pledged or hypothecated to the bank. Demand promissory notes were signed by the borrower in favour of the guarantor, which was in turn endorsed to the bank. Lending against shares of the banks or on the mortgage of houses, land or other real property was, however, forbidden.

Indians were the principal borrowers against deposit of Company's paper, while the business of discounts on private as well as salary bills was almost the exclusive monopoly of individuals Europeans and their partnership firms. But the main function of the three banks, as far as the government was concerned, was to help the latter raise loans from time to time and also provide a degree of stability to the prices of government securities.

India witnessed rapid commercialisation in the last quarter of the nineteenth century as its railway network expanded to cover all the major regions of the country. New irrigation networks in Madras, Punjab and Sind accelerated the process of conversion of subsistence crops into cash crops, a portion of which found its way into the foreign markets. Tea and coffee plantations transformed large areas of the eastern Terais, the hills of Assam and the Nilgiris into regions of estate agriculture par excellence. All these resulted in the expansion of India's international trade more than six-fold. The three presidency banks were both beneficiaries and promoters of this commercialisation process as they became involved in the financing of practically every trading, manufacturing and mining activity in the subcontinent. While the Banks of Bengal and Bombay were engaged in the financing of large modern manufacturing industries, the Bank of Madras went into the financing of small-scale industries in a way which had no parallel elsewhere. But the three banks were rigorously excluded from any business involving foreign exchange. Not only was such business considered risky for these banks, which held government deposits, it was also feared that these banks enjoying government patronage would offer unfair competition to the exchange banks which had by then arrived in India. This exclusion continued till the creation of the Reserve Bank of India in 1935."

### *Government Savings Banks (Postal Savings Banks)*

"Before concluding this account of Indian banking, a brief reference may be made to postal savings banks, which also played some role in mobilising savings and developing the banking habit. Savings bank business in India was conducted by Government right from the time of the East India Company. Government savings banks were established first in the three Presidency towns between 1833 and 1835 and later at selected district Treasuries in 1870. In 1882 and 1883, savings banks were opened at post offices throughout the country and these took over the business of the district savings banks in 1886 and of Presidency savings banks in 1896. The rate of interest on these deposits was reduced steadily from $4^1/_6$% in 1879 to 3% in 1905 and to 2½% in 1933". (*Source*: RBI History.)

Besides establishing Three Presidency Banks as commercial banks, the British also created Three Presidency Savings Banks in the year 1833 and 1835 and few District Savings Banks at few district treasuries in the year 1870. This is the forerunner of the present postal savings bank accounts at post offices. Post Offices started opening savings bank accounts in the year 1882 and 1883. Subsequently the business of Presidency Savings Banks and District Savings Banks were transferred to post offices. Post office savings bank accounts are the only exception today in the country where running savings account with cheque book facility is provided by someone other than banks.

### *Other Banks*

As per records available, many Joint stock banks were established during the period 1801 to 1860. Some of them were:

| Year | Name | Place | Remarks |
|---|---|---|---|
| 1804 | The Asiatic Bank | Madras | Amalgamated to form Bank of Madras in 1843 |
| 1806 | The Madras Bank | Madras | Amalgamated to form Bank of Madras in 1843 |
| 1819 | The Commercial Bank | Calcutta | Failed in 1828 |
| 1824 | The Calcutta Bank | Calcutta | Failed in 1829 |
| 1828 | Bank of India * | | Unknown |
| 1829 | Union Bank of Calcutta # | Calcutta | Failed in 1848 |
| 1833 | The Agra and United Service Bank Ltd. (Earlier The Agra Bank and later The Agra and Masterman's Bank, London) | Agra | Failed in 1866 |
| 1835 | The Bank of Mirzapore | Mirzapur | Failed in 1837 |
| 1840 | North Western Bank of India | Mussoorie | Failed in 1859 |
| 1842 | The Oriental Bank Corporation (Earlier, Bank of Western India) + @ | Bombay | Failed in 1884 |
| 1842 | The Agra Savings Fund | Agra | Failed in 1863 |
| 1844 | Delhi Bank Corporation Ltd. | Delhi | Unknown |
| 1844 | The Benares Bank | Banaras | Failed in 1850 |
| 1844 | Simla Bank Ltd. | Simla | Failed in 1893 |
| 1845 | The Commercial Bank of India @ | Bombay | Failed in 1866 |
| 1845 | The Cownpore Bank | Kanpur | Failed in 1851 |
| 1846 | Dacca Bank (merged into Bank of Bengal) | Dacca | Merged in 1862 |
| 1846 | Uncovenanted Service Bank Ltd. | Agra | Failed in 1894 |

(*Sources*: Cooke, Brunyate, Tandon, Maharashtra State Archives and RBI.)

* A person named Ramakishen Dutt set up the first Bank of India in Calcutta (now Kolkata) in 1828, but nothing more is known about this bank.

\# Few Indian merchants in Calcutta, established the Union Bank of Calcutta in 1829, and when it failed in 1848 because of the economic crisis of 1848-49, it triggered the failure of about 42 agency houses by 1850. It opened a branch in Singapore in 1840 and was also issuing bank notes. It is said to have been started by Dwaraknath Tagore, a wealthy businessman and an ancestor of Guru Rabindranath Tagore. It is informed that it took over the business of the Commercial Bank and the Calcutta Bank which had failed.

\+ The bank was established in 1842 in Bombay, under the name Bank of Western India. After the headquarters was moved to London in 1845, the name was changed to the Oriental Bank Corporation. It was chartered in 1851 to allow competition with the East India Company's opium billing monopoly, which was unpopular in England at the time.

@ The Orient Bank Corporation established in Bombay as the Bank of Western India in 1842 was authorised to issue bank notes. The Commercial Bank of India established in 1845 in Bombay (also an Exchange Bank) also issued bank notes.

Financial Chapter in the History of Bombay City by D.E.Wacha in 1910 has recorded the presence of 25 banks in Bombay in the year 1864. They were:

| Sl. No. | Bank |
|---|---|
| 1. | Alliance Bank of Bombay |
| 2. | Asiatic Banking Corporation |
| 3. | Bank of China |
| 4. | Bank of India |
| 5. | Bombay City Bank |
| 6. | Bombay Presidency Bank |
| 7. | Bombay Trading and Banking Association |
| 8. | Bombay Warrant Banking Co. |
| 9. | Brokers' Loan and Discount Banking Co. |
| 10. | Central Bank of Western India |
| 11. | East India Bank |
| 12. | Imperial Bank of Bombay |
| 13. | Imperial Banking and Trading Co. |
| 14. | Indian Peninsula, London and China Bank |
| 15. | Indo-Egyptian, London and Bombay Bank |
| 16. | London and Bombay Bank and General, Financial and Insurance Agency Corporation |
| 17. | Royal Bank of India |
| 18. | Union Bank of Bombay |
| 19. | Universal Bank and Financial Association |
| 20. | Bank of Guzerat |
| 21. | East Indian Trading and Banking Co. |
| 22. | Bank of Bombay |
| 23. | Agra and Masterman Bank |
| 24. | Bank of Hindustan, China and Japan |
| 25. | Commercial Bank Corporation of India and the East |

Most of these banks were started in late 1850s or early 1860s. It is reported that Bombay witnessed a business boom in sixties triggered by the American Civil War when demand and price for cotton went up. This benefitted cotton exporters from Bombay. Further, during this period, Bombay also witnessed hectic land reclamation activity and many companies sprang up for cashing this boom. It appears banks also followed the trend. However, the boom was short-lived and by the year 1865, it crashed. Many of these banks failed during this period after remaining in business for very short period. Many of these banks were Exchange banks and had their head office/branch in London.

### *Banks After 1860—Joint Stock Banks with Limited Liability*

An act to allow formation of "joint stock" banks, as limited liability corporations was passed in 1860. The first Indian joint stock bank of this variety was the Bank of Upper India, established in 1863, and survived until 1913. When it failed some of its assets and liabilities were transferred to the Alliance Bank of Simla (opened in 1875), an exchange bank, which itself was later closed in 1923.

The Punjab Bank also opened in the year 1863, was another first native Indian bank, formed at Rawal Pindee by Punjabi Hindus, with branches in Peshawer, Multan and Poona. It was capitalized at 5 million rupees. It failed subsequently and the exact year of its failure is not known.

The Allahabad Bank, was established in 1865 and is the Oldest Joint Stock Bank in India still functioning. Few Europeans started this bank.

- Allahabad Bank was founded on April 24, 1865 by a group of Europeans at Allahabad. Head office of the bank was shifted in the year 1923 to Calcutta. This bank is the surviving Oldest Joint Stock Bank of the country.

  In 1920, the Bank became a part of P & O Banking Corporation, which took over the Bank but ran it as separate entity under its group. In 1927, Chartered Bank acquired the controlling interest in the P & O

Banking Corporation and Allahabad Bank became a part of Chartered Bank Group. Bank was nationalized in the year 1969. In the year 1989, United Industrial Bank was merged with it.

The bank is one of the leading nationalized banks today and as at March 2010 it had 2286 branches with deposits of ₹ 1,06,056 crores and advances of ₹ 72,437 crores.

The New Bank of Bombay was established in January 1868 (in place of Bank of Bombay started in 1840 and failed in 1868) which became later a presidency bank.

Another entirely Indian Joint Stock Bank (started by Indians) was the Oudh Commercial Bank, established in 1881, in Faizabad. It failed in 1958.

The next was the Punjab National Bank, established in Lahore in 1895, which has survived and is now one of the largest banks in India. It was promoted by the veteran freedom fighter Lala Lajpat Rai as part of swadeshi movement.

- Punjab National Bank Ltd. Bank was founded as a national bank by patriots, like Lala Lajpat Rai, Mr. E.C. Jessawala, Babu Kali Prasono Roy, Lala Harkishan Lal and Sardar Dyal Singh Majithia. It was incorporated under the Act VI of 1882, Indian Companies Act, and the Bank commenced operations on April 12, 1895 from Lahore, with an authorised total capital of ₹ 2 lakhs and working capital of ₹ 20,000. The Bank withstood various financial crises and at the time of partition of India in 1947, the Bank had to close 92 offices in West Pakistan. The registered office was then shifted to Delhi.

  Bank was nationalised in the year 1969. In the year 1993, another nationalised bank viz., New Bank of India was merged with this bank.

  Bank is a leading nationalised bank now and as at March, 2010, bank had 5002 branches with deposits of ₹ 2,49,330 crores and advances of ₹ 1,86,601 crores.

Another present day bank—Nedungadi Bank also came in into existence in the year 1899 (this bank started in Kerala was incorporated in the year 1913 and later merged with PNB in 2003).

- Nedungadi Bank was established in 1899 at Calicut in Kerala by Rao Bahadur T.M. (Thalakodi Madathil) Appu Nedungadi. It was the first private sector commercial bank to be set up in South India. The bank was incorporated in 1913 and in 1965 it took over selected assets and liabilities of the Coimbatore National Bank Ltd.

  In 2003, this bank was merged with Punjab National Bank. At the time of merger, the bank had some 174 branches.

It appears that after the year 1860 many banks came up and functioned. However, most of them lived for a short period of 20 to 30 years. Between the years 1915 to 1938 due to various factors like the First World War, The Great Depression and also the mismanagement, these banks were closed. Some of the banks established during 1860 to 1899 and closed are as below:

| Sl. No. | Name | Year established | Year closed |
|---|---|---|---|
| 1. | Kayastha Mercantile Banking Corporation Delhi | 1881 | 1916 |
| 2. | Kashmiri Bank Faizabad | 1882 | 1916 |
| 3. | Pabna Bank | 1883 | 1930 |
| 4. | Meerut Bank | 1884 | 1932 |
| 5. | Nanjangud Sri Nanjundeswara Bank | 1885 | 1936 |
| 6. | Chickballapur Rajdhani Bank | 1886 | 1917 |
| 7. | Jwala Prakash Meerut Bank, Meerut | 1888 | 1920 |
| 8. | Rajdhany Bank Bangalore | 1889 | 1915 |
| 9. | Deccan Bank | 1890 | 1916 |
| 10. | Gudibanda Ooperhalli Shri Hanumantarayaswami Bank | 1890 | 1918 |
| 11. | Mercantile Bank, Bangalore | 1892 | 1927 |
| 12. | Poona Mercantile Bank | 1893 | 1923 |
| 13. | Mandya Lakshmi Vilasa Bank | 1894 | 1922 |
| 14. | Devanalli Sri Adinarayanaswamy Bank | 1895 | 1929 |
| 15. | Gorakhpur Bank, Gorakhpur | 1895 | 1917 |
| 16. | Trinnevelly Bank | 1896 | 1932 |
| 17. | Bombay Banking Company | 1898 | 1913-14 |
| 18. | Poona Bank, Poona | 1898 | 1924 |

(*Source*: Modern Banking in India by S.K. Muranjan-Sydenham College, 1st August 1940.)

Though Indians and British started many banks during the century, only three banks, besides presidency banks, survived to present date. They are: Allahabad Bank established in the year 1865, Punjab National Bank established in the year 1895, and Nedungadi Bank in south that came into existence in the year 1899 (later merged with PNB in 2003).

### *Exchange Banks*

Prior to 1935, commercial banks including the Presidency banks in the country were not allowed to transact foreign exchange business, as it were felt very risky for them. A new type of banks called—Exchange banks were only allowed to undertake foreign exchange business. These were mainly foreign banks of British, French and other origin. These banks undertook exchange business. This monopoly of exchange banks continued until the year 1935.

The colonial rules by Britain, France and Portugal witnessed the opening of few exchange bank branches in the second half of nineteenth century by the banks from these nations. Few newly established banks mainly promoted by foreigners also appeared to take up banking business in the regions like India, Myanmar, Sri Lanka, Hongkong, China, and Japan then under the colonial rules. These banks opened branches in Mumbai or Calcutta or at both the places. Some banks have subsequently expanded by opening branches in more cities. These banks were sometimes called Anglo-Indian banks to distinguish them from the other existing operating foreign banks.

### *Chartered Banks*

Many of the Exchange banks have tried and received Royal Charters, which gave them some status in the eyes of the public. These banks were called the Chartered Banks. There were two types of chartered banks. One type was those banks, which were constituted under the Royal charter. The second type was those banks, which came into existence first and later received Royal charter. Royal charters also helped these banks, as under it, the liability of the shareholders was made limited on certain conditions. Royal charters also enabled these banks to issue bank notes, which was a privilege then. The requirement of use of words like—'Ltd' or 'Plc' in their names were waived. These banks also could use the word 'Chartered' in their name. Some of the banks who received Royal charters between the years 1840 to 1864 for operating in India were as under:

| Royal Charter Date | Bank | Present status |
|---|---|---|
| 10 Aug 1840 | Bank of Ceylon | Closed |
| 07 Aug 1851 | Oriental Bank Corporation | Closed |
| 19 Aug 1853 | Chartered Bank of Asia | Closed |
| 19 Aug 1853 | Chartered Bank of India, Australia and China | Now Standard Chartered Bank |
| 18 Oct 1854 | London and Eastern Banking Corporation | Closed |
| 06 May 1857 | Agra and United Service Bank | Closed |
| 27 Aug 1857 | Chartered Mercantile Bank of India, London and China | Now HSBC |
| 03 Feb 1864 | Commercial Bank Corporation of India and the East | Closed |
| 03 Feb 1864 | Asiatic Banking Corporation | Closed |

(*Source:* Wikipedia)

As per available information, following exchange banks were started/arrived during the years 1840 to 1900.

| Sl. No. | In India | Bank | Head office | Brief status |
|---|---|---|---|---|
| 1. | 1842 | The Oriental Bank Corporation (Earlier Bank of Western India) | London | The bank was established in 1842 in Bombay under the name Bank of Western India. After the headquarters was moved to London in 1845, the name was changed to the Oriental Bank Corporation. The Oriental Bank Corporation received Royal charter in 1851 and was authorised to issue bank notes. The Bank failed in 1884. |
| 2. | 1846 | Delhi and London Bank | London | The Delhi and London Bank was established in London in 1844, and the Bank operated at Delhi from 1846.<br>The Delhi and London Bank was absorbed by the |

(*Contd*...)

| | | | | |
|---|---|---|---|---|
| | | | | Alliance Bank of Simla in 1916. |
| 3. | 1852 | Chartered Bank of Asia | | The bank was started in 1852 under Royal charter and it failed in 1855. |
| 4 | 1853 | Mercantile bank of India | London | Originally established in Bombay as the Mercantile Bank of Bombay in 1853, the bank was granted a Royal charter in 1857 and it was later renamed in 1868 as the Chartered Mercantile Bank of India, London and China. Its Head office was moved to London in 1858. It was renamed the Mercantile Bank of India in 1893.<br>This oldest exchange bank has survived. In 1959, HSBC acquired this bank and the branches are now continuing as HSBC branches. |
| 5. | 1858 | Chartered Bank of India, Australia and China | London | Chartered Bank of India, Australia and China was founded in 1853 by a Scotsman- James Wilson under the Royal Charter by Queen Victoria.<br>The Chartered Bank opened its first branches in Mumbai, and Kolkata in 1858.<br>In the year 1969, Chartered Bank and Standard Bank, both British banks, merged to form Standard Chartered Bank. Now the branches are functioning as Standard Chartered Bank. |
| 6. | 1860 | The Comptoire d'Escompte de Paris | Paris | This French bank opened a branch in Calcutta in 1860, and another in Bombay in 1862. It also opened branches in Madras and Pondicherry and many other places. Kolkata branch was closed in 1903 and was reopened in the year 1948. This bank has survived and later known as Banque National De Paris |

(*Contd...*)

| | | | | |
|---|---|---|---|---|
| | | | | from 1966 and now as BNP Paribas from the year 2000. |
| 7. | 1863 | National Bank of India | London | The National Bank of India was established in 1863 as the Calcutta Banking Corporation, a name that was changed in 1864 to National Bank of India. The head office was transferred from Calcutta to London in 1866.<br>*(source:* Indian Finance And Banking by V. Findlay Shirras)<br>This bank survived and undergone many changes in its ownership. In 1948, the National Bank of India, took over Grindlays Bank operations in India. Name was changed to National & Grindlays Bank Ltd. in 1959, Grindlays Bank Ltd in 1975, Grindlays Bank plc in 1982 and ANZ Grindlays Bank in 1989.<br>In 2000, Standard Chartered Bank acquired Grindlays Bank from ANZ Bank and the branches are now Standard Chartered Bank. |
| 8. | 1864 | Hong Kong and Shanghai Banking Corporation | London | The Hong Kong and Shanghai Banking Corporation Limited, was established in 1865 in Hong Kong to finance the growing trade between Europe, India and China. The bank opened branch in India in 1864.<br>It acquired the Mercantile Bank of India and the British Bank of the Middle East in 1959.<br>In the 1980s, it acquired Marine Midland Bank in the US and in 1992 it acquired Midland bank of UK. After this, the head office of the bank was moved to London. |

*(Contd...)*

| | | | | |
|---|---|---|---|---|
| 9. | 1865 | The Agra & Masterman's Bank | London | The bank was started as the Agra Bank in 1833 later changed to Agra & United services Bank Ltd. and received Royal charter in 1857. It became Agra & Masterman's Bank in 1865. This Bank was reported to have failed in 1866. |
| 10. | 1868 | *Banco Nacional Ultramarino* | Lisbon | *Banco Nacional Ultramarino* (National Overseas Bank) was a Portuguese bank with operations throughout the world, especially in Portugal's former overseas provinces. The bank opened a branch in Goa in 1868 and a representative office in Bombay in 1920. It was merged with Caixa Geral de Depósitos, the Portugal government-owned savings bank, in 2001. In 1952, BNU closed its branches in India. |
| 11. | 1869 | Agra Bank Ltd. | London | Bank was started in 1868 at London and opened its Bombay branch in 1869. It is reported to have closed after the year 1890. |
| 12. | 1875 | Indo-China Bank (*Banque de L'Indochine),* | Paris | It was the first French bank to be established in Pondicherry on 21 January 1875. It enjoyed the privilege of issuing notes for French colony. The bank withdrew from Pondicherry in March 1955. |
| 13. | 1894 | Yokohama Specie Bank | Yokohama | Yokohama Specie Bank was a Japanese bank founded in Yokohama, Japan in the year 1880. It opened a branch in Bombay in 1894. It later became the Bank of Tokyo Ltd. in 1947. |
| 14. | 1896 | Deutsch-Asiatische Bank<br>. | Berlin | Deutsch-Asiatische Bank in Berlin was promoted in 1889 by a German bank syndicate led by *Disconto-Gesellschaft* and *Deutsche Bank*, as a special institution for the East Asian |

(*Contd...*)

| | | | | |
|---|---|---|---|---|
| | | | | market. This bank opened its first branch for India in Calcutta (now Kolkata) in 1896. In the year 1914, the Calcutta branch was closed due to the beginning of World War I. |

Out of these banks, only five banks i.e. Mercantile Bank of India (now HSBC) Chartered Bank of India, Australia and China (now Standard Chartered Bank), The Comptoire d'Escompte de Paris (now BNP Paribas), National Bank of India (now Standard Chartered Bank) and Hong Kong and Shanghai Banking Corporation continued till date. These banks have however undergone mergers and formed into new foreign banks.

As per available records there were also few new exchange banks started by foreigners for doing business in India in 19th century. They were:

| Sl. No | In India | Bank | Head office | Brief status |
|---|---|---|---|---|
| 15. | 1840 | North Western Bank of India | Mussoorie | Bank opened London office in 1849. It was reported to have failed in 1859 |
| 16. | 1841 | Bank of Asia | | Reportedly opened in 1841 and was closed in 1842. |
| 17. | 1841 | The Bank of Ceylon | | The bank was started in 1841 under Royal Charter issued in 1840 and merged with the Oriental Bank Corporation in 1849. |
| 18. | 1845 | The Commercial Bank of India. | Bombay | The Commercial Bank of India established in 1845 in Bombay was an Exchange Bank and also issued bank notes.<br>Bank received Royal Charter in 1864 and started a branch in 1865 in London. The name was changed to Commercial Bank Corporation of India and the East. It was closed in 1866. |
| 19. | 1854 | London and Eastern Banking Corporation | | Bank received Royal Charter in 1854. It had branches in Bombay and |

(*Contd*...)

| | | | | |
|---|---|---|---|---|
| | | | | Calcutta. Bank also had a branch in London. Bank was probably closed in 1858. |
| 20. | 1860 | The Central Bank of Western India | Bombay | Central Bank of western India with its head office at Bombay was Yokohama based Japanese bank. It had branches in London, Calcutta, Madras, China, Japan and Melbourne. It was said to have issued bank notes (*Source*: The Argus-Saturday 25, 1865). It opened its London branch in 1863.<br>In 1867 bank went in to liquidation |
| 21. | 1860 | Bank of China | Bombay | The book-*Banking Reform in India and China* by Lawrence Saez in 2004, records the existence of one Royal Bank of China incorporated in Bombay in 1860.<br>HSBC history also mentions about the efforts of Bombay financiers to set up Bank of China and this in fact prompted the establishment of HSBC in 1865.<br>However, no confirmation is available about these facts, and whether it is the same bank. |
| 22. | 1862 | Scinde, Punjab and Delhi Bank Corporation | London | Scinde, Punjab and Delhi Bank Corporation was established in 1862 with head office at London. It had branches in Bombay and Karachi. It is reported to have gone in for liquidation in 1866 and perhaps National Bank of India took over the bank. (*Source*: Allens India Mail of December 6, 1866) |
| 23. | 1863 | Bank of Hindustan, China and Japan | London | An Exchange Bank with HO in London started in 1863 as Bank of Hindustan and renamed |

(*Contd*...)

| | | | | |
|---|---|---|---|---|
| | | | | as Bank of Hindustan, China and Japan in 1864. Bank probably closed in 1866. |
| 24. | 1864 | Asiatic Banking Corporation | | An Exchange bank It was originally promoted in 1863 and christened as the Bombay Joint Stock Bank, the promoters were Mess` Michael Scott, Gavin Steel and Cowasji Jehanghir Readymoney. The Bank obtained a Royal Charter in 1864. Bank was closed in 1869. |
| 25. | 1864 | Bank of India | Bombay | Established in 1864 in Bombay and London branch was opened in 1865. Probably the bank failed in 1867. |
| 26. | 1864 | Bombay City Bank | Bombay | Bombay City Bank Limited was started in 1864. It opened a branch in London in 1866. The bank closed in 1867. |
| 27. | 1864 | Royal Bank of India | Bombay | Royal bank of India had head office in Bombay with authorised capital of one million Pound sterling and had branches in London, Calcutta, Ahmedabad, Surat, Belgaum and Melbourne. The bank was established in 1864. Mr. Andrew Grant who came to Bombay in 1858 was said to be its first chairman. (*Source*: the Argus-Saturday 25, 1865). Bank was closed in 1868. |
| 28. | 1866 | East India Bank | | Bank Opened a branch in London in 1866. Bank was closed in 1867. |
| 29. | 1866 | Indian Peninsula, London and China Bank | | Bank opened a branch in London in 1866. Bank was closed in 1867. |
| 30. | | Indo-Egyptian, London and Bombay Bank | | No information is available on this bank. |
| 31. | 1866 | London and Bombay Bank | . | Bank opened branch in London in 1866 and in |

(*Contd*...)

| | | | | |
|---|---|---|---|---|
| | | and General, Financial and Insurance Agency Corporation | | 1867 bank was put under liquidation |
| 32. | 1875 | The Alliance Bank of Simla | Simla | The Alliance Bank of Simla was a British-run though India-registered bank that commenced operations in Simla in 1875. Early In 1913, it acquired some of the assets and liabilities of the Bank of Upper India (which had been founded in Meerut in 1863 and was the first Joint Stock Bank in India). Then in 1916 it acquired the Delhi and London Bank (est. 1844), and the Punjab Banking Company (est. 1889—founded by Sir David P. Masson in Lahore). The next year Alliance Bank acquired the Bank of Rangoon (est. 1906). The Alliance Bank failed in 1923 due to speculations by its management. At the time it failed, it had 36 branches, including ones in Lahore, Lucknow, Peshawar, Rawalpindi, and Rangoon. (*Sources*: RBI, Indian finance, currency and banking (1914) by Doraiswami S.V. and Wikipedia.) |

All these banks (15 to 32) were closed subsequently. Most of them failed during the period 1860 to 1870.

It is reported that in the year 1866, there were 24 exchange banks in Mumbai and 22 banks in Kolkata. Mostly these are new banks established by foreigners to take up exchange business in the country. This number gradually came down as many of the exchange banks failed and closed down. However, few foreign banks that came survived and continued, though many of them have undergone mergers and acquired new names.

Exchange banks of foreign origin that opened their branches during the years 1901 to 1925 were as under:

| Sl. No. | In India | Bank | Head office | Brief status |
|---|---|---|---|---|
| 33. | 1902 | The National City Bank of New York | New York | City Bank of New York (now Citibank) was established on June 16, 1812 in New York City. In 1865, it was named The National City Bank of New York. Bank opened its branch in Kolkata in 1902 and at Bangalore in the year 1903. In 1955, the bank changed its name to The First National City Bank of New York. In 1976, First National City Bank became Citibank, N.A. (for National Association). Branches of the bank are continuing now as Citi Bank |
| 34. | 1904 | International Banking Corporation | New York | International Banking Corporation of USA opened its branch in Bombay in 1904. In 1918 this U.S. overseas bank, became a wholly owned subsidiary of National City Bank of New York. It continued as the First National City Bank of New York and now as Citi Bank. |
| 35. | 1908 | Grindlay & Co. | London | The firm opened offices at Calcutta in 1854 and at Bombay in 1865 and in 1908 these were transformed into branches, administered directly from London. In 1912 it added a branch in Simla; In 1923, the UK's National Provincial Bank (now National Westminster and a subsidiary of Royal Bank of Scotland) acquired Grindlay & Co., and registered it as a limited company, but ran it as a separate company. |

(*Contd…*)

| | | | | |
|---|---|---|---|---|
| | | | | Grindlay & Co. changed its name to Grindlays Bank Ltd in 1947. In 1948, National Provincial decided to withdraw from overseas banking and sold Grindlays Bank to the National Bank of India (NBI). In 1958, National Bank of India and Grindlays Bank merged and became National Overseas & Grindlays Bank. In 1959, the bank changed its name to National & Grindlays Bank (NGB). In 1961, NGB acquired Lloyds Bank's Eastern branches including Indian branches. |
| 36. | 1910 | Russo-Asiatic Bank | Russia | The Russo-Asiatic Bank was established in 1895 and collapsed in 1926. It had a branch in Bombay opened in the year 1910. |
| 37. | 1910 | The Eastern Bank of India | London | The Eastern Bank Limited was founded in London as a limited company at the end of 1909 as a new Eastern 'exchange' bank, to help finance trade with the East. It had two overseas branches, established in 1910 in Bombay and Calcutta. From 1957, Eastern Bank became a wholly-owned subsidiary of Chartered Bank. In 1971, it was absorbed by Chartered Bank, which later became Standard Chartered Bank. The branches are now continuing as Standard Chartered Bank. |
| 38. | 1916 | Sumitomo Bank | Osaka Japan | Bank opened a branch in Delhi in 1916. In 2001, this bank and Mitsui Bank were merged to form Sumitomo Mitsui Banking Corporation. *(see Mitsui bank below)* |
| 39. | 1924 | Mitsui bank Ltd. | Tokyo | As per records, Mitsui Bank Limited had an |

*(Contd...)*

| | | | | |
|---|---|---|---|---|
| | | | | agency office in Bombay opened in the year 1924. The bank opened its branch office in Bombay on 28th May 1955. In 2001, Mitsui Bank merged with Sumitomo Bank to form Sumitomo Mitsui Banking Corporation. The new bank had two branches in India one each at Delhi and Mumbai. In 2005 bank closed its branches in India. |
| 40. | 1917 | Bank of Taiwan | Taipeh | The Bank of Taiwan was established as Taiwan's central bank in 1899 by Taiwan's Japanese government. In 1917, it opened a branch in Mumbai. |
| 41. | 1920 | Netherland Trading Society | Holland | The Netherlands Trading Society (*Nederlandsche Handel-Maatschappij* or NHM) was a Dutch trading company established in 1824 by King Willem I of the Netherlands. It was also engaged in banking operations. In 1920 NHM opened branches in Bombay (Mumbai) and Calcutta (Kolkata) primarily to work with clients in the diamond business.<br>In 1964 NHM merged with the *Dutch Twentsche Bank* to form Algemene Bank Nederland (ABN), which subsequently merged with ABN AMRO.<br>In 2007, The Royal Bank of Scotland NV took over ABN AMRO. The branches are continuing now as The Royal Bank of Scotland NV. |
| 42. | 1920 | Netherlands India Commercial Bank (The Nederlandsch-Indische Handelsbank) | Amsterdam | Netherlands India commercial bank was established in 1863 to finance and handle trade with the Netherlands East Indies (NEI). It had its head |

(*Contd*...)

| | | | | |
|---|---|---|---|---|
| | | | | office in Amsterdam.<br>In 1920, The bank established branches in Bombay and Calcutta.<br>In 1950, The bank changed its name to Nationale Handelsbank. In 1965, again the name was changed to Nationale Bank Voor Middellang Krediet (National Bank for Medium-Term Credit).<br>In 1967, this bank was absorbed by AMRO Bank, which later became ABN AMRO.<br>In 2007, The Royal Bank of Scotland NV took over. |
| 43. | 1920 | The Peninsular & Oriental Banking Corporation | London | The Peninsular and Oriental Steam Navigation Company established the Peninsular & Oriental Banking Corporation in 1920. In the same year, Lloyds Bank and National Provincial Bank took shares in this Bank. P&O Banking Corporation acquired Allahabad Bank (est. 1865) in 1920. However, P&O Bank ran Allahabad Bank separately.<br>In 1920, P&O Bank established branches in Calcutta, Bombay, Madras and Karachi in India and Colombo, Shanghai, Hong Kong, Singapore, and Canton. The bank was unable to progress and ended up with bad debts.<br>In 1927, Chartered Bank of India, Australia, and China (now Standard Chartered Bank) acquired 75% of P&O Bank and later acquired the remaining shares. For some time, Chartered Bank continued to run the two Banks, P&O Bank and Allahabad Bank, separately. In 1937, P&O Bank was merged with |

(*Contd*...)

| | | | | |
|---|---|---|---|---|
| | | | | Chartered Bank, but Allahabad bank remained separate bank. |
| 44. | 1922 | American Express Bank Ltd. | USA | This US Bank opened a branch in Mumbai in 1922 and is continuing. |
| 45. | 1923 | Lloyds Bank | UK | Lloyds Bank an old British bank established in 1765, acquired the business of Cox's & King's in 1923. Cox's & King's had been bankers to the British Army since 1758 and had branches in India and other places. Lloyds Bank took over the business in 1923, acquiring branches in India, Egypt and Burma. In 1961, Lloyds Bank transferred its Eastern Division including business in India to National and Grindlays Bank in exchange for a 25% share in National and Grindlays Bank (renamed Grindlays Bank in 1975). |
| 46. | 1924 | Thomas Cook & Sons (Bankers) | UK | Thomas Cook & Sons, a UK firm engaged in travel and other business, set up a separate company under the name of Thomas Cook & Sons (Bankers) Ltd. in 1924 to undertake banking business. It had offices in Bombay, Delhi and Calcutta.<br>In 1942, Grindlays & Co. took over Thomas Cook & Sons (Bankers). |

From these banks (year 1901 to 1925) only few Banks survived to the present. They are: National City Bank of New York (now Citi Bank), International Banking Corporation (now Citi Bank), The Eastern Bank of India (now Standard Chartered Bank), Netherland Trading Society (now The Royal Bank of Scotland NV), American Express Bank and the P&O Bank (merged with Chartered Bank now Standard Chartered Bank).

Operations of Llyods Bank, Grindlays & Co, and Thomas Cook & Sons (Bankers) were all merged with National and Grindlays Bank which is now Standard Chartered Bank.

There were few exchange banks started by Indians, which did not survive. They were:

| Sl. No. | In India | Bank | Head office | Brief status |
|---|---|---|---|---|
| 47. | 1906 | Indian Specie Bank | Bombay | The bank was started by Chunilal Saraya in the year 1906 and the bank was liquidated in 1914 after it was found involved in speculation in silver. |
| 48. | 1917 | Tata Industrial Bank established in 1917 | Bombay | Tata Industrial Bank, promoted by Tata group was amalgamated with Central Bank of India in 1923. |
| 49. | 1936 | Central Exchange Bank of India | London | Bank was promoted by Central Bank of India in 1936. London branch of Central Exchange Bank of India was taken over by Barclays Bank in 1938. |

As per Report of Bengal Provincial Banking Enquiry Committee, 1929-30, there were total 18 Exchange banks in the country in the year 1929 and 15 Exchange banks were present in Calcutta out of this 18. They were:

1. The Chartered Bank of India, Australia and China,
2. The National Bank of India,
3. The Mercantile Bank of India,
4. The Peninsular and Oriental Banking Corporation,
5. The Eastern Bank,
6. Messers Thomas Cook and Sons (Bankers).
7. Lloyds Bank,
8. Hong Kong and Shanghai Banking Corporation,
9. Yokohama Specie Bank,
10. The Bank of Taiwan,
11. National City Bank of New York,
12. Nederlandsch Indische Handelsbank (Netherlands India Commercial Bank),
13. Nederlandsche Haudel-Maatschappij (Netherlands Trading Society),

14. American Express Company
15. Messers Grindlay & Co.

Three exchange banks which had branches at other places than Calcutta were:

16. The Sumitomo Bank
17. The Mitsui Bank
18. Bank National de Paris (though this bank had a branch in Calcutta opened in the year 1860, it was closed in the year 1903 and was reopened only in 1948. It had branches in Bombay and other places).

After the year 1935, the separate distinction of exchange banks was removed as Indian commercial banks were allowed to do exchange business. Then with enactment of Foreign Exchange Regulation Act 1947, banks were given separate licence to deal in foreign exchange as Authorised Dealer.

### Banks in India During 20th Century

Most of the present day banks in the country have their origins in this century. The period between 1906 and 1911, saw the establishment of banks inspired by the Swadeshi movement, which inspired many local businessmen and political figures to found banks. A number of banks established then have survived to the present. In fact, most of the present day banks were established between 1900 and 1950.

There were also many banks established in the beginning of the century, which did not survive. Their lifespan was again 20 to 30 years on an average and most of them failed between the years 1913 and 1938. Some of these banks were as under:

| Sl. No. | Name | Year established | Year closed |
|---|---|---|---|
| 1. | The Kyastha Trading and Banking Corporation | 1900 | 1920 |
| 2. | Bank of Trichinopally | 1900 | 1921 |
| 3. | Gundlupet Sri Raja-rajeswari Bank | 1900 | 1929 |
| 4. | Pretoria Bank | 1901 | 1923 |
| 5. | The Peoples Bank of Lahore | 1901 | 1913 |
| 6. | Gundlupet Sri Himavat Gopalakrishnaswamy Bank | 1901 | 1926 |
| 7. | Allahabad Union Bank. | 1904 | 1924 |

| Sl. No. | Name | Year established | Year closed |
|---|---|---|---|
| 8. | Vellore Commercial Bank | 1904 | 1926 |
| 9. | Trichinopally Bank | 1905 | 1932 |
| 10. | Banking and Ornament Manufacturing Co. | 1906 | 1935 |
| 11. | Lahore Bank | 1906 | 1935 |
| 12. | The Hindustan Bank, Multan | 1906 | 1914 |
| 13. | The Bengal National Bank | 1906 | 1927 |
| 14. | The Indian Specie Bank * | 1906 | 1914 |
| 15. | Lyallpur Bank | 1907 | 1931 |
| 16. | Pabna Union Bank | 1908 | 1930 |
| 17. | Co-operative Hindusthan Bank | 1908 | 1932 |
| 18. | Bharat National Bank | 1908 | 1934 |
| 19. | Chinese Merited Company | 1909 | 1931 |
| 20. | The Credit Bank of India | 1909 | 1916 |
| 21. | Karachi Bank | 1910 | 1930 |
| 22. | Mufassil Bank U.P. | 1910 | 1935 |
| 23. | Kathiawar and Ahmedabad Corporation | 1910 | 1913 |
| 24. | Hazaribag Bank | 1911 | 1935 |
| 25. | Madaripur Bank | 1911 | 1936 |
| 26. | The British India Bank | 1911 | 1913 |
| 27. | The Pioneer Bank, Bombay | 1911 | 1916 |
| 28. | Travancore National and Quilon Bank | 1912, 1919 | 1938 |
| 29. | Coimbatore Sabanati Bank | 1913 | 1935 |
| 30. | Dawsons Bank $ | 1914 | # |
| 31. | Midnapore Bank | 1915 | 1935 |
| 32. | The Tata Industrial Bank | 1917 | 1923 |
| 33. | Darbhanga Bank | 1921 | 1932 |
| 34. | Amritsar National Bank | 1922 | 1923 |
| 35. | Peoples Bank of Northern India | 1925 | 1931 |
| 36. | The Sivarama Ayyar Bank, Madras | # | 1932 |
| 37. | The Amritsar Bank, Lahore @ | # | # |
| 38. | The Bank of Burma | # | # |

$ year not known.

* Indian Specie Bank was reported to have started immediately after Bank of India was started in 1906.

@ The Amritsar Bank was established before the year 1910 and it collapsed along with Peoples Bank (closed in 1931).

(*Source:* Modern Banking in India by S.K. Muranjan-Sydenham College, 1st August 1940.)

$ Dawson bank is a Burmese bank started by Lawrence Dawson a European with its head office at Pyapon. Head office was later shifted to Rangoon. In 1937, Burma was separated from India. The functioning of the bank was disturbed in 1942 when Japan invaded Burma and occupied it for some time. Again, bank restarted its activities and continued till 1962. Subsequently the assets of the bank were reported to have been seized by the Govt. and sold.

(*Source:* Fiery dragons-Banks, moneylenders and micro finance in Burma by Sean Turnell.)

As stated earlier the origin of most of the present day banks are traced to the period 1900 to 1950 as given hereunder.

South Canara (South Kanara) district in Karnataka state now bifurcated to Dakshina Kannada district and Udupi district is known as "Cradle of Indian Banking". Four nationalised banks and a leading private sector bank were started in this district. They are Canara Bank, Syndicate Bank, Corporation Bank and Vijaya Bank, now in public sector and Karnataka Bank in private sector. This is a unique occurrence in the history of Indian banking.

Bank of Bengal, Bank of Bombay, and Bank of Madras were merged in the year 1921 to form Imperial Bank of India, which later on became State Bank of India. State Bank of India came into existence under an act, in the year 1955. Imperial Bank (later SBI) functioned as central bank, banker to the Govt and as a commercial bank until the time RBI came into existence in 1935.

## Present day Banks

### *1904-City Union bank*

The bank, 'The Kumbakonam Bank Limited' as it was then called was incorporated as a limited company on 31st October, 1904. It was promoted by twenty devoted and prominent citizens of Kumbakonam including Sarvashri R. Santhanam Iyer, S. Krishna Iyer, V. Krishnaswami Iyengar and T.S. Raghavachariar.

Shri S. Mahalinga Iyer earlier Secretary subsequently became the First Full-time Managing Director of the bank in 1929. He held the position of Managing Director from 1929 to 1963. The Bank was included in the Second Schedule of Reserve Bank of India Act, 1934, on 22nd March 1945.

In 1957, the bank took over the assets and liabilities of the Common Wealth Bank Limited which had five Branches.

Bank is a leading private sector bank today and as at March 2010, Bank had 225 branches, with deposits of ₹ 10,285 crores, and advances of ₹ 6,833 crores.

### 1906-Canara Bank

Bank was founded as 'Canara Bank Hindu Permanent Fund' in 1906, by Late Sri Ammembal Subba Rao Pai, a philanthropist, in Mangalore in Karnataka State. In 1910, it became a limited company as 'Canara Bank Ltd.'.

Bank was nationalised in the year 1969. As at March 2010, Bank had 3046 branches with deposits of ₹ 2,34,651 crores and advances were ₹ 1,69,335 crores.

### 1906-Bank of India

Bank of India was founded on 7th September, 1906. The lead promoter of the Bank of India was Sir Sassoon J. David. He was a member of the Sassoons—a part of Bombay community of Baghdadi Jews. Bank began with one office in Mumbai, with a paid-up capital of ₹ 50 lakh and with 50 employees. Sir David was the Chief Executive of the bank from its founding in 1906 until his death in 1926.

Bank was nationalised in the year 1969. The Bank had 3207 branches in India as at the end of March 2010 and 24 branches and 5 representative offices in foreign countries. Bank's deposits were ₹ 2,29,762 crores and advances were ₹ 1,71,317 crores.

### 1906-Corporation Bank

Corporation Bank came into being as Canara Banking Corporation (Udipi) Limited, on 12th March, 1906, in the temple town of Udupi, by the pioneering efforts of a group of visionaries.

The Founder President was Khan Bahadur Haji Abdullah Haji Kasim Saheb Bahadur. The Bank started functioning with just ₹ 5000 as its capital. The Bank's name changed from Canara Banking Corporation (Udipi) Ltd., to "Canara Banking Corporation Ltd., in 1939 and the second change in the name of the Bank occurred in 1972, to 'Corporation Bank Limited'.

Bank was nationalised in the year 1980. As at March 2010 Bank had 1155 branches. Bank's deposits were ₹ 92,734 crores and advances were ₹ 63,203 crores.

### *1907-Indian Bank*

Indian Bank was founded by Sh. Annamalai and Sh. Ramaswami Chettiar on 15 August 1907. The fall of Arbuthnot's, an agency house and banker for very long time prompted the promoters to float the bank to fill in the void created. Bank was established in Madras now Chennai, in Tamil Nadu State.

Bank was nationalised in the year 1969. As at March 2010 Bank had 1756 branches. Bank's deposits were ₹ 88,228 crores and advances were ₹ 62,658 crores.

### *1908-Bank of Baroda*

Bank of Baroda was established on 20th July 1908, under the Companies Act of 1897, with a paid up capital of ₹ 10 lakhs. Founder of the bank was the Maharaja Sayajirao Gaekwad of the princely State of Baroda.

Bank was nationalised in the year 1969. Now it is one of the leading banks. As at March 2010 Bank had 3100 domestic branches and 48 overseas branches. Bank's deposits were ₹ 2,41,044 crores and advances were ₹ 1,75,035 crores.

### *1908-Punjab & Sind Bank*

The bank was started in 1908 by luminaries like Bhai Vir Singh, Sir Sunder Singh Majithia and Sardar Tarlochan Singh. They enjoyed the highest respect with the people of Punjab.

The bank was nationalised in the year 1980. As at March 2010 Bank had 916 branches. Bank's deposits were ₹ 49,155 crores and advances were ₹ 32,738 crores.

### *1911-Central Bank of India*

Bank was established on 21st December 1911 at Mumbai, was the first Indian commercial bank, which was wholly owned and managed by Indians. Sir Sorabji Pochkhanawala, was the founder of the Bank. Sir Pherozesha Mehta was the first Chairman of this 'Swadeshi Bank'.

The bank was nationalised in the year 1969. As at March 2010 bank's deposits were ₹ 1,62,107 crores and advances were 1,05,383 crores. Bank had 3728 branches as at March 2011.

### 1916-Karur Vysya Bank

Karur Vysya Bank was started in 1916 by two promoters: Late Shri M.A. Venkatarama Chettiar and Late Shri Athi Krishna Chettiar with rupees one lakh as capital. The bank was started in Karur, a small textile town in Tamil Nadu.

The bank is a private sector bank today. As at March 2010 Bank had 367 branches with deposits of ₹ 19,271 crores and advances of ₹ 13,675 crores.

### 1916-Sangli Bank

The bank was established in the year 1916 at Sangli in Maharashtra State. The Bhate family of Sangli almost held 30% of share capital. The bank was merged with ICICI Bank in the year 2006. At the time of merger, the bank had about 190 branches.

### 1919-Union Bank of India

Union Bank of India was established on 11th November 1919 with its headquarters in the city of Bombay now known as Mumbai. The new head office building was inaugurated by the Father of the Nation, Mahatma Gandhi in the year 1922.

The bank was nationalised in the year 1969. As at March 2010 Bank had 2805 branches. Bank also has branches in few countries. Bank's deposits were ₹ 1,69,670 crores and advances were ₹ 1,18,272 crores.

### 1920-Catholic Syrian Bank

Catholic Syrian Bank is one of the private banks in India; it was started in 1920, 26th November in Thrissur district, in Kerala. The bank started its work on January 1st, 1921 with a capital of ₹ 5 lakhs and paid capital of ₹ 45,270. In August 1960, the bank took over the liabilities and assets of other banks in Kerala. Catholic Syrian Bank became a scheduled bank in 1960.

The bank is a leading private sector bank today. As at March 2010 Bank had 377 branches and had deposits of ₹ 6,978 crores and advances of ₹ 4,466 crores.

### 1921-Tamil Nadu Mercantile Bank

The bank was promoted by Nadar business community at Tuticorin in 1920. The bank was registered on May 11, 1921 as "The Nadar Bank Ltd". The name was later changed to Tamil Nadu Mercantile Bank. Shri M.V. Shanmugavel Nadar was the first Chairman elected on Nov. 04, 1921. The bank was opened by Shri T.V. Balagurusamy Nadar, the then President of the Nadar Mahajana Sangam.

It is one of the private sector banks today. As at Sept. 2011, Bank had about 233 branches with deposits of ₹ 14,494 crores and advances of ₹ 11,266 crores.

### 1922-Nainital Bank

Nainital Bank was founded by Sh. Govind Ballabh Pant and a few other prominent men in the year 1922 in Nainital, Uttarakhand State. It is one of the private sector banks today. Bank has its Head Office at Nainital, Uttarakhand and one Regional Office in New Delhi. The bank has about 103 branches in Uttarakhand, Rajasthan, Delhi and Haryana states.

In 1975 Government-owned Bank of Baroda (BOB), acquired 98.6% stake in the bank and made it a subsidiary. As at March 2010, total assets of the bank were ₹ 2877 crores.

### 1923-Andhra Bank

The eminent freedom fighter and a multifaceted genius, Dr. Bhogaraju Pattabhi Sitaramayya, founded Andhra Bank. The Bank was registered on 20th November 1923 and commenced business on 28th November 1923 with a paid up capital of ₹ 1.00 lakh and an authorised capital of ₹ 10.00 lakh. Bank's head office is located in Hyderabad.

The bank was nationalised in the year 1980. As at September 2010 Bank had 1652 branches. Bank's deposits were ₹ 78,584 crores and advances were ₹ 61,020 crores.

### *1924- Karnataka Bank*

This bank is located in Mangalore town of Karnataka. The bank was established in the year 1924 on this coastal town in Dakshina Kannada district of the olden Madras Presidency with B. R. Vysarayachhar as one of its founder.

The bank is a leading private sector bank today. As at March 2010, the bank had 486 branches. The deposits of the bank stood at ₹ 23,730 crores and advances at ₹ 14,435 crores.

### *1925- Syndicate Bank*

Syndicate Bank was established in 1925 in Udupi, in coastal Karnataka with a capital of ₹ 8000 by three visionaries—Sri Upendra Ananth Pai, a businessman, Sri Vaman Kudva, an engineer and Dr. T.M.A. Pai, a physician. Bank started an innovative Pigmy Deposit Scheme in 1928 under which small amount of deposit was collected daily from depositor's from their doorsteps. This scheme is the Bank's brand equity today. The bank is also one of the first banks to lend to agriculture.

The bank was nationalised in the year 1969. As at March 2010 Bank had about 2210 branches and a branch in London. Bank's deposits were ₹ 1,17,026 crores and advances were ₹ 82,599 crores.

### *1926-Laxmi Vilas Bank*

Seven people of Karur under the leadership of Shri V.S.N. Ramalinga Chettiar founded the Lakshmi Vilas Bank Limited (LVB) in 1926. The bank was incorporated on November 03, 1926 under the Indian Companies Act, 1913 and obtained the certificate to commence business on November 10, 1926. The Bank obtained its license from RBI in June 1958 and in August 1958, it became a Scheduled Commercial Bank. During 1961-65, LVB took over nine Banks and raised its branch network considerably.

The bank is in private sector. As at March 2010 Bank had 279 branches with deposits at ₹ 9075 crores and advances at ₹ 6277 crores.

### *1927-Dhanlaxmi Bank*

A group of enterprising entrepreneurs at Thrissur, a city of Kerala, founded Dhanlaxmi bank on 14th November 1927. The group started with around ₹ 11,000 and with only seven employees. Today the branches of the bank are spread over the States of Kerala, Tamil Nadu, Karnataka, Andhra Pradesh, Maharashtra, Gujarat, Delhi and West Bengal.

It is now a private sector bank. As at March 2010 Bank had 256 branches with deposits of ₹ 7,098 crores and advances at ₹ 5,056 crores.

### *1929-South Indian Bank*

South Indian Bank came into being during the Swadeshi movement. The bank was established by a group of enterprising men who joined together at Thrissur, a town in Kerala State. It became a scheduled bank in 1946.

The bank is a leading private sector bank today. As at March 2010 bank had 575 branches. The bank had deposits of ₹ 23,012 crores and advances of ₹ 15,970 crores.

### *1930-Vysya Bank* (later became ING Vysya Bank in 2002)

ING Vysya Bank Ltd., is an entity formed with the coming together of erstwhile, Vysya Bank Ltd., a premier bank in the Indian Private Sector and a global financial powerhouse, ING of Dutch origin, during Oct. 2002. The origin of the erstwhile Vysya Bank was in the year 1930 when it was set up in Bangalore. It became a scheduled bank in 1948.

The bank is one of the leading private sector banks today. As at March 2010, the Deposits was ₹ 25,865 crores and advances of ₹ 18,507 crores. The bank had 493 branches.

### *1931-Vijaya Bank*

Vijaya Bank, was founded on 23rd October 1931 by Late Shri A.B. Shetty and other enterprising farmers in Mangalore, Karnataka. The bank became a scheduled bank in 1958.

The bank was nationalised in the year 1980. As at March 2010 Bank had 1158 branches. Bank's deposits were ₹ 61,932 crores and advances were ₹ 41,935 crores.

### 1936-Bank of Maharashtra

Bank was established in Pune, Maharashtra State and commenced its operations on 08-02-1936 in Pune. Prof V.G. Kale was the first chairman of the bank.

The bank was nationalised in the year 1980. As at March 2010 Bank had about 1564 branches. Bank's deposits were ₹ 63,304 crores and advances were ₹ 40,314 crores.

### 1936-United Western Bank

United Western Bank was one of the private banks in India incorporated in 1936, in the State of Maharashtra. The head office was at Satara in Maharashtra State. It had about 230 branches.

The bank was merged with IDBI Bank in the year 2006.

### 1937-Indian Overseas Bank

Indian Overseas Bank (IOB) was founded on February 10$^{th}$, 1937, by Shri M.Ct.M. Chidambaram Chettyar, a pioneer in many fields—Banking, Insurance and Industry with the twin objectives of specialising in foreign exchange business and overseas banking.

The bank was nationalised in the year 1969. In the year 2007, Bharat Overseas Bank was merged with this bank. As at March 2010 Bank had 2002 branches and 13 establishments abroad. Bank's deposits were ₹ 1,10,795 crores and advances were ₹ 80,782 crores.

### 1938-Dena Bank

Dena Bank was founded on 26th May, 1938 by the family of Devkaran Nanjee under the name Devkaran Nanjee Banking Company Ltd. It became a Public Ltd. Company in December 1939 and later the name was changed to Dena Bank Ltd. Its head office is in Mumbai.

The bank was nationalized in the year 1969. As at March 2010 Bank had 1223 branches with deposits of ₹ 51,344 crores and advances of ₹ 35,462 crores.

### *1938-Jammu & Kashmir Bank*

The Bank was incorporated in 1938. Jammu & Kashmir Bank is the only Bank in the country with majority ownership vested with a State Government—the Government of Jammu & Kashmir. Bank functions as a universal bank in Jammu & Kashmir and as a specialised bank in the rest of the country. It is also the only private sector bank designated as RBI's agent for banking business, and carries out banking business of the Central Government.

As at March 2010 Bank had 536 branches with deposits of ₹ 37,237 crores and advances of ₹ 23,057 crores.

### *1940-Federal Bank*

Federal Bank was established in the year 1940 and was initially known as the Travancore Federal Bank. It gradually transformed into a full-fledged bank under the leadership of its Founder, Mr. K.P. Hormis. The name was changed to Federal Bank Limited in the year 1947. The bank is situated in Alwaye, bordering Kochi in Kerala.

It is one of the leading private sector banks today. As at March, 2010 Bank had 699 branches. Bank's deposits stood at ₹ 36,057crores and Advances at ₹ 26,950 crores.

### *1940-Lord Krishna Bank*

Lord Krishna Bank was established at Kodungallur in Thrissur District, Kerala in 1940. During the 1960's, Lord Krishna Bank acquired three commercial banks: Thiyya Bank, Josna Bank and Kerala Union Bank.

This bank merged with Centurion Bank of Punjab in the year 2006.

### *1943-Oriental Bank of Commerce*

Bank was founded in Lahore in the year 1943 by the Founder-Late Rai Bahadur Lala Sohan Lal, the first Chairman of the Bank. Within four years of coming into existence, the Bank had to face partition and after partition of the country, the head office of the bank was moved to Amritsar and later again moved to Delhi.

The bank was nationalised in the year 1980. As at March 2010 Bank had 1508 domestic branches. Bank's deposits stood at ₹ 1,20,257 crores and advances were ₹ 83,489 crores.

### 1943-Uco Bank

Mr. G.D. Birla, the doyen of Indian Industrial renaissance, started this bank on 6th of January 1943. The United Commercial Bank Ltd. has its Registered and Head Office at Kolkata.

The bank was nationalised in the year 1969. As at March 2010 bank's deposits were ₹ 1,22,415 crores and advances were ₹ 82,504 crores. Bank had 2231 domestic branches and 4 overseas branches as on 30-09-11.

### 1943-Bank of Rajasthan

Bank was set up at Udaipur in 1943 with an initial capital of ₹ 10.00 lakhs. An eminent Industrialist Late Seth Shri Govind Ram Seksaria was the founder Chairman. It was classified as Scheduled Bank in 1948.

This bank merged with ICICI Bank in the year 2010 and at the time of merger, it had 463 branches.

### 1943-Hindustan Commercial Bank

Hindustan Commercial Bank was established in the year 1943 and its head office was in Kanpur in Uttar Pradesh. This bank was merged with Punjab National Bank in the year 1986. At the time of merger, this bank had 142 branches.

### 1943-Bank of Madura

The bank was established in 1943 by Karumuttu Thiagarajan Chettiar at Madurai in Tamil Nadu State. It acquired Chettinad Mercantile Bank (est. 1933) and Illanji Bank (est. 1904) in the 1960s.

The bank was merged with ICICI Bank in the year 2001. At the time of merger, this bank had 280 branches and 40 ATMs.

### 1943-Ratnakar Bank

The Ratnakar Bank Ltd. was established by Shri Babgonda Bhujgonda Patil a distinguished Advocate of Sangli and Shri.

Gangaram Siddhappa Chougule, a renowned merchant of Kolhapur. The bank was set up on 6th August 1943. In 1959 RBI granted the status of Scheduled bank to it. The head office of the bank is at Kolhapur in Maharashtra State.

The bank is in private sector and as at March 2010, the bank had about 90 branches. It had deposits of ₹ 1,585 crores and advances of ₹ 1,170 crores.

### *1947-New Bank of India*

The bank was established in Lahore prior to independence (1947). After partition of the country, the head office of the bank was moved to Amritsar and then to New Delhi. The bank was nationalised in the year 1980 along with five other banks.

The bank was merged with Punjab National Bank, a nationalised bank in the year 1993. At the time of merger, it had 591 branches. It is the only instance when a nationalised bank was merged with another bank.

### *1947-Laxmi Commercial Bank*

This bank was also established before independence (1947) as a private bank. This bank was merged with Canara Bank in the year 1985.

### *1950-United Bank of India*

The bank was formed in 1950 by merging four fairly big banks. On October 12, 1950, the name of Bengal Central Bank Limited (established in 1918 as Bengal Central Loan Company Limited) was changed to United Bank of India Limited and three other banks were amalgamated with it on December 18, 1950. They are Comilla Banking Corporation Limited (established in 1914), The Comilla Union Bank Limited (established in 1922), and The Hooghly Bank (established in 1932). Subsequently, other banks namely, Cuttack Bank Limited, Tezpur Industrial Bank Limited, Hindustan Mercantile Limited (merged in 1973), and Narang Bank of India Limited (merged in 1976) were merged with United Bank of India.

The bank was nationalized in the year 1969. As at March 2010 Bank had 1534 branches. Bank's deposits were ₹ 68,180 crores and advances were ₹ 42,756 crores.

All these present day banks have been started between years 1900 to 1950 as private banks and as joint stock companies. Two more banks in private sector came into existence after 1950 and they are:

### *1973-Bharat Overseas Bank*

The bank was established in 1973 in order to take over the Bangkok branch of the Indian Overseas Bank. The head office of the bank was in Chennai. It was one of the few private banks, permitted by Reserve Bank of India to have a branch outside of India. It was owned by seven banks viz., Indian Overseas Bank (30% stake), Bank of Rajasthan (16%), Vysya Bank (14.66%), Karur Vysya Bank (10%), Federal Bank (19.67%), South Indian Bank (10%), and Karnataka Bank (8.67%).

In 2007, this bank was merged with Indian Overseas Bank and at the time of merger, the bank had about 75 branches.

### *1994-SBICI Bank Ltd.*

State Bank of India Commercial and International Bank Ltd. (SBICI Bank Ltd.) is a wholly owned subsidiary of SBI, which was set up in 1994 after taking over the Indian operations of the erstwhile Bank of Credit & Commerce International Ltd. (BCCI), which went into liquidation in 1991. SBICI Bank Ltd. has only two branches, both in Mumbai

On 21-07-2011, The Union Cabinet approved acquisition of the State Bank of India Commercial and International Bank Ltd. (SBICI Bank Ltd.) by State Bank of India (SBI), in terms of sub-section (2) of section 35 of the State Bank of India Act, 1955.

From 29-07-2011, State Bank of India Commercial and International Bank Limited Branches started to operate as SBI Branches.

Another bank in public sector—IDBI Bank, came into existence in the year 1994.

### *1994-IDBI Bank*

IDBI was the apex Development Financial Institution (DFI) constituted under an act in the year 1964 and functioned as a development bank for industrial growth. It along with SIDBI promoted IDBI Bank as a commercial bank in the year 1994. The bank became operational from 13th November 1995 and the registered office is in Indore, MP. In 2004, IDBI a statutory corporation became a company and the name was changed to IDBI Ltd., to facilitate its merger with IDBI Bank. Subsequently in the year 2005, by a reverse merger process, the parent IDBI Ltd. was merged with IDBI bank. As the majority ownership is vested with Govt of India, the bank is a public sector bank from the date of origin. However, it is a new generation bank coming on the scene after the reforms were introduced. Later in the year 2006, it took over the ailing United Western Bank, a private sector bank. Bank's Head office is in Mumbai.

It is leading public sector bank today and as on March 31, 2011, the Bank had a network of 816 Branches and 1372 ATMs. The Bank's total business, during FY 2010-11, reached ₹ 3,37,584 crores, Balance Sheet reached ₹ 2,53,377 crores.

## Associate Banks of SBI

During the same period (1900-1950) all the eight banks that later became subsidiary banks of State Bank of India also came into existence. These banks are:

### *State Bank of Saurashtra [1902]*

Origin of State Bank of Saurashtra is traced to Bhavnagar Durbar Bank established in the year 1902 in the princely state of Bhavnagar in Saurashtra region in Gujarat State.

Prior to 1948, the region of Saurashtra, which at present forms a part of Gujarat State, comprised many small, medium and large princely states. Bhavnagar, Rajkot and Porbandar, which were among the larger states, and two smaller states, Palitana and Vadia, had established their own Darbar (meaning Palace) Banks, the oldest of which was Bhavnagar

Darbar Bank, established in 1902. These banks mainly catered to the needs of the governments of their respective princely states, and acted as depositories for local savings. After the establishment of Saurashtra state in 1948, there was a parallel amalgamation of these banks. The Bhavnagar Darbar Bank became the State Bank of Saurashtra, under the Saurashtra State Bank (Amalgamation) Ordinance, 1950, and the four Darbar Banks—Rajkot State Bank, Porbandar State Bank, Palitana Darbar Bank and Vadia State Bank—were merged with it with effect from 1 July, 1950 as its branches. At the close of 1950 the Bank had only 9 branches and deposits of ₹ 7 crores (*Source*: State Bank of Saurashtra).

State Bank of Saurashtra became a subsidiary of SBI in 1960 under the State Bank of India (Subsidiary Banks) Act, 1959. In the year 2008, the bank was merged with State Bank of India.

### *State Bank of Mysore [1913]*

State Bank of Mysore was established in the year 1913 as Bank of Mysore Ltd. under the patronage of the erstwhile Govt of Mysore. It was established on the recommendations of the banking committee headed by the great Engineer-Statesman, Late Dr. Sir M. Visvesvaraya. In March 1960, the Bank became an Associate of State Bank of India. State Bank of India held 92.33% of shares.

As at March 2010, the bank had Deposits of ₹ 43,225 crores and advances of ₹ 29,236 crores and had 689 branches.

### *State Bank of Patiala [1917]*

The bank was established in the year 1917 in Patiala, Punjab as Patiala state bank. It was founded by Late His Highness Bhupinder Singh, Maharaja of erstwhile Patiala state, with one branch known as 'Chowk Fort, Patiala'. It was a state owned bank.

It became subsidiary of the State Bank of India on 1st April 1960, when it was named as the State Bank of Patiala.

As at March 2010 the bank had 886 Branches, had Deposits of ₹ 64,551 crores, and advances of ₹ 46,347 crores.

### *State Bank of Indore [1920]*

In 1920, The Bank of Indore was incorporated under a special charter from Maharaja Tukoji Rao Holkar III, who was the ruler from 1903 to 1927 of the former princely state of Indore. Indore State awarded the Bank a monopoly for 10 years, granted it certain concessions and subscribed to the Bank's share capital. Indore Bank's main branch and headquarters was in the city of Indore, Madhya Pradesh State.

The Bank of Indore became a subsidiary of State Bank of India w.e.f. 1 January 1960 and was renamed as State Bank of Indore. State Bank of Indore acquired the Bank of Dewas (established in 1936), in 1962 and Dewas Senior Bank (established in 1941) in 1965.

State Bank of Indore was merged with State Bank of India in the year 2010.

### *State Bank of Hyderabad [1941]*

State Bank of Hyderabad was constituted as Hyderabad State Bank on 08-08-1941 under Hyderabad State Bank Act, 1941. The Bank started with the unique distinction of being the central bank of the erstwhile State of Hyderabad, covering present-day Telangana region of Andhra Pradesh, Hyderabad—Karnataka of Karnataka State and Marathwada of Maharashtra State, to manage its currency—Osmania Sikka and public debt apart from the functions of commercial banking. The first branch of the bank was opened at Gunfoundry, Hyderabad on 5th April, 1942.

In 1953, the Bank took over the assets and liabilities of the Hyderabad Mercantile Bank Ltd. In the same year, the Bank started conducting Government and Treasury business as agent of Reserve Bank of India. In 1956, the Bank was taken over by Reserve Bank of India as its first subsidiary and its name was changed from Hyderabad State Bank to State Bank of Hyderabad. The Bank became a subsidiary of State Bank of India on the 1st October 1959 and is now the largest Associate Bank of State Bank of India.(*Source*: State Bank of Hyderabad)

As at March 2010, the bank had 1185 branches. The bank had Deposits of ₹ 72,970 crores and advances of ₹ 52,824 crores.

### *State Bank of Travancore [1945]*

State Bank of Travancore (SBT) was originally established as Travancore Bank Ltd. in 1945 sponsored by the erstwhile princely state of Travancore. It became an Associate of the State Bank of India under SBI subsidiary Banks Act 1959. Its head office is situated in Trivandrum in Kerala State.

As at March 2010, the bank had had 748 branches with deposits of ₹ 50,883 crores and advances of ₹ 38,461 crores.

### *State Bank of Bikaner and Jaipur [1963]*

State Bank of Jaipur was established in 1943 and State Bank of Bikaner was established in 1944 by the respective princely states of Jaipur and Bikaner. Both the banks became subsidiaries of SBI in 1960 under the Subsidiary Banks Act 1959. On January 1, 1963, these two subsidiary banks were merged and State Bank of Bikaner and Jaipur was formed. The Bank took over the business of the Govind Bank Pvt. Ltd., Mathura on 25th April, 1966.

As at March 2010 the bank had 861 Branches with deposits of ₹ 46,059 crores and advances of ₹ 35,563 crores.

All the above banks were started in the princely states of erstwhile Indian rulers and also functioned as bankers to the respective princely states.

### Other Banks

1. The co-op movement was witnessed mainly during the period 1900 to 1950 wherein many urban co-op banks came up and other co-op sector banks were also created for rural development. (See under urban coop banks and coop sector for rural development)
2. Concept of development banks was introduced in the country in 1948. The First Institution established in the field of Development Banking was The Industrial Finance Corporation of India, in 1948. After this

beginning, many Development Banks came to be established. They are basically term lending institutions for industries or other sectors of economy. (See under development banks)

3. Regional Rural Banks (RRBs) were started from the year 1975. These banks were sponsored as commercial banks by nationalised banks for the purpose of rural development. (See under regional rural banks)
4. After the financial sector reforms were introduced from the year 1991, new generation private sector banks made their appearances in 1994 and onwards. (See under new private sector banks)
5. Few Local Area Banks (LABs) made their appearances from the year 1996 onwards as commercial banks. (See under local area banks)

### Banks in India During 2001-2010

First decade of 21st century witnessed many more changes. Kotak Mahindra Bank came in 2003, converted from NBFC to bank. Yes Bank came in the year 2004. (See under private sector banks). Many foreign banks came to India and opened branches.

In 2002, The Reserve Bank of India has cancelled the licence issued to Vinayak Local Area Bank Ltd., Sikar, Rajasthan, prohibiting it to carry on banking business.

Nedungadi Bank, a private sector bank, was merged with PNB in the year 2003. GTB one of the new generation private sector banks, failed in the year 2004 and the business was merged with Oriental Bank of Commerce. South Gujarat Local Area Bank was merged with Bank of Baroda in 2004. In the year 2006, two banks were merged—Sangli Bank with ICICI bank and United Western Bank with IDBI Bank. In the year 2008, Centurion Bank of Punjab was merged with HDFC Bank. (Lord Krishna Bank {1940} merged with Centurion Bank of Punjab in 2007. Centurion Bank of Punjab itself was formed in the year 2005 by merging Centurion Bank (1994) and Bank of Punjab {1995}.)

Two of the subsidiaries of State Bank of India i.e. State Bank of Saurashtra and State Bank of Indore were merged with SBI in 2008 and 2010. Bank of Rajasthan was merged with ICICI bank in 2010.

Regional rural banks which were 196 in number came down to 82 as many of them were merged with other RRBs.

## Creation of State Bank of India (SBI)

State Bank of India is the India's largest bank and occupies a unique position in banking industry. In terms of network of branches and the reach, it has no competitors and other banks are far behind it. It has a unique history and place in Indian banking.

The roots of the State Bank of India are traced to the Carnatic Bank (estb: 1788), the British Bank of Madras (estb: 1795), the Asiatic Bank (estb: 1804), the Madras Bank (estb:1806). (The Bank of Madras was formed in 1843 by the amalgamation of these four banks) and the Bank of Calcutta, established on 2 June 1806. Later Bank of Calcutta was renamed as the Bank of Bengal. The Bank of Bengal was one of three Presidency banks; the other two were the Bank of Bombay (incorporated on 15 April 1840 and failed in 1968 and New Bank of Bombay created the same year) and the Bank of Madras (incorporated on 1 July 1843). All three Presidency banks were incorporated as joint stock companies by the Royal Charters. These three banks received the exclusive right to issue paper currency in 1861, on behalf of Govt under the Paper Currency Act, a right they retained until the formation of the Reserve Bank of India. The Presidency Banks Act came into operation on 1 May 1876, and brought the three presidency banks under a common statute. These presidency banks dominated banking scene in 19th century and acted as govt bank, central bank and as commercial banks. All the three presidency banks were merged to form Imperial Bank of India in the year 1921.

State Bank of India Act was passed by Parliament in May 1955 and the State Bank of India was constituted on 1 July 1955. It took over Imperial Bank. Imperial Bank at the time had 480 offices comprising branches, sub-offices and three Local Head Offices. In terms of business, more than 25% of the resources of the Indian banking system came under the direct control of the State. Later, the State Bank of India (Subsidiary Banks) Act was passed in 1959, and the State Bank of India took over eight former State-Associated banks as its subsidiaries (later named Associates). After formation of RBI, State Bank of India acted as agent to RBI for conducting govt business and managed Clearing Houses, wherever RBI did not had its offices. Even now, SBI is managing Clearing Houses at many places.

At the time of formation, State Bank of India was owned by the Government through RBI, which held more than 95% of the share capital. Then in the year 1994, SBI issued fresh shares to public and the RBI holding came down to nearly 60%. In 2008, the Government of India took over the stake held by the Reserve Bank of India. At present, Govt holding is 59.40% of the total capital.

Immediately after its formation, SBI was asked by the Govt to expand its branch network and open 400 new branches in order to provide banking support to Govt for its development plans. Branch expansion of SBI has no parallel in the history. From a mere 480 offices at the time of its formation, branch network expanded to over 13000 branches. This expansion of SBI, along with other nationalized banks, is the main reason for economic development of the country as it enabled Govt to join all parts of the country in the development process.

State Bank Group had the monopoly over govt business. Even after formation of RBI, it managed govt business at all centres where RBI's presence was not there. This monopoly continued for long time and only in nineties other banks were allowed to handle govt business.

The bank maintained its lead and branch expansion was impressive. As on March 2011, SBI had 13542 domestic branches and 156 foreign branches. Deposits were ₹ 9,33,933 crores and advances were ₹ 7,56,719 crores. SBI has 14 Local

Head Offices and 57 Zonal Offices that are located at important cities throughout the country.

The State Bank Group, with over 19347 branches, and over 25005 ATMs has the largest banking branch network in India.

Presently the bank is planning to merge all its associate banks with it. In the process, State Bank of Saurashtra was merged with SBI in 2008, and State Bank of Indore was merged with it in 2010.

## Creation of Reserve Bank of India

The need for a central banking authority was felt since very long and was recommended by Hilton-Young Commission. The commission submitted its report in the year 1926, and in the year 1934, the Reserve Bank of India Act 1934, was enacted. RBI came into existence in the year 1935. It was created as a joint stock company with government holding some shares.

The Preamble of the Reserve Bank of India describes the basic functions of the Reserve Bank as "to regulate the issue of bank notes, to keep reserves with a view to securing monetary stability in India and generally to operate the currency and credit system in the best interests of the country".

The Central Office of the Reserve Bank was initially established in Kolkata, but was permanently moved to Mumbai in 1937. The Reserve Bank continued to act as the central bank for Myanmar till Japanese occupation of Burma and later up to April 1947, though Burma seceded from the Indian Union in 1937. After partition, the Reserve Bank served as the central bank for Pakistan until June 1948, when the State Bank of Pakistan commenced operations. Now the RBI is fully owned by the Government of India since its nationalization in 1949.

Though the act defined the role and function of RBI, in the absence of any banking companies act, its role was not very effective. In fact, it had no mandatory authority over banks. In view of this, the role became advisory. In the year 1949, RBI was nationalized and was made an autonomous authority as central bank of the country. To streamline the functioning and activities of commercial banks, the Government of India enacted The Banking Companies Act, 1949 which was later changed to Banking Regulation Act 1949 as per amending Act of 1965 (Act No. 23 of 1965) and this act gave vast powers to RBI over banking sector.

Main functions of RBI are:

- RBI is the Monetary Authority of the country, which formulates implements and monitors the monetary policy with the objective for maintaining price stability and ensuring adequate flow of credit to productive sector.
- Regulator and supervisor of the financial system: Prescribes broad parameters of banking operations within which the country's banking and financial system functions with the objective to maintain public confidence in the system, protect depositors' interest and provide cost-effective banking services to the public.
- RBI is the Manager of Foreign Exchange and manages the Foreign Exchange Management Act, 1999 with objective to facilitate external trade and payment and promote orderly development and maintenance of foreign exchange market in India.
- RBI is the Issuer of currency with objective to give the public adequate quantity of supplies of currency notes and coins and in good quality.
- Banker to the Government: performs merchant banking function for the Central and the State Governments and acts as their banker.
- Banker to banks and the banker of last resort: maintains banking accounts of all scheduled banks. Also acts as the banker of last resort. In this role, the central bank injects funds into the system to help banks tide over temporary mismatches of funds. RBI moved to an auction system of repos and reverse repos to suck-out and inject liquidity to the market.

In the year 1960, Reserve Bank of India was vested with extensive powers for the supervision of banking in India as the Central Banking Authority and was given powers to compulsorily merge weak banks with other banks to safeguard the public interest as the country experienced periodic failures of banks.

Large co-operative banks with paid-up share capital and reserves of ₹ 1 lakh were brought under the purview of the Banking Regulation Act 1949 with effect from 1st March 1966 and within the ambit of the Reserve Bank's supervision. With this Banking related functions (viz. licensing, area of operations, interest rates, etc.) for co-op banks are now governed by RBI. However, Registration, management, audit and liquidation, etc. of coop banks are governed by State Governments as per the provisions of respective State Acts.

RBI has largely succeeded in streamlining and consolidating banking sector in the country. It became proactive to safeguard interests of the depositors and managed to enforce mergers to save the weak banks from closing down.

From period 1949 to 1991 it monitored banking operations by framing rules and guidelines for every aspect of banking and involved itself in micro management of banks. From the year 1991, financial sector reforms were introduced and RBI played a stellar role in transforming Indian banking to global banking standards. In the process, it distanced itself from micro management of banks and moved to macro management of the banks.

# Banking Crisis and Consolidation

# 3

Joint stock banks in India came into existence from the year 1720 onwards. However, all the banks that came into existence till 1900, were closed subsequently barring few banks. Only three presidency banks, three private banks, and a coop bank that came into existence prior to 1900 survived.

"By the end of December 1913, the total number of reporting commercial banks in the country reached 56 comprising 3 Presidency banks, 18 Class 'A' banks (with capital of greater than ₹ 5 lakhs), 23 Class 'B' banks (with capital of ₹ 1 lakh to 5 lakhs) and 12 exchange banks. Exchange banks were foreign owned banks that engaged mainly in foreign exchange business in terms of foreign bills of exchange and foreign remittances for travel and trade. Class A and B were joint stock banks. The banking sector during this period, however, was dominated by the Presidency banks as was reflected in paid-up capital and deposits" (*Source*: RBI-evolution of banking in India).

"Apart from commercial and co-operative banks, several other types of banks existed in India. This was because the term "bank" was an omnibus term and was used by the entities, which, strictly speaking, were not banks. These included loan companies, indigenous bankers and nidhis some of which were registered under the Companies Act, 1913. Although very little information was available about such banks, their number was believed to be very large. Even the number of registered entities was enormous. Many doubtful companies registered themselves as banks and figured in the statistics of bank failures. Consequently, it was difficult to define in strict legal terms the scope of organised banking, particularly in the period before 1913 (Chandavarkar, 2005)" (*Source*: RBI-Evolution of banking in India).

During the end of 19th century and in the first two decades of 20th century, there was mushrooming growth in number of banks. This was because till the year 1935, there was no central banking authority in the country. RBI came in that year. Many loan companies, indigenous bankers, and nidhis registered themselves as banks under the Companies Act 1913. They were not the commercial banks in true sense. The real authority of RBI on banking sector became effective in the year 1949, after nationalization of the RBI and after passing of Banking Companies Act (later renamed as Banking Regulation Act) in the same year. After Banking Regulation Act 1949 came into force, banks were distinguished and above-mentioned financial companies were barred from using the word 'bank' or 'banking' in their name.

## Banking Crisis

The first banking crisis was during the years of the First World War, and it took its toll as at least 94 banks collapsed between 1913 and 1918.

Next crisis was when the Great Depression gripped the world economy during the period from 1928 to 1934. This also had an impact on the Indian banking industry and number of banks failed due to their loans going bad.

By 1930, the number of commercial banks increased to 107 with the Imperial Bank of India dominating the Indian banking sector. At end-March 1929, 158 co-operative banks also existed. However, many indigenous bankers were also registered themselves as banks and hence for statistics, the number of banks, including them, was very high. In fact, by the year 1930, 1258 entities were registered as banks. Some were banks in genuine terms; others were indigenous bankers, like nidhis and loan companies. During those years, in a large number of towns and villages, indigenous banks were the main source of credit. It was informed that many indigenous bankers worked along modern lines and transacted all kinds of business like the joint-stock banks, and even issued passbooks and cheque books. Further, many of this type of smaller banks also existed who did not register themselves.

By the year 1940 the country had nearly 1200 commercial banks—small and big, operating. Then came the banking crisis triggered by the Second World War. Nearly half the number of banks who could not withstand the crisis was closed. In 1947, the country got independence and faced partition. Partition of the country also triggered failure of many banks mostly in west Bengal and Punjab. Between the years 1940 to 1951, nearly 634 banks had failed and closed. It was a big jolt to the banking business. Total number of banks came down to 566 in 1951, out of this, 76 were scheduled banks, 16 were foreign banks and 474 banks were under non-scheduled category.

### Bank Failures

Bank failures were regular feature due to weak financials and poor and mis-managements of these banks. Further, due to the effect of First World War, the Great Depression, Second World War, and the partition of country, large number of banks failed. During the period 1913 to 1966, total of 1585 banks failed as under:

| Years | No. of banks failed |
|---|---|
| 1913 to 1922 | 123 |
| 1923 to 1936 | 357 |
| 1937 to 1939 | 255 |
| 1940 to 1946 | 392 |
| 1947 to 1951 | 242 |
| 1952 to 1953 | 62 |
| 1954 to 1959 | 106 |
| 1960 to 1966 | 48 |
| **Total** | 1585 |

A major bank failure was in the year 1938 when Kerala based Travancore National and Quilon Bank (TNQ bank) was liquidated on the orders of Dewan of Travancore. This bank was formed in the year 1937 by amalgamating two banks—Travancore National Bank (established in 1912) and Quilon

Bank (established in 1919) and was considered as greatest banking amalgamation in south India. The failure of this bank created a scare in south India, the role of RBI came under public and media gaze. This led to the collapse of more than 60 small banks at that time.

In the absence of Banking Companies Act, which came only in 1949, RBI had little control on banks. RBI at the time did not have the authority to inspect these banks and these banks were not submitting their affairs to RBI. Though the failure of TNQ Bank in 1938 highlighted the requirement of better control on banks, it took more than 10 years for bringing in banking companies act for strengthening the authority of RBI over banks.

Even after the Banking Companies Act came in the year 1949, it had not much impact as the period coincided with after-effects of Second World War and Partition of the country. Till the year 1951 many banks failed. Only after this crisis period, the effect of the Banking Companies Act 1949 was felt and things improved.

Again, in the year 1960 two more fairly big banks failed. The failures of Palai Central Bank# in Kerala and Laxmi Bank of Akola in the year 1960 triggered some action by the Govt and RBI was given powers to enforce merger and amalgamations of banks. RBI started using its authority to merge banks from the year 1961 onwards. The major problems were in Kerala (167 banks in Madras province in 1930) and West Bengal (919 banks in 1930) where large number of small banks existed. The period from 1960 to 1967 was the period of consolidation of banks in the country with the active intervention of RBI.

# Palai Central Bank was founded in 1927 as a commercial bank with its headquarters in Palai, Kerala. Although it was started in a small remote town, the Bank grew up to become the biggest bank in Kerala and the 17th largest among the 94 scheduled banks in India. It was ordered to be liquidated in 1960 by Kerala High Court on a petition moved by the Reserve Bank of India.

RBI actively undertook strengthening of the banking sector and the process involved weeding out the unviable banks by liquidation or the taking of assets of the non-functioning banks by other banks.

"During the period 1954 to 1959 as many as 106 banks were liquidated. Of these, 73 banks went into voluntary liquidation and 33 went into compulsory liquidation. Between 1960 to 1966, another 48 banks went into liquidation" (*Source*: RBI-Evolution of banking in India).

### Mergers

Besides liquidation of weak banks, RBI managed to amalgamate many banks, also to transfer business of many weak banks to other banks for consolidating banking sector and to protect depositors of the banks. The mergers and consolidation of banks during 1954 to 1966 was as under:

| Year | Compulsory amalgamation | Voluntary amalgamation | Business transferred to other banks | Total |
|---|---|---|---|---|
| 1954 | | | 17 | 17 |
| 1955 | | | 11 | 11 |
| 1956 | | | 6 | 6 |
| 1957 | | 1 | 10 | 11 |
| 1958 | | 4 | 10 | 14 |
| 1959 | | 4 | 20 | 24 |
| 1960 | | 2 | 15 | 17 |
| 1961 | 30 | | 9 | 39 |
| 1962 | 1 | 3 | 22 | 26 |
| 1963 | 1 | 2 | 15 | 18 |
| 1964 | 9 | 7 | 63 | 79 |
| 1965 | 4 | 5 | 24 | 33 |
| 1966 | | | 7 | 7 |
| | 45 | 28 | 229 | 302 |

(*Source*: RBI)

The policy of strengthening of the banking sector through compulsory amalgamation and mergers helped in consolidating the banking sector. Between the years, 1961 and 1966 RBI managed to merge nearly 202 banks and streamlined the banking system. Number of banks in 1967 came down to 91 from 566.

To protect depositors of banks, Deposit Insurance Corporation of India was started in the year 1962, which provided insurance cover for bank depositors. With this insurance cover and effective authority of RBI, bank failures were kept under check and after 1967, not many bank failures were witnessed.

After nationalization of 14 banks in the year 1969, RBI again became active in enforcing mergers and managed to merge many weak banks with nationalized banks. About 15 banks were merged with other banks between 1969 and 1992 and about 23 more banks were merged with other banks between 1993 and 2010.

Most of these mergers were forced and weak banks were merged with nationalised banks to protect the depositors of those banks. However, there was one case of New Bank of India, a nationalized bank, merged with PNB a bigger nationalized bank. Two of the subsidiaries of SBI were merged with SBI, which was a strategic move by SBI. Only five mergers have been voluntary as shown hereunder. There were few mergers with private sector banks also.

**Bank mergers from 1969 to 2010**

| Sl. No. | Merger year | Target bank | Acquirer bank | Reason |
|---|---|---|---|---|
| 1. | 1969 | Bank of Bihar | SBI | forced merger |
| 2. | 1969 | Indo Commercial Bank | PNB | forced merger |
| 3. | 1970 | National Bank of Lahore | SBI | forced merger |
| 4. | 1973 | Hindustan Mercantile Bank | United Bank | forced merger |
| 5. | 1974 | Krishnaram Baldeo Bank | SBI | forced merger |
| 6. | 1976 | Narrang Bank of India | United Bank | forced merger |
| 7. | 1985 | Bank of Cochin | SBI | forced merger |
| 8. | 1985 | Laxmi Commercial Bank | Canara Bank | forced merger |
| 9. | 1986 | Hindustan Commercial Bank | PNB | forced merger |
| 10. | 1986 | Parur Central Bank | Bank of India | forced merger |
| 11. | 1986 | Bank of Cochin | SBI | forced merger |
| 12. | 1988 | Bank of Tamilnadu | IOB | forced merger |
| 13. | 1988 | Bank of Tanjore | Indian Bank | forced merger |
| 14. | 1988 | Traders Bank | Bank of Baroda | forced merger |
| 15. | 1989 | Purbanchal bank | Central Bank | forced merger |
| 16. | 1993 | New Bank of India | Punjab National Bank | forced merger |
| 17. | 1994 | Bank of Karad Ltd. | Bank of India | forced merger |
| 18. | 1995 | Kashinath Seth Bank | State Bank of India | forced merger |
| 19. | 1996 | Punjab Co-op Bank Ltd. | Oriental Bank of Commerce | forced merger |

*(Contd...)*

| | | | | |
|---|---|---|---|---|
| 20. | 1997 | Bari Doab Bank Ltd. | Oriental Bank of Commerce | forced merger |
| 21. | 1999 | Bareilly Corp Bank Ltd. | Bank of Baroda | forced merger |
| 22. | 1999 | Sikkim Bank Ltd. | Union Bank of India | forced merger |
| 23. | 2000 | Times Bank Ltd. | HDFC Bank Ltd | voluntary merger |
| 24. | 2001 | Bank of Madura | ICICI Bank | voluntary merger |
| 25. | 2002 | Benaras State Bank Ltd. | Bank of Baroda | forced merger |
| 26. | 2003 | Nedungadi Bank Ltd. | Punjab National Bank | forced merger |
| 27. | 2004 | South Gujarat Local Area Bank | Bank of Baroda | forced merger |
| 28. | 2004 | Global Trust Bank Ltd. | Oriental Bank of Commerce | forced merger |
| 29. | 2005 | Centurion Bank | Bank of Punjab | voluntary merger |
| 30. | 2006 | Ganesh Bank of Kurandwad | Federal Bank | forced merger |
| 31. | 2006 | United Western Bank | IDBI Bank | forced merger |
| 32. | 2006 | Lord Krishna Bank | Centurion Bank of Punjab | voluntary merger |
| 33. | 2006 | Sangli Bank | ICICI Bank | voluntary merger |
| 34. | 2007 | Bharat Overseas Bank | Indian Overseas Bank | forced merger |
| 35. | 2008 | Centurion Bank of Punjab | HDFC Bank | forced merger |
| 36. | 2008 | State Bank of Saurashtra | SBI | merger with parent |
| 37. | 2010 | State Bank of Indore | SBI | merger with parent |
| 38. | 2010 | Bank of Rajasthan | ICICI Bank | forced merger |

RBI extensively used merger route now to protect customers and the experiment has proved to be success. Even though, the bank taking over has to bear some loss initially, it is worth it as they get new branches and client base of the merged bank. Initial loss suffered is more than compensated subsequently. Banks like SBI, PNB, Bank of India, Bank of Baroda, Canara Bank, Oriental Bank of Commerce, United Bank of India and IDBI Bank in the public sector and ICICI Bank & HDFC Bank in private sector have benefitted by mergers in growing faster.

There were few cases of voluntary mergers in private sector. HDFC Bank was the major beneficiary and within short span of 10-15 years the bank has grown in size and at present has more than 2000 branches. Times Bank was merged with it in 2000. Then Centurion Bank of Punjab merged with it in 2008. The Centurion Bank of Punjab itself was a merged entity of three banks; Centurion Bank, Bank of Punjab, and Lord Krishna Bank.

ICICI bank acquired Bank of Madura in 2001, Sangli Bank in 2006, and Bank of Rajasthan in 2010.

## Changes in Structure and Constitution of Banks

### *Banking Business and Bank*

Banking business basically is accepting deposits for the purpose of giving loans or investments. Now the question is who can undertake this business and whether whosoever undertakes this business can be called a bank?

Until the enactment of Banking Companies Act 1949 (later renamed as Banking Regulation Act 1949), banking business was conducted by anyone either as a company or partnership or as proprietary firm. Most of the indigenous bankers were partnership or proprietary firms. There was no bar for anyone carrying banking business. Many of them had named themselves as banks.

As there were no controls on the structures and the ownership of banks, many entered into the business of banking and this weakness in the system was a major cause for bank failures. This position was changed slowly over a period starting from year 1949. The progress in this respect to change the structure of banks and make them corporate entities can be traced to following developments.

Banking Regulation Act 1949 framed detailed guidelines for banking companies and gave RBI authority over banking companies.

Banking Regulation Act 1949 defined "banking", "banking company" and "company" as under:

*Section 5. Interpretation*

(b) "banking" means the accepting, for the purpose of lending or investment, of deposits of money from the public, repayable on demand or otherwise, and withdrawal by cheque, draft, order or otherwise;

(c) "banking company" means any company which transacts the business of banking in India.

*Explanation*—Any company which is engaged in the manufacture of goods or carries on any trade and which accepts deposits of money from the public merely for the purpose of financing its business as such manufacturer or trader shall not be deemed to transact the business of banking within the meaning of this clause;

(d) "company" means any company as defined in section 3 of the Companies Act, 1956 (1 of 1956); and includes a foreign company within the meaning of section 591 of that Act;).

This section defined 'banking' and the criteria are accepting deposit from the public for the purpose of lending or investment. Repayment can be by cheque, draft or order or otherwise. This section recognises only companies registered under the Companies Act 1956 and doing banking business as 'banking company'. Though other entities like associations, partnerships, and proprietary concerns are not expressly prohibited from carrying on banking business, they are placed under some restrictions as under:

Section 7 of Banking Regulation Act 1949 placed prohibition for use of word "bank", "banker", "banking", or "banking company" as under:

"["Section 7. Use of words "bank", "banker", "banking" or "banking company".

(1) No company other than a banking company shall use as part of its name or in connection with its business any of the words "bank", "banker" or "banking" and no company shall carry on the business of banking in India unless it uses as part of its name at least one of such words.

(2) No firm, individual or group of individuals shall, for the purpose of carrying on any business, use as part of its or his name any of the words "bank", "banking" or "banking company".

(3) Nothing in this section shall apply to—

(a) a subsidiary of a banking company formed for one or more of the purposes mentioned in sub-section (1) of section 19, whose name indicates that it is a subsidiary of that banking company;

(b) any association of banks formed for the protection of their mutual interests and registered under section 25 of the Companies Act, 1956 (1 of 1956).]"

Under this section, it is compulsory for banking companies to use these words in its name and all others are prohibited from use of any of these words in their names with the exception of the word "banker". Because of this restriction, even when the entities are in banking business they cannot call themselves as "banks". However, they can call themselves as "banker".

Facility of withdrawing by cheque is recognised as an exclusive right of the banking company, distinguishing it from others as per section 49A of Banking Regulation Act 1949.

> "Section 49A. Restriction on acceptance of deposits withdrawable by cheque.
>
> No person other than a banking company, the Reserve Bank, the State Bank of India or any other banking institution, firm or other person notified by the Central Government in this behalf on the recommendation of the Reserve Bank shall accept from the public deposits of money withdrawable by cheque:
>
> Provided that nothing contained in this section shall apply to any savings bank scheme run by the Government."

This section was introduced in the year 1959 and permits the use of cheques exclusively by banking companies. The exception provided in this section is for post office savings accounts conducted by the government. Only govt on the recommendations from RBI, can allow any others for using cheques for withdrawals. This section prohibited other entities in banking business to issue cheque books.

Thus under the provisions of Banking Regulation Act 1949, any entity other than a banking company cannot use the word "bank", "banking" or "banking company" in its name and also cannot issue cheque book to its customers.

The Companies Act 1956 (replacing the Companies Act 1913) also placed one restriction on entities in banking business. The section 11(1) of this act stipulated as under:

> "Section 11. Prohibition of associations and partnerships exceeding certain number.
>
> (1) No company, association or partnership consisting of more than ten persons shall be formed for the purpose of carrying on the business of banking, unless it is registered as a company under this Act, or is formed in pursuance of some other Indian Law."

This section prohibited any business concern with more than 10 persons to carry on banking business unless it is registered as a company under the act.

It is to be noted that though only companies were allowed to function as banks under the Banking Regulation Act 1949, there was no legal bar on individuals, firms or other entities to carry on deposit taking or loaning business. The Companies Act 1956 only restricted the number of persons to less than 10 persons for carrying on banking business. In fact, this activity continued and only they were not called banks and they could not issue cheque book to their customers.

This situation allowed such entities to remain outside the control of RBI. This position was changed subsequently.

In the year 1963, by an amendment to RBI Act, a new Chapter III-B was inserted in the RBI Act. Non-Banking Institutions and Financial Institutions were brought under the control of RBI and they were made to get themselves registered with RBI as non-banking financial company (NBFC). RBI was given effective control on their activities like prescription of minimum capital, reserve funds, SLR requirement and inspection. RBI was also empowered to wind up NBFCs in case their continuation is not found tenable.

However, individuals, firms engaged in deposit taking and loans business were still without control and only in the year 1997, such non-corporate bodies were prohibited from accepting deposits by an amendment to RBI act and a new

Chapter III C was inserted in the act. The new section 45S stipulated as under:

> "Section 45S. Deposits not to be accepted in certain cases.—
>
> (1) No person, being an individual or a firm or an unincorporated association of individuals shall, accept any deposit—
>
> (i) If his or its business wholly or partly includes any of the activities specified in clause (c) of section 45-I; or
>
> (ii) if his or its principal business is that of receiving of deposits under any scheme or arrangement or in any other manner, or lending in any manner;".

This section exempted the loans taken by individuals or firms from any of their relatives. Deposits taken earlier were required to be repaid within a period of three years. Further from the 1st day of April 1997, persons referred to in subsection (1) were prohibited to issue any advertisement in any form for soliciting deposit.

Hence, now the banks in the country are companies registered under Companies' Act 1956 or Societies registered under State Coop Societies Acts (Coop banks) or banks created by statutes like RBI, SBI, Exim Bank, etc. All others engaged in financial business (accepting deposits and/or giving loans) are called NBFCs (non-banking financial companies). No individual, or a firm, or an unincorporated association of individuals can accept any deposit from public now.

# Different Types of Banks in India

# 4

Today Banks in our country can be classified into following categories:

## Public Sector Banks

The three presidency banks started by the British, the first in the year 1806, can be considered as state owned banks so also the merged entity of these three banks—Imperial Bank of India in 1921. The subsidiaries of SBI, eight in numbers were also state owned banks owned by erstwhile rulers of princely states. State Bank of India came into existence in the year 1955, under an Act of Parliament, and took over Imperial Bank of India. In 1959, eight banks functioning as govt banks of princely states were made subsidiaries of SBI, by an Act of Parliament. Two of the banks State Bank of Bikaner and State Bank of Jaipur were merged in 1963, to form State Bank of Bikaner and Jaipur. Two subsidiaries, State Bank of Saurashtra and State Bank of Indore were later merged with SBI in the year 2008 and 2010, leaving now five subsidiaries.

Govt. nationalised 14 Banks in 1969 and another 6 banks in 1980. Out of this one bank, New Bank of India was merged in the year 1993 with Punjab National Bank leaving 19 banks under this category.

IDBI promoted IDBI Bank in 1994 and subsequently merged itself with IDBI Bank. As IDBI was state owned development bank, the new universal bank became a public sector bank from inception.

Many private sector banks have been merged with these banks since 1969. At present following public sector banks, are functioning:

| Sl. No. | Year started | Year nation-alised | Name | Banks merged with it after nationalisation with year of merger |
|---|---|---|---|---|
| 1. | 1865 | 1969 | Allahabad Bank | |
| 2. | 1895 | 1969 | Punjab National Bank | 2003 - Nedungadi Bank Ltd.<br>1993 - New Bank of India<br>1986 - Hindustan Commercial Bank<br>1969 - Indo Commercial Bank |
| 3. | 1906 | 1969 | Canara Bank | 1985 - Laxmi Commercial Bank |
| 4. | 1906 | 1969 | Bank of India | 1994 - Bank of Karad Ltd.<br>1986 - Parur Central Bank |
| 5. | 1906 | 1980 | Corporation Bank | |
| 6. | 1907 | 1969 | Indian Bank | 1988 - Bank of Tanjore |
| 7. | 1908 | 1969 | Bank of Baroda | 2004 - South Gujarat Local Area Bank<br>2002 - Benaras State Bank Ltd.<br>1999 - Bareilly Corp Bank Ltd.<br>1988 - Traders Bank |
| 8. | 1908 | 1980 | Punjab & Sind Bank | |
| 9. | 1911 | 1969 | Central Bank | 1989 - Purbanchal Bank |
| 10. | 1922 | 1969 | Union Bank of India | 1999 - Sikkim Bank Ltd. |
| 11. | 1923 | 1980 | Andhra Bank | |
| 12. | 1925 | 1969 | Syndicate Bank | |
| 13. | 1931 | 1980 | Vijaya Bank | |
| 14. | 1936 | 1980 | Bank of Maharashtra | |
| 15. | 1937 | 1969 | Indian Oversea Bank | 2007 - Bharat Overseas Bank<br>1988 - Bank of Tamilnadu |
| 16. | 1938 | 1969 | Dena Bank | |
| 17. | 1943 | 1980 | Oriental Bank of Commerce | 2004 - Global Trust Bank Ltd.<br>1997 - Bari Doab Bank Ltd.<br>1996 - Punjab Co-op Bank Ltd. |
| 18. | 1943 | 1969 | UCO Bank | |
| 19. | 1950 | 1969 | United Bank of India | 1976 - Narrang Bank of India<br>1973 - Hindustan Mercantile Bank |
| 20. | 1806 | 1955 | State Bank of India | 2010 - State Bank of Indore<br>2008 - State Bank of Saurashtra<br>1995 - Kashinath Seth Bank |

*(Contd...)*

| | | | | |
|---|---|---|---|---|
| | | | | 1986 - Bank of Cochin<br>1985 - Bank of Cochin<br>1974 - Krishnaram Baldeo Bank<br>1970 - National Bank of Lahore<br>1969 - Bank of Behar |
| 21. | 1941 | 1959 | State Bank of Hyderabad | |
| 22. | 1917 | 1959 | State Bank of Patiala | |
| 23. | 1913 | 1959 | State Bank of Mysore | |
| 24. | 1943/ 1944 | 1959 | State Bank of Bikaner & Jaipur | |
| 25. | 1945 | 1959 | State Bank of Travancore | |
| 26. | 1994 | | IDBI Bank | 2006 - United Western Bank |

As at March 2010 there were 27 public sector banks (State Bank of Indore merged with SBI after the date), and their deposits were ₹ 33,44,935 crores which was 72.15% of scheduled banks deposits. Advances were ₹ 24,14,137 crores 72.33% share of total advances and branches were 61301.

## Private Sector Banks

Until nationalisation of banks in 1969 and 1980, all banks, barring State Bank of India and its subsidiaries, were in private sector. State Bank of India group were in public sector as they were state owned banks. Though, there were large number of banks in private sector, over a period many banks disappeared mostly by mergers with other banks. 20 of these banks were nationalised in the year 1969 and 1980. By the year 1993, there were about 25 private sector banks operating in the country. From the year 1994, a new breed of private sector banks came into existence after financial sector reforms, and RBI's decision to allow new banks to come up. Purpose was to open up the economy, and to end the near monopoly of public sector banks in the country. Private sector banks are now categorised in to 'old private sector banks' i.e. banks that were existing prior to reform period and 'new private sector banks' i.e. banks that came after the reforms. As on March 2010, there were total 22 private sector banks (both old and new) and these banks had total branch network of 10387 branches.

Thereafter one Bank, Bank of Rajasthan was merged with ICICI Bank in the year 2010, leaving total 21 banks at present.

### Old Private Sector Banks

As on March 2011, following old private sector banks numbering 14 are in business:

| Sl. No. | Started in the year | Bank | No. of branches as at March 2010 |
|---|---|---|---|
| 1. | 1904 | City Union Bank | 225 |
| 2. | 1916 | Karur Vysya Bank | 367 |
| 3. | 1920 | Catholic Syrian Bank | 377 |
| 4. | 1921 | Tamilnadu Mercantile Bank | 233 |
| 5. | 1922 | Nainital Bank | 103 |
| 6. | 1924 | Karnataka Bank | 486 |
| 7. | 1926 | Laxmi Vilas Bank | 279 |
| 8. | 1927 | Dhanalaxmi Bank | 256 |
| 9. | 1929 | South Indian Bank | 575 |
| 10. | 1930 | ING Vysya Bank@ | 493 |
| 11. | 1938 | Jammu and Kashmir Bank$ | 510 |
| 12. | 1940 | Federal Bank | 699 |
| 13. | 1943 | Ratnakar Bank | 90 |
| 14. | 1994 | SBI Commercial & international Bank# | 2 |

@ Vysya Bank started in the year 1930, later became ING Vysya Bank in 2002 after ING group joined it.

$ Jammu & Kashmir Bank is considered as private sector bank though the majority ownership is vested with a State Government—the Government of Jammu & Kashmir. It is also the only private sector bank designated as RBI's agent for banking business, and carries out banking business of the Central Government.

# SBI Commercial & International Bank Ltd. was set up in 1994 as a private sector bank for taking over the Indian operations of the erstwhile Bank of Credit & Commerce International Ltd. (BCCI), which went into liquidation in 1991. This bank is fully owned subsidiary of SBI. The bank has two branches. SBI wanted to merge the bank with it and only in July 2011, GOI has approved the merger. This bank is merged with SBI in the year 2011.

As at March 2010, 15 old private sector banks (Bank of Rajasthan merged with ICICI Bank later) had deposits of ₹ 2,09,590 crores 4.53% share of all scheduled banks, advances of ₹ 1,53,035 crores 4.59% share and 5174 branches.

### New Private Sector Banks

After the financial sector reforms were introduced from the year 1991, RBI allowed new private sector banks to come on the scene. Taking advantage of the new policy of RBI, many financial institutions promoted new banks. Few other promoters from business also floated new banks.

HDFC, ICICI, UTI and IDBI promoted new banks—HDFC Bank, ICICI Bank, UTI Bank (now Axis Bank) and IDBI Bank. ICICI, the parent, merged with ICICI Bank in 2002.

IDBI Bank came into existence in 1994 and IDBI, the parent, merged with IDBI Bank in 2005. However, this bank is considered as public sector bank in view of govt holding.

The new generation private sector banks that came into existence are:

#### 1. HDFC Bank (1994)

HDFC is India's premier housing finance company established in 1977. HDFC, taking advantage of RBI's policy to encourage new private sector banks, was amongst the first to promote a bank. It promoted HDFC Bank Ltd. as a private sector bank in the year 1994. The bank was incorporated in August 1994 with its registered office in Mumbai. HDFC Bank commenced operations as a Scheduled Commercial Bank in January 1995.

The bank has grown very fast since then. Another new generation private sector bank, Times Bank was merged with it in the year 2000. Subsequently Centurion Bank of Punjab, another private bank was also merged with it in the year 2008.

At present, it is a leading private sector bank and as at March 2011 had 1986 branches and 5471 ATMs. Banks deposits stood at ₹ 2,08,586 crores and advances at ₹ 1,59,982 crores.

#### 2. Axis Bank, Earlier Known as UTI Bank (1994)

UTI Bank is one of the new private banks to have begun operations in 1994. The Bank was promoted jointly by the Administrator of the specified undertaking of the Unit Trust of India (UTI-I), Life Insurance Corporation of India (LIC),

General Insurance Corporation of India (GIC) and other four PSU insurance companies, i.e. National Insurance Company Ltd., The New India Assurance Company Ltd., The Oriental Insurance Company Ltd. and United India Insurance Company Ltd. All the promoters are public sector undertakings. The Bank's Registered Office is at Ahmedabad and its Central Office is located at Mumbai. The bank changed its name to Axis Bank in April 2007.

The Bank is a leading private sector bank today and as at March 2010 had 1035 branches. The Bank has a network of over 7591 ATMs (as on 30th September 2011). Bank's business as at March 2010 was deposits ₹ 1,41,300 crores and advances at ₹ 1,04,343 crores.

### 3. Indusind Bank (1994)

The bank was promoted by Mr. Srichand P. Hinduja, a leading Non-Resident Indian businessman and head of the Hinduja Group. Dr. Manmohan Singh, Honourable Prime Minister of India who was then the country's Finance Minister, formally inaugurated the Bank in April 1994. It started with a capital base of ₹ 100 crores of which ₹ 60 crores was raised through private placement from Indian Residents and ₹ 40 crores was by Non-Resident Indians.

As at March 2010, the bank had 210 branches and 497 ATMs. Banks deposits stood at ₹ 26,710 crores and advances at ₹ 20,551 crores.

### 4. Global Trust Bank (1994)

Global Trust Bank was another new generation private sector bank, which commenced operations in 1994. The main promoters were Shri Jayanta Madhab, who was associated with the Asian Development Bank (ADB), and Shri Ramesh Gelli, a former executive at Vysya Bank. Its head office was at Hyderabad in Andhra Pradesh State. Bank did well initially and later it ran into trouble. In the year 2004, the business of the bank was taken over by Oriental Bank of Commerce, a nationalised bank. At the time of merger, this bank had over 100 branches.

### 5. Times Bank (1994)

Times Bank Limited was a new private sector bank promoted by Bennett, Coleman & Co., (Times Group) in the year 1994. This bank was merged with HDFC Bank Ltd., effective February 26, 2000. This was the first merger of two banks in the New Generation Private Sector Banks.

### 6. Centurion Bank (1994)

Centurion Bank, a new private sector bank was established in June 30, 1994 as a joint venture between 20th Century Finance Corporation and Keppel Group of Singapore through Kephinance Investment. It started with a network of ten branches. In the following year, 20th Century Finance Corporation was amalgamated with Centurion Bank.

On June 29, 2005, the Centurion Bank and the Bank of Punjab merged to form Centurion Bank of Punjab.

### 7. Bank of Punjab (1995)

Bank of Punjab was a new private sector bank established in April 1995 and its first branch was opened in Chandigarh. On June 29, 2005, the Centurion Bank and the Bank of Punjab merged to form Centurion Bank of Punjab.

### 8. Development Credit Bank (1995)

Development Credit Bank (DCB) is a new generation private sector bank. DCB, which was originally a coop bank was converted into a Scheduled Commercial Bank on May 31, 1995, in the wake of India's economic liberalisation. Its promoter the Aga Khan Fund for Economic Development (AKFED) holds over 23% stake in the bank. Development credit bank originally started in 1930 as a co-operative bank and converted into a commercial bank in the year 1995, is the only such case in Indian banking history.

As at March 2010, the bank had about 80 branches and 134 ATMs. The deposits stood at ₹ 4,787 crores and advances at ₹ 3,459 crores.

### 9. ICICI Bank (1996)

ICICI Bank is India's second-largest bank next to State Bank of India. It was promoted by ICICI, a development bank (see under development banks) in the year 1996 as a new generation private sector bank. By a reverse merger, the parent ICICI then merged with ICICI Bank in the year 2002. ICICI Bank is the number one private sector bank today. ICICI bank has taken over Bank of Madura in 2001, Sangli Bank in 2006 and Bank of Rajasthan in 2010.

As at March 2010 the bank had deposits of ₹ 20,20,17 crores and Advances of ₹ 18,12,06 crores.

At March 31, 2011 total assets of the bank were ₹ 40,62,34 crores (US$ 91 billion) and the Bank has a network of 2552 branches and 7440 ATMs, and has presence in 19 countries, including India.

### 10. Kotak Mahindra Bank (2003)

In 2003, Kotak Mahindra Finance Ltd. was permitted by RBI to be converted into a commercial bank in private sector. This company belonged to the Kotak Mahindra group one of India's reputed financial conglomerates. Kotak Mahindra Finance Ltd. was established in 1985 by the promoter Shri Uday Kotak. Kotak Mahindra Finance Ltd. is the first non-banking finance company in India to convert itself into a bank as Kotak Mahindra Bank Ltd.

As at March 2010, the bank had 249 branches and 492 ATMs with deposits of ₹ 23,886 crores and Advances of ₹ 20,775 crores.

### 11. Yes Bank (2004)

Yes Bank is a new generation private sector bank started in the year 2004 and Shri Rana Kapoor, is the Founder of the bank. He is the Managing Director & CEO of the bank.

As at March 2010 bank had Deposits of ₹ 26,798 crores and advances of ₹ 22,193 crores with about 150 branches.

All these banks succeeded in growing very fast and started with total computerization in their operations. The only failure amongst them was Global Trust Bank, which though succeeded in carving a niche in banking services, failed subsequently, and its business was merged with Oriental Bank of Commerce in 2004. The new private sector banks brought in sea change in banking and galvanized the slow moving public sector banks to sit up and take notice. As the competition offered by these new banks were fierce, the public sector banks were made to come out of their slumber and respond. Computerization and technology was brought in and this has improved the service levels of entire banking industry benefiting the customers. ATMs, core banking, and internet banking was introduced by all banks in public sector and old private sector banks. Even urban coop banks adopted the new technology, as this has become a matter of survival for existing banks in the country.

Business growth rate of the new private sector bank was phenomenal and ICICI Bank that came into existence in 1996 has grown by the year 2010, to a size next only to SBI—the public sector giant bank. The new private banks have adopted both organic and inorganic growth, which saw many mergers of existing banks with them. These banks leveraged technology for growth and were instrumental in popularizing ATMs and internet banking in the country. As they had small branch network to begin with, they relied on ATMs for delivery of services and created large network of ATMs. This forced public sector banks and other banks to start ATMs and internet banking services in order to retain customers. Number of ATMs of leading new private banks as on March 31, 2011 was Axis Bank - 6270, ICICI Bank - 6,104, and HDFC Bank- 5,471. Only State Bank Group and Punjab National Bank have matched them in numbers as 25,060 ATMs of State Bank of India group, and 5050 of Punjab National Bank have been set up. Every bank in the country became active and started setting up ATMs. The number of ATMs linked to the National Financial Switch (NFS) which consists of 54 member banks in the country, was 75,178 as of March 31, 2011.

ICICI Bank and HDFC Bank have also adopted merger route for growth. ICICI bank has taken over Bank of Madura in 2001, Sangli Bank in 2006 and Bank of Rajasthan in 2010.

Times Bank merged with HDFC Bank in the year 2000. Centurion Bank (1994) and Bank of Punjab (1995) voluntarily merged to form Centurion Bank of Punjab in the year 2005.

Lord Krishna Bank {1940} merged with Centurion Bank of Punjab (CBOP) in 2007. Later on CBOP merged with HDFC bank in 2008. All these mergers have propelled HDFC Bank as a leading bank and it has over 2000 branches at present.

As of now, there are seven new generation private sector banks, as shown below, in addition to 14 old private sector banks.

1. HDFC Bank (1994)
2. Axis Bank earlier known as UTI Bank (1994)
3. Indusind Bank (1994)
4. Development Credit Bank (1995)
5. ICICI Bank (1996)
6. Kotak Mahindra Bank (2003)
7. Yes Bank (2004).

As at March 2010, 7 new private sector banks had deposits of ₹ 5,67,848 crores—12.25% share of all scheduled banks, advances of ₹ 4,31,668 crores—12.93% share and 5213 branches.

**Urban Co-operative Banks**

The origin of the urban cooperative banking movement in India can be traced to the close of nineteenth century and was inspired by the success of the experiments related to the co-operative movement in Britain and the co-operative credit movement in Germany. Co-operative societies are based on the principles of co-operation, mutual help, democratic decision-making, and open membership. Co-operatives represented a new and alternative approach to organisation as against proprietary firms, partnership firms and joint stock companies, which represent the dominant form of commercial organisation.

Anyonya Co-operative Bank Limited (ACBL) located at Vadodara (formerly Baroda) in Gujarat, was the first co-operative bank in India established in 1889 with the name Anyonya Sahayakari Mandali Co-operative Bank Limited, by Shri Vithal L. Kavthekar with a primary objective of providing an alternative to exploitation by moneylenders for Baroda's residents. In fact, this bank was said to be the first co-op bank in Asia also. This bank was functioning until recently and in 2007, Reserve Bank of India ordered the bank to stop its operations. Subsequently bank was closed in March 2008.

However, the real impetus to the co-operative movement in the country came with the enactment of Co-operative Credit Societies Act, 1904.

The first registered urban co-operative credit society was the Conjeevaram Urban Co-operative Bank, organised in Conjeevaram, in the then Madras Presidency in 1904. The second urban co-operative bank was the Peoples' Co-operative Society in 1905 in Bangalore city in the princely State of Mysore.

Co-op credit societies were the forerunners of urban co-op banks as many of them became co-op banks later.

The term Urban Co-operative Banks (UCBs), is not formally defined and refers to primary co-operative banks located in urban and semi-urban areas. These banks, till 1996, were not allowed to lend money for purposes of agriculture. This restriction does not exist today. These banks are traditionally centered on communities, localities, work place groups. They essentially lend to small borrowers and businesses. Today, their scope of operations has widened considerably. There is not much difference today between them and commercial banks.

It is observed that the urban co-op banking movement in the country has been uneven in geographical spread as most banks came up in the States of Maharashtra (557 banks), Karnataka (270 banks) and Gujarat (249 banks). Most banks are unit banks without any branch network. Generally, these banks operated on regional basis and were allowed to open branches in the same State. In 1985, RBI allowed multi-state banking and some of the larger banks then established their presence in many states. Now some of these banks are also 'Authorised Dealers' in Foreign Exchange.

Many prominent Banks in co-operative sector came into existence. They are:

- Shamrao Vithal Co-op Bank in 1906
- Cosmos Co-op Bank also in 1906
- Saraswat Co-op Bank in 1918
- Development Credit Bank in 1930 (this bank has started as co-op bank and converted as commercial bank in the year 1995—probably the only such case in Indian banking history)
- Bombay Mercantile Co-op Bank in 1941.

Cooperative Credit Societies Act, 1904 was a Central Act and the constitutional reforms, which led to the passing of the Government of India Act in 1919, transferred the subject of "Cooperation" from Government of India to the Provincial Governments (State Govts). Thereafter coop societies are now registered and controlled under state acts.

Urban co-op banks have become a useful and integral part of the financial system in our country. There is large number of smaller banks functioning and at times, they created scare. There were cases of failures, which is comparatively more in this sector. Since creation of Deposit Insurance scheme in 1962, DICGC has settled the claims in respect of 176 urban coop banks that have failed.

There were two major bank failures. In 2001 a large multistate co-operative bank in the State of Gujarat, the Madhavpura Mercantile Coop Bank established in the year 1968, witnessed a sudden 'run' on its branches, following rumours of its large exposure to a leading stock broker who had suffered huge losses in the share market. The Central Government enforced an order of moratorium on the bank. The bank was subsequently placed under a scheme of reconstruction with the approval of Reserve Bank of India.

Another major crisis was in the State of Andhra Pradesh in 2002, when one of the largest co-operative banks in the State, Prudential Coop Bank established in the year 1920, faced a run, following a case registered by police against the chairman and three directors of the bank. The bank was in a weak position, and ultimately, after attempts for its revival failed, its licence was cancelled by the Reserve Bank in 2004.

The number of UCBs came down to 1793 in 2007 from 1926 in 2004. However public confidence in UCBs is continuing to rise though at times shaken a little, as evidenced by the business growth of these banks.

In March 2005, Reserve Bank brought out a draft 'Vision Document' for UCBs, setting out the broad approach and strategies needed to strengthen the sector. This is now under implementation.

As on March 2010, there are around 1674 Urban Coop Banks operating in India, with 6884 branches spread across the country. The total number of customers with these UCBs exceeds 20 million. UCB deposits were recorded at ₹ 1,82,862 crores and advances of ₹ 1,10,304 crore as on March 2010. (State-wise spread of UCBs are given in table on next page.)

RBI grades these UCBs into four categories based on capital structure. The functioning of UCBs are similar to commercial banks. In the year 2010, their major advances are to agriculture and allied activities (5.8%), small enterprises (26.5%), housing loans (16.2%) and retail trade (9.5%). Priority sector advances stood at 64.7% of their total advances. Gross NPA of UCBs is over 11% and net NPA is over 4%. (See table below)

53 out of 1674 UCBs are under scheduled bank category and they have major share in total business. As at 2010, these 53 UCBs accounted for ₹ 77,224 crores in deposits and ₹ 49,522 crores in advances. List of scheduled urban coop banks with brief status of these banks are given in the table below.

**Profile of UCBs as at March 2010**

(₹ in crores)

| | | % |
|---|---|---|
| No. of UCBs | 1674 | |
| No. of scheduled UCBs | 53 | |
| Total branches | 6884 | |
| Total ATMs | 840 | |
| Capital & Reserves | 30,743 | |
| Deposits | 1,82,862 | |
| Advances | 1,10,304 | |

*(Contd...)*

| | | |
|---|---|---|
| Gross NPA | 12,727 | |
| Net NPA | 4724 | |
| Coverage ratio | | 62.9 |
| Priority sector advances of which | 71,385 | 64.7 |
| Agriculture & allied activities | 6383 | 5.8 |
| Small enterprise | 29,279 | 26.5 |
| Housing loans | 17,923 | 16.2 |
| Retail trade | 10,429 | 9.5 |
| (*Source*: Development in coop banking date 8-11-2010, publication by RBI-Table V.12) | | |

**State-wise and Centre-wise details of UCBs**

| **Spread of Urban Coop Banks** | | | | | | | | | |
|---|---|---|---|---|---|---|---|---|---|
| (As at end-March 2010) | | | | | | | | | |
| **State** | **Centre/s** | **Grades** | | | | **Number of** | | | |
| | | I | II | III | IV | All UCBs | Branches | Extension Counters | ATMs |
| 1 | 2 | 3 | 4 | 5 | 6 | 7 | 8 | 9 | 10 |
| Gujarat | Ahmedabad | 118 | 98 | 12 | 21 | 249 | 874 | 10 | 69 |
| Karnataka | Bangalore | 126 | 90 | 38 | 16 | 270 | 848 | 9 | 19 |
| Madhya Pradesh | Bhopal | 13 | 24 | 11 | 5 | 53 | 91 | 1 | - |
| Orissa | Bhubaneswar | 2 | 5 | 2 | 3 | 12 | 45 | 4 | - |
| PB/HR/HP | Chandigarh | 7 | 5 | 1 | 3 | 16 | 40 | 3 | 2 |
| Tamil Nadu | Chennai | 98 | 27 | 1 | 4 | 130 | 313 | - | 4 |
| Uttarakhand | Dehradun | 4 | 1 | - | - | 5 | 54 | 2 | 3 |
| Assam/ North East | Guwahati | 9 | 6 | 1 | 1 | 17 | 40 | 1 | - |
| Andhra Pradesh | Hyderabad | 65 | 34 | 4 | 8 | 111 | 245 | 5 | 2 |
| Rajasthan | Jaipur | 26 | 10 | 1 | 2 | 39 | 189 | 3 | - |
| Jammu and Kashmir | Jammu | 3 | - | - | 1 | 4 | 16 | 4 | - |
| West Bengal/ Sikkim | Kolkata | 30 | 4 | 3 | 11 | 48 | 101 | 2 | 1 |
| Uttar Pradesh | Lucknow | 48 | 6 | 9 | 7 | 70 | 190 | 28 | 8 |
| Maharashtra | Mumbai | 216 | 91 | 51 | 45 | 557 | 3,407 | 122 | 731 |
| | Nagpur | 59 | 38 | 37 | 20 | | | | |
| New Delhi | New Delhi | 11 | 2 | 1 | 1 | 15 | 65 | 1 | - |
| Bihar/ Jharkhand | Patna | 5 | - | - | - | 5 | 6 | 1 | - |
| Chhattisgarh | Raipur | 7 | 3 | 2 | 1 | 13 | 21 | 2 | 1 |
| Kerala | TVM | 32 | 21 | 5 | 2 | 60 | 339 | 2 | - |
| Total | | 879 | 465 | 179 | 151 | 1,674 | 6,884 | 200 | 840 |
| TVM: Thiruvananthapuram. PB: Punjab. HR: Haryana. HP: Himachal Pradesh. '-': Nil. | | | | | | | | | |

*Note*:

(1) Data are provisional.

(2) Branches include head office-cum-branch.

(3) Out of 840 ATMs, 26 were off-site ATMs and rest were onsite ATMs. Offsite ATMs are located in four States, i.e., 16 in Maharashtra, 6 in Uttar Pradesh, 3 in Gujarat and one in Karnataka.

### Scheduled Urban Cooperative Banks

| Sl. No. | Bank Name | Year std. | Bank Head Office | Brief status |
|---|---|---|---|---|
| 1. | Ahmedabad Mercantile Co-op Bank Ltd. | 1966 | Ahmedabad | A Multi-state scheduled coop bank established by Shri Mohanbhai C. Patel in 1966 at Ahmedabad. It became scheduled bank in 1996. Bank has branches mainly in the state of Gujarat and one branch in Mumbai, Maharashtra. Bank had 24 branches as at March 2010 with deposits of ₹ 551 crores and advances of ₹ 229 crores. |
| 2. | Kalupur Commercial Coop. Bank Ltd. | 1970 | Ahmedabad | Late Shri Baldevbhai Dosabhai Patel and the Ahmedabad Grain Merchants' Association founded the bank in the year 1970 at Ahmedabad. Bank became a scheduled bank in 1988 and a multi-state bank in 1995. As at March 2006 bank had 31 branches in Gujarat and Mumbai with deposits of ₹ 1083 crores and advances of ₹ 579 crores. Bank is authorised dealer for undertaking foreign exchange business. |
| 3. | Madhavpura Mercantile Co-op Bank Ltd. | 1968 | Ahmedabad | Madhavpura Mercantile Co-operative Bank was established on October 10, 1968. In 2001, the Bank witnessed a sudden 'run' on its branches, following rumours of its large exposure to a leading stockbroker who had suffered huge losses in the share market. The Central Government enforced an order of moratorium on the bank. Bank is not continuing banking business now. |
| 4. | Mehsana Urban Co-op Bank Ltd. | 1983 | Mehsana | The bank was started in 1983 at Mehsana, Gujarat State and became a scheduled bank in the year 2000. Bank has about 26 branches all in the State of Gujarat. As at March 2010, the bank had deposits of ₹ 1000 crores and advances of ₹ 587 crores. |

(*Contd*...)

| | | | | |
|---|---|---|---|---|
| 5. | Nutan Nagarik Sahakari Bank Ltd. | 1971 | Ahmedabad | The bank was established in the year 1971 in Ahmadabad. It was promoted by Late Shri Atmaram Bhogilal Sutaria and Late Shri Kalyanbhai P. Fadia. Bank became a scheduled bank in the year 2000. It is now a multi-state bank and has 20 branches in Gujarat state and one branch in Mumbai. As at March 2010, bank had deposit of ₹ 508 crores and advances of ₹ 255 crores. |
| 6. | Rajkot Nagrik Sahakari Bank Ltd. | 1953 | Rajkot | The bank was established in the year 1953 in Rajkot by Late Keshavlal Amrutlal Parekh and Late Janmashankar Antani. It became a scheduled bank in 1988. It became a multi state bank in 2001 and opened a branch in Mumbai. As at March 2010 bank had 27 branches with deposits of ₹ 1344 crores and advances of ₹ 913 crores. |
| 7. | Sardar Bhiladwala Pardi Peoples Coop Bank Ltd. | 1929 | Pardi - 396 125 | Sardar Bhiladwala Pardi People's Co-operative Bank was established in 1929 in Pardi, Gujarat state by Late Sardar Khan Bahadur Vikajl Pirojsha Bhiladwala supported by Late Gulabbhai Makanji Desai. Bank became a scheduled bank in the year 2000. Bank has 10 branches and deposits of the bank were about ₹ 350 crores in 2011. |
| 8. | Surat Peoples Coop Bank Ltd. | 1922 | Surat | One of the old coop banks, it was established in the year 1922 at Surat. It was one of the first coop banks to become a scheduled bank. It has about 23 branches mainly in Surat city and one each in Vapi and Navsari in Gujarat state. As at March 2010 deposits were ₹ 1200 crores and advances were ₹ 665 crores. |
| 9. | Amanath Co-operative Bank Ltd. | 1977 | Bangalore | The bank was established in the year 1977 by promoters Janab Dr. Mumtaz Ahmed Khan and Janab K. Rahman Khan at Bangalore. Bank is a scheduled bank since the year 2000 and has 15 branches in the state of Karnataka. As at 2008 bank had deposits of ₹ 331 crores and advances of ₹ 180 crores. |
| 10. | Andhra Pradesh Mahesh Co-op | 1978 | Hyderabad | Bank has commenced its operations on 9th August 1978 in |

*(Contd...)*

| | | | | |
|---|---|---|---|---|
| | Urban Bank Ltd. | | | Hyderabad. It became a scheduled bank in 1996. The Bank has been registered as a Multi-state Co-operative Bank in 2001. Bank has about 36 branches mainly in the state of Andhra Pradesh and one branch each in Jaipur and Mumbai. As at March 2010 bank had deposit of ₹ 1243 crores and advances of ₹ 785 crores. |
| 11. | Charminar Co-operative Urban Bank Ltd. | 1985 | Hyderabad | The bank was established in the year 1985 in Hyderabad. It ran into trouble in 2001 and finally RBI cancelled the license in November 2011. In 2001 bank had 21 branches in Hyderabad with a deposit base of about ₹ 500 crores. |
| 12. | Vasavi Coop Urban Bank LImited. | 1982 | Hyderabad | The bank was started in the year 1982 at Hyderabad and was a scheduled bank. Bank faced liquidity crisis in 2003 and had to shut all its 17 branches in Hyderabad. RBI has restricted the bank from accepting fresh deposits. The fate of the bank is undecided. |
| 13. | Indian Mercantile Co-operative Bank Ltd., | 1989 | Lucknow | Bank was established in Lucknow, UP in the year 1989. Bank has 9 branches in the state. |
| 14. | Abhyudaya Co-operative Bank Ltd., | 1964 | Mumbai | The bank was started in the year 1964 in Mumbai and now it is one of the leading coop banks in the country. It became multi state bank in 2007 and has branches in the States of Maharashtra, Gujarat, and Karnataka. Bank holds Authorised Dealer license issued by RBI to deal in foreign exchange business. As at March 2011 bank had deposits of ₹ 5260 crores and advances of ₹ 3452 crores. Bank has about 105 branches. |
| 15. | Bassein Catholic Co-operative Bank Ltd. | 1918 | Vasai | One of the old coop banks, The bank was established by Rev. Msgr. P.J. Monis on 6th February 1918 at vasai, Maharashtra. It became a scheduled bank in 1990. As at March 2011 bank had 28 branches with deposits of ₹ 2192 crores and advances of ₹ 1383 crores. |
| 16. | Bharat Co-operative Bank (Mumbai) Ltd. | 1978 | Mumbai | The bank was established in the year 1978 at Mumbai by social workers associated with The |

(*Contd...*)

| | | | | |
|---|---|---|---|---|
| | | | | Billawar Association, Mumbai, a leading Charitable Institution. It is a scheduled multi-state bank with branches in Maharashtra and Karnataka. As at March 2010 bank had, 34 branches with deposits of ₹ 2664 crores and advances were ₹ 1834 crores. Bank is an authorised dealer for undertaking foreign exchange business. |
| 17. | Bharati Sahakari Bank Limited | 1971 | Pune | Dr. Patangrao Kadam who is also the founder of Bharati Vidyapeeth, started the bank at Pune in the year 1971. The bank has about 18 branches in Maharashtra state and one extension counter in New Delhi. Bank attained the status of multi state scheduled bank in the year 2002. |
| 18. | Bombay Mercantile Co-operative Bank Limited | 1939 | Mumbai | Bank is one of the leading urban coop banks established in the year 1939 by the founder Shaikh Mohammedally Allabaux, the founder chairman along with Padmashri Zain G. Rangoonwala. Bank's head office is in Mumbai. It became a scheduled bank in the year 1988. Bombay Mercantile Co-operative Bank Ltd. is a multi-state bank and has its' branch network spread across the country in the States of Maharashtra, Gujarat, Delhi, Jammu & Kashmir, Rajasthan, Madhya Pradesh, Andhra Pradesh, Uttar Pradesh, Bihar and West Bengal. The Bank has presently 52 Branches. As at March 2010 banks deposits stood at ₹ 1945 crores and advances of ₹ 939 crores. Bank is an authorized dealer and undertakes foreign exchange business. |
| 19. | Citizen Credit Co-operative Bank Ltd. | 1920 | Mumbai | Bank was established in the year 1920 in Mumbai. Bank became a scheduled bank in 1996 and multi state bank in 1998. As at March 2010 bank had 31 branches in Maharashtra and Goa with deposits of ₹ 1432 crores and advances of ₹ 700 crores. |
| 20. | Cosmos Co-operative Urban Bank Ltd. | 1906 | Pune | The bank is one of the oldest urban coop banks, established in the year 1906. Banks head office is in Pune. It is scheduled multi state bank since 1997 with branches in 5 states— |

(*Contd*...)

| | | | | |
|---|---|---|---|---|
| | | | | Maharashtra, Madhya Pradesh, Andhra Pradesh, Karnataka and Gujarat. As at March 2010 bank had 104 branches with deposit of ₹ 7212 crores and advances of ₹ 4621 crores. Bank is second largest next to only Saraswat Coop Bank. Bank is an authorized dealer and carries on foreign exchange business. |
| 21. | Dombivli Nagari Sahakari Bank Ltd. | 1970 | Dombivli | Bank was established in the year 1970 at Dombivli, Maharashtra. It became scheduled bank in 1996. As at March 2010, it had 10 branches in the state with deposits of ₹ 1002 crores and advance of ₹ 662 crores. |
| 22. | Goa Urban Co-operative Bank Limited | – | Panji | Bank is a leading urban coop bank of Goa. It is a scheduled bank and has over 14 branches in the state. As at March 2009 bank had deposits of ₹ 563 crores and advances of ₹ 312 crores. |
| 23. | Gopinath Patil Parsik Janata Sahakari Bank Ltd. | 1972 | Thane | Bank was established in 1972 at Thane, Maharashtra by the founder Late Gopinath Shivram Patil. It became a scheduled bank in 1998. The bank has the network of 35 branches and two extension counters in six districts of Maharashtra. As at March 2011 bank had deposits of ₹ 1398 crores and advances of ₹ 722 crores. |
| 24. | Greater Bombay Co-operative Bank Limited | 1952 | Mumbai | The bank was established in the year 1952 at Mumbai. It became a scheduled bank in 1996. As at March 2010 it had 21 branches with deposits of ₹ 1209 crores and advances of ₹ 818 crores. |
| 25. | Jalgaon Janata Sahakari Bank Ltd. | 1979 | Jalgaon | Bank was established in the year 1979 at Jalgaon, Maharashtra and became a scheduled bank in 2000. Bank has 10 branches. |
| 26. | Janakalyan Sahakari Bank Ltd. | 1974 | Mumbai | The bank was established in the year 1974 in Mumbai and became a scheduled bank in 1998. Presently it has 26 branches in Maharashtra state. As at March 2010 bank had deposits of ₹ 1314 crores and advances of ₹ 811 crores. |
| 27. | Janalaxmi Co-operative Bank Ltd. | 1976 | Nashik | The bank was established in the year 1976 at Nashik, Maharashtra. It became a scheduled bank in 2000. At present, it has 30 branches and extension counters |

*(Contd...)*

| | | | | |
|---|---|---|---|---|
| | | | | in the state. As at March 2010 bank had deposits of ₹ 349 crores and advances of ₹ 145 crores. |
| 28. | Janata Sahakari Bank Ltd. | 1949 | Pune | The bank was established in the year 1949 at Pune and is one of the leading banks. It became a scheduled bank in 1988. As at March 2010 bank had ₹ 2825 crores deposits and advances of ₹ 1789 crores. Bank has 39 branches including ECs in the state. |
| 29. | Kallappanna Awade Ichalkaranji Janata Sahakari Bank Ltd. | 1963 | Ichalkaranji | Bank was started as Ichalkaranji Janata Sahakari Bank Ltd. in the year 1963 at Ichalkaranji, Maharashtra by the founder Late Dattajirao Kadam along with Late Shankarrao Hupare and Shri. Kallappanna Awade. It became a scheduled bank in 2000. The bank was renamed in 2007. As at March 2011 bank had 33 branches in the state with deposits of ₹ 803 crores and advances of ₹ 524 crores. |
| 30. | Kalyan Janata Sahakari Bank Ltd. | 1973 | Kalyan | The bank was started in the year 1973 at Kalyan Maharashtra and became scheduled bank in 2000. Presently bank has 23 branches in the state and it has a business mix of over ₹ 1500 crores as at March 2011. |
| 31. | Karad Urban Co-operative Bank Ltd. | 1917 | Karad | Bank is one of the old urban coop banks. It was established in the year 1917 by the Late Dr. D.S. Erram and Shri Subhashrao Joshi at Karad, Maharashtra. Bank became a scheduled bank in the year 2000. As at March 2010, it had 47 branches in the state with ₹ 1066 crores of deposits and advances at ₹ 660 crores. |
| 32. | Mahanagar Co-operative Bank Ltd. | 1973 | Mumbai | The bank was started by Solicitor Shri. G.S.Shelke in the year 1973 at Mumbai as The Ahmednagar Sahakari Bank Ltd. The name was changed to Mahanagar Coop Bank Ltd. in 1998. Same year the bank became a scheduled bank. The bank has about 32 branches. |
| 33. | Mapusa Urban Co-operative Bank of Goa Ltd. | 1967 | Mapusa, Goa | The bank was started in the year 1967 in Goa and is a scheduled bank. Since the year 2002, bank is in problem and became sick. Bank is now looking for revival with the help of State Government. As at March 2009 |

*(Contd...)*

| | | | | |
|---|---|---|---|---|
| | | | | the bank had 24 branches with deposit of ₹ 309 crores and advances of ₹ 143 crores |
| 34. | Nagar Urban Co-operative Bank Ltd. | 1910 | Ahmednagar | Bank was started in Ahmednagar, Maharashtra state in 1910. It became a scheduled bank in 2000. As at March 2008, the bank had 33 branches in the district Ahmednagar with deposit of ₹ 429 crores and advances of ₹ 284 crores. |
| 35. | Nasik Merchant's Co-operative Bank Ltd. | 1959 | Nasik | The bank was started in Nasik, Maharashtra in the year 1959. It became a scheduled bank in 1996 and a multi-state bank in 2000. As at March 2010 bank had 56 branches with deposits of ₹ 713 crores and advances of ₹ 361 crores. |
| 36. | New India Co-operative Bank Ltd. | 1968 | Mumbai | Bank was established in the year 1968 in Mumbai. It is a multi state scheduled coop bank with about 19 branches in Maharashtra and one branch in Surat. |
| 37. | NKGSB Co-operative Bank Ltd. | 1917 | Mumbai | One of the old banks founded by Sheth Shantaram Mangesh Kulkarni in the year 1917 in Mumbai. It is now a Multi-State Bank having its branches in the States of Maharashtra, Karnataka, Goa, Gujarat and Union territories of Daman, Diu, Dadra and Nagar Haveli. It has about 56 branches now. As at March 2010 bank had deposits of ₹ 2298 crores and advances of ₹ 1370 crores. |
| 38. | Pravara Sahakari Bank Ltd. | 1975 | At & Post Loni Bk., Dist. Ahmednagar | The bank was founded by Padmabhushan Shri Balasaheb Vikhe Patil in the year 1975 at Loni, dist. Ahmednagar, Maharashtra. Bank became a scheduled bank in 2003.<br>As at March 2008, the bank had 14 branches in the district of Ahmednagar with deposit of ₹ 228 crores and advances of ₹ 135 crores. |
| 39. | Punjab & Maharashtra Co-operative Bank Ltd. | 1984 | Mumbai | The bank was established in the year 1984 in Mumbai and became a scheduled bank in the year 2000. Now it is a multi state bank with total 55 branches in New Delhi, Karnataka and Maharashtra. As at March 2010 bank had deposit of ₹ 2540 crores and advances of ₹ 1897 crores. Bank is an authorised dealer and |

(*Contd...*)

| | | | | |
|---|---|---|---|---|
| | | | | undertakes foreign exchange business. |
| 40. | Rupee Co-operative Bank Ltd. | 1912 | Pune | One of the earliest urban coop banks established in the year 1912. The bank was promoted by Late Shri Govindrao Dharap, Late Shri. Keshavrao Doke and Late Shri. Kalurambhau Naik. Head office of the bank is in Pune. Bank became a scheduled bank in 1988 and has about 36 branches in the State of Maharashtra. |
| 41. | Sangli Urban Co-operative Bank Ltd. | 1935 | Sangli | Bank was established in the year 1935 in Sangli, Maharashtra under the leader Late Shri. M.H. Godbole. It is a scheduled bank with 35 branches in the state. As at March 2011, total business was about ₹ 850 crores. |
| 42. | Saraswat Co-operative Bank Ltd. | 1918 | Mumbai | Saraswat coop bank is one of the oldest and the largest urban coop bank of the country. It was started in the year 1918 and was founded by Mr. J.K. Parulkar, Mr. N.B. Thakur, Mr. P.N. Warde, and Mr. Shivram Gopal Rajadhyaksha. Bank's head office is in Mumbai. It is a scheduled and multi-state bank with branches in six states viz. Maharashtra, Gujarat, Madhya Pradesh, Karnataka, Goa and Delhi. As at March 2010 the bank had 200 branches, the largest network amongst urban coop banks with deposits of ₹ 14,266 crores and advances of ₹ 9250 crores. In September 2011, banks business has crossed ₹ 29000 crores. Bank is an authorised dealer and undertakes foreign exchange business. |
| 43. | Shamrao Vithal Co-operative Bank Ltd. | 1906 | Mumbai | The bank was one of the oldest urban coop banks of the country started in the year 1906 by the founder Rao Bahadur Shripad Subbarao Talmaki. The head office of the bank is in Mumbai. It is a scheduled and multi-state bank with branches in 6 States—Maharashtra, Karnataka, Goa, Delhi, Tamilnadu and Gujarat. As at March 2010 bank had 89 branches with deposits of ₹ 5257 crores and advances of ₹ 3397 crores. Bank is authorised dealer to transact foreign exchange business. |
| | | | | |

(*Contd*...)

| | | | | |
|---|---|---|---|---|
| 44. | Solapur Janata Sahakari Bank Ltd. | – | Solapur | Solapur Janata Sahakari Bank is having 31 branches in Maharashtra and In 2011, total business exceeded ₹ 1200 crores. |
| 45. | Thane Bharat Sahakari Bank Ltd. | – | Thane | The Thane Bharat Sahakari Bank was established in Thane and has 13 branches in Thane and Mumbai. |
| 46. | Thane Janata Sahakari Bank Ltd. | 1972 | Thane | Bank was established in the year 1972 in Thane. Bank is a scheduled multi-state bank. Bank has 55 branches in the State of Maharashtra and one each at Goa and Belgaum-, Karnataka. As at March 2010 the deposits were ₹ 2799 crores and advances of ₹ 1679 crores. It is one of the very few co-operative banks to get authorised dealer license to deal in Foreign exchange business. |
| 47. | The Kapol Co-operative Bank Ltd. | 1939 | Mumbai | Late Rajratna Shri Khushaldas Kurji Parekh established the bank in the year 1939. The head office is in Mumbai. The bank became scheduled bank in the year 1991. As at March 2010, the bank had deposits of ₹ 814 crores and advances of ₹ 468 crores. Bank has 15 branches. |
| 48. | Zoroastrian Co-operative Bank Ltd. | 1927 | Mumbai | The bank was established in 1927 in Mumbai. It is a scheduled bank and presently has 10 branches and one extension counter in the state. |
| 49. | Nagpur Nagrik Sahakari Bank Ltd. | 1962 | Nagpur | The bank was established in the year 1962 in Nagpur. Bank became a scheduled bank in 1999 and multi-state bank in 2001. It has branches in Maharashtra, Madhya Pradesh and Chhattisgarh states. As at March 2010 bank had 33 branches with deposits of ₹ 663 crores and advances of ₹ 370 crores. |
| 50. | Shikshak Sahakari Bank Ltd. | – | Nagpur | The bank was established in Nagpur. It ran into liquidity problem in 2006 and is said to have recovered. The bank has deposits to the tune of ₹ 560.60 crores and loans at ₹ 410.47 crores in the year 2011. |
| 51. | The Akola Janata Commercial Co-operative Bank Ltd. | 1969 | Akola | The Akola Janata Commercial Co-op Bank Ltd., was established in Akola in the year 1969. It became a scheduled bank in 1999 and now is a multi-state bank with 34 branches and 4 extension counters |

(*Contd...*)

| | | | | |
|---|---|---|---|---|
| | | | | in the states of Maharashtra and Madhya Pradesh. As at March 2010 bank had deposits of ₹ 1001 crores and advances of ₹ 609 crores. |
| 52. | The Akola Urban Co-operative Bank Ltd. | – | Akola | Established in Akola Maharashtra, Bank has 30 branches in the state. |
| 53. | The Khamgaon Urban Co-operative Bank Ltd. | 1963 | Khamgaon | The Bank was founded by Dr. M.G. Saoji in 1963 in Khamgaon, Maharashtra. It is a multi-state scheduled bank with about 34 Branches in Maharashtra and MP states. |

## Co-operative Sector for Rural Development

Government identified and preferred Cooperative sector, for the purpose of rural development in the country and a system for providing credit to agriculture was evolved over the years. The credit structure as under was created:

- Primary agriculture credit societies at village levels (PACs)
- District Central Coop Banks at district levels
- Apex Co-op Banks (State Central Coop Banks) at state levels
- Land Mortgage Banks at taluka, district and state levels
- NABARD.

After passing the Land Mortgage Banks Act in 1930's, land mortgage banks were created for taking care of long-term loan requirement of farmers.

PACs were created by the year 1951, and nearly 115462 PACs came into existence. However, as on 31 March 2010, their number came down to 94,647.

Setting up of district central coop banks and apex coop banks have started along with setting up of PACs, but it was only after the states were reorganised in the year 1956, the objectives for setting up Apex Coop Banks and District Central Coop Banks at state level and district level have been achieved.

This set up, financed the farmers for their short-term loan requirements in coordinated manner and credit linkage was created between PACs, district central coop banks, and state level apex coop bank.

As at 2010, there are 370 District Central Coop Banks and 31 State Coop Banks in the country. Business figures of these banks and PACs as at 31st march 2010 were as under:

(₹ in crores)

| | Nos. | Deposits | Advances |
|---|---|---|---|
| PACs | 94647 | 35286 | 74938 |
| DCCBs | 370 | 147109 | 123221 |
| SCBs | 31 | 82311 | 49199 |

(*Source*: NABARD)

### Land Development Banks

The special banks created for providing long-term loans to agriculture were called Land Development Banks (LDB). The history of LDB's is quite old. The first LDB was started at Jhang in Punjab in 1920. However, the real impetus to these banks was received after passing the Land Mortgage Banks Act in 1930's (LDB's were originally called Land Mortgage Banks). After passing of this Act, LDB's were started in different states of India.

These banks in due course diversified their activities and at the instance of the NABARD, they started financing agriculture and rural development activities including wastelands. In late eighties and the beginning of nineties, LDBs started financing long-term loans for some more rural development activities like, village and cottage industries, rural artisans, etc.

In view of broader role of LDBs, they are now known as State Co-operative Agriculture and Rural Development Banks (SCARDBs).

These Banks have two-tier structure:

1. **Primary Land Development Bank**—at district level with branches at taluka level.
2. **State Land Development Bank**—Central Land Development Bank at the State Level with all primary Land Development Banks in the state affiliated to it. In some States, there is "Unitary structure" wherein, there is only one State Land Development Bank at the

state level operating through its branches and sub-branches at district and taluka levels.

Hence, the long-term cooperative credit structure consists of the State Cooperative Agriculture & Rural Development Banks (SCARDBs) and Primary Cooperative Agriculture & Rural Development Banks (PCARDBs), which are affiliated to the SCARDBs.

As on March 31st 2010, total No. of SCARDB's are 20 (No. of branches—750) and No. of PCARDBs are 697 (No. of branches—1132). Annual lending during the year was ₹ 3188 crores. Business figures of these banks as on 31st March 2010 were as under:

(₹ in crores)

| | Nos | Deposits | Advances |
|---|---|---|---|
| PCARDBs | 697 | 447 | 11377 |
| SCARDB's | 20 | 756 | 16879 |

(*source*-NABARD)

All these banks put together are called Rural Cooperative Banks. These banks are under the control of NABARD, which is the apex institution for rural credit. Tables below give the profile of rural coop banks for March 2009, number of banks and branches as at 2009 and comparative business figures for the year 2009 and 2010.

**A Profile of Rural Cooperative Banks (At end-March 2009)**

(Amount in ₹ crores)

| | Item | Short-Term | | | Long-Term | | Total |
|---|---|---|---|---|---|---|---|
| | | StCBs | DCCBs | PACs | SCARDBs | PCARDBs | |
| A. | No. of Cooperative Banks | 31 | 370 | 95,633 | 20 | 697 | 96,751 |
| B. | Balance Sheet Indicators | | | | | | |
| | (i) Owned Funds (Capital + Reserves) | 11,726 | 29,792 | 11,806 | 4,003 | 5,007 | 62,334 |
| | (ii) Deposits | 68,659 | 1,27,623 | 26,245 | 711 | 400 | 2,23,638 |
| | (iii) Borrowings | 20,874 | 27,664 | 48,938 | 15,849 | 12,365 | 1,25,690 |
| | (iv) Loans and Advances Issued* | 93,883 | 90,105 | 58,787 | 2,585 | 1,195 | 2,46,555 |
| | (v) Loans and Advances Outstanding | 48,079 | 99,429 | 64,044 | 16,421 | 11,268 | 2,39,241 |
| | (vi) Investments | 45,230 | 64,709 | - | 2,941 | 1,122 | 1,14,002 |

(*Contd...*)

| | | | | | | | |
|---|---|---|---|---|---|---|---|
| | (vii) Total Liabilities/Assets | 1,06,321 | 1,95,684 | 94,585+ | 25,386 | 24,846 | 4,46,822 |
| C. | Financial Performance | | | | | | |
| | (i) Institutions in Profit | | | | | | |
| | (a) No. | 26 | 320 | 37,291 | 11 | 303 | 37,951 |
| | (b) Amount of Profit | 385 | 1,603 | 843 | 398 | 177 | 3,406 |
| | (ii) Institutions in Loss | | | | | | |
| | (a) No. | 5 | 50 | 45,869 | 8 | 309 | 46,241 |
| | (b) Amount of Loss | -71 | -287 | -1,915 | -349 | -375 | -2,997 |
| | (iii) Overall Profit (+)/Loss (-) | 314 | 1,316 | -1,072 | 49 | -198 | 408 |
| | (iv) Accumulated Loss | 459 | 5,213 | - | 1,108 | 3,678 | 10,458 |
| D. | Non-performing Assets | | | | | | |
| | (i) Amount | 5,764 | 17,929 | 37,937++ | 4,938 | 4,393 | 70,961 |
| | (ii) As Percentage of Loans Outstanding | 12.0 | 18.0 | 59.2 | 30.1 | 39.0 | 29.7 |
| | (iii) Recovery of Loans to Demand (Per cent) | 92 | 72 | - | 49 | 39 | - |

StCBs: State Cooperative Banks, DCCBs: District Central Cooperative Banks, PACs: Primary Agricultural Credit Societies, SCARDBs: State Cooperative Agriculture and Rural Development Banks, PCARDBs: Primary Cooperative Agriculture and Rural Development Banks.

*: April- March, '-' : Not available. +: Working capital. ++ : Total overdues.

*Note*:

(1) Data are provisional.

(2) Data for StCBs in Bihar, West Bengal and Tripura are repeated for the year 2008-09.

(3) Data for DCCBs in Bihar, Jharkhand, West Bengal and Kerala are repeated for the year 2008-09.

(4) During 2008-09, 12,473 PACS were in no-profit no-loss position.

(5) Data for SCARDBs in Maharashtra are repeated for 2008-09 from the year 2007-08.

(6) SCARDB in Manipur is defunct.

*Source*: NABARD and NAFSCOB-RBI-.Table V.13.

**Business per Branch of Rural Cooperatives (As at end-March 2009)**

(Amount in ₹ crores)

| Category | Number of Banks | Number of Branches | Business per Branch |
|---|---|---|---|
| StCBs | 31 | 943 | 123.8 |
| DCCBs | 370 | 12,939 | 17.5 |
| SCARDBs | 20 | 844 | 20.3 |
| PCARDBs | 697 | 1,227 | 9.5 |

Note: Data are provisional.

*Source*: NABARD-RBI—**Table V.30.**

**Comparative position for years 2009 and 2010**

| | **Rural Cooperative Banks**—At end-March 2009 and 2010 | | | | | | |
|---|---|---|---|---|---|---|---|
| | | | | | | | (Amount in ₹ crores) |
| | **Item** | **Short-Term** | | | **Long-Term** | | **Total** |
| | | **StCBs** | **DCCBs** | **PACS** | **SCARDBs** | **PCARDBs** | |
| 2009 | No. of Cooperative Banks | 31 | 370 | 95,633 | 20 | 697 | 96,751 |
| **2010** | | **31** | **370** | **94,747** | **20** | **697** | **95,865** |
| 2009 | Owned Funds (Capital + Reserves) | 11,726 | 29,792 | 11,806 | 4,003 | 5,007 | 62,334 |
| **2010** | | | | | | | |
| 2009 | Deposits | 68,659 | 1,27,623 | 26,245 | 711 | 400 | 2,23,638 |
| **2010** | | **82,311** | **1,47,109** | **35,286** | **756** | **447** | **2,65,909** |
| 2009 | Loans and Advances Outstanding | 48,079 | 99,429 | 64,044 | 16,421 | 11,268 | 2,39,241 |
| **2010** | | **49,199** | **1,23,221** | **74,938** | **16,879** | **11,377** | **2,75,614** |

## Performance of Rural Coop Banks

Rural coop banks are created to lend and support agriculture. These banks are not to be compared with commercial banks. Profitability is not the driving force for them as achievement of agriculture lending is the sole purpose. These banks are financially weak, and are burdened with high level of NPA. Collectively NPA was 29.7% of advances as at March 2009. NPA were high in case of PCARDBs & SCARDBs.

Out of 96751 banks, 46241 were loss making as at March 2009, mainly PACs & PCARDBs. Out of 31 state coop banks, 5 were in loss. Fifty of district central coop banks out of total 370 DCCBs were in loss. Total accumulated losses of rural coop banks amounted to ₹ 10,458 crores against the net owned funds of ₹ 62,334 crores at March 2009.

## State Co-operative Banks

The concept of apex coop bank at state level came into effect from fifties. Many of the present day state coop banks were started much earlier from the year 1905 onwards and they were converted as apex banks in fifties. Some new state coop banks were started as and when a new state was created.

State Cooperative Banks are conceived as apex bodies at state level for cooperative sector and are umbrella organisations to which all the District Central Coop Banks in the state and PACs at village level are affiliated. This is a three-tier set up created for providing short-term agriculture credit to farmers with the State Coop Bank at the top which provides refinance support to DCCBs. As the purpose was to support the captive needs of farming sector, these banks are not visualised as commercial banks and are also not encouraged to develop on commercial line. In fact, State Coop Banks are discouraged to open branches, as they are to use the network of DCCBs and PACs for development. DCCBs are allowed to open branches within the districts they operate, to support PACs. Hence, State Coop Banks were not required to increase branch network.

However, over a period, things have changed to some extent. Depending on development needs of the state and districts, State Coop Banks were allowed to open branches to complement the branch network of DCCBs. Wherever DCCBs are not existing, the state coop bank was allowed to fill the gap. This feature is mostly seen in smaller States or Union Territories. RBI has been allowing State Coop Banks, on selective basis, to expand branch network. Today there are many state coop banks with more than 50 branches. Himachal Pradesh State Coop Bank has about 190 branches. As at March 2009, 31 State Coop Banks had total of 943 branches.

Banking licences were also issued to many state coop banks to carry on regular banking business. This was necessitated to help state coop banks to finance in urban areas they operate and to garner resources by mobilising retail deposits. State coop banks were made eligible to become scheduled banks for this purpose and today 16 out of 31 state coop banks have achieved the status of scheduled banks. Maharashtra State Coop Bank, which is the leading state coop bank in the country is also authorised to undertake foreign exchange business as an authorised dealer.

Five state coop banks out of 31 are in loss making in the year 2009. These state coop banks besides being apex bodies for cooperative sector are now developing themselves as regular commercial banks.

The list and brief profile of state coop banks is as under:

| Sr. No. | State Co-operative Bank | Head office | Status | Profile |
|---|---|---|---|---|
| 1. | The Andaman and Nicobar State Co-operative Bank Ltd. | Port Blair-744 101. | | Andaman & Nicobar State Cooperative Bank Ltd, was established in 1965 to which 28 PACs and 31 other Co-operative organisations were affiliated.<br>Bank has 29 branches and as at March 2010, the deposits were ₹ 372 crores and advances were ₹ 146 crores. |
| 2. | The Andhra Pradesh State Co-operative Bank Ltd. | Hyderabad-500 001 | Scheduled bank | The Andhra Pradesh State Cooperative Bank Limited (APCOB) is a Scheduled State Cooperative Bank for the State of Andhra Pradesh. 22 District Cooperative Central Banks (DCCBs), having 557 Branches and 2748 Primary Agricultural Cooperative Societies (PACs) are affiliated to it.<br>Bank has a network of 26 branches.<br>As on 31-3-10 Deposits were ₹ 3566 crores and Loans & Advances were ₹ 4035 crores. |
| 3. | The Arunachal Pradesh State co-operative Apex Bank Ltd. | Naharlagun-791 110 | – | Bank was started about 22 years back and The state government revived the bank three years ago, as the bank was in difficulties. The Bank had a total deposit of ₹ 63.65 crores, the bank's outstanding loans at ₹ 109.59 crores in 2011. |

*(Contd...)*

| | | | | |
|---|---|---|---|---|
| | | | | Bank has about 32 branches. |
| 4. | The Assam Co-operative Apex Bank Ltd. | Guwahati-781 001. | – | Established in 1948, the bank, today, has a network of 68 branches.<br>The bank which has been accumulating losses over the years is expected to turn around after making profits last fiscal (2010-11) after almost a decade.<br>In March, 2009 bank had deposits of ₹ 823 crores and advances of ₹ 311 crores.<br>In 2011, the deposits amounted to about ₹ 1,200. |
| 5. | The Bihar State Co-operative Bank Ltd. | Patna-800 004 | Scheduled bank | The Bihar State Co-operative Bank Ltd. was established in Patna in 1914. This Bank was included in the second schedule of Reserve Bank of India in the month of July 1966. The Bank is presently doing its business through its 14 branches and 30 DCCBs affiliated to it.<br>After bifurcation of Jharkhand from unified Bihar in the year 2000 its five branches are now located in Jharkhand state and 9 in Bihar State. Out of existing 30 DCCBs affiliated to it, 8 DCCBs are located in Jharkhand State and 22 DCCBs in Bihar State. Since the Jharkhand State Co-operative Bank has not yet been established, present area of operation of the Bank is both Jharkhand and Bihar States.<br>In March, 2009 bank had deposits of ₹ 899 crores and advances of ₹ 628 crores. |

(*Contd...*)

| | | | | |
|---|---|---|---|---|
| 6. | The Chandigarh State Co-operative Bank Ltd. | Chandigarh-160 022 | | The Chandigarh State Co-op Bank Ltd., Chandigarh was registered on 2-11-1966. The bank has 13 branches in Union Territory, Chandigarh.<br>In March, 2009 bank had deposits of ₹ 162 crores and advances of ₹ 52 crores. |
| 7. | The Delhi State Co-operative Bank Ltd. | New Delhi-110 002 | – | The Delhi State Co-operative Bank Ltd. was established in 1921 and currently has 47 branches and extension counters in the national capital. The state government has 24% stake in the bank.<br>In March, 2009 bank had deposits of ₹ 685 crore and advances of ₹ 349 crores. |
| 8. | The Goa State Co-operative Bank Ltd. | Panaji - 403 001. | Scheduled bank | The Goa State Co-operative Bank Ltd. was founded on 7th November 1963 as Apex financing agency in the co-operative sector in the then Union territory of Goa, Daman and Diu.<br>The Bank has 67 branches. In 1994, Reserve Bank of India conferred the bank with "Scheduled" status.<br>In March, 2009 bank had deposits of ₹ 754 crores and advances of ₹ 494 crores. |
| 9. | The Gujarat State Co-operative Bank Ltd. | Ahmedabad-380 001 | Scheduled bank | The Gujarat State Coop. Bank Ltd. came into existence and started banking business from 10th May, 1960 with the establishment of Gujarat State on 1st May, 1960.<br>18 District Central Coop. Banks (DCCBs) with its 1144 branches and 8103 Primary Agricultural Cooperative Societies |

(*Contd...*)

| | | | | |
|---|---|---|---|---|
| | | | | (PACs) are associated with this bank.<br>In March, 2009 bank had deposits of ₹ 3209 crores and advances of ₹ 1763 crores. |
| 10. | The Haryana State Co-operative Apex Bank Ltd. | Chandigarh - 160 017 | Scheduled bank | The Haryana State Cooperative Apex Bank Ltd. commonly called as HARCO BANK was established in November 1966.<br>Bank has 13 branches and 2 extension counters at Chandigarh and Panchkula. 19 Central Cooperative Banks with their 594 branches and 634 PACs (Mini Banks) are affiliated to it.<br>In March 2010 bank had deposits of ₹ 1935 crores and advances of ₹ 2988 crores. |
| 11. | The Himachal Pradesh State Co-operative Bank Ltd. | Shimla – 171 001 | – | In 1953 Himachal Pradesh State Co-operative Bank was established after amalgamating Mahasu Central Co-operative Bank, The Mandi Central Co-operative Bank Ltd. and The Chamba Central Co-operative Bank Ltd., which were functioning prior to independence. Bank has a network of 190 branches and Extension Counters and one branch at Azadpur, New Delhi for the benefits of horticulturists of the State.<br>In March, 2009 bank had deposits of ₹ 4075 crores and advances of ₹ 1549 crores. |

*(Contd...)*

| | | | | |
|---|---|---|---|---|
| 12. | The Jammu and Kashmir State Co-operative Bank Ltd. | Srinagar-190 005 | – | The J&K State Co-operative Bank came into establishment in the year 1917. It was originally named Srinagar Central Co-operative Bank. It was given the status of apex bank in the year 1954. The bank currently has 17 branches.<br>It also offers refinance facility to 3 District Central Coop. Banks in the State i.e. Jammu Central Coop. Bank, Baramulla C.C. Bank and Anantnag Central Coop Bank.<br>In March, 2009 bank had deposits of ₹ 364 crores and advances of ₹ 87 crores. |
| 13. | The Karnataka State Co-operative Apex Bank Ltd. | Bangalore-560 018 | Scheduled bank | The Bank was registered on 10th November 1915 under the name and style of The Mysore Provincial Cooperative Bank Limited.<br>In 1925, it was converted into an Apex Bank with the jurisdiction extending over the entire State for financing the co-operative societies exclusively and the Bank thereafter was named as the Mysore Provincial Co-operative Apex Bank Ltd., and later renamed as Karnataka State Coop Apex Bank.<br>As at March 2010 banks deposits were ₹ 4479 crores and advances were ₹ 3146 crores. Bank has 40 branches. |
| 14. | The Kerala State Co-operative Bank Ltd. | Thiruvananthapuram-695 033 | Scheduled bank | Origin of the bank dates back to the year 1915 when The Trivandrum Central Cooperative Bank was registered in the year 1915. |

*(Contd...)*

| | | | | |
|---|---|---|---|---|
| | | | | Later in 1943, the bank was converted into the Travancore Central Cooperative Bank. The State 'Kerala' was formed in the year 1956. Then the bank became The Kerala State Cooperative Bank Ltd. Bank has 19 branches.<br>In July 1966, the RBI approved the Bank as a 'Scheduled State Cooperative Bank'.<br>In March, 2009 bank had deposits of ₹ 4593 crores and advances of ₹ 2410 crores. |
| 15. | The Madhya Pradesh Rajya Sahakari Bank Maryadit | Bhopal-462 003 2010 | Scheduled bank | M.P. State Coop Bank Ltd. was registered on 02-04-1912 at Jabalpur later on its Head Office has been transferred to Nagpur.<br>In the year 1956 Madhya Pradesh Cooperative Bank Ltd. Nagpur has been divided and "Mahakaushal Coop Bank", Jabalpur came into existence.<br>In the year 1956, after formation of new Madhya Pradesh state Mahakaushal Coop Bank has been renamed as M.P. Rajya Sahakari Bank Mydt. (M.P. State Coop Bank Ltd.). Now 38 Districts Central Coop Banks are affiliated with Madhya Pradesh State Coop Bank.<br>The Apex Bank is operating with its 20 branches in the state. As at March 2010 banks deposits were ₹ 3290 crores and advaces were 2503 crores. |

*(Contd...)*

| | | | | |
|---|---|---|---|---|
| 16. | The Maharashtra State Co-operative Bank Ltd. | Fort Mumbai-400 023 | Scheduled bank Authorised dealer for forex business | Bank was established in the year 1911 and now functions as apex coop bank for the state. Bank has about 50 branches.<br>As at March 2010 bank had deposits of ₹ 21420 crores and advances of ₹ 7997 crores.<br>The bank is the only state coop bank authorised as authorised dealer for undertaking all types of forex business. |
| 17. | The Manipur State Co-operative Bank Ltd. | Imphal-795 001 | | Manipur State Co-operative Bank has about 9 branches in the state.<br>In March, 2009 bank had deposits of ₹ 78 crores and advances of ₹ 153 crores. |
| 18. | The Meghalaya Co-operative Apex Bank Ltd. | Shillong-793 001 | | The Meghalaya Co-operative Apex Bank Ltd. (MCAB) was established in 1971, with the formation of Meghalaya State after bifurcation of the erstwhile Assam State. Today, the Bank has a wide network of 43 branches, spread throughout the State. Banks deposits were ₹ 911 crores and advances over ₹ 263 crores as on 31-03-2010. |
| 19. | The Mizoram Co-operative Apex Bank Ltd. | Aizawl-796 001 | | The bank was established in 1994.<br>In March, 2009 bank had deposits of ₹ 216 crores and advances of ₹ 127 crores. |
| 20. | The Nagaland State Co-operative Bank Ltd. | Dimapur-797 112. | | Bank Commenced Banking Business on 21-04-1967.<br>Bank has 22 branches and as at March 2010, total business of the bank was ₹ 350 crores with deposits of ₹ 281 crores. |

*(Contd...)*

| | | | | |
|---|---|---|---|---|
| 21. | The Orissa State Co-operative Bank Ltd. | Bhubaneswar-751 001 | Scheduled bank | Orissa State Co-operative Bank Ltd. was set up in 1948. Bank has 8 branches. 17 Districts Central Co-operative Banks at the District level with 323 branches and 2726 PACS including 218 large size Adivasi Multi Purpose Societies (LAMPS) are affiliated to it. In March, 2009 bank had deposits of ₹ 2310 crores and advances of ₹ 1981 crores. |
| 22. | The Pondichery State Co-operative Bank Ltd. | Pondicherry-605 001 | Scheduled bank | The Pondicherry State Co-operative Bank Ltd., was registered as a Co-op. Society on 10th October 1958 and started functioning on 30th October 1958. Bank is functioning with its 20 branches and one extension in counter In March, 2009 bank had deposits of ₹ 334 crores and advances of ₹ 208 crores. |
| 23. | The Punjab State Co-operative Bank Ltd. | Chandigarh-160 022 | Scheduled bank | The Punjab State Cooperative Bank came into existence in the year 1949 as a part of the cooperative movement of Punjab. The Head office of the bank was shifted to Jalandhar in the year 1951 and later on to Chandigarh in 1963. The bank has 18 branches and 3 extension counters in Chandigarh. There are 19 District Central Cooperative Banks having 813 branches all over Punjab, mostly in rural areas of the State affiliated to it. In March, 2009 bank had deposits of ₹ 1935 crores and advances of ₹ 4729 crores. |

(*Contd*...)

| | | | | |
|---|---|---|---|---|
| 24. | The Rajasthan State Co-operative Bank Ltd. | Jaipur-302 003 | Scheduled bank | Bank was started on 14th October 1953.<br>Bank has 5 Regional Branches and 8 Branches. In 2010, bank's deposits were ₹ 2576 crores and advances were ₹ 1825 crore. |
| 25. | The Sikkim State Co-operative Bank Ltd. | Gangtok-737 101 | – | The Bank was setup in 1999.<br>The bank currently has 634 member cooperative societies under its umbrella. Currently the Bank has branches at district head quarters viz. Namchi, Gyalshing and Mangan, Jorethang and Singtam. (5 branches)<br>In March, 2009 bank had deposits of ₹ 86 crores and advances of ₹ 33 crores. |
| 26. | The Tamil Nadu State Apex Co-operative Bank Ltd. | Chennai-600 001 | Scheduled bank | Bank was registered on 23-11-1905. The Bank commenced its business on 26.11.1905 and is the oldest state coop bank.<br>The deposits of the Bank as on 31-12-2009 stood at ₹ 5581 crores and total advances of the bank stood at ₹ 3971 crores. Bank has about 45 branches. |
| 27. | The Tripura State Co-operative Bank Ltd. | Agartala-799 001 | | The Tripura State Cooperative Bank Limited (TSCB) was established on 21-01-1957 with its headquarters at Agartala.<br>Now the bank has over 39 branches and extension counters all over the state.<br>In March, 2009 bank had deposits of ₹ 483 crores and advances of ₹ 155 crores. |
| 28. | The Uttar Pradesh Co-operative Bank Ltd. | Lucknow-226 001 | Scheduled bank | Bank is functioning as apex coop bank for the state and 50 DCCBs with 1277 |

(*Contd*...)

| | | | | |
|---|---|---|---|---|
| | | | | branches affiliated to it. The bank has sponsored a regional rural bank- Kshetriya Kisan Gramin Bank. It is the only coop bank that has sponsored a RRB.<br>In March, 2009 bank had deposits of ₹ 3830 crores and advances of ₹ 3258 crores. Bank has about 29 branches. |
| 29. | The West Bengal State Co-operative Bank Ltd. | Kolkata–700 069 | Scheduled bank | The bank was originally registered in 1918 as the Bengal Provincial Co-op. Federation Ltd. It was renamed as the West Bengal State Cooperative Bank Limited in 1967. Bank has about 48 branches.<br>In March, 2009 bank had deposits of ₹ 3368 crores and advances of ₹ 2170 crores. |
| 30. | The Chhattisgarh Rajya Sahakari Bank Maryadit | Raipur-492 001 | | The Chhattisgarh Rajya Sahakari Bank Mydt. was formed after the reformation of state on 30-10-2000.<br>In march, 2009 bank had deposits of ₹ 1592 crores and advances of ₹ 373 crores. Bank has about 5 branches. |
| 31. | The Uttaranchal Rajya Sahakari Bank Ltd. | Dehradun-248 001 | | RBI permitted in 2003 establishment of the bank by bifurcating UP coop bank.<br>In March, 2009 bank had deposits of ₹ 920 crores and advances of ₹ 1294 In March, 2009 bank had deposits of ₹ 899 crores and advances of ₹ 628 crores. |

## NABARD

National Bank for Agriculture and Rural Development was set up in the year 1982, as an apex Development Bank with a mandate for facilitating credit flow for promotion and development of agriculture, small-scale industries, cottage and village industries, handicrafts and other rural crafts. It took over the functions, which hitherto were performed by RBI and ARDC.

NABARD is also the regulator and controller for Regional Rural Banks and Co-op banks (except urban coop banks) and coordinates with RBI on agriculture and rural development credits.

(Also see under Development banks.)

### Banks in Cooperative Sector

Hence, at present, there are four categories of Cooperative banks in the country.

1. Primary cooperative banks or urban cooperative banks

   (These were mostly started by a group of people to cater banking needs of the group. They were public limited companies with share capital collected from the members and can only lend to a member. However, they can make new members by issuing new shares to them and then lend to them.)

2. District central coop banks at district levels
3. State coop banks at apex state levels.
4. Land development banks (PCARDBs & SCARDBs).

The last three categories of banks are semi public sector undertakings, as they are under administrative control of State Governments and with capital contribution by State Governments.

To encourage cooperative movement, rules were framed so that the money mobilized by coop banks remains with coop sector and lent to members. Investment by coop banks with other commercial banks was put under some restrictions. They were even allowed better terms like higher interest for both deposit and advances as compared to commercial banks so that growth in the sector is sustained and improved. RBI has control over the entire banking sector. While RBI is very particular about commercial banking sector as regards stipulations and directives for changes, it is more tolerant of coop sector and allows it liberal time schedule for implementation of guidelines. Generally, the guidelines for new changes are issued separately for commercial banks, and coop banks. Many of the stipulations applicable to commercial banks are either not applicable or diluted for coop banks. The reason behind this treatment is that the co-op movement is very important and that these banks do not have the infrastructure and trained manpower. Until such time these banks come up of age this favourable treatment may continue.

## Regional Rural Banks (RRBs)

The Government of India allowed to set up Regional Rural Banks (RRBs) on October 2, 1975 with the purpose to provide credit to the weaker sections of the rural areas, particularly the small and marginal farmers, agricultural labourers, artisans and small entrepreneurs.

Initially, five RRBs were set up sponsored by Syndicate Bank, State Bank of India, Punjab National Bank, United Commercial Bank and United Bank of India. Capital for RRBs was subscribed 50% by the Central Government, 15% by the State Government, and 35% by the sponsoring bank. The total authorized capital was fixed at ₹ One crore which has since been raised to ₹ Five crores.

RRBs are given specific mandates to operate within the area of operation fixed for them. Generally, few districts are allocated to a RRB and the bank has to open branches within the area. RRBs are not allowed to operate in metro areas and are required to open most of the branches in rural areas.

RRBs enjoys several concessions by the Reserve Bank of India such as lower interest rates and lower cash reserve ratio, lower statutory liquidity ratio, lower rate of interest on loans taken from sponsoring banks, managerial and staff assistance from the sponsoring bank and reimbursement of the expenses on staff training.

The RRBs are under the control of NABARD. NABARD has the responsibility of laying down the policies for the RRBs, to oversee their operations, provide refinance facilities, to monitor their performance and attend to their problems. Earlier Reserve Bank of India had laid down ceilings on the rate of interest to be charged by these RRBs. However, from August 1996 the RRBs have been granted freedom to fix rates of interest, which is usually in the range of 14-18% for advances.

The number of branches of RRBs increased to 14,494 as on 31 March 2006. Deposits stood at ₹ 71,329 crores and advances were ₹ 39,713 crores.

There were 196 RRBs and many of them became weak financially with burdens of sizeable bad loans. Govt of India initiated the process of structural consolidation of RRBs by amalgamating RRBs sponsored by the same bank within a State as per the recommendations of the Vyas Committee (2004). Amalgamations helped RRBs to provide better customer service due to better infrastructure, computerization of branches, pooling of experienced work force, common publicity/marketing efforts, etc. RRBs also derived the benefits of a large area of operation, enhanced credit exposure limits and more diverse banking activities. Because of the amalgamation, the number of RRBs was reduced from 196 to 133 as on 31st March 2006, and to 82 as on year ending 2010-11. At present State bank and its associate banks have 22 RRBs sponsored by them. Two RRBs are sponsored by private banks and one by a state coop bank. Remaining 57 RRBs have been sponsored by nationalised banks.

RRBs are commercial banks and all of them are scheduled banks. Due to majority ownership being with central and state governments (65%), they are public sector undertakings.

As on 31st March 2010, 82 RRBs had 15723 branches and the business figures of these RRBs were, deposits ₹ 1,35,814 crores and advances ₹ 79,086 crores. Growth of business of RRBs from the year 1982 to 2010 is given in the table on the next page. List of RRBs with brief profile of banks, names of sponsoring banks is also given under.

Though the structural consolidation and amalgamations carried out in the years 2005 and 2006 has reduced the number of banks and has improved their performance, still some more reorganisation of RRBs may be needed. Due to amalgamations, some RRBs have become big in sizes. For example: Uttar Bihar Gramin Bank has 865 branches (sponsored by Central Bank of India) and Baroda Uttar Pradesh Gramin Bank has about 700 branches (sponsored by Bank of Baroda). There are many RRBs with less than hundred branches.

**Important Banking Indicators—Regional Rural Banks**

(₹ Crores)

| Year | Deposits | Bank Credit |
|---|---|---|
| 1981-82 | 352 | 439 |
| 1982-83 | 494 | 606 |
| 1983-84 | 689 | 813 |
| 1984-85 | 973 | 1134 |
| 1985-86 | 1314 | 1465 |
| 1986-87 | 1754 | 1852 |
| 1987-88 | 2271 | 2328 |
| 1988-89 | 2927 | 2858 |
| 1989-90 | 3815 | 3409 |
| 1990-91 | 4560 | 3497 |
| 1991-92 | 5271 | 3951 |
| 1992-93 | 6370 | 4451 |
| 1993-94 | 8045 | 5024 |
| 1994-95 | 10,848 | 6201 |
| 1995-96 | 13,370 | 7289 |
| 1996-97 | 16,971 | 8544 |
| 1997-98 | 20,977 | 9687 |
| 1998-99 | 25,428 | 11,016 |
| 1999-00 | 30,051 | 12,663 |
| 2000-01 | 35,995 | 15,211 |
| 2001-02 | 42,494 | 18,033 |
| 2002-03 | 47,644 | 21,359 |
| 2003-04 | 53,390 | 25,057 |
| 2004-05 | 58,286 | 31,651 |
| 2005-06 | 64,195 | 36,050 |
| 2006-07 | 81,620 | 48,420 |
| 2007-08 | 94,412 | 57,417 |
| 2008-09 | 1,13,828 | 64,011 |
| 2009-10 | 1,35,814 | 79,086 |

(*Source*: RBI)

**List of RRBs with the Names of Sponsoring Banks in 2011**

| Sl. No. | Name of RRB | Name of Sponsor Bank | Head office location | Brief profile |
|---|---|---|---|---|
| 1. | Chaitanya Godavari Grameena Bank | Andhra Bank | Dist. Guntur-522 202 (Andhra Pradesh) | Bank was formed by amalgamating Chaitanya Grameena Bank and Godavari Grameena Bank on 1-3-2006. Its head office is in Guntur. The Bank's operational area is spread across Guntur, East Godavari and West Godavari districts. Bank has about 105 branches. In March 2011 bank had deposits of ₹ 759 crores and advances of ₹ 847 crores. |
| 2. | Saptagiri Grameena Bank | Indian Bank | Chittoor-517 001 (Andhra Pradesh) | Saptagiri Grameena Bank has been formed with the merger of Sri Venkateswara Grameena Bank, Chittoor, Chittoor district and Kanakadurga Grameena Bank, Gudivada, Krishna District w.e.f., from 01-07-2006. Banks Head office is at Chittoor, Andhra Pradesh. Bank has about 144 branches and in March 2010 deposits were ₹ 1243 crores and advances were ₹ 1371 crores. |
| 3. | Deccan Grameena Bank | State Bank of Hyderabad | Hyderabad-500 060 (Andhra Pradesh) | The Bank was established by amalgamating four RRB's viz. (1) Sri Saraswathi Grameena Bank, Adilabad, (2) Sri Satavahana Grameena Bank, Karimnagar (3) Sri Rama Grameena Bank, Nizamabad and (4) Golconda Grameena Bank, Ranga Reddy (Hyderabad) with an aggregate network of 215 branches. The area of operation of the bank covers the districts of Adilabad, Karimnagar, Nizamabad, hyderabad and Ranga Reddy districts of Andhra Pradesh. As at March 2010 bank had deposits of ₹ 2261 crores and advances of ₹ 1610 crores. |
| 4. | Andhra Pradesh Grameena Vikas Bank | State Bank of India | Warangal-506 001 (Andhra Pradesh) | Bank was formed on 31-3-2006 by amalgamating Sri Visakha Grameena Bank (Established on 30-09-1976), Nagarjuna Grameena Bank (Established on 30-04-1976), Sangameswara Grameena Bank (Established on 31-03-1982), Manjira Grameena Bank (Established on 31.03.1982), Kakathiya Grameena Bank |

(*Contd...*)

| | | | | |
|---|---|---|---|---|
| | | | | (Established on 28-06-1982). Bank has about 523 branches. Area of operation of the bank is 7 districts: Warangal, Vizianagaram, Visakhapatnam, Srikakulam, Medak, Mahabubnagar, Nalgonda and Khammam in AP. As at March 2010 bank had deposits of ₹ 3804 crores and advances of ₹ 3822 crores. |
| 5. | Andhra Pragathi Grameena Bank | Syndicate Bank | Kadapa-516 001 (Andhra Pradesh) | Bank came into existence on 1-6-2006 by amalgamating Sri Rayalaseema Grameen Bank, Pinakini grameena bank and Anantha grameena bank. The head office of the bank is in Kadapa with jurisdiction over districts of Kurnool, Kadapa, Nellore, Prakasam and Ananthpur. Bank has about 393 branches. As at march 2011 bank had deposits of ₹ 4079 crores and advances of ₹ 4291 crores. |
| 6. | Arunachal Pradesh Rural Bank | State Bank of India | Naharlagun-791 110 (Arunanchal Pradesh) | Arunachal Pradesh Rural Bank was established on 30th November 1983. The bank had shifted its Head Office from Pasighat to Naharlagun in 2004 and the area of operation of the bank has been expanded from six districts of Arunachal Pradesh to entire state of Arunachal Pradesh. Bank has about 23 branches. In March, 2011 bank had deposits of ₹ 231 crores and advances of ₹ 48 crores. |
| 7. | Langpi Dehangi Rural Bank | State Bank of India | Diphu, P.O. Diphu, Dist. Karbi Anglong-782 460 (Assam) | Langpi Dehangi Rural Bank was established on 27th January 1982. The Head Office of the bank is situated at Diphu. The bank has a total network of 42 branches and 1 satellite office, operating in Karbi Anglong District and in N.C. Hills District. As at March 2011 bank had deposits of ₹ 276 crores and advances of ₹ 156 crores. |
| 8. | Assam Gramin Vikash Bank | United Bank of India | Guwahati-781 001 (Assam) | Assam Gramin Vikash Bank was established on the 12th of January 2006 by amalgamating Pragjyotish Gaonlia Bank (Estd. 06-07-1976), Lakhimi Gaonlia Bank (Estd. 29-07-1980), Cachar Gramin Bank (Estd. 31-03-1981) |

*(Contd...)*

| | | | | |
|---|---|---|---|---|
| | | | | and Subansiri Gaonlia Bank (Estd. 30-03-1982). The Bank covers 25 out of 27 districts of the State. Bank has about 360 branches.<br>In March 2011 bank had deposits of ₹ 4376 crores and advances of ₹ 2072 crores. |
| 9. | Uttar Bihar Gramin Bank | Central Bank of India | Muzaffarpur-842 001 (Bihar) | The central government has amalgamated Uttar Bihar Kshetriya Gramin Bank and Kosi Kshetriya Gramin Bank in the state of Bihar into a single regional rural bank called as Uttar Bihar Gramin Bank with its head office at Muzaffarpur. Now area of operation of Uttar Bihar Gramin Bank is the districts of Araria, Katihar, Kishanganj, Darbhanga, East Champaran, Gopalganj, Madhepura, Madhubani, Muzaffarpur, Purnea, Saharsa, Saran, Sheohar, Sitamarhi, Siwan, Supaul, West Champaran and Vaishali in the state of Bihar. 'Uttar Bihar Gramin Bank is one of the largest regional rural banks in India in terms of branch network, staff strength and area. Bank has about 865 branches.<br>As at March 2010 deposits stood at ₹ 7233 crores and advances at ₹ 2619 crores. |
| 10. | Madhya Bihar Gramin Bank | Punjab National Bank | Patna-800 001 (Bihar) | The bank was established on 10-02-2006 by amalgamating four RRBs viz. Bhojpur Rohtas Gramin Bank, Magadh Gramin Bank, Nalanda Gramin Bank and Patliputra Gramin Bank. The bank has about 423 branches. The area of operation of the bank is the districts of Ara, Patna, Bihar sharif, Nawada, Gaya, Aurangabad, and Sasaram.<br>Deposits of the bank stood at ₹ 3867 crores as on March' 2010 and advances of the Bank stood at ₹ 1536 crores. |
| 11. | Samastipur Kshetriya Gramin Bank | State Bank of India | Samastipur-848 101 (Bihar) | Samastipur Kshetriya Gramin Bank was started in 1980 in the state of Bihar. The bank has over 65 branches across various districts. Head office of the bank is in Samastipur.<br>Deposits of the bank stood at ₹ 423 crores and advances at ₹ 213 crores in March 2010. |

*(Contd...)*

| | | | | |
|---|---|---|---|---|
| 12. | Bihar Kshetriya Gramin Bank | Uco Bank | Monghyr-811 201 (Bihar) | Bihar Kshetriya Gramin Bank came into existence on 12-09-2005 by amalgamating 3 RRBs namely: Monghyr Kshetriya Gramin Bank (established on 12-03-1977), Bhagalpur-Banka Kshetriya Gramin Bank (established on 22-03-1985) and Begusarai Kshetriya Gramin Bank (established on 23-03-1985). The area of operation of the Bank is 8 districts of Bhagalpur, Banka, Munger, Lakhisarai, Jamui, Sheikhpura, Begusarai and Khagaria in the state of Bihar. Bank is having 164 branches at March 2011. The Head Office of the bank is situated in Munger.<br>In March 2011 bank's deposits stood at ₹ 1395 crores and advances at ₹ 499 crores. |
| 13. | Surguja Kshetriya Gramin Bank | Central Bank of India | Ambikapur, Distt. Surguja-497 001 (Chhattisgarh) | Surguja Kshetriya Gramin Bank was formed on 24th of October, 1979, The bank is headquartered in Ambikapur in Surguja District of Chhattsigarh state. The bank operates in two districts of Chhattisgarg namely Surguja and Korea.<br>Bank has 85 branches. Banks deposits stood at ₹ 851 crores and advances at ₹ 255 crores in March 2010. |
| 14. | Durg-Rajnandgaon Gramin Bank | Dena Bank | Rajnandgaon-491 441 (Chhatisgarh) | .The Bank was established on 12th March 1980, the area of operation of the Bank is Durg, Rajnandgaon and Kawardha Districts in the State of Chhattisgarh.<br>The Bank is having 110 branches, As at March 2010 bank had Deposit of ₹ 953 crores and Advances of ₹ 248 crores. |
| 15. | Chhattisgarh Gramin Bank | State Bank of India | Raipur- 492 009 (Chhattisgarh) | Chhattisgarh Gramin Bank was established on 30-06-2006 with the amalgamation of three RRBs namely; erstwhile Bilaspur-Raipur Kshetriya Gramin Bank, Bastar Kshetriya Gramin Bank and Raigarh Kshetriya Gramin Bank.<br>Now the bank is operating in 19 districts namely; Bilaspur, Kawardha, Korba, Raipur, Janjgir-Champa, Dhamtari, Mahasamund, Raigarh, Jashpur, Kanker, Narayanpur, Bastar, |

(Contd...)

| | | | | |
|---|---|---|---|---|
| | | | | Dantewada, Bijapur, Baloda Bazar, Mungeli, Sukma, Gariaband and Kondagaon.<br>Bank has about 294 branches plus 37 Satellite offices.<br>In March 2010 bank had deposits of ₹ 2023 crores and advances of ₹ 647 crores. |
| 16. | Baroda Gujarat Gramin Bank | Bank of Baroda | Bharuch-392 001 (Gujarat) | The bank was formed on 12-9-2005 by amalgamating three RRBs namely: Panchmahal Vadodara Gramin Bank, Surat Bharuch Gramin Bank and Valsad Dangs Gramin Bank, into a single Regional Rural Bank and named as Baroda Gujarat Gramin Bank with its Head office at Bharuch.<br>Bank has about 141 branches and as at March, 2010 had deposits of ₹ 1158 crores and advances of ₹ 466 crores. |
| 17. | Dena Gujarat Gramin Bank | Dena Bank | Gandhinagar-382 016 (Gujarat) | The Bank came into existence on 12-09-2005 following the amalgamation of the three Regional Rural Banks viz. Banaskantha Mehsana Gramin Bank, Kutch Gramin Bank and Sabarkantha Gandhinagar Gramin Bank. The Bank has a network of 143 branches and 23 satellite offices.<br>The area of operation of the Bank is spread over seven districts of Gujarat State, viz. Ahmedabad, Banaskantha, Gandhinagar, Kutch, Mehsana, Patan and Sabarkantha.<br>As at March, 2010 Bank had deposits of ₹ 1571 crores and advances of ₹ 463 crores. |
| 18. | Saurashtra Gramin Bank | State Bank of Saurashtra | Rajkot-360 002 (Gujarat) | Saurashtra Gramin Bank came into existence w.e.f. 02-01-2006 with amalgamation of following three erstwhile RRBs:<br>(1) Jamnagar–Rajkot Garmin Bank<br>(2) Surendranagar–Bhavnagar Garmin Bank<br>(3) Junagadh–Amreli Garmin Bank (all started in 1978).<br>The Bank has its presence at 7 districts of Gujarat namely: Jamnagar, Surendranagar, Junagadh, Amreli, Porbandar, Bhavnagar and Rajkot. Bank has a Network of 169 Branches. |

(Contd...)

| | | | | |
|---|---|---|---|---|
| | | | | As at March 2010 the bank had deposits of ₹ 1220 crores and advances of ₹ 719 crores. |
| 19. | Haryana Gramin Bank | Punjab National Bank | Rohtak-124 001 (Haryana) | Haryana Gramin Bank came into existence on 21st December 2005 by amalgamation of following three RRB's in the State:<br>1. Haryana Kshetriya Gramin Bank: Established on 02nd October 1975, one of the first five RRBs in India.<br>2. Hisar Sirsa Kshetriya Gramin Bank: Established on 02nd October 1984.<br>3. Ambala Kurukshetra Gramin Bank: Established on 18th January 1985.<br>Presently Haryana Gramin Bank has 229 branches in 16 districts.<br>In March 2011 bank had deposits of ₹ 3481 crores and advances of ₹ 3287 crores. |
| 20. | Gurgaon Gramin Bank | Syndicate Bank | Gurgaon-122 002 (Haryana) | Gurgaon Gramin Bank is a Regional Rural Bank, having its Head Office at Gurgaon. It came into existence in the year 1976. Bank has operational area covering seven Districts i.e. Gurgaon, Faridabad, Palwal, Mewat, Rewari, Mahendergarh and Sonepat having network of 186 Branches.<br>In March 2011 bank had deposits of ₹ 3967 crores and advances of ₹ 1820 crores. |
| 21. | Himachal Gramin Bank | Punjab National Bank | Mandi, District: Mandi-175 001 (Himachal Pradesh) | The bank came into existence on 23 December 1976, with its Head Office at Mandi (H.P.). The bank is sponsored by Punjab National Bank. The bank has 127 branches including 2 satellite branches. As at March 2010 bank had deposits of ₹ 1099 crores and advances of ₹ 375 crores. |
| 22. | Parvatiya Gramin Bank | State Bank of India | Chamba, Dist. Chamba-176 310 (Himachal Pradesh) | Parvatiya Gramin Bank with its Head Office at Chamba, Himachal Pradesh was established on 2nd November 1985 under the Regional Rural Banks Act 1976. Presently, the bank is operating in the district of Chamba. Bank has about 33 branches.<br>In March, 2011 bank had deposits of ₹ 225 crores and advances of ₹ 165 crores. |

*(Contd...)*

| | | | | |
|---|---|---|---|---|
| 23. | Ellaquai Dehati Bank | State Bank of India | Srinagar-190 008 (Jammu &Kashmir) | Ellaquai Dehati Bank has been established on the 16th July 1979 under the RRBs Act 1976. Bank has its presence in both the divisions of the J&K State and has at present a branch network of 111 branches spread in thirteen districts of the State.<br>In March 2010 bank had deposits of ₹ 422 crores and advances of ₹ 168 crores. |
| 24. | J&K Grameen Bank | J&K Bank Ltd. | Jammu-180 006 (Jammu & Kashmir) | J&K Grameen Bank (JKGB), was established on 30th June 2009 after amalgamation of two RRBs viz. JRB and KRB. The area of operation of the bank is extended to 11 Districts (Baramulla, Bandipora, Kupwara, Jammu, Kathua, Rajouri, Poonch, Leh, Kargil, Samba and Kishtwar), besides some parts of District Srinagar and Ganderbal of J&K State. The bank has network of 176 branches with 7 extension counters in 2011.<br>As at March 2010 bank had deposits of ₹ 1397 crores and advances of ₹ 436 crores. |
| 25. | Jharkhand Gramin Bank | Bank of India | Ranchi-834 001 (Jharkhand) | Jharkhand Gramin Bank, was established on 12th June, 2006, consequent upon amalgamation of four erstwhile Regional Rural Banks—namely, Ranchi Kshetriya Gramin Bank, Singhbhum Kshetriya Gramin Bank, Hazaribag Kshetriya Gramin Bank, and Giridih Kshetriya Gramin Bank. Head Office of Jharkhand Gramin Bank (JGB) is located in Ranchi, the capital of Jharkhand State. JGB is operating in 15 out of 24 districts in the State of Jharkhand, and it has a network of 224 branches.<br>Bank had deposits of ₹ 1660 crores and Advances of ₹ 451 crores in March 2010. |
| 26. | Vananchal Gramin Bank | State Bank of India | Dangalpara, Dumka-814 101 (Jharkhand) | Bank was established on 30-06-2006 with the amalgamation of Santhal Parganas Gramin Bank and Palamau Kshetriya Gramin Bank. The bank is operating in 9 districts of Jharkhand State with its Head Office at Dumka (sub-capital of Jharkhand State). It has 195 branches functioning at |

(Contd...)

| | | | | |
|---|---|---|---|---|
| | | | | Deoghar, Godda, Daltonganj and Garhwa Districts.<br>The bank had ₹ 1411 crores as deposits and ₹ 446 crores as advances in March 2010. |
| 27. | Pragathi Gramin Bank | Canara Bank | Bellary-583 103 (Karnataka) | Pragathi Gramin Bank came into existence on 12-09-2005 by amalgamating four RRBs namely: Tungabhadra Gramin Bank (started in 1976), Chitradurga Gramin Bank, Kolar Gramin Bank and Sahyadri Gramin Banks in Karnataka State.<br>Bank has about 368 branches in 2011. Area of operation of the bank is 8 districts: Bellary, Chitradurga, Davanagere, Kolar, Chikkaballapura, Koppal, Raichur, Shimoga in Karnataka state.<br>As at March 2011 bank had deposits of ₹ 4812 crores and advances of ₹ 4349 crores. |
| 28. | Chikmagalur Kodagu Grameena Bank | Corporation Bank | Chikmagalur-577 101 (Karnataka) | Bank was established in the year of 1984 under the RRB Act 1976. The operational area of the bank is the districts Chikmagalur and Kodagu. The bank has its Head Office at Chikmagalur, Karnataka, State.<br>The bank has a network of 52 branches i.e. 34 branches in Chikmagalur and 18 in Kodagu Districts. As at March 2010 bank had deposits of ₹ 300 crores and advances of ₹ 205 crores. |
| 29. | Krishna Grameena Bank | State Bank of India | Gulbarga-585 105 (Karnataka) | The Bank was established on 01-12-1978. The area of operation of the bank comprises three districts viz., Gulbarga, Bidar and Yadgir. The present branch network is 139,<br>In March 2011 bank had deposits of ₹ 1286 crores and advances of ₹ 1224 crores. |
| 30. | Cauvery Kalpatharu Grameena Bank | State Bank of Mysore | Mysore-570 017 (Karnataka) | Cauvery Kalpatharu Grameena Bank came into existence on 24th May 2006 by amalgamation of Cauvery Grameena Bank and Kalpatharu Grameena Bank<br>The operational area of the Bank spreads to seven districts viz., Mysore, Hassan, Bangalore Rural, Ramanagar, Bangalore Urban, Tumkur and Chamarajanagar districts. The bank has 215 branches. |

*(Contd...)*

| | | | | |
|---|---|---|---|---|
| | | | | In March 2011 bank had deposits of ₹ 2187 crores and advances of ₹ 1708 crores. |
| 31. | Karnataka Vikas Grameena Bank | Syndicate Bank | Dharwad-580 008 (Karnataka) | The four RRBs viz. Malaprabha Grameena Bank, Bijapur Grameena Bank, Varada Grameena Bank and Netravathi Grameena Banks sponsored by Syndicate Bank in the State of Karnatak were amalgamated to form the Karnatak Vikas Grameena Bank in 2005. The combined business level of this Bank was ₹ 3263.73 crores with Deposits of ₹ 1620.46 crores and Advances of ₹ 1643.27 Crores as on 12-09-2005<br>The bank has a network of 451 branches in nine districts forming its area of operation.<br>In March 2011 bank had deposits of ₹ 5405 crores and advances of ₹ 3640 crores. |
| 32. | Visveshvaraya Grameena Bank | Vijaya Bank | Mandya-571401 (Karnataka) | Vishveshwarya grameena bank was established in 27-3-1985 having Head office at Mandya. Bank has a total network of 25 branches in Mandya District of Karnatak State.<br>Total deposits of the bank were ₹ 242 crores as at March 2011, and aggregate advances were ₹ 158 crores as at March 2011. |
| 33. | South Malabar Gramin Bank | Canara Bank | Malappuram-676 505 (Kerala) | South Malabar Gramin Bank (SMG) is operational since 1976 with headquarters in Malappuram. It has around 235 branches across 8 districts of Kerala namely: 1. Malappuram 2. Kozhikode, 3. Wynad (2 blocks), 4. Thrissur, 5. Palakkad, 6. Pathanamthitta, 7. Idukki 8. Trivandrum.<br>As at June 2011 bank had deposits of ₹ 3029 crores and advances of ₹ 3144 crores. |
| 34. | North Malabar Gramin Bank | Syndicate Bank | P.O. Pallikunnu, Kannur-670 004 (Kerala) | The Bank was established on the 12th of December 1976 with its Headquarters in Kannur (Kerala-India). The Bank currently has 185 branches with 2 Extension counters. Area of operation of the bank is, 82 branches in Kannur District, 51 branches in Kasargod district, 9 branches and 1 extension counter in Waynad district, 17 branches in |

(*Contd...*)

| | | | | |
|---|---|---|---|---|
| | | | | Ernakulam, 19 branches in Kottayam district, 10 branches in Alappuzha district and 12 branches in Kollam district.<br>Bank had deposits of ₹ 2078 crores and advances of ₹ 2025 crores in March 2010. |
| 35. | Sharda Gramin Bank | Allahabad Bank | Satna-485 001 (Madhya Pradesh) | Sharda Gramin Bank was established on 31-03-1979 under section 3(I) of Regional Rural Bank Act 1976, The bank started business on 21st May 1979.<br>The area of operation of the bank is Satna District (M.P.) comprising of 5 tehsils and 8 blocks. Bank has 64 branches.<br>In March 2011 bank had deposits of ₹ 720 crores and advances of ₹ 216 crores. |
| 36. | Jhabua Dhar Kshetriya Gramin Bank | Bank of Baroda | Jhabua-457 661 (Madhya Pradesh) | Jhabua Dhar Kshetriya Gramin Bank was established on 20th June 1980 with its Head Office at Jhabua, in South-Western Madhya Pradesh. Bank has 80 branches and 3 satellite branches covering in 3 districts viz. Jhabua, Dhar and Alirajpur. As at March 2010 bank had deposits of ₹ 603 crores and advances of ₹ 250 crores. |
| 37. | Narmada Malwa Gramin Bank | Bank of India | Indore-452 001 (Madhya Pradesh) | The bank operates in 10 districts of Madhya Pradesh state.<br>Bank has 222 branches and as at March 2010 deposits were ₹ 1838 crores and advances were ₹ 1211 crores. |
| 38. | Satpura Narmada Kshetriya Gramin Bank | Central bank of India | Chhindwara-480 001 (Madhya Pradesh) | Satpura Narmada Kshetriya Gramin Bank came into existence on 1-6-2006 by amalgamation of four RRBs namely: "Hoshangabad, Kshetriya Gramin Bank", "Chhindwara-Seoni Kshetriya Gramin Bank", "Mandla-Balaghat Kshetriya Bank", "Shahdol Kshetriya Gramin Bank".<br>Its working area is 11 Districts namely: Hoshangabad, Raisen, Harda, Chhindwara, Seoni, Mandla, Balaghat, Dindori, Shahdol, Umaria and Anuppur. Its head office is at Chhindwara. Bank has about 347 branches.<br>In March 2010 the deposits of the bank stood at ₹ 2942 crores and advances were ₹ 1364 crores. |

(*Contd*...)

| | | | | |
|---|---|---|---|---|
| 39. | Vidisha Bhopal Kshetriya Gramin Bank | State Bank of India | Vidisha-464 001 (Madhya Pradesh) | Bank was established in the year 1986. The area of operation of the bank is the districts of Vidisha and Bhopal. Bank has about 22 branches<br>As at March 2009 bank had deposits of ₹ 271 crores and advances of ₹ 143 crores. |
| 40. | Madhya Bharat Gramin Bank | State Bank of India | Sagar-470 001 (Madhya Pradesh) | Madhya Bharat Gramin Bank was established on 30-06-2006 by amalgamation of 3 Regional Rural Banks namely Damoh Panna Sagar Kshetriya Gramin Bank, Shivpuri Guna Kshetriya Gramin Bank and Bundelkhand Kshetriya Gramin Bank.<br>The Head office of the bank is at Sagar (M.P.). The Bank has 221 branches covering 8 districts of state of Madhya Pradesh namely Sagar, Damoh, Panna, Shivpuri, Guna, Ashoknagar, Tikamgarh and Chhatarpur.<br>In March 2011 the deposits were ₹ 1802 crores and advances were ₹ 1059 crores. |
| 41. | Mahakaushal Kshetriya Gramin Bank | Uco Bank | Jabalpur-482 002 (Madhya Pradesh) | Mahakaushal Kshetriya Gramin Bank was incorporated on 01-04-84 and the area of operation is Jabalpur/Katni/ Narsinghpur districts.<br>The position of total deposits as on 31st March 2011 was ₹ 279 crores and advances were ₹ 88 crores. Bank has about 43 branches as at March 2011. |
| 42. | Rewa-Sidhi Gramin Bank | Union Bank of India | Rewa-486 001 (Madhya Pradesh) | Rewa Sidhi Gramin Bank was established on 20th Dec. 1976 at Rewa. The area of operation was two backward and undeveloped districts of M.P. namely Rewa and Sidhi. Area of the bank now covers 3 districts by coming into existence of new Singrauli distt..<br>Bank has a branch network of 100 branches with 3 satellite offices. 59 branches in Rewa district, 22 full fledged and 3 satellite branches in Sidhi district and 19 branches of the Bank are in Singrauli district.<br>As at March 2010 bank had deposits of ₹ 949 cores and advances of ₹ 218 crores. |
| 43. | Maharashtra Gramin Bank | Bank of Maharashtra | Nanded-431 602 (Maharashtra) | Maharashtra Gramin Bank came into existence w.e.f. 25-03-2008 by amalgamating two RRBs i.e. |

*(Contd...)*

| | | | | |
|---|---|---|---|---|
| | | | | Aurangabad Jalna Gramin Bank & Thane Gramin Bank.<br>Bank has 327 branches as at the end of February 2011. The service area of the bank includes 16 districts covering Nanded, Latur, Beed, Osmanabad, Parbhani, Hingoli, Aurangabad, Jalna, Pune, Thane, Jalgaon, Ahmednagar, Nasik, Dhule, Nandurbar and Raigad.<br>As at March 2010 Deposits were ₹ 2457 crores and advances were ₹ 1192 crores. |
| 44. | Wainganga Krishna Gramin Bank | Bank of Maharashtra | Solapur-413 001 (Maharashtra) | Wainaganga Krishna Gramin Bank came into existence on 15th December 2008 through amalgamation of Wainganga Kshetriya Gramin Bank, Chandrapur, Solapur Gramin Bank- Solapur and Ratnagiri-Sindhudurg Gramin Bank-Ratnagiri.<br>The area of operation of the bank covers 12 districts of Maharashtra state viz. Chandrapur, Gadchiroli, Wardha, Bhandara, Gondia, Nagpur, Ratnagiri, Sindhudurg, Kolhapur, Solapur, Satara and Sangli.<br>The bank has 182 branches and 4 extension counters spread across the area of operation.<br>As at March 2010 bank had deposits of ₹ 1059 crores and Advances of ₹ 569 crores. |
| 45. | Vidharbha Kshetriya Gramin Bank | Central Bank of India | Akola-444 005 (Maharashtra) | Vidharbha Kshetriya Gramin Bank, was established on 12-09-2005 by amalgamating three RRBs working in Akola, Washim, Buldhana and Yavatmal districts from 1983-84. Bank has about 97 branches.<br>In March 2010 bank had deposits of ₹ 609 crores and advances were ₹ 311 crores. |
| 46. | Manipur Rural Bank | United Bank of India | Imphal-795 001 (Manipur) | Manipur Rural Bank [MRB] was established by the Government of India sponsored by United Bank of India with headquarter located at Imphal. At present it has 30 branches at the districts of Manipur viz. Imphal East, Imphal West, Thoubal, Bishenpur, Chandel, Senapati, Ukhrul, Tamengong and Churachandpur. |

(*Contd...*)

| | | | | |
|---|---|---|---|---|
| | | | | In March 2011 bank had deposits of ₹ 95 crores and advances of ₹ 32 crores. |
| 47. | Meghalaya Rural Bank | State Bank of India | Shillong-793 001 (Meghalaya) | Meghalaya Rural Bank was established on 29th December 1981 under the Regional Rural Banks Act, 1976 with its Head Quarter at Shillong, the capital of Meghalaya.<br>The bank has 58 branches in the State and its area of operation comprises six districts of the State, namely, 1. East Khasi Hills, 2. West Khasi Hills, 3. Jaintia Hills, 4. Ribhoi District, 5. West Garo Hills and 6. East Garo Hills District.<br>As at March 2010 bank had deposits of ₹ 532 crores and advances of ₹ 154 crores. |
| 48. | Mizoram Rural Bank | State Bank of India | Zarkawt, Aizawl-796 007 (Mizoram) | The Mizoram Rural Bank established on 27th September 1983 under the Regional Rural Bank Act 1975 is having a spread in all the districts and blocks of the state. It covers 8 districts. Bank has about 61 branches. As at March 2010 bnak had deposits of ₹476 crores and advances of ₹ 234 crores. |
| 49. | Nagaland Rural Bank | State Bank of India | Kohima-797 001 (Nagaland) | Nagaland Rural Bank was, established on March 3, 1983 and 5 districts are covered by the bank. Bank has 8 branches.<br>In March, 2011 bank had deposits of ₹ 42 crores and advances of ₹ 10 crores. |
| 50. | Rushikulya Gramya Bank | Andhra Bank | Berhampur, Ganjam-760 001 (Orissa) | Rushikulya Gramya Bank, was established on 14th day of February, 1981 under provision of Section 3 of the Regional Rural Bank Act, 1976 with its Head Office at Berhampur (Ganjam), Orissa.<br>Bank has 81 branches and the area of operation is two districts—Ganjam and Gajapati districts in Orissa.<br>As at June 2009 bank had deposits of ₹ 700 crores and advances were ₹ 298 crores. |
| 51. | Baitarani Gramya Bank | Bank of India | AT & PO.: Baripada- 757 001 District-Mayurbhanj (Orissa) | Baitarani Gramya Bank was established on 23rd June 1980 to serve the people of the two districts of Mayurbhanj and Keonjhar, dominated by tribal |

*(Contd...)*

| | | | | |
|---|---|---|---|---|
| | | | | population. Head office is located at Baripada. BGB has a network of 106 branches in Orissa.<br>In March, 2011 bank had deposits of ₹ 1130 crores and advances of ₹ 642 crores. |
| 52. | Neelachal Gramya Bank | Indian Overseas Bank | Bhubaneswar-751 020 (Orissa) | Neelachal Gramya Bank was established on 31st August 2007 by amalgamation of the two Banks namely: Puri Gramya Bank (established on 25th February 1976) and Dhenkanal Gramya Bank (estblished on August 12, 1981).<br>Bank has about 174 branches in Orissa and as at March 2010 deposits were ₹ 2144 crores and advances were ₹ 1010 crores. |
| 53. | Utkal Gramya Bank | State Bank of India | Bolangir-767 001 (Orissa) | Utkal Gramya Bank (UGB) came into existence with effect from 31st July 2006 with its Head Office at Bolangir by amalgamating three RRBs namely: Bolangir Anchalik Gramya Bank (BAGB), Kalahandi Anchalik Gramya Bank (KAGB) and Koraput Panchabati Gramya Bank (KPGB).<br>The Bank operates in 15 districts of Western and Southern Orissa viz. Bolangir, Sonepur, Bargarh, Sambalpur, Deogarh, Jharsuguda, Sundargarh, Kalahandi, Nuapada, Kandhamal, Boudh, Koraput, Malkangiri, Rayagada and Nabarangpur districts.<br>Bank has about 332 branches and as at March 2010 had deposits of ₹ 2417 crores and advances of ₹ 1408 crores. |
| 54. | Kalinga Gramya Bank | Uco Bank | Cuttack-753001(Orissa) | Kalinga Gramya Bank, was established in 1975. As at March 2011 bank had 183 branches situated at different districts of Orissa with deposits of ₹ 1692 crores and advances of ₹ 962 crores. |
| 55. | Puduvai Bharathiar Grama Bank | Indian Bank | Puducherry-605 003 (Union Territory) | Puduvai Bharathiar Grama Bank was established on 26-3-08.<br>Area of operation of the bank is the entire Union Territory of Puducherry covering all the four regions viz. Puducherry, Karaikal, Mahe and Yanam. Bank has 25 branches, and as at March 2010 had deposits of ₹ 40 crores and advances of ₹ 44 crores. |

*(Contd...)*

| | | | | |
|---|---|---|---|---|
| 56. | Sutlej Kshetriya Gramin Bank | Punjab & Sind Bank | Bathinda-151 001 (Punjab) | Faridkot Bathinda Kshetriya Gramin Bank was established on 22-03-1986. The name of bank has since been changed to Sutlej Gramin Bank.<br>The bank has 30 branches. Its functional jurisdiction consists of 6 districts namely Bathinda, Mansa, Faridkot, Muktsar, Moga and Ludhiana.<br>As at March 2010 bank had depsoits of ₹ 195 crores and advances of ₹ 116 crores. |
| 57. | Malwa Gramin Bank | State Bank of Patiala | Sangrur, District Sangrur-148 001 (Punjab) | Malwa Gramin Bank a Regional Rural Bank was established on 27-02-1986. It has total 54 branches in five districts of Punjab, out of which 49 are in rural area, 4 in semi urban area and 1 in urban area. Its deposits and advances as on 31-03-2011 are ₹ 563 crores and ₹ 471 crores respectively. |
| 58. | Punjab Gramin Bank | Punjab National Bank | Kapurthala-144 601 (Punjab) | Punjab Gramin bank has come into existence on 12-09-2005 after the amalgamation of three erstwhile Regional Rural Banks of Punjab State.<br>The area of operation of the bank extends to 11 districts of state of Punjab namely, Kapurthala, Ferozpur, Moga, Gurdaspur, Amritsar, Hoshiarpur, Ropar, Mohali, Tarn Taran and Nawanshahar. Bank has Total 178 Branches and 2 Extn. Counters.<br>As at March 2010 bank had deposits of ₹ 1869 crores and advances of ₹ 1214 crores. |
| 59. | Baroda Rajasthan Gramin Bank | Bank of Baroda | Ajmer-305 006 (Rajasthan) | Baroda Rajasthan Gramin Bank, was established on 03-02-2006, by amalgamating 5 Regional Rural Banks viz. Marudhar Kshetriya Gramin Bank, Aravali Kshetriya Gramin Bank, Bundi Chittorgarh Kshetriya Gramin Bank, Bhilwara Ajmer Kshetriya Gramin Bank and Dungarpur Banswara Kshetriya Gramin Bank. The Head Office of the bank is at Ajmer. The Bank has 274 branches and 20 satellite offices.<br>The operational area of the bank is spread in 13 districts of Rajasthan viz. Sawai Madhopur, Dausa, Tonk, Karauli, Ajmer, Bundi, Bhilwara, Chittorgarh, |

*(Contd...)*

| | | | | |
|---|---|---|---|---|
| | | | | Dungarpur, Banswara, Pratapgarh, Churu and Bikaner.<br>As at March 2010 bank had deposit of ₹ 2061 crores and Advances of ₹ 1396 crores. |
| 60. | Mewar Anchalik Gramin Bank | Bank of Rajasthan Now ICICI Bank | Udaipur-313 002 (Rajasthan) | Mewar Aanchalik Gramin Bank was established on 25th June 1983. Bank has 59 branches.<br>The area of operation of the bank is two districts namely: Udaipur and Rajsamand districts. As at March 2010 bank had deposit of ₹ 435 crores and advances of ₹ 144 crores. |
| 61. | Hadoti Kshetriya Gramin Bank | Central Bank of India | Kota-324 007 (Rajasthan) | The bank was set up on 14th October 1982 with its head office at Kota city in the State of Rajasthan. The operation area of the bank is Kota, Baran and Jhalawar districts. Bank has about 96 branches.<br>Total Deposit as on 31st March 2010 was ₹ 764 crores. Total Advances as on 31st March 2010 was ₹ 445 crores. |
| 62. | Marwar Ganganagar Bikaner Gramin Bank | State Bank of Bikaner & Jaipur | Pali-Marwar-306 401 (Rajasthan) | MGB Gramin Bank came into existence on June 12, 2006 and July 14, 2006 when the government amalgamated three RRBs namely: Marwar Gramin Bank, Shriganganagar Kshetriya Gramin Bank and Bikaner Kshetriya Gramin Bank into a single bank called Marwar Ganganagar Bikaner Gramin Bank. The bank is operating with a network of 218 branches spread over six south western and north eastern districts of Rajasthan—Pali, Sirohi, Jalore, Bikaner, Hanumangarh and Sriganganagar.<br>In March 2011 bank had deposits of ₹ 2001 crores and advances of ₹ 1626 crores. |
| 63. | Jaipur Thar Gramin Bank, | Uco Bank | Jaipur-302 001 (Rajasthan) | Jaipur Thar Gramin Bank came in to existence w.e.f. 27-01-2006 by amalgamating two RRBs namely: Jaipur Nagaur Aanchalik Gramin Bank and Thar Aanchalik Gramin Bank. The area of operation of the bank is four districts; Amber, Jhotwara, Jodhpur and Nagaur.<br>Bank has about 210 branches and as at March 2010 bank had deposits of ₹ 1669 crores and advances of ₹ 869 crores. |

*(Contd...)*

| | | | | |
|---|---|---|---|---|
| 64. | Rajasthan Gramin Bank | Punjab National Bank | Alwar-301 001 (Rajasthan) | Rajasthan Gramin Bank (RGB) having its Head Office at Alwar (Rajasthan) came into existence on 24-1-2006 by amalgamating two RRBs: the erstwhile Shekhawati Gramin Bank having its Head Office at Sikar and Alwar Bharatpur Anchlik Grainin bank having its Head Office at Bharatpur. The area of operation of the bank comprises of five districts i.e. Alwar, Bharatpur, Dholpur, Jhunjhunu and Sikar of Rajasthan State. Bank has about 225 branches.<br>As at March 2010 bank had deposits of ₹ 1915 crores and advances of ₹ 1132 crores. |
| 65. | Pallavan Grama Bank | Indian Bank | Salem-636 007 (Tamil Nadu) | Pallavan Grama Bank, sponsored by Indian Bank was formed on 31-08-2006 by amalgamation of erstwhile Adhiyaman Grama Bank, Dharmapuri and Vallalar Grama Bank, Cuddalore.<br>Area of operation of the bank is 15 districts viz. Dharmapuri.<br>Krishnagiri Cuddalore, Villupuram, Coimbatore, (Tiruppur) Erode, Kancheepuram, Karur, Namakkal, Nilgiris, Salem, Thiruvallur, Thiruvannamalai and Vellore.<br>The bank has about 110 branches.<br>As at March 2010 bank had deposits of ₹ 528 crores and advances of ₹ 608 crores. |
| 66. | Pandyan Grama Bank | Indian Overseas Bank | Virudhunagar-626 002 (Tamil Nadu) | Bank was established on 9th March 1977, with Head Quarters at Sattur, and later shifted to Virudhunagar, Tamilnadu state.<br>Bank operates in 15 districts with, 210 branches. As on 30-09-2011bank had deposits of ₹ 2156 crores and advances of ₹ 3051 crores. |
| 67. | Tripura Gramin Bank | United Bank of India | Agartala- 799 005 (Tripura ) | Tripura Gramin Bank was set up with four branches on 21st December 1976 under the Regional Rural Bank Act 1976 in the state of Tripura.<br>Tripura Gramin Bank is having a net work of 119 branches spread across all the four districts of the state.<br>As at March 2010 bank had deposits of ₹ 2050 crores and advances of ₹ 799 crores. |

(*Contd...*)

| | | | | |
|---|---|---|---|---|
| 68 | Allahabad UP Gramin Bank | Allahabad Bank | Banda-210 001 (Uttar Pradesh) | Allahabad UP Gramin Bank, came into its existence after the amalgamation of 2 RRBs viz. Lucknow Kshetriya Gramin Bank, Sitapur and Triveni Kshetriya Gramin Bank, Orai on 2nd March 2010 with its Head Office at Banda.<br>Prior to this amalgamation erstwhile Lucknow Kshetriya Gramin Bank was formed on 1st March 2006 with the amalgamation of Bhagirath Gramin Bank (Sitapur), Sarayu Gramin Bank (Lakhimpur Kheri) and Shrawasti Gramin Bank (Bahraich)<br>Similarly, erstwhile Triveni Kshetriya Gramin Bank was also formed on 1st March 2006 after the amalgamation of Tulsi Gramin Bank, (Banda), Vindhyawasini Gramin Bank, (Mirzapur) abd Chatrashaal Gramin Bank (Orai).<br>Hence the bank is amalgamated entity of six RRBs. The Bank was having a business of over ₹ 7000 crore as on date of amalgamation. Bank has a large network of 507 branches and 4 extension counters spread over 11 districts of Uttar Pradesh viz. Sitapur, Bahraich, Shrawasti, Lakhimpur, Banda, Hamirpur, Jalaun, Chitrakoot, Mirzapur, Sonabhadra and Mahoba.<br>In March 2011 bank had deposit of ₹ 5301 crores and advances of ₹ 3120 crores. |
| 69 | Baroda Uttar Pradesh Gramin Bank | Bank of Baroda | Raibareli-229 001 (Uttar Pradesh) | Govt of India vide its notification dt. 23-02-2006 amalgamated 7 RRBs of Eastern Uttar Pradesh namely Allahabad Kshetriya Gramin Bank, Sultanpur Kshetriya Gramin Bank, Faizabad Kshetriya Gramin Bank, Pratapgarh Kshetriya Gramin Bank, Kanpur Kshetriya Gramin Bank, Raebareli Kshetriya Gramin Bank, Fatehpur Kshetriya Gramin Bank, and 2 RRBs of Western Uttar Pradesh namely Bareilly Kshetriya Gramin Bank, Shahjahanpur Kshetriya Gramin Bank sponsored by Bank of Baroda. Thus emerged two new corporates called Baroda Eastern |

*(Contd...)*

| | | | | |
|---|---|---|---|---|
| | | | | Uttar Pradesh Gramin Bank and Baroda Western Uttar Pradesh Gramin Bank with their Head Offices in Raebareli and Bareilly respectively. Govt of India on 31st March 2008, amalgamated the two banks to form a new entity called Baroda Uttar Pradesh Gramin Bank with its Head Office in Raebareli.<br>Bank has about 700 branches.<br>As at March 2010 bank had deposits of ₹ 7142 crores and advances of ₹ 2223 crores. |
| 70 | Aryavart Gramin Bank | Bank of India | Lucknow-226 010 (Uttar Pradesh) | Aryavart Gramin Bank, a Regional Rural Bank, was constituted on 3rd October 2006 after amalgamation of three Regional Rural Banks (RRBs) namely Avadh Gramin Bank (constituted on 07-06-1977 as Hardoi-Unnao Gramin Bank. The name was subsequently changed to Avadh Gramin Bank on 04-12-1987), Barabanki Gramin Bank (constituted on 26-03-1976) and Farrukhabad Gramin Bank (constituted on 29-03-1976).<br>Bank has 325 branches. The bank operates in 6 districts namely Lucknow, Barabanki, Farrukhabad, Hardoi, Kannauj and Unnao in the State of Uttar Pradesh.<br>As at March 2010 bank had deposits of ₹ 3306 crores and advances of ₹ 1566 crores. |
| 71. | Shreyas Gramin Bank | Canara Bank | Aligarh-202 001 (Uttar Pradesh) | Shreyas Gramin Bank, came into existence on 1st June 2006 after amalgamation of three RRBs i.e. Aligarh Gramin Bank, Etah Gramin Bank and Jamuna Gramin Bank.<br>The Bank is operating in seven districts viz. Aligarh, Mahamaya Nagar (Hathras), Etah, Manyawar Kanshiram Nagar, Agra, Mathura and Firozabad.<br>Bank has a network of 203 branches. As at Sept. 2010 bank had deposits of ₹ 2517 crores and advances of ₹ 1488 crores. |
| 72. | Ballia-Etawah Gramin Bank | Central Bank of India | Ballia-277 001 (Uttar Pradesh) | Ballia-Etawah Gramin Bank came into existence on 01 January 2010 consequent upon the amalgamation of two RRBs viz. Ballia Kshetriya Gramin Bank and |

*(Contd...)*

| | | | | |
|---|---|---|---|---|
| | | | | Etawah Kshetriya Gramin Bank. The bank's operational area is spread over four districts i.e. Ballia, Mau (only in one block namely Ratanpura), Etawah and Auraiya of Uttar Pradesh.<br>The bank is operating with network of 139 branches spread over four districts.<br>As at March 2010 bank had deposits of ₹ 1193 crores and advances of ₹ 433 crores. |
| 73. | Sarva UP Gramin Bank | Punjab National Bank | Meerut-250 002 (Uttar Pradesh) | Sarva U.P. Gramin Bank was established on 30th Nov. 2007. It came into existence by amalgamation of 4 RRB's (Uttar Pradesh Gramin Bank (Meerut), Kisan Gramin Bank, (Budaun), Rani Laxmi Bai Gramin Bank (Jhansi) and Devi Patan Gramin Bank (Gonda).<br>The bank has 297 branches. The bank's operational area spreads in 14 districts viz. Bulandshahar, Ghaziabad, Meerut, Gautam Budh Nagar, Bijnor, Gonda, Balrampur, Budaun, Haridwar, Bagpat, Saharanpur, Jhansi, Lalitpur and Muzaffaranagar.<br>As at March 2011 bank had deposits of ₹ 2902 crore and advances of ₹ 1601 crore. |
| 74. | Purvanchal Gramin Bank | State Bank of India | Gorakhpur-273 008 (Uttar Pradseh) | Purvanchal Gramin Bank came in to existence on 12-9-2005 by amalgamation of two RRB's i.e., Gorakhpur Kshetriya Gramin Bank and Basti Gramin Bank.<br>The bank has a network of 380 branches spread over in seven districts of U.P. (Gorakhpur, Mahrajganj, Deoria, Kushinagar, Basti, Siddharthnagar and Sant Kabir Nagar) as at March 2010 bank had deposits of ₹ 2988 crores and advances of ₹ 1220 crores. |
| 75. | Prathama Bank | Syndicate Bank | Moradabad-244 001 (Uttar Pradesh) | Prathama bank, was the first Regional Rural Bank of the country established on 2nd Otcober, 1975 with its Head Office at Moradabad in terms of the ordinance issued by the Government of India in 1975.<br>The bank is presently serving the people in three districts of UP namely Moradabad, Jyotiba Phule Nagar and Rampur. |

*(Contd...)*

| | | | | |
|---|---|---|---|---|
| | | | | The bank has 212 branches. In March 2011 bank had deposits of ₹ 2816 crores and advances of ₹ 2199 crores. |
| 76. | Kashi Gomti Samyut Gramin Bank | Union Bank of India | Varanasi-221 001 (Uttar Pradesh) | Kashi Gomti Samyut Gramin Bank, a new RRB, created on 12-9-2005 after the amalgamation of three erstwhile RRBs Kashi Gramin Bank-Varanasi, Samyut Kshetriya Gramin Bank, Azamgagh and Gomti Gramin Bank, Jaunpur. Kashi Gomti Samyut Gramin Bank with its head office at Varanasi has a network of 365 Branches spread over 8 districts of eastern Uttar Pradesh.<br>At the end of Financial Year 2011 total deposits stood at ₹ 4586 crores and advances were ₹ 1311 crores. |
| 77. | Kshetriya Kisan Gramin Bank | UP State Coop. Bank | Mainpuri-205 001 (Uttar Pradesh) | This is the only RRB sponsored by a state coop bank. The bank operates in two districts and has a network of 63 branches.<br>In March, 2011 bank had deposits of ₹ 476 crores and advances of ₹ 241 crores. |
| 78. | Nainital Almora Kshetriya Gramin Bank | Bank of Baroda | Nainital-263 139 (Uttarakhand) | Nainital-Almora Kshetriya Gramin Bank (NAKGB) was established on 26th March, 1983. Presently the bank has over 58 branches across 4 districts of Uttarakhand, namely: Udham Singh Nagar, Nainital, Bageshwar and Almora.<br>As at March 2010 bank had deposits of ₹ 548 crores and advances of ₹ 293 crores. |
| 79 | Uttarakhand Gramin Bank | State Bank of India | Dehradun-248 001 (Uttaranchal) | Uttarakhand Gramin Bank was established on June 30th 2006, after amalgamation of three erstwhile Regional Rural Banks viz. Ganga Yamuna Gramin Bank, Alaknanda Gramin Bank and Pithoragarh Kshetriya Gramin Bank,<br>Bank's area of operation is nine districts: Dehradun, Tehri, Uttarakashi, Haridwar, Pauri, Chamoli, Rudraprayag of Garhwal Division and Pithoragarh and Champawat districts of Kumaun Division in Uttarakhand.<br>Bank has 148 branches. As at March 2010 bank had deposits of ₹ 831 crores and advances of ₹ 523 crores. |

*(Contd...)*

| 80. | Uttar Banga Kshetriya Gramin Bank | Central Bank of India | P.O. & District Cooch Behar-736 101 (West Bengal) | Bank has about 119 branches in west Bengal state. In March 2010 bank had deposits of ₹ 1006 crores and advances of ₹ 546 crores. |
|---|---|---|---|---|
| 81. | Bangiya Gramin Vikash Bank | United Bank of India | Chuanpur, P.O. Berhampur, Dist. Murshidabad-742 101 (West Bengal) | Bangiya Gramin Vikash Bank started on 21-02-2007 following amalgamation of five RRBs in West Bengal. Bank operates in 11 districts of West Bengal with a network of 552 branches and 2 Extension Counters.<br>In March 2011 bank had deposit of ₹ 5989 crores and advances of ₹ 2864 crores. |
| 82. | Paschim Banga Gramin Bank | Uco Bank | Howrah-711 101 (West Bengal) | Paschim Banga Gramin Bank was established on 26th February 2007 by amalgamation of three RRBs namely; Howrah Gramin Bank, Bardhaman Gramin Bank and Mayurakshi Gramin Bank. Bank is having its Head Office at Howrah.<br>Paschim Banga Gramin Bank has four districts viz. Howrah, Hooghly, Burdwan and Birbhum as its area of operation. Bank has over 216 branches.<br>As at March, 2010 bank had deposits of ₹ 2347 crores and advances of ₹ 734 crores. |

## Local Area Banks (LABs)

In the year 1996 with a view to providing institutional mechanisms for promoting rural savings as well as for the provision of credit for viable economic activities in the local areas, Government of India has decided to allow the establishment of new local banks in the private sector. The objective was to set up Local Area Banks in private sector in the rural and semi-urban areas to cater to the credit needs of the local people and to provide efficient and competitive financial intermediation services in their area of operation. It is expected that their lendings will be to agriculture and allied activities, SSI, agro-industrial activities, trading activities and the non-farm sector with a view to ensuring the provision of timely and adequate credit to the local clientele in the area of operation. The banks are required to observe the priority sector lending targets at 40% of net bank credit (NBC) as applicable to other domestic banks. Within the above target, these banks are required to adhere to the requirement of lending at least 25% of their priority sector deployments (10% of NBC) to the weaker sections.

RBI had introduced the Local Area Bank scheme in 1996 to encourage financial activities in unbanked areas. The scheme envisaged setting up of LABs with a minimum capital of ₹ 5 crores, to operate in an area comprising three contiguous districts.

Few licences were issued by RBI to open LABs, and five such banks came into existence as under:

1. Coastal Local Area Bank Ltd, Vijayawada, Andhra Pradesh in 1999.
2. Capital Local Area Bank Ltd., Nakodar, Punjab; in 2000.
3. South Gujarat Local Area Bank Ltd., Gujarat in 2000.
4. Vinayak Local Area Bank Ltd., Sikar, Rajasthan in 2000.
5. Krishna Bhima Samruddhi Local Area Bank (Karnataka and Andhra Pradesh) in 2001.

However, the experiment to promote local area banks did not succeed and in the year 2002, RBI decided not to encourage opening of such banks. Two of the banks: South Gujarat Local Area Bank and Vinayak Local Area Bank ran into problems in very short time. This led to merger of South Gujarat Local Area Bank with Bank of Baroda in 2004. In 2002, The Reserve Bank of India has cancelled the licence issued to Vinayak Local Area Bank Ltd., Sikar, Rajasthan, prohibiting it to carry on banking business.

### Coastal Local Area Bank Ltd.

This was the first local area bank to be approved by RBI in the year 1999. Bank was set up in Vijayawada in Andhra Pradesh and was allowed to have branches in three districts of Krishna, Guntur and West Godavari in Andhra Pradesh. The Bank has 23 branches at present. As at March 2010, bank had deposits of ₹ 132 crores and advances of ₹ 112 crores.

### Capital Local Area Bank Ltd.

Presently this is the largest local area bank and was started in the year 2000. Head office of the bank is in Nakodar, Punjab. Bank has branches in three districts; Jalandhar, Kapurthala and Hoshiarpur in Punjab state. Bank has 24 branches at present. As at March 2010, bank had deposits of ₹ 531 crores and advances of ₹ 346 crores.

### Krishna Bhima Samruddhi Local Area Bank

The bank was established in the year 2001. The bank operates in four districts of Mahabubnagar, Gulbarga, Yadgir and Raichur in Andhra Pradesh and Karnataka states. The head office is in Mahabubnagar. The bank was promoted by and is presently owned entirely by Bhartiya Samruddhi Investments and Consulting Services Ltd. (BASICS Ltd.). Bank has 14 branches including one mobile branch. As at March 2010 bank had deposits of ₹ 74.56 crores and ₹ 78.11 crores as advances.

### Foreign Banks

Entry of foreign banks into the country was during British rule. They were then called 'Exchange Banks' and they alone were allowed to handle foreign exchange business. Most of these banks opened their branches in Mumbai and Kolkata, as they were the major trading centres those days.

Many Exchange Banks of British origin came to the country. They were: Mercantile Bank of India (now HSBC) in 1853, Chartered Bank of India, Australia and China (now Standard Chartered Bank) in 1858, National Bank of India in 1863, Hong Kong and Shanghai Banking Corporation in 1864, and Eastern Bank (now Standard Chartered Bank) in 1910.

In Kolkata The Comptoire d'Escompte de Paris, a French bank (now BNP Paribas) opened a branch in 1860, and another in Bombay in 1862. It also opened branches in Madras and Pondicherry (then a French colony). Another French bank, Indo-China Bank (Banque de L'Indochine), opened its branch in 1875 at Pondicherry. Banco Nacional Ultramarino, a Portuguese bank opened a branch in Goa in 1868.

At the end of 19th century one Japanese bank—Yokohama Specie Bank opened its branch in 1894 and one German bank: Deutsch-Asiatische Bank opened its branch in 1896.

During the years 1900 to 1925, few more foreign banks came to the country as under.

Three US banks viz. National City Bank of New York, International Banking Corporation and American Express Bank.

Two Japanese banks viz. Sumitomo Bank and Mitsui Bank.

One bank from Taiwan i.e. Bank of Taiwan.

One Russian bank i.e. Russo-Asiatic Bank.

One bank from UK i.e. the Eastern Bank.

Two Dutch banks viz. Netherland Trading Society and Netherlands India Commercial Bank. (*See* under Exchange banks)

Many of the above banks closed their branches subsequently. Thereafter entry of foreign banks to the country was minimal. This position continued till 1990. No new bank opened branch in the country during 1925 to 1952. In the year, 1951 there were 16 foreign banks having branches in the country.

About 12 more foreign banks opened their branches during 1953 to 1990. However many other foreign banks opened their representative offices in the country.

Another two banks viz. The British Bank of the Middle East and The Bank of Credit and Commerce International (BCCI) also came during this period. BBME was later absorbed by HSBC in 1999 and BCCI was ordered to be liquidated in 1991.

## British Bank of the Middle East

The bank was of British origin and was established in September 1889 as The Imperial Bank of Persia and acted as banker to the Govt of Persia (Iran). In the year 1949, it withdrew from Iran and was named The British Bank of the Middle East. In 1952, the bank obtained a new Royal Charter. The bank had branches in many Middle East countries and opened one branch in Bombay, opened around the year 1939. Later it opened branches in Delhi and Trivandrum. HSBC acquired this bank in the year 1959. It was then known as HSBC Bank Middle East Limited. However, the Indian branches continued under the name of The British Bank of the Middle East. In the year 1999, the Indian branches of this bank were merged with HSBC.

### The Bank of Credit and Commerce International (BCCI)

The Bank of Credit and Commerce International (BCCI) was a major international bank founded in 1972 by a Pakistani financier. The Bank was registered in Luxembourg with head offices in Karachi and London. The group held under it, BCCI SA (Luxembourg) and BCCI Overseas (Grand Cayman). BCCI expanded from 19 branches in five countries in 1973 to 108 branches in 1976. Within a decade, BCCI touched its peak. It operated in 78 countries, had over 400 branches, and had assets in excess of US$20 billion, making it the seventh largest private bank in the world by assets. The bank opened its branch in Mumbai in the year 1983.

BCCI came under the scrutiny of numerous Financial Regulators and Intelligence Agencies in the 1980s due to concerns that it was poorly regulated. Subsequent investigations revealed that it was involved in massive money laundering and other financial crimes, and illegally gained controlling interest in a major American bank. In 1991, regulators in various countries decided to liquidate BCCI. Bank's business in India was also liquidated in 1991 and SBI took over the business in 1994 through its subsidiary.

After the financial sector reforms were introduced, foreign banks were encouraged and 14 foreign banks came to the country and opened branches during the years 1994 to 2010.

In the year 2010, there are 32 foreign banks in India with 310 branches all over the country. Twenty-seven among these 32 foreign banks are headquartered in Mumbai. Two banks have headquarters in New Delhi and remaining three banks are headquartered in Kolkata, Chennai and Gurgaon.

Standard Chartered Bank is the largest foreign bank in India in terms of branches with 95 branches in 2010, followed by Hong Kong & Shanghai Banking Corp with 50 branches, Citibank with 43 branches and Royal Bank of Scotland with 31 branches. These four banks are leading in business also and their workings in March 2010 were as under:

(₹ In crore)

| Sl. No. | Bank | Deposits | Advances |
|---|---|---|---|
| 1. | HSBC | 55,748 | 23,475 |
| 2. | Citi Bank NA | 54,452 | 36,655 |
| 3. | Standard Chartered Bank | 48,192 | 41,552 |
| 4. | The Royal Bank of Scotland NV | 16,601 | 13,406 |

The last bank to open branch till the year 2010 was First Rand Bank in Mumbai. Few more foreign banks opened branches in 2011. The 32 foreign banks till the year 2010 are listed under:

| Sl. No. | Foreign Bank | Country | In India since Year |
|---|---|---|---|
| 1. | The Hongkong and Shanghai Banking Corporation Ltd. | UK | 1853 |
| 2. | Standard Chartered Bank | UK | 1858 |
| 3. | BNP Paribas | France | 1862 |
| 4. | Citibank NA | USA | 1903 |
| 5. | The Royal Bank of Scotland NV (earlier ABN AMRO) | UK | 1920 |
| 6. | American Express Banking Corporation | USA | 1922 |
| 7. | The Bank of Tokyo-Mitsubishi UFJ Ltd. | Japan | 1953 |
| 8. | Bank of America NA | USA | 1964 |
| 9. | Sonali Bank | Bangladesh | 1974 |
| 10. | Deutsche Bank AG | Germany | 1980 |
| 11. | Abu Dhabi Commercial Bank Limited | UAE | 1980 |
| 12. | Mashreqbank psc | UAE | 1980 |
| 13. | Credit Agricole Corporate & Investment Bank | France | 1981 |
| 14. | The Bank of Nova Scotia | Canada | 1984 |
| 15. | Oman International Bank S.A.O.G. | Oman | 1985 |
| 16. | Societe Generale | France | 1985 |
| 17. | Bank of Bahrain and Kuwait B.S.C. | Bahrain | 1986 |
| 18. | Barclays Bank PLC | UK | 1990 |
| 19. | JPMorgan Chase Bank | USA | 1994 |
| 20. | The Development Bank of Singapore Ltd. | Singapore | 1995 |

*(Contd...)*

| | | | |
|---|---|---|---|
| 21. | Bank of Ceylon | Sri Lanka | 1995 |
| 22. | Arab Bangladesh Bank Limited. | Bangladesh | 1996 |
| 23. | Bank Internasional Indonesia | Indonesia | 1996 |
| 24. | Chinatrust Commercial Bank | Taiwan | 1996 |
| 25. | MIZUHO Corporate Bank Ltd. | Japan | 1996 |
| 26. | Shinhan Bank | Korea | 1996 |
| 27. | Krung Thai Bank Public Company Limited. | Thailand | 1997 |
| 28. | State Bank of Mauritius Ltd. | Mauritius | 1997 |
| 29. | Antwerp Diamond Bank N.V. | Belgium | 2002 |
| 30. | JSC VTB Bank | Russia | 2008 |
| 31. | UBS AG | Switzerland | 2009 |
| 32. | First Rand Bank Ltd. | South Africa | 2009 |

Besides the above foreign banks, 47 other foreign banks are having representative offices in India as at June 2011.

As at 2010 there were 32 foreign banks and they had deposits of ₹ 2,34,639 (5.06% share) and advances of ₹ 1,66,860 crores (5% share). Total number of branches was 310.

## Repco Bank Ltd. (A Govt of India Enterprise)

Repco Bank Ltd. was commenced in the year 1969 by Govt of India with the main objective of rehabilitating repatriates from Burma and Srilanka. The Schemes are open to all on admission as members of the bank so as to enable the bank serve its main objective effectively. The bank is governed by the Ministry of Home Affairs, Govt of India. The area of operation of the bank covers the south Indian states viz., Tamil Nadu, Andhra Pradesh, Karnataka, Kerala, and the Union Territory of Pondicherry. The Share Capital of the bank constitutes subscription by the Govt of India and the state Govts. of Tamil Nadu, Andhra Pradesh, Karnataka, Kerala besides individual Repatriate members. It is working as a cooperative for the benefits of repatriates.

As at 31-12-2010 the bank had deposits of ₹ 2611 crores and advances of ₹ 1965 crores.

## Post Office Savings Bank

Indian post is a department of Govt of India. The Department of Posts comes under the Ministry of Communications and Information Technology. It also works as bank apart from its primary function of postal work. Post offices across the country act like banks and maintain savings bank accounts for individuals just like a bank. It offers chequebook facility to its savings customers. It also participates in clearing. This is the only exception in our country where someone other than bank is offering banking services to the public.

Besides savings accounts, post offices also accept term deposits from the public just like banks. It also offers recurring deposit accounts and monthly income deposit scheme to public. These are the four deposit products similar to banks.

Post offices also manage many other investment schemes on behalf of govt of India. They are national savings schemes where deposit is accepted for 4-6 years and national savings certificates (NSC) are issued. It also manages Indira Vikas Patra (IVP) scheme and Kisan Vikas Patra (KVP) scheme similar to NSC scheme on behalf of Govt. It also manages public provident fund (PPF)—an investment scheme for public. Many of the schemes carry tax benefits for the public.

Post offices are into money order business, a remittance facility, which it managed since long and the service has no parallel. It connected the entire country for remittance and till recently it was the only mode of remittance to large number of villages and other places.

Origin of Post office banking can be traced to East India Company rule of the country. Savings bank business in India was conducted by Government right from the time of the East India Company. Government savings banks were established in the three Presidency towns between 1833 and 1835 and later at selected district Treasuries in 1870. These were separate banks and played some role in mobilising savings and developing the banking habit.

Post offices started opening savings bank accounts in 1882 and 1883, throughout the country and took over the business of the district savings banks in 1886 and of Presidency savings banks in 1896. The rate of interest paid on savings deposits were $4\frac{1}{6}\%$ in 1879 and was reduced steadily to 3% in 1905 and to 2.5% in 1933. The interest rates after nineties were 5.5% from September 1993, 4.5% from January 1999, 3.5%

from March 2001. At present, the interest rate is 3.5% (now increased to 4% in November 2011).

Funds mobilised by the post offices are on behalf of the central govt and the funds are used by the govt who is responsible to the depositors.

Indian post is managing many other deposit schemes for public and also offers insurance products.

Various deposit schemes managed by post offices at present is given in the following table along with amount of deposits mobilised by it.

(₹ In crores)

| Sl. No. | Name of the Scheme | Interest Since Mar. 1, 2003 % | Amount Outstanding at end-Mar. 2010 (Provisional figures) |
|---|---|---|---|
| 1. | Post Office Savings Bank Accounts | 3.50 | 26458 |
| 2. | Public Provident Fund 1968 | 8.00 | 26096 |
| 3. | Post Office Time Deposit Account | 6 .25 to 7.50 | 27573 |
| 4. | Post Office Recurring Deposit Account | 7.50 | 62818 |
| 5. | National Savings Scheme 1992 | - | 577 |
| 6. | Post Office Monthly Income Scheme | 8.00 | 201693 |
| 7. | NSC VIII issue | 8.00 | 54776 |
| 8. | Indira Vikas Patra | - | 1022 |
| 9. | Kisan Vikas Patra | 8.41 | 153933 |
| 10. | Senior Citizens Saving Scheme | 9.00 | 24989 |
| | **Total** | | 579935 |

(*Source*: RBI)

(Interest rates are revised upwards in November 2011.)

## Development Banks

Development banks were set up in India at various points of time starting from the year 1948 to cater to the medium to long-term financing requirements of industry. This was needed as the capital market in India had not developed sufficiently and the commercial banks were not allowed in the past to provide long-term finance due to their limited resources. These banks were different from commercial banks, as they are not allowed to undertake retail-banking business.

The First Institution established in the field of Development Banking was The Industrial Finance Corporation of India, in

1948. After this beginning, a battery of Development Banks came to be established. There are many development banks and financial institutions created by central and state governments. They are basically term lending institutions for industries or other sectors of economy.

These development banks are state owned. Few of them are created by passing necessary acts by the govt and hence are statutory bodies. Some are registered as govt companies under companies act with share capital provided by govt or other govt agencies. Few of the development banks contain the word "bank" in their name while others are named as finance/development corporations. Their basic function is to provide long-term finance, either directly to units, or indirectly by giving refinance to banks and institutions providing loans.

Until the year 1990, developments banks and commercial banks were demarcated with a clear line drawn between the functional areas. Each operated within the assigned areas. However, the liberalisation and opening up of the economy started and the resource position of the banks changed. Commercial banks were no longer short of resources and Development Banks were short of resources. Both wanted to encroach upon other's domain. Commercial banks wanted larger share in term lending and development banks wanted access to public deposits to shore up their resources. This was the time when the demarcating line between them became blurred. While commercial banks can undertake term lending as their legitimate function, developments banks are not universal banks and had no authority to do retail banking. As the scenario changed, and RBI accepted the changed equations between development banks and commercial banks, few development banks started commercial banking through their subsidiaries. They promoted new commercial banks, taking advantage of RBI's policy to allow entry of new banks from the year 1994. ICICI and IDBI are the leaders in this and promoted new banks: ICICI Bank and IDBI Bank. Later, in unique reverse mergers, both the parent organisations: ICICI and IDBI merged with their subsidiaries ICICI Bank and IDBI Bank.

Few of the national level development banks are as under:

### 1. The Industrial Finance Corporation of India, (IFCI)

At the time of independence in 1947, India's capital market was relatively underdeveloped. Although there was significant demand for new capital, there was a dearth of providers. Merchant bankers and underwriting firms were almost non-existent and commercial banks were not equipped to provide long-term industrial finance in any significant manner.

It is against this backdrop that the government established the Industrial Finance Corporation of India (IFCI) on July 1, 1948, as the first Development Financial Institution in the country to cater to the long-term finance needs of the industrial sector. IFCI was provided access to low-cost funds through the central bank's Statutory Liquidity Ratio (SLR), which in turn enabled it to provide loans and advances to corporate borrowers at concessional rates.

By the early 1990s, it was also felt that IFCI should directly access the capital markets for its funds needs. For this purpose, the constitution of IFCI was changed in 1993 from a statutory corporation to a company under the Indian Companies Act, 1956. Subsequently, the name of the company was also changed to "IFCI Limited" with effect from October 1999.

Financial indicators as at March 2010

| | | (₹ Crores) |
|---|---|---|
| **Sl. No.** | **Particulars** | **Amount** |
| 1. | Capital | 1002 |
| 2. | Reserves | 3608 |
| 3. | Borrowings—bonds and debentures | 7864 |
| 4. | Loans and advances | 14400 |
| 5. | Total assets | 26365 |

### 2. Industrial Credit and Investment Corporation of India (ICICI)

(Now ICICI Bank)

ICICI was formed in 1955 at the initiative of the World Bank, the Government of India and representatives of Indian industry. The principal objective was to create a development financial institution for providing medium-term and long-term project financing to Indian businesses.

In the 1990s, ICICI transformed its business from a development financial institution offering only project finance to a diversified financial services group offering a wide variety of products and services, both directly and through a number of subsidiaries and affiliates like ICICI Bank.

ICICI promoted ICICI Bank as a private sector bank in 1996. In a move towards universal banking, the managements of ICICI and ICICI Bank decided to merge ICICI with ICICI Bank and merger took place in 2002. Consequent to the merger, the ICICI group's financing and banking operations, both wholesale and retail, have been integrated into a single entity.

### 3. Industrial Development Bank of India (IDBI)

(Now IDBI Bank)

Industrial Development Bank of India (IDBI) was constituted under Industrial Development Bank of India Act, 1964 as a Development Financial Institution (DFI) and came into being as on July 01, 1964 vide GOI notification dated June 22, 1964. It was wholly owned by RBI till 1976 and thereafter the ownership was transferred to GOI. After formation, IDBI took over the functions of Refinance Corporation of India, a development bank established earlier for providing refinance to boost industrial activities. It continued to serve as a DFI for 40 years till the year 2004 when it was transformed into a Bank.

IDBI is the premier term lending institution for industrial units including small-scale units. Subsequently SIDBI came into existence, which took up financing small-scale units and IDBI concentrated on to finance bigger units.

IDBI promoted IDBI Bank in the year 1994. Later, it was decided to transform IDBI into a Bank. For the purpose, Industrial Development Bank (transfer of undertaking and Repeal) Act, 2003 was passed repealing the Industrial Development Bank of India Act, 1964. In terms of the provisions of the Repeal Act, a new company under the name of Industrial Development Bank of India Limited (IDBI Ltd.)

was incorporated as a Govt Company under the Companies Act, 1956 on September 27, 2004. Later, IDBI Ltd. was amalgamated with IDBI Bank Ltd. The merger became effective from April 02, 2005.

### 4. Industrial Investment Bank of India (IIBI)

IIBI was initially set up as Industrial Reconstruction Corporation Limited (IRC) during 1971. It was renamed as Industrial Reconstruction Bank of India w.e.f. Mar. 20, 1985 under IRBI Act, 1984 to take over the function of IRC. During 1997, the bank was converted to a joint stock company by naming it Industrial Investment Bank of India. Its head office is in Kolkata.

The main objective of the bank is to revive and revitalize industrial units closed or facing closure. Besides sanctioning advances, IIBI also provides underwriting of shares and debentures, providing technical and managerial support to the assisted units.

The bank was burdened with bad loans and became financially weak. Between the years, 2004 and 2006 there were active news that the bank shall be merged with some other banks like Allahabad bank or other development banks like IDBI, ICICI, IFCI, etc. Now it is learnt that IIBI is in the process of voluntary winding up.

### 5. Export-Import Bank of India (EXIM Bank)

Export-Import Bank of India is the premier export finance institution of the country, set up in 1982 under the Export-Import Bank of India Act, 1981. Government of India launched the institution with objectives for providing financial assistance to exporters and importers, and for functioning as the principal financial institution for coordinating the working of institutions engaged in financing export and import of goods and services with a view to promoting the country's international trade. Since its inception, Exim Bank has been both a catalyst and a key player in the promotion of cross border trade and investment.

Exim Bank plays a major role in partnering Indian industries, particularly the Small and Medium Enterprises, in their globalisation efforts, through a wide range of products and services offered at all stages of the business cycle, starting from import of technology and export product development to export production, export marketing, pre-shipment and post-shipment and overseas investment.

Exim Bank offers export credit facilities (which can be availed of by Indian companies for executing contracts overseas) like Pre-shipment credit, Supplier's Credit for Project Exporters, for Exporters of Consultancy and Technological Services, and Guarantee Facilities. For commercial Banks, Exim Bank offers rediscounting facility, enabling them to rediscount export bills and Refinance of Supplier's Credit, enabling commercial banks to offer credit to Indian exporters.

Financial indicators as at March 2010

| | | (₹ Crores) |
|---|---|---|
| **Sl. No.** | **Indicators** | **Amount** |
| 1. | Capital | 1700 |
| 2. | Reserves | 2832 |
| 3. | Borrowings—bonds and debentures | 27,204 |
| 4. | Total assets | 48,194 |

### 6. The Agricultural Refinance and Development Corporation (ARDC)

The Agricultural Refinance Corporation was established by an Act of Parliament in 1963 and started functioning from 1st July 1963. Although primarily a refinancing agency, the Corporation had also assumed certain functions, which are essentially developmental and promotional in nature. In order to emphasise the developmental and promotional role of the Corporation, it was renamed as Agricultural Refinance and Development Corporation (ARDC) by amending the original Act in 1975.

According to the statute, the Corporation is to "provide such financial assistance to eligible institutions as it considers necessary for promoting the development of agriculture in India" and agriculture has been defined as including animal husbandry, dairy farming, poultry farming and pisciculture involving development of both inland and marine fisheries, catching of fish and activities connected therewith or incidental thereto.

After formation of NABARD in 1982, the entire undertaking of ARDC was merged with NABARD.

### 7. National Bank for Agriculture and Rural Development (NABARD)

NABARD was set up on 12th July 1982 under an act of Parliament by initially merging the A.C.D. and R.P. cell of RBI and the entire undertaking of ARDC. NABARD is an Apex Development Bank of the country with a mandate for facilitating credit flow for promotion and development of agriculture, small-scale industries, cottage and village industries, handicrafts and other rural crafts. It also has the mandate to support all other allied economic activities in rural areas, promote integrated and sustainable rural development, and secure prosperity of rural areas.

Till the formation of NABARD some areas of rural development and agriculture was looked after by RBI and ARDC acted as development bank for the sector. It was felt that a new arrangement would be necessary at the national level for achieving the desired focus and thrust towards integration of credit activities in the context of the strategy for Integrated Rural Development. Against the backdrop of the massive credit needs of rural development and the need to uplift the weaker sections in the rural areas within a given time horizon the arrangement called for a separate institutional set-up. The Reserve Bank had onerous responsibilities to discharge in respect of its many basic functions of central banking in monetary and credit regulations and was not in a position to devote undivided attention to the operational details of the emerging complex credit problems of agriculture. This paved the way for the establishment of NABARD. The Parliament, through the Act 61 of 81, approved setting up of NABARD. It was set up in the year 1982 with an initial capital of ₹ 100 crores, which was enhanced to ₹ 2000 crores, fully subscribed by the Government of India and the RBI.

NABARD is set up as an apex Development Bank with a mandate for facilitating credit flow for promotion and development of agriculture and other area. In discharging its role as a facilitator for rural prosperity, NABARD is entrusted with main functions as under:

1. Providing refinance to lending institutions in rural areas.
2. Bringing about or promoting institutional development, and
3. Evaluating, monitoring and inspecting the client banks.

NABARD is also the regulator and controller for Regional Rural Banks and Co-op banks (except urban coop banks) and coordinates with RBI on agriculture and rural development credits.

Financial indicators as at March 2010

| | | (₹Crores) |
|---|---|---|
| **Sl. No.** | **Indicators** | **Amount** |
| 1. | Capital | 2000 |
| 2. | Reserves | 10,675 |
| 3. | RIDF funds | 59,869 |
| 4. | Total assets | 1,36,292 |

## 8. Housing and Urban Development Corporation (HUDCO)

The Housing and Urban Development Corporation Ltd. (HUDCO) was incorporated on April 25, 1970 under the Companies Act, 1956, as a fully owned enterprise of the Government of India.

Towards the close of the 1960s, a need was realized for setting up a housing organisation in the country as the availability and cost of bank credit were the prime constraints in this development. It was found at that time there was no institution to provide housing finance to the rural and urban poor or even to meet the credit needs of housing boards, development authorities and other urban bodies set up by the State Governments.

It was in this context that a decision was taken to set a Housing and Urban Development Corporation (HUDCO) which could take a comprehensive look at the need of the sector and find workable and effective solutions. The establishment of HUDCO in 1970 was for comprehensively dealing with the problems of growing housing shortages, rising number of slums and for fulfilling the pressing needs of the economically weaker section of the society.

Apart from financing housing schemes, HUDCO is also contributing to improve the quality of life by augmenting basic community facilities and infrastructure services through its financial assistance for core infrastructure. It also promotes Projects involving self-help by the beneficiaries, and shelter upgradation. Financial assistance for basic sanitation schemes is also being extended on liberalised items in order to provide basic facilities in the existing houses where adequate sanitary disposal system are not available. The objectives also include to finance or undertake, wholly or partly, the setting up of new or satellite town and to finance or undertake the setting up of industrial enterprises of building material.

Financial indicators as at March 2010

| | | (₹ Crores) |
|---|---|---|
| **Sl. No.** | **Indicators** | **Amount** |
| 1. | Capital | 2001 |
| 2. | Reserves | 3095 |
| 3. | Borrowings—bonds and debentures | 15,520 |
| 4. | Loans and advances | 19,026 |
| 5. | Total assets | 21,929 |

### 9. National Housing Bank (NHB)

The Hon'ble Prime Minister of India, while presenting the Union Budget for 1987-88 on February 28, 1987 announced the decision to establish the National Housing Bank (NHB) as an apex level institution for housing finance. Following this, the National Housing Bank Bill (91 of 1987) providing the legislative framework for the establishment of NHB was passed by Parliament in the winter session of 1987 and with the assent of the Hon'ble President of India on December 23, 1987, became an Act of Parliament.

In pursuance of the above, NHB was set up on July 9, 1988 under the National Housing Bank Act, 1987. NHB is wholly owned by Reserve Bank of India, which contributed the entire paid-up capital. The Head Office of NHB is at New Delhi.

NHB developed model housing loan scheme for banks and made available refinance to banks for housing loans sanctioned by them. In a way, this started the housing loans by banks as hitherto this segment was financed by other housing finance companies.

NHB is also a regulatory body over housing finance companies in the country. In terms of the National Housing Bank Act, 1987, National Housing Bank is expected, in the public interest, to regulate the housing finance system of the country to its advantage or to prevent the affairs of any housing finance institution being conducted in a manner detrimental to the interest of the depositors or in a manner prejudicial to the interest of the housing finance institutions.

For this purpose, National Housing Bank has been empowered to determine the policy and give directions to the housing finance institutions and their auditors. National Housing Bank has issued the Housing Finance Companies (NHB) Directions, 2001 as also Guidelines for Asset Liability Management System in Housing Finance Companies. These are periodically updated through issue of circulars and notifications. As part of the supervisory process, an entry-level regulation is achieved through a system of registration of housing finance companies. National Housing Bank supervises the sector through a system of on-site and off-site surveillance.

NHB supports housing finance sector by extending refinance to different primary lenders in respect of eligible housing loans extended by them to individual beneficiaries, and for project loans extended by them to various implementing agencies. NHB also lends directly in respect of projects undertaken by public housing agencies for housing construction and development of housing related infrastructure.

Financial indicators as at March 2010

| | | (₹ Crores) |
|---|---|---|
| **Sl. No.** | **Indicators** | **Amount** |
| 1. | Capital | 450 |
| 2. | Reserves | 1769 |
| 3. | Borrowings—bonds and debentures | 10,833 |
| 4. | Loans and advances | 19,837 |
| 5. | Total assets | 22,753 |

## 10. The Small Industries Development Bank of India (SIDBI)

SIDBI was established on April 2, 1990. The Small Industries Development Bank of India Act, 1989 envisaged SIDBI to be "the principal financial institution for the promotion, financing and development of industry in the small scale sector and to co-ordinate the functions of the institutions engaged in the promotion and financing or developing industry in the small scale sector and for matters connected therewith or incidental thereto.

The head office of the bank is situated in Lucknow.

Prior to setting up of SIDBI, the functions of financing small-scale sector were looked after by IDBI. As a Principal Development Financial Institution for Promotion Financing and Development of Industries in the small-scale sector, SIDBI coordinates the functions of other institutions engaged in similar activities.

SIDBI is providing refinance to State Level Finance Corporations/State Industrial Development Corporations/ Banks, etc., against their loans granted to small-scale units. SIDBI has also taken up the financing of SSI projects directly on a selective basis. SIDBI has evolved itself as a supplier of a range of products and services to the Small & Medium Enterprises [SME] sector. In addition, SIDBI also assists the transport, health care, and tourism sectors and to the professional and self-employed persons setting up small-sized professional ventures.

Small-scale industrial units, contribute significantly to the national economy in terms of production, employment, and exports. Small-scale industries are the industrial units in which the investment in plant and machinery does not exceed ₹ 10 million. As per SIDBI report, about 3.1 million such units, employing 17.2 million persons account for a share of 36% of India's exports and 40% of industrial manufacture.

Financial indicators as at March 2010

| | | (₹ Crores) |
|---|---|---|
| **Sl. No.** | **Indicators** | **Amount** |
| 1. | Capital | 450 |
| 2. | Reserves | 5457 |
| 3. | Borrowings—bonds and debentures | 5312 |
| 4. | Borrowings—Govt and others | 14,019 |
| 5. | Loans & advances | 35,718 |
| 6. | Total assets | 51,217 |

# Business Growth, Spread and Evolution of Banks

5

## Business Growth of Commercial Banks

Business growth of commercial banks in the country is phenomenal between the years 1947 to 2010. In these six decades, banks have grown keeping in line with economic development in the country. Main reasons for such astronomical growth is growth in agriculture, industry and service sectors, and expansion of bank network into all parts of country.

Commercial banks includes public sector banks, private sector banks, foreign banks, local area banks and regional rural banks but does not include coop banks. Business figures of urban coop banks and other coop banks are compiled separately. (RBI also publishes business figures of scheduled banks, which include all scheduled commercial banks as mentioned above and scheduled urban coop banks and scheduled state coop banks.)

For our study purpose, business figures of following years have been taken and compared:

1947—year of independence, 1949—the year banking companies act came into force and RBI was nationalised, 1955—the year when SBI came into existence, 1959—when subsidiaries of SBI came into existence, 1969—the year when social control on banks was brought in and 14 major banks were nationalised, 1980—the year when six more banks were nationalised, 1986, 1991—the eve of financial sector reforms, and 1997, 2002, 2005, and 2010. It may be noted that accounting year-end for banks was December till 1987 and was changed to March from the year 1989. All the data presented is according to this.

### Deposits

Deposit growth of commercial banks received a boost from 1969 due to nationalisation and fast expansion of bank branches in the country. Deposits rose from ₹ 4646 crores in 1969 to ₹ 33,377 in 1980 and to ₹ 44,92,826 crores by 2010. Deposits as percentage to GDP, was just 8.7% in 1955 has increased to 33.8% by the year 1991. By 2010, commercial banks' deposits were 68.6% of GDP. This again shows the outreach of commercial banks and development and progress of banking habits in the country.

(₹ in crores)

| Year | Deposits | As % to GDP |
|---|---|---|
| 1947 | 989 | |
| 1949 | 829 | |
| 1955 | 1159 | 8.7 |
| 1959 | 2000 | 10.8 |
| 1969 | 4646 | 11.0 |
| 1980 | 33,377 | 26.0 |
| 1986 | 91,828 | 30.4 |
| 1991 | 2,01,199 | 33.8 |
| 1997 | 5,36,342 | 36.7 |
| 2002 | 11,31,188 | 48.4 |
| 2005 | 17,00,198 | 52.4 |
| 2010 | 44,92,826 | 68.6 |

(*Source*: RBI)

### Bank Branches

Total bank branches were 8262 in the year 1969 and by 1991; it increased to 60220 and to 87768 by the year 2010. The following table gives the progress in branch expansion by commercial banks. Population covered by branches was about 65000 per branch in 1969 and has come down to about 14000 per branch in the year 2010.

| Year | No. of banks | No. of branches | Population in thousands per branch |
|---|---|---|---|
| 1947 | 625 | | |
| 1949 | 585 | | |
| 1955 | 456 | | |
| 1959 | 355 | | |
| 1969 | 85 | 8262 | 65 |
| 1980 | 153 | 32419 | 20 |
| 1986 | 276 | 53287 | |
| 1991 | 276 | 60220 | |
| 1997 | 296 | 63550 | |
| 2002 | 298 | 68195 | |
| 2005 | 288 | 70373 | |
| 2010 | 167 | 87768 | 14 |

(*Source*: RBI)

## Advances

Advances of commercial banks were mere ₹ 432 crores in 1947 and was ₹ 3599 crores in 1969 when 14 major banks were nationalised. It rose sharply to ₹ 33,377 crores by 1980 keeping in line with deposit growth. Thereafter advances showed consistent growth over the years to reach ₹ 32,44,788 crores in the year 2010.

Advances to priority sector were promoted from the year 1969. It was just ₹ 504 crores and 14% of total bank advances in 1969. It rose to whopping ₹ 44,572 crores by the year 1991 and in percentage terms, it reached 37.7% of bank advances. By 2010 advances to priority sector was staggering ₹ 10,91,574 crores and 31.2% of advances.

Credit Deposit ratio was 77.4% in 1969, which was quite high as there were not much investments by banks and CRR and SLR was quite low then. CD ratio started falling as RBI increased CRR and SLR progressively in terms of its monetary policy relevant to the periods. Just before the reforms, the SLR was as high as 38.5% and the Cash Reserve Ratio (CRR) was as high as 15%. Taken together, banks needed to maintain 53.5% of their resources in CRR & SLR and this seriously restricted banks capacity to lend. CD ratio was low at 60.0% in 1991.

CRR and SLR were reduced gradually from the year 1992, after financial sector reforms were introduced, as this was one of the major recommendations for reforms. By the year 2006, CRR was down to 5% and SLR to 25% and CD ratio bounced to 71.5%. CD ratio of banks rose to 73.6% in 2010.

(₹ In crores)

| Year | Advances | Priority Sector advances | % Priority Sector advances to total advance | CD ratio % |
|---|---|---|---|---|
| 1947 | 432 | | | 43.7 |
| 1949 | 393 | | | 47.4 |
| 1955 | 703 | | | 60.6 |
| 1959 | 1045 | | | 52.2 |
| 1969 | 3599 | 504 | 14.0 | 77.4 |
| 1980 | 22,068 | 7278 | 37.0 | 66.1 |
| 1986 | 57,229 | 22,844 | 41.0 | 62.3 |
| 1991 | 1,21,865 | 44,572 | 37.7 | 60.6 |
| 1997 | 2,93,104 | 84,880 | 28.7 | 55.1 |
| 2002 | 6,09,053 | 1,77,718 | 27.5 | 53.8 |
| 2005 | 11,00,428 | 3,70,603 | 32.2 | 62.6 |
| 2010 | 32,44,788 | 10,91,574 | 31.2 | 73.6 |

(*Source*: RBI)

## Capital

Capital and Reserves of commercial banks came to focus after prudential norms were introduced and Basel accord on capital was made applicable. Until then the size of bank capital was not considered relevant. Capital and reserves were just ₹ 533 crores in 1980. It increased to ₹ 6788 crores by 1991. Post reforms, it went up steeply to ₹ 41,774 crores in 1997. Thereafter, again there was phenomenal increase in capital and reserves to ₹ 4,30,124 crores by the year 2010. This increase in banks capital and reserves underlines the strengths of commercial banks in the country.

(₹ In crores)

| Year | Capital + Reserves |
|---|---|
| 1947 | 70 |
| 1949 | 76 |
| 1955 | 72 |
| 1959 | 75 |
| 1969 | 113 |
| 1980 | 533 |
| 1986 | 2412 |
| 1991 | 6788 |
| 1997 | 41,774 |
| 2002 | 85,292 |
| 2005 | 1,49,610 |
| 2010 | 4,30,124 |

(Source: RBI)

Capital adequacy ratio was prescribed at 8% till 1999 and 9% from the year 2000. At present as at year 2010, scheduled commercial banks excluding RRBs have achieved CRAR of 13.6% much above the minimum prescribed. All the banks, barring one old private sector bank, have CRAR above 10%. CRAR of scheduled commercial banks from the year 1998 to 2010 were as under:

| Year | CRAR of 81 SCBs % | Year | CRAR of 81 SCBs % |
|---|---|---|---|
| 1998 | 11.5 | 2005 | 12.8 |
| 1999 | 11.3 | 2006 | 12.3 |
| 2000 | 11.1 | 2007 | 12.4 |
| 2001 | 11.4 | 2008 | 13 |
| 2002 | 12 | 2009 | 13.2 |
| 2003 | 12.7 | 2010 | 13.6 |
| 2004 | 12.9 | | |

(*Source*: RBI)

## All Scheduled Banks

All scheduled banks position as at last reporting Friday of March 2010 is given below. Public sector banks accounted for 72.15% of deposits and 72.33% of advances of all scheduled banks. Private sector banks accounted for 16.78% of deposits and 17.52% of advances. Foreign banks accounted for 5.06% of deposits and 5% advances. RRBs are state owned and when their figures are added, public sector accounts for 75.09% of deposits and 74.70% of advances of all scheduled banks in India.

(₹ In crores)

| Group | No. of reporting banks | Deposits | % | Advances | % | No. of Branches |
|---|---|---|---|---|---|---|
| SBI group | 7 | 1034889 | 22.32 | 749977 | 22.47 | 18114 |
| Nationalised banks | 20 | 2310046 | 49.83 | 1664160 | 49.86 | 43187 |
| **P.S. Banks** | **27** | **3344935** | **72.15** | **2414137** | **72.33** | **61301** |
| Old private sector banks | 15 | 209590 | 4.53 | 153035 | 4.59 | 5174 |
| New private sector banks | 7 | 567848 | 12.25 | 431668 | 12.93 | 5213 |
| **Private sector banks** | **22** | **777438** | **16.78** | **584703** | **17.52** | **10387** |
| Foreign banks | 32 | 234639 | 5.06 | 166860 | 5.00 | 310 |
| RRBs | 82 | 135814 | 2.94 | 79085 | 2.37 | 15723 |
| **SCBs** | **163** | **4492826** | **96.93** | **3244785** | **97.22** | **87721** |
| State coop banks | 16 | 65175 | 1.40 | 43350 | 1.30 | |
| Urban coop banks | 53 | 77224 | 1.67 | 49522 | 1.48 | |
| **All Scheduled banks** | **232** | **4635225** | **100.00** | **3337657** | **100.00** | |

(*Source*: RBI)

*Note*: As on March 2010, 4 commercial banks are in non-scheduled category and have 47 branches. Their business figures are not included in the above table.

## Spread of Banks in India in 20th Century

It can be observed that historically banking developments followed trading activities in the country. After the coming of British into the country, Kolkata became a big trading centre. The origin of banking in organized sector also took place there. Bank of Calcutta was opened in 1806 and Allahabad bank in 1865. Few foreign banks have also opened their branches there. Besides large number of smaller banks came on the scene. Most of these smaller banks perished or were merged. The present day nationalized banks—UCO Bank (1943) and United Bank of India (1950) hail from this centre.

Mumbai as an important trading centre witnessed establishment of banks like Bank of Bombay (1840), Bank of India (1906), Central Bank of India (1911), Union Bank of India (1922), Dena Bank (1938). Other prominent banks established in Maharashtra state were Sangli bank (1916), United Western Bank (1936), Bank of Maharashtra (1936), and Ratnakar Bank (1943).

Swadeshi movement to open Indian banks became a driving force to open banks and this trend is more visible in undivided Punjab and southern states.

Punjab National Bank (1895), Punjab & Sind Bank (1908), State Bank of Patiala (1917), Oriental Bank of Commerce (1943), New Bank of India and Laxmi Commercial Bank were all established in undivided Punjab and Lahore.

So-called cradle of Indian banking—South Kanara district in Karnataka gave birth to Canara Bank (1906), Corporation Bank (1906), Karnataka Bank (1924) Syndicate Bank (1925), and Vijaya Bank (1931). State Bank of Mysore (1913) also came into existence.

Kerala like West Bengal witnessed large number of small banks coming up and many of them did not survive. Prominent among the present day banks are Nedungadi Bank (1899), Catholic Syrian Bank (1920) Dhanalaxmi Bank (1927), South Indian Bank (1929), Federal Bank (1940), Lord Krishna Bank (1940) and State Bank of Travancore (1945).

State of Tamil Nadu witnessed opening of Bank of Madras (1843), City Union Bank (1904), Indian Bank (1907), Karur Vysya Bank (1916), Tamil Nadu Mercantile Bank (1921), Laxmi Vilas Bank (1926) and Indian Overseas Bank (1937).

Another important trading centre—Ahmedabad and Gujarat saw opening of banks like State Bank of Saurashtra (1902), and Bank of Baroda (1908). However, growth of urban cooperative banks and continuance of indigenous bankers was very prominent in Gujarat and the trend is even now visible.

Hyderabad region saw opening of Andhra Bank (1923), Vysya Bank (1930), and State Bank of Hyderabad (1941).

At present bank branches are evenly spread at all parts of the country. No. of commercial bank branches stood at 87768 as at March 2010. Rural centres account for maximum 32528 branches followed by semi urban branches—20771, urban branches—18171, and metro branches—16298.

State of Uttar Pradesh has maximum branches at 10550, followed by State of Maharastra - 8427 branches, Andhra Pradesh - 7208 branches, Tamil Nadu - 6527 branches, and Karnataka - 6336 branches. Southern states put together have 24658 branches which is 28.1% of total branches in the country.

State-wise number of branches is given in the following table.

| Region | No. of offices/ (%) | State/Union territory | No. of offices | No. of offices | No. of offices | No. of offices | No. of offices |
|---|---|---|---|---|---|---|---|
| | | | Rural | Semi urban | Urban | Metro | Total |
| **Northern Region** | **15221** (17.3) | Chandigarh | 24 | 1 | 304 | - | 329 |
| | | Delhi | 56 | 37 | - | 2400 | 2493 |
| | | Haryana | 742 | 548 | 1030 | 136 | 2456 |
| | | Himachal Pradesh | 765 | 184 | 77 | - | 1026 |
| | | Jammu & Kashmir | 550 | 207 | 281 | - | 1038 |
| | | Punjab | 1192 | 1064 | 808 | 567 | 3631 |
| | | Rajasthan | 1779 | 1067 | 939 | 463 | 4248 |
| **North Eastern Region** | **2292** (2.6) | Arunachal Pradesh | 51 | 30 | - | - | 81 |
| | | Assam | 799 | 368 | 326 | - | 1493 |
| | | Manipur | 35 | 20 | 26 | - | 81 |
| | | Meghalaya | 126 | 33 | 54 | - | 213 |
| | | Mizoram | 55 | 14 | 30 | - | 99 |
| | | Nagaland | 38 | 53 | - | - | 91 |
| | | Tripura | 115 | 61 | 58 | - | 234 |
| **Eastern Region** | **14479** (16.5) | Andaman & Nicobar | 18 | 21 | - | - | 39 |
| | | Bihar | 2399 | 933 | 518 | 306 | 4156 |
| | | Jharkhand | 996 | 419 | 455 | - | 1870 |

*(Contd...)*

| | | | | | | | |
|---|---|---|---|---|---|---|---|
| | | Orissa | 1703 | 572 | 628 | | 2903 |
| | | Sikkim | 48 | 26 | - | | 74 |
| | | West Bengal | 2369 | 665 | 1026 | | 5437 |
| **Central Region** | **17417** (19.8) | Chhattisgarh | 673 | 277 | 398 | | 1348 |
| | | Madhya Pradesh | 1779 | 1054 | 866 | | 4309 |
| | | Uttar Pradesh | 4944 | 1951 | 1956 | | 10550 |
| | | Uttarakhand | 592 | 342 | 276 | | 1210 |
| **Western Region** | **13701** (15.6) | Dadra & Nagar Haveli | 7 | 20 | - | - | 27 |
| | | Daman & Diu | - | 20 | - | - | 20 |
| | | Goa | 167 | 278 | - | - | 445 |
| | | Gujarat | 1535 | 1084 | 697 | 1466 | 4782 |
| | | Maharashtra | 2180 | 1550 | 1296 | 3401 | 8427 |
| **Southern Region** | **24658** (28.1) | Andhra Pradesh | 2477 | 1676 | 1890 | 1165 | 7208 |
| | | Karnataka | 2159 | 1278 | 1404 | 1495 | 6336 |
| | | Kerala | 341 | 2871 | 1218 | - | 4430 |
| | | Lakshadweep | 8 | 3 | - | - | 11 |
| | | Puducherry | 34 | 37 | 75 | - | 146 |
| | | Tamil Nadu | 1772 | 2007 | 1535 | 1213 | 6527 |
| **All India** | **87768** | | **32528** | **20771** | **18171** | **16298** | **87768** |
| | **(100)** | | | | | | |

(*Source*: RBI)

## Evolution of Banking in India (after 1935—RBI as Regulator)

Until the year 1969, there were State Bank of India and its subsidiaries in Government sector, few foreign banks, many banks in private sector, which were joint stock companies and private bankers—mostly proprietary concerns, in the country. The financial activities have increased to such an extent that these banks and bankers became backbones of financial system. Banks grow based on their reputation that they have generated and built over the years. However, due to many failures and non-accountability of these private sector banks, public confidence was low. Slowly the Government started feeling the requirement of some control and accountability in the system. This is when the need for a central bank with authority and jurisdiction over entire financial system was felt and the Government created the Reserve Bank of India (RBI Act of 1934) in the year 1935 as a joint stock company. Reserve bank was later nationalized in the year 1949.

Reserve bank started to streamline the banking system, framed rules for the conduct of business by banks, and started issuing guidelines. It was felt that banking business cannot be left entirely to market forces and in private hands as failure of banks have cascading effect on the economy and nightmarish for people. Though it is not possible to take responsibility of banks by the Government/central bank, some control in the larger public interest is required.

First step in this direction started by RBI was by classifying banks on certain parameters as scheduled banks (banks whose names are listed in the second schedule of RBI Act) and non-scheduled banks. Banks were required to take license from Reserve bank for carrying on banking business.

## Scheduled Banks

Scheduled Banks are those banks, which have been included in the Second Schedule of Reserve Bank of India (RBI) Act, 1934. RBI in turn includes only those banks in this schedule which satisfy the criteria laid down vide section 42(6)(a) of the Act. The banks to be included in this schedule list should fulfill mainly two conditions as per this section:

1. The paid capital and collected funds of bank should not be less than ₹ 5 lakh.
2. Any activity of the bank will not adversely affect the interests of depositors.

Scheduled bank becomes eligible for debts/loans at bank rate from RBI. Scheduled banks are bound to maintain CRR & SLR, submit periodical returns to RBI about their business status and are subjected to inspection by RBI.

Scheduled banks are considered more compliant to the rules for banking like minimum capital, maintenance of CRR & SLR, etc. This created status consciousness and every existing bank tried to become a Scheduled bank so that it can leverage on this exalted status for business growth. Existing Foreign incorporated banks were also allowed the status of scheduled bank and allowed to continue but their expansion was kept under check.

Today scheduled banks comprise of State Bank of India and its Associates, Nationalised Banks, Foreign Banks, Private Sector Banks, Urban Co-operative Banks, State Coop Banks and Regional Rural Banks.

By 2010, out of 167 commercial banks in country including RRBs, 163 have attained the status of scheduled banks. Four banks having 47 branches are still under non-scheduled bank category. By 2010, 16 State Coop Banks and 53 Urban Coop Banks were under scheduled bank category.

### Consolidation of Banking Sector

The important task before RBI since its inception in 1935, was to streamline banking sector as large number of small banks existed which were poorly managed. Bank failures were a regular feature. Many finance firms and companies also had registered themselves as banks and doing banking business. Strengthening the banks and weeding out weak banks was on the top of agenda. There were many private banks organised as joint stock companies prior to 1935. Most banks were small and had private shareholding and were closely held. They were largely local banks and many of them were weak. They came under the purview of the Reserve Bank. However, the scope of regulation and supervision was limited to the provisions of the Reserve Bank of India Act, 1934 and the Companies Act, 1913 which were not enough.

Prior to 1935, Forex business was exclusively in the domain of foreign banks called as exchange banks. Even imperial bank (SBI) was not allowed to undertake foreign exchange business until the year 1934. After RBI came, this distinction between exchange banks and commercial banks was removed. Indian banks were allowed to undertake foreign exchange business. Foreign exchange regulation act was enacted in 1947 and banks were authorized as 'authorized dealers' for transacting in foreign exchange.

The real authority of RBI over banking sector came after the Banking Companies Act 1949 (later renamed as Banking Regulation Act 1949) was passed. RBI was nationalized in the same year. The Banking companies act clearly demarcated

Banks and NBFCs. Only corporate entities in banking business are named as banks and all other providers of financial services are termed as non-banking financial companies. Banks are required to obtain licenses from RBI. Banks are made to disclose the word 'bank' or 'banking' in their name so that the public can recognize their status immediately and without confusion. All others are prohibited to use the word 'bank' and "banking" in their name (section 7 of Banking Regulation Act 1949).

The difference between a bank and NBFC is that only banks can maintain current or savings accounts i.e. running accounts for customers and issue chequebooks for operating these accounts. Others cannot use cheques for withdrawing. (Section 49 A of Banking Regulation Act 1949). Only exception is post office savings bank accounts. *(See* under post office savings bank)

Bank failures were regular feature starting from 1913 to 1966. About 1585 banks failed during these years shaking the confidence of the public. Though RBI did address this issue within its competence, and managed to merge many weak banks with other banks, the problem remained. When again in 1960 two more banks failed, Govt took steps and empowered RBI to force mergers on weak banks to protect depositors of the banks. Govt also created Deposit Insurance Corporation of India to provide insurance cover to bank depositors in the year 1962.

These two measures helped greatly and RBI managed to merge nearly 202 banks between 1961 and 1966. This brought stability to the banking system and bank failures thereafter became minimal. 15 more banks were merged during 1969 to 1992, and another 23 banks were merged between 1993 to 2010.

Cooperative sector banks until then were under the control of State Governments and in the year 1966, these banks were brought under the control of RBI for all their banking activities. State Govt control on them on other matters was continued. A system of dual control on coop banks came into existence. This helped to bring stability in coop sector banks.

State Bank of India came into existence in the year 1955 by taking over Imperial Bank of India and in 1959, eight banks that functioned as durbar banks in erstwhile princely states were made subsidiaries of SBI. These banks became public sector banks. Besides these banks, there were foreign banks, cooperative banks, and commercial banks in private sector.

### Social Control on Banks

In sixties, it was observed that most of the banks were promoted and owned by business houses and though they were joint stock companies, the control of promoter was present, which at times was misused and misdirected. Sanctioning of loans was management decisions and was a weak area. It was seen that the loans were not sanctioned on merits, but as favours or to the group companies. Banks were not lending to the needy as rigidity in lending was apparent and the approach was security oriented. It was difficult to say whether the loans given were in the interest of the society as a whole or in the interests of few individuals only. Few individuals were controlling the resources of the banks.

To address this problem, Govt brought in social control on banks in the year 1969. Banking Regulation Act 1949 was amended and it was prescribed that banks shall have professional bankers as full time Chairman & Managing Director and not the promoter businessmen/industrialists as prevalent then. Effective management of the bank was given to career bankers. Further, the appointment of Chairman/ Managing Director also required prior approval of Reserve Bank. Stringent rules were prescribed for sanctioning loans to promoter group and permission was required to do the same. Banks were advised to disclose such loans in its financial reports. Thus, sanction of loan to promoter group companies was kept under check.

India after independence adopted a constitution as democracy with adult suffrage and the constitution provided that the governing shall be for the purpose of creating a welfare state. Government is supposed to direct its policies for this purpose. While industrial growth was identified as important, the country was largely dependent on agriculture and large population lived in villages. Food grain production was deficient and country had to import the same. Green revolution was the need of the hour. Development of rural area and uplifting the rural poor was the top priority economically and politically.

On this backdrop, Government felt that its intervention in the banking business is necessary so that the uses of resources, mobilized by banks are dovetailed for development purpose as enshrined in the constitution. To achieve this objective, 14 major banks with deposit base over ₹ 50 crores were nationalized in the year 1969. At the time, total deposits of commercial banks were ₹ 4646 crores. Subsequently in the year 1980 another six banks were nationalized. At this time, the cut off limit of deposits was fixed at ₹ 200 crores. With this, major share of banking business came under the control of public sector. These 20 banks and SBI group put together accounted for more than 91% of total banking business. One of the nationalized banks, New Bank of India was later merged with PNB in 1993.

The period after nationalization witnessed unprecedented growth in banking business mainly due to aggressive branch expansions undertaken by these banks. The deposit base of ₹ 4646 crores of all commercial banks in the year 1969 showed mind-boggling increase to ₹ 44,92,826 crores by the year 2010. Total number of branches, which were 8262 in the year 1969, has increased over ten times to 87,768 by the year 2010.

With Government control on banks, the social banking and development banking took front seat. Social banking is mass banking and providing banking services to the society and providing loans for genuine requirements. Development banking is to identify the sectors of economy where growth is desired and providing loans for such identified sectors for development purpose. In line with the Government directives, Reserve Bank came out with priority sector concept in the year 1974 and fixed targets for banks to achieve. Sectors like Agriculture, Small Scale Industries (SSI) and Services were recognized as Priority Sectors and a certain percentage of bank lending was earmarked to this sector. Initially starting with

33.3%, it was increased to 40% and Government banks were asked to achieve it. Even other banks were also goaded to lend to this sector.

After nationalisation of the banks, business growth was exponential and priority sector lending became buzzword for banks. Rural lending brought in green revolution and country achieved self-sufficiency in food grain production. Small-scale industries, having great employment potential, got financial support, and shown very good growth.

Security oriented approach was given way to purpose oriented approach for sanctioning loans. For the rural poor, Government came out with many loan schemes linked with subsidies and banks were asked to take active part in those schemes created for self-employment and income generation. As nationalized banks cannot reach all the rural areas, they were advised to sponsor regional rural banks (RRBs) and penetrate rural area. Large number of RRBs came into existence from the year 1975 onwards.

### Govt Stake in Banks

Financial sector reforms were introduced from the year 1991. For banks, prudential norms like asset classification, income recognition, provisioning and capital adequacy were introduced from that year which changed the entire perception of bank's strengths and weaknesses. During the same time, Basel Accord prescribed minimum capital requirements for the banks at 8% on risk weighted assets. RBI prescribed minimum 9% norms for Indian banks from the year 2000. This new norms identified many banks including few nationalized banks as weak banks. Government of India (GOI) had to infuse capital to few nationalized banks in order to strengthen their capital base.

This was the time when GOI had to take a fresh look on the future status of nationalized banks. GOI fully owned these banks and any fresh capital required had to come from GOI. Further, as banks are growing the requirement of additional capital is a continuous process and has to be provided periodically. It was felt that GOI cannot keep on pumping in fresh capital for nationalized banks from its budgetary resources. The only option available was to reduce govt holding in banks and allow banks to raise capital from the public. This decision was taken around the year 1993 and GOI allowed the nationalized banks to bring down GOI holding to 51% and issue fresh capital to public. In the year 1994 two banks, State Bank of India, and Oriental Bank of Commerce went public and collected fresh share capital from the public. Many other nationalized banks followed suit in the following years.

### Deregulation of Interest Rates

To start with, almost every activity of banking was under the control of Reserve Bank of India. RBI fixed all deposit rates period wise (prior to 1997), and lending rates category-wise (prior to 2003). Banks were competing with each other only based on services, as the interest rates are same. Banks had assured net interest margins. Reserve Bank of India issued detailed directives on almost all subjects.

In early nineties Reserve Bank of India wanted to deregulate deposit interest rates and asked banks to decide for themselves. However, it did not work as all banks ended up paying maximum interest on short-term deposits and proved that banks are not yet ready for the freedom. Reserve Bank of India had to intervene and again prescribe deposit rates. Again, in the year 1997, Reserve Bank of India deregulated deposit interest rates and this time banks were mature enough to take up the responsibility. Now the banks individually decide the deposit rates. Only savings bank interest is fixed by Reserve Bank of India. Savings interest was paid on minimum balance between 10th and last day of the month. Since 1-4-2010, banks were asked to pay interest on savings bank accounts on daily products basis. This decision was taken as banks are now on CBS and such calculation will not pose any problem for them. There is a move to free savings interest. (Savings interest has been freed w.e.f. 24th October 2011 by RBI.)

Likewise Reserve Bank of India deregulated interest rates on loans in the year 2003, with the condition that banks fix their Benchmark Prime Lending Rate (BPLR) and fix the spread over and above PLR. This was applicable for loans above ₹ 2 lakhs. This system worked well for some time but as envisaged, the BPLR did not move with changes in interest rate scenario. BPLR became rigid and unchanging.

Initially banks were not allowed to lend below BPLR except in case of directed lending. Subsequently looking at market dynamics, Reserve Bank of India allowed sub PLR lending. Here again banks were driven by competition and increased their sub PLR lending to an alarmingly high percentage and were caught in a web of their own making. Sub PLR lending affects the earnings of the banks.

In view of this in April 2010, Reserve Bank of India advised the banks to move to base rate concept. Under 'Base Rate' concept, banks cannot lend below base rates. Base rates are calculated based on cost of funds and loading it with some other factors. Very few exemptions are there for lending below base rate. With this change, banks are now required to review the base rate at least once in a quarter and expected to change the base rate in tandem with the interest rate movements.

## Financial Sector Reforms

The year 1991 was the turning point in banks control and supervision. Until then banking was dominated by public sector banks almost fully owned by GOI. Every aspect of banking was under control of RBI. Banks had practically no discretion on anything or had very little discretion. It was during 1991 and afterwards, financial sector reforms were introduced with purpose to open up the economy and move towards globalization. Globalization required liberalization and freeing the shackles on industry and trade. Having accepted the need to move towards globalization, the perception on controls necessarily had to be changed. Banks have come up of age and are fairly stable now. For further growth, and to keep abreast with the developed economies, freeing of micro level controls was necessary. Future of banking sector was to be decided. Nationalization though has not outlived its purpose, yet changes were called for as banks are now required to constantly upgrade themselves to meet the needs of customers and required to increase capital base in proportion to its business level.

Hence, for Indian banking, post-1990 is the period of decontrol. Firstly, 100% ownership of GOI in public sector banks was diluted. There was even thinking for privatization of banks. Banking sector was opened up and monopoly of public sector was broken. New private sector banks were encouraged to come into existence and foreign banks are allowed to expand their operations in the country. RBI also went into liberalization mode and started scrapping many controls. Interest rates were freed, lending norms were liberalized to include all the emerging sectors of the economy like personal loans, real estate sector, etc. RBI started issuing broad policy guidelines with minimum restrictions and asked banks to create a system of corporate governance. Banks were asked to seek guidance from the bank's Board, who are required to frame policies on different matters and then oversee the implementation of it. RBI has now moved to issue only macro level guidelines and only mandatory directives for banking sector.

# Priority Sector

6

Reserve Bank of India formally came up with definition of priority sector in the year 1974. Priority sector was mainly divided to three sub sectors. They are agriculture, small-scale industries, and tertiary sector comprising services. These were identified, as these sectors were very crucial for the development of our economy at the time. Agriculture was the backbone of the economy and large population depended on it for livelihood. However, farmers were an exploited lot and they were not getting support. There was shortfall in food grain production and country had to import the same. Hence, agriculture was recognised as the first priority for bank loans.

At the time of independence, country was industrially backward and Govt had the task of promoting industries in the country. Govt started many basic industries, as private initiatives were not there. It was felt that setting up of large industries alone will not solve the problem. Private entrepreneurs were to be encouraged. It was also realised that small industrial units needed to be encouraged to promote entrepreneurship. Such smaller units are best suited as they provide more employment than the organised large industries and contribute significantly to the production of goods and services. Govt policy was to promote smaller units also along with large industries. On this backdrop, the term small-scale industry was coined and was identified as new growth centre.

Tertiary sector is important as it is providing self-employment to skilled and semi-skilled people. These include retail trade, transport, professional services, small business and enterprises. All these activities are identified as necessary to build the economy.

### Targets for Priority Sector Lending

Initially there was no specific target fixed in respect of priority sector lending. In November 1974, banks were advised to raise the share of these sectors in their aggregate advances to the level of 33.33% by March 1979. Banks achieved the same and at December 1980, priority sector advances were 37% of total advances.

Subsequently, based on the recommendations of the Working Group on the Modalities of Implementation of Priority Sector Lending and the Twenty-Point Economic Programme by Banks, all commercial banks were advised to achieve the target of priority sector lending at 40% of aggregate bank advances by 1985. Sub-targets were also fixed for lending to agriculture and the weaker sections within the priority sector. Banks again achieved the target and as at March 1986, priority sector advances were 41% of total advances.

Initially banks felt that Reserve Bank of India would further increase percentage target of 40% for the priority sector. Slowly it was realized that largely the demand in this sectors are met by banks. Reserve Bank of India kept expanding the coverage of borrowers under priority sector by increasing monetary limits and also by adding new activities from time to time. In addition, with increase in banks lendable resources every year by good amount, banks are obliged to sanction fresh loans each year to this sector to maintain the target of 40%.

This 40% target for commercial banks for priority sector lending remained thereafter with a change that it is calculated on Net Bank Credit (NBC) i.e. excluding the food credit by banks. Banks were to achieve 40% target on ongoing basis at any given date. Subsequently in the year 2007, this was changed to 40% target, based on Adjusted Net Bank Credit (ANBC) as at the close of previous financial year. In arriving at ANBC certain items as prescribed by RBI, were added to NBC.

**RIDF**—Priority sector target was made mandatory from the year 1995-96 and banks were penalised for not achieving the targets by asking them to deposit amount equal to the shortfall with NABARD in Rural Infrastructure Development Fund at low interest rates. Banks are thus forced to lend directly to this sector to avoid the penalty. The first RIDF was established with NABARD in 1995-96, to provide loans to the State Governments for financing rural infrastructure projects. Many banks were failing in fulfilling the targets and were obliged to deposit default amount in RIDF every year. Thus, RIDF became the main instrument to channelize bank funds for financing rural infrastructure.

In case of foreign banks, the shortfall amount was to be deposited with SIDBI or any other Financial Institutions, as specified by the Reserve Bank. This is because they have no target for agriculture lending and in their case; targets are given for SSI and other priority sector only.

### Agriculture

Even prior to formally announcing the priority sector concept for bank lending, RBI was actively pursuing with banks for loans to agriculture. To give boost to rural lending RBI introduced lead bank scheme in the year 1969. Under this scheme, all the districts of the country are covered and a bank having larger presence in the district is made the lead bank. District Consultative Committees (DCC) have been formed in all districts. The District Collector is made the convener and chairman of the committee. The committee has membership of all banks, other financial institutions and Govt development depts. in the district. Lead bank is to prepare an annual action plan for the district, incorporating all developmental activities planned, make assessment of bank finance required and present the plan to DCC for approval. Targets for each bank in the district are fixed for each type of loans under priority sector and govt sponsored schemes. The District Collector takes up review of performance regularly. Subsequently in 1988, RBI introduced service area approach by modifying the lead bank scheme.

Under Service Area Approach, every village has been allocated to some bank branch, which will be known as service area branch. The primary responsibility for financing borrowers within the Service Area will be that of the concerned Service Area branch. Borrowers will first approach their Service Area branch for credit facilities. In the event of the concerned Service Area branch not being in a position to finance them, it will be incumbent on it to give a 'No Dues Certificate' to the concerned borrower, who will then be free to approach any other branch in the block for credit support.

Banks were asked to lend to farmers for all their farming needs like for growing of crop, farm development, farm mechanization, and lift irrigation, etc. Banks were advised to achieve 18% sub target for agriculture loans within priority sector target of 40% of total bank credit.

Farmers are identified as tenant farmers, sharecroppers, small and marginal farmers (land holding up to 5 acres) and large farmers (land holding above 5 acres) and priority was given to small and marginal farmers, sharecroppers, and tenant farmers. Landless labourers in rural area are also given special consideration for loans. Finance to allied activities like fishing, poultry, piggery, animal husbandry, dairy, etc. were also added to the definition of agriculture.

Banks were advised to finance trading activity like traders in fertilizers and pesticides, supplying to farmers. Banks were also advised to give loans to others whose activities are supportive to farmers like storage units for agriculture produces and to Electricity Boards for rural electrification programmes, etc. These advances were given the status of indirect agriculture loans. A sublimit was prescribed for indirect finance to agriculture at 4.5% of total credit within overall target of 18% for agriculture loans.

Banks were asked to penetrate rural area by starting Regional Rural Banks (RRBs). The Government of India allowed setting up of Regional Rural Banks in 1975 with the purpose to provide credit to the weaker sections of the rural areas, particularly the small and marginal farmers, agricultural labourers, artisans and small entrepreneurs.

Integrated Rural Development Programme (IRDP) was started by the Govt of India in 1980 in all the blocks of the country to help rural poor. Target group was small and medium farmers, agricultural labourers and rural artisans living below the poverty line. Beneficiaries were identified from farming and other rural activities for suitable credit support depending on their vocation and banks were asked to give loans to them. Govt supported them by giving subsidies.

To make bank borrowing easy and less costly, all State Governments waived stamp duty on mortgages by farmers and made the procedure simple. To reduce the interest burden on farmers, concessional rate of interest was charged and the compounding of interest was made half yearly. NPA norms were also liberalized for loans to agriculture and repayment was linked to crop harvest. Insurance scheme for crops were introduced to protect farmers against the vagaries of nature.

Reserve bank started Agriculture Refinance Corporation in the year 1963, which later became ARDC in the year 1975 to provide refinance to banks for their agriculture lending. In the year 1982, NABARD was created by an Act of Parliament to support the agriculture sector for all its requirements and it took over ARDC and some functions from RBI.

### APMCs and Minimum Support Price

Problem faced by farmers was that they were not getting fair price for their produce and, as they are bound to sell the produce immediately on harvesting, merchants and middlemen fleeced them. To overcome this, govt encouraged setting up of Agriculture Produce Markets and many state govts passed acts around 1963 for creation of Agriculture Produce Marketing Committees (APMCs). This enabled farmers to sell their produces at organized mandis. In many States, such markets were created much earlier. From the year 1964, govt also started fixing up minimum support prices for major agriculture produces so that the farmers could get fair price for their produce.

### Food Credit

Food Corporation of India (FCI) was created in the year 1964 to hold buffer stock of food grains that can be used in time of famine and other natural disasters. GOI authorized FCI to avail credit from banks under a consortium led by SBI. Banks are obliged to provide credit to FCI based on its requirement. This credit by banks is called Food Credit and is shown separately by banks and monitored separately.

Food credit by banks started from the year 1969-70 and was ₹ 56 crores that year. It rose to ₹ 2010 crores in 1979, to ₹ 25,691 crores in 2000 and to ₹ 48,489 crores in 2010. In percentage terms, it was high in the years 1975 to 1979 and low in the years 2006 to 2010. In 2010 it accounted for 1.49% of total bank credit. (*See* Table 1, page 191)

### Kisan Credit Card

In the year 1998, NABARD introduced an innovative credit scheme for farmers by the name of Kisan Credit Card (KCC). Kisan Credit Card is a credit delivery system for providing adequate and timely credit to farmers under single window. It is flexible with simplified procedure, adopting whole farm approach. Credit limit is set up for the short-term credit, medium term and long-term credit needs of the borrowers for agriculture and allied activities including a reasonable component for consumption needs. Farmers under the Scheme are issued with a credit card and a pass book or a credit card-cum-pass book incorporating the name, address, particulars of land holding, borrowing limit, validity period, and facilitate recording of transactions on an ongoing basis.

Kisan Credit Card (KCC) Scheme provides Revolving cash credit facility involving any number of drawals and repayments within the limit. Limit is fixed based on land holding, cropping pattern and scale of finance. Entire production credit needs for full year and ancillary activities related to crop production is considered while fixing limit. Sub-limits to cover short-term, medium term as well as long-term credit are fixed at the discretion of banks. Card is generally valid for 3 to 5 years subject to annual review.

This scheme has become very popular and now efforts are made to cover all the farmers of the country under this scheme. Since launching in August 1998, around 9.36 crore Kisan Credit

Cards with limits of ₹ 4,27,748 crores have been issued up to 31 March 2010 by Cooperative Banks, Regional Rural Banks and Commercial Banks put together. (*See* Table 3, page 193)

## Commercial Banks' Share in Agriculture Lending

Banks and other institutional lending to agriculture have brought in "green revolution" in the country. The Green Revolution resulted in a record grain output of 131 million tons in 1978-79. This established India as one of the world's biggest agricultural producers.

Commercial banks' advance to agriculture under priority sector was just ₹ 485 crores in 1973, it increased to ₹ 4615 crores in 1981-82 and to ₹ 4,16,133 crores in 2010. As at 2010 advance to agriculture under priority sector amounted to 13.69% of total non-food credit of banks. (*See* Table 2, page 192)

Commercial banks started lending to agriculture in a significant way after 1969. Originally, agriculture was earmarked for rural coop banks created earlier for this purpose. Commercial banks entry into the field of agriculture loans was to augment the availability of finance and was perceived as complimentary in nature. However, as the years passed, commercial banks overtook the rural coop banks in financing agriculture. From the year 2000 and today, they are the major players in financing agriculture. The following table shows the dominance of commercial banks' lending to agriculture.

(₹ in crores)

| Year | Agriculture loans | Agriculture loans | | | | | |
|---|---|---|---|---|---|---|---|
| | SCBs | PACs | DCCBs | St. CBs | SCARDBs | PCARDBs | Total (3 to 7) |
| 1 | 2 | 3 | 4 | 5 | 6 | 7 | 8 |
| 2008-09 | 3,75,595* | 64,045 | 99,429 | 48,079 | 16,279 | 11,229 | 2,39,061 |
| 2009-10 | 4,63,321* | 76,480 | 1,23,221 | 49,199 | 16,999 | 11,512 | 2,77,411 |

* Figures are for total credit to agriculture including under priority sector and others.

SCBs—Scheduled commercial banks
PACs—Primary agriculture credit societies
DCCBs—District central coop banks
St.CBs—State central coop banks
SCARDBs—State Co-operative Agriculture and Rural Development Banks
PCARDBs—Primary Cooperative Agriculture & Rural Development Banks

## Small-Scale Industries/Small Enterprises

Small-scale industry (SSI) has been defined as a unit manufacturing, processing, and preserving of goods and services with a certain monetary limit (which was changed from time to time in line with government policies) of investment in plant and machinery and banks were asked to finance them. District Industrial Centres (DIC) were opened to assist the SSI units. Small Industries Service Institutes (SISI) were created to provide marketing support to SSI units. Registration system for SSI units was introduced—however it was not made mandatory. Even non-registered units are eligible for bank loans. IDBI operated a refinance window for banks and subsequently in the year 1990, this function was taken over by SIDBI. Govt gave special preferences to SSI units for supply to govt depts. RBI also defined ancillary industries under this category with a higher investment limits. Ancillary units are the identified units supplying to a bigger industrial unit either their entire production or a large part of their production. Very small units are identified as tiny sector and given special treatment. Artisans and village industries are also covered under this segment.

In the year, 2005 Govt of India came out with concept of small and medium enterprise (SME) and banks were asked to encourage these sectors. On this line, RBI made changes and created the concept of Micro and small enterprises in place of existing SSI sector. Small enterprises concept is much more liberal than the definition of SSI and besides manufacturing, all service sector units are also now covered by the definition of small enterprises.

As per SIDBI reports small-scale industrial units, contribute significantly to the national economy in terms of production, employment and exports. As at 2010, about 3.1 million such units, employing 17.2 million persons accounted for a share of 36% of India's exports and 40% of industrial manufacture.

Commercial banks advances to small-scale industry, which was ₹ 576 crores in 1972, and ₹ 3901 crores in 1981-82, rose sizeable to ₹ 2,06,401 crores in 2010. In percentage terms, it accounted for 6.79% of non-food credit as at 2010. (*See* Table 2, page 192)

### Other Priority Sector (tertiary sector)

Tertiary sector comprised of small road and water transport, small business, business enterprises, small traders, professionals and self-employed. Later on education and housing loan were also added to the list. Definition and limits for each category was prescribed. Transporters of passengers or goods with single vehicle or with fleet up to six vehicles were covered under the definition.

Commercial banks advances to tertiary sector have been increasing particularly since 2000-01 when it was 10.83% of total advances, and increased to 15% of total advances in 2010-11. This is mainly due to housing loans started by banks which is a major portfolio for banks now.

After 2005, most of these activities are reclassified under priority sector and covered as small enterprises—service units.

### Credit Guarantee Schemes for Priority Sector Advances

To encourage banks to lend to priority sector two guarantee schemes were launched—one for small-scale industries and another for other priority sector advances. These schemes gave relief to banks by settling claims in case of loans becoming non-recoverable. However, the claim was generally restricted to average of 70-75% except in very few cases. Guarantee scheme for SSI was administered by Reserve Bank of India since the year 1960 on behalf of the Government and for other guarantee scheme, Credit Guarantee Corporation of India was formed in the year 1971.

Deposit Insurance Corporation was formed in the year 1962 to guarantee repayment of deposits by banks. This corporation gave insurance cover up to ₹ one lakh per account in case of bank failure. Deposit Insurance Corporation and Credit Guarantee Corporation were merged in the year 1978 to form a single entity called Deposit Insurance and Credit Guarantee Corporation (DICGC)—now a fully owned subsidiary of Reserve Bank. The credit guarantee scheme for SSI operated by RBI was also taken over by DICGC from the year 1981. Subsequently banks were given the choice to opt out of credit guarantee schemes but not from deposit insurance scheme. Many banks opted out of credit guarantee schemes due to unsatisfactory claim payment record and that the scheme did not provide support to banks for bad loans in priority sector as intended.

In the year 2000, Government with SIDBI started another credit guarantee scheme under the aegis of a trust named Credit Guarantee Trust for Medium and Small Enterprises (CGTMSE). This scheme is at present operative as it has many attractive features, online claim lodging and settlement system. Presently it is getting acceptance by banks. This trust is encouraging banks to give loans without insisting for collateral security as it is found that small borrowers are unable to fulfil banks' demand for the same.

### Other Aspects of Priority Sector

Govt started many sponsored schemes to help the poor and unemployed and advised banks to finance them. These schemes are beneficiaries under Integrated Rural Development Programme (IRDP), Prime Minister Rozgar Yojna (PMRY), Swarnjayanti Gram Swarozgar Yojana (SGSY), Swarna Jayanti Shahari Rozgar Yojana (SJSRY), Khadi & Village Industries Commission (KVIC), Rehabilitation of Manual Scavengers (SRMS); wherein Govt provided subsidies to the borrowers. All these schemes were included under priority sector lending based on activities and the ceilings prescribed for it under priority sector definition.

**DRI Advances:** In the year 1972, RBI also created a special segment of borrowers under priority sector who were below the poverty line and banks were asked to extend 1% of their total credit to this segment of borrowers at a special concessional rate of interest of 4%. These advances are called DRI (differential rate of interest scheme) advances.

### Weaker Sections Within Priority Sector

RBI also created a weaker section concept within priority sector who are identified based on economic and social backwardness and banks were advised to take care of their credit needs on top priority basis. Guidelines were also issued to earmark sub-limits for them within the overall limit for priority sector.

The weaker sections under priority sector include the following:

(a) Small and marginal farmers with land holding of 5 acres and less, and landless labourers, tenant farmers and sharecroppers;

(b) Artisans, village and cottage industries where individual credit limits do not exceed ₹ 50,000;

(c) `Beneficiaries of Swarnjayanti Gram Swarozgar Yojana (SGSY) now National Rural Livelihood Mission (NRLM);

(d) Scheduled Castes and Scheduled Tribes;

(e) Beneficiaries of Differential Rate of Interest (DRI) scheme;

(f) Beneficiaries under Swarna Jayanti Shahari Rozgar Yojana (SJSRY);

(g) Beneficiaries under the Scheme for Rehabilitation of Manual Scavengers (SRMS);

(h) Advances to Self Help Groups;

(i) Loans to distressed poor to prepay their debt to informal sector, against appropriate collateral or group security.

(j) Loans granted under (a) to (i) above to persons from minority communities as may be notified by Government of India from time to time.

In States, where one of the minority communities notified is, in fact, in majority, item (j) will cover only the other notified minorities. These States/Union Territories are Jammu & Kashmir, Punjab, Meghalaya, Mizoram, Nagaland and Lakshadweep.

## Performance of Commercial Banks under Priority Sector Lending

Commercial banks performance from the year 1981-82 to 2009-10 is given in the Table 2. From the year 1981 to 1990 banks advances to priority sector was 40% and over as required. Thereafter percentage achievement has come down. This is due to faster growth in resources and credit of banks, post liberalisation, and the demand in priority sector has not picked up to this level. Achievement was lowest at 33.02% in 1995-96. As the base figure for target purpose has been changed to preceding year's ANBC from the year 2007, banks have achieved targets from the year 2007-08 onwards till the year 2010-11 as under:

**Priority Sector Advances by Scheduled Commercial Banks**—(achievements based on previous year's non-food bank credit)

(₹ in crores)

| Year | Agriculture | | SSI | | Other priority sector | | Total Priority Sector | | Non-food Gross Bank Credit amount |
|---|---|---|---|---|---|---|---|---|---|
| | Amount | % Achieve-ment | Amount | % Achieve-ment | Amount | % Achieve-ment | Amount | % Achieve-ment to previous year's non-food credit | |
| 2007-08 | 275343 | 15.29 | 132698 | 7.37 | 340032 | 18.88 | 748073 | 41.53 | 2204801 |
| 2008-09 | 338656 | 15.36 | 168997 | 7.66 | 424806 | 19.27 | 932459 | 42.29 | 2601825 |
| 2009-10 | 416133 | 15.99 | 206401 | 7.93 | 469645 | 18.05 | 1092179 | 41.98 | 3040007 |
| 2010-11 | 460333 | 15.14 | 229101 | 7.54 | 549952 | 18.09 | 1239386 | 40.77 | 3667354 |

Achievements under agriculture are less than the stipulated 18% target. From 1981-82 till 1989-90 it was over 16% and thereafter it came down and it was lowest at 11.83% in the year 1999-00. Even after the change in base figure from 2007-08, it is now little above 15%. Shortfall amount is now being deposited with NABARD in RIDF. Here also, while-quantum wise commercial banks lending to agriculture has shown sizeable increase over the years and commercial banks have even become predominant players in agriculture loans, banks resources have grown much faster and hence percentage achievement has come down.

The above analysis is based on non-food bank credit, however for target purpose RBI considers ANBC, which is separately arrived at.

## Priority Sector—New Definition

Now (after 2005) priority sector has been redefined by RBI and comprises five sub sectors. They are (1) Agriculture, (2) Micro & small enterprises, (3) Micro credit (up to individual limit of 50,000 to SHGs or MFIs), (4) Education loans, (5) Housing loans. The tertiary sector as defined earlier has now been merged with small enterprises.

Reserve Bank of India changed the definition of segments of priority sector and in place of SSI, concept of micro and small enterprises (MSE) has been introduced. The definition of SSI as manufacturing unit is diluted and MSE are identified as manufacturing or service units. Any enterprises providing some services is eligible for treatment as MSE under priority sector and get favourable treatment by banks.

Micro and small enterprises are defined now as under:

### Micro (Manufacturing) Enterprises

Enterprises engaged in the manufacture/production, processing or preservation of goods and whose investment in plant and machinery [original cost excluding land and building and the items specified by the Ministry of Small Scale Industries vide its notification no. S.O. 1722 (E) dated October 5, 2006] does not exceed ₹ 25 lakh, irrespective of the location of the unit.

### Small (Manufacturing) Enterprises

Enterprises engaged in the manufacture/production, processing or preservation of goods and whose investment in plant and machinery [original cost excluding land and building and such other items excluded by Govt. Notification No. S.O.1722(E) dated October 5, 2006] is more than ₹ 25 lakh but does not exceed ₹ 5 crore, irrespective of the location of the unit.

### Micro (Service) Enterprises

Enterprises engaged in providing/rendering of services and whose investment in equipment (original cost excluding land and building and furniture, fittings and other items not directly related to the service rendered or as may be notified under the MSMED Act, 2006) does not exceed ₹ 10 lakh, irrespective of the location of the unit.

## Small (Service) Enterprises

Enterprises engaged in providing/rendering of services and whose investment in equipment [original cost excluding land and building and furniture, fittings and such other items excluded by Govt. Notification No. S.O.1722(E) dated October 5, 2006] is more than ₹ 10 lakh but does not exceed ₹ 2 crore, irrespective of the location of the unit.

## Targets/Sub-Targets

Under priority sector, RBI has fixed overall target and sector-wise sub-targets to be achieved by commercial banks and foreign banks. Agriculture has a separate target of 18% within the overall target of 40% for priority sector. Within agriculture, targets have been fixed for direct lending and indirect lending. In case of advances for micro & small enterprises, sub-targets have been fixed for micro manufacturing enterprises. Besides these targets, 10% target for weaker section advances and 1% target for DRI advances have also been fixed.

The targets and sub-targets set under priority sector lending for domestic and foreign banks operating in India as applicable now are furnished below:

## Targets

| | Domestic commercial banks | Foreign banks |
|---|---|---|
| Total Priority Sector advances | 40% of Adjusted Net Bank Credit (ANBC) or credit equivalent amount of Off-Balance Sheet Exposure, whichever is higher.. | 32% of ANBC or credit equivalent amount of Off-Balance, Sheet Exposure, whichever is higher. |
| Total agricultural advances | 18% of ANBC or credit equivalent amount of Off-Balance Sheet Exposure, whichever is higher. | No target. |
| | Of this, indirect lending in excess of 4.5% of ANBC or credit equivalent amount of Off-Balance Sheet Exposure, whichever is higher, will not be reckoned for computing performance under 18% target. However, all agricultural advances under the categories 'direct' and 'indirect' will be reckoned in computing performance under the overall priority sector target of 40% of ANBC or credit equivalent amount of Off-Balance Sheet Exposure, whichever is higher. | |
| Micro & Small Enterprise | Advances to micro and small enterprises sector will be reckoned | 10% of ANBC or credit equivalent amount of Off- |

*(Contd...)*

| | | |
|---|---|---|
| advances (MSE) | in computing performance under the overall priority sector target of 40% of ANBC or credit equivalent amount of Off-Balance Sheet Exposure, whichever is higher. | Balance Sheet Exposure, whichever is higher. |
| Micro Enterprises within Micro and Small Enterprises sector | (i) 40% of total advances to micro and small enterprises sector should go to micro (manufacturing) enterprises having investment in plant and machinery up to ₹ 5 lakh and micro (service) enterprises having investment in equipment up to ₹ 2 lakh;<br>(ii) 20% of total advances to micro and small enterprises sector should go to micro (manufacturing) enterprises with investment in plant and machinery above ₹ 5 lakh and up to ₹ 25 lakh, and micro (service) enterprises with investment in equipment above ₹ 2 lakh and up to ₹ 10 lakh. (Thus, 60% of micro and small enterprises advances should go to the micro enterprises).<br>(iii) The increase in share of micro enterprises in MSE lending to 60% should be achieved in stages, viz. 50% in the year 2010-11, 55% in the year 2011-12 and 60% in the year 2012-13. | Same as for domestic banks. |
| Export credit | No target. | 12% of ANBC or credit equivalent amount of Off-Balance Sheet Exposure, whichever is higher. |
| Advances to weaker sections | 10% of ANBC or credit equivalent amount of Off-Balance Sheet Exposure, whichever is higher. | No target. |
| Differential Rate of Interest Scheme | 1% of total advances outstanding as at the end of the previous year. It should be ensured that not less than 40% of the total advances granted under DRI scheme go to scheduled caste/scheduled tribes. At least two third of DRI advances should be granted through rural and semi-urban branches. | No target. |

It can be seen that while domestic commercial banks have a target of 40% for priority sector advances, in case of foreign banks it is 32% and also some sub targets are different or not applicable to them. Export finance has been included as priority sector advance for foreign banks whereas for domestic banks, it is not considered for target purpose.

## Micro Credit

Micro credit or micro finance is a term coined for informal small loans to the poor for any purpose under the concept of self-help groups—groups of persons from same locality or vocation. It started in India in the early 1980s by forming informal self-help groups (SHG) to provide access to much-needed savings and credit services to the poor. Non-Governmental Organisations (NGO) took the initiative for the same. Subsequently RBI and NABARD took up the matter and many studies were made on the subject. It was realised that in rural area, informal credit played an important role, and the formal credit delivery structure put in place through banks and RRBs, are not enough. Poor households still depend on this informal credit and it was accepted that there is a need to bring this system of credit delivery through SHGs into mainstream. It was decided that credit linkages to SHGs be provided by banks to encourage the system. This type of credit delivery structure is suitable and the experiences of many other countries like Bangladesh Indonesia, Thailand, and Bolivia was considered worth emulating.

In 1991-92, a pilot project for linking about 500 SHGs with banks was launched by NABARD in consultation with the RBI, which advised the banks to actively participate in it. In 1994, RBI advised that the banks' financing of SHGs would be reckoned as part of their lending to weaker sections and as priority sector lending. RBI made formal policy announcements in 1999. Banks were urged to make all out efforts for providing micro-credit and forging linkages with Self-Help Groups (SHGs), either at their own initiative or by enlisting support of Non-Governmental Organisations (NGOs). The micro-credit extended by the banks is treated as part of their priority sector lending. Within short period credit linkage of SHGs with banks picked up.

The cumulative number of SHGs 'credit-linked' to the banks increased from 255 as at end-March 1993 to 16.18 lakh as at end-March 2005. Total loans disbursed till the year 2005 was around ₹ 6,898 crores and an estimated 2.42 crores poor families were brought within the fold of banking services.

Year-wise loans sanctioned under this linkage programme are given in the Table 4 below. In the year 2009-10, 1586822 SHGs have been sanctioned loans of ₹ 14,453.30 crores. Cumulative refinance from NABARD up to the year 2010 amounted to ₹ 12,861.65 crores.

Keeping in view the importance of micro credit, a separate category under priority sector has been created. RBI and govt have recognised the importance of this credit linkage for rural development and upliftment of the poor everywhere. Loans of very small amounts, not exceeding ₹ 50,000 per borrower provided by banks either directly or indirectly through a SHG/JLG mechanism for on-lending up to ₹ 50,000 per borrower is considered as priority sector advance.

A new breed of organisations called Micro Finance Institutions (MFI) have made appearances and are now allowed to play a role in providing linkage between banks and SHGs. Even foreign investments in MFIs are being encouraged.

**Table 1:** Food Credit by Commercial Banks

(Amount in ₹ Crores)

| Year | Food Credit | Non-Food Credit | Bank Credit | Food credit to total credit % |
|---|---|---|---|---|
| 1969-70 | 56 | 3915 | 3971 | 1.41 |
| 1970-71 | 214 | 4469 | 4684 | 4.57 |
| 1971-72 | 345 | 4918 | 5263 | 6.56 |
| 1972-73 | 340 | 5775 | 6115 | 5.56 |
| 1973-74 | 367 | 7032 | 7399 | 4.96 |
| 1974-75 | 613 | 8149 | 8762 | 7.00 |
| 1975-76 | 1521 | 9356 | 10877 | 13.98 |
| 1976-77 | 2191 | 10982 | 13173 | 16.63 |
| 1977-78 | 1984 | 12955 | 14939 | 13.28 |
| 1978-79 | 2210 | 16075 | 18285 | 12.09 |
| 1979-80 | 2100 | 19437 | 21537 | 9.75 |
| 1980-81 | 1759 | 23612 | 25371 | 6.93 |
| 1981-82 | 2127 | 27555 | 29682 | 7.17 |
| 1982-83 | 2965 | 32528 | 35493 | 8.35 |
| 1983-84 | 4022 | 37272 | 41294 | 9.74 |
| 1984-85 | 5665 | 43287 | 48953 | 11.57 |
| 1985-86 | 5535 | 50533 | 56067 | 9.87 |
| 1986-87 | 5104 | 58204 | 63308 | 8.06 |
| 1987-88 | 2190 | 68346 | 70536 | 3.10 |
| 1988-89 | 769 | 83950 | 84719 | 0.91 |

*(Contd...)*

| 1989-90 | 2006 | 99446 | 101453 | 1.98 |
|---|---|---|---|---|
| 1990-91 | 4506 | 111795 | 116301 | 3.87 |
| 1991-92 | 4670 | 120922 | 125592 | 3.72 |
| 1992-93 | 6743 | 145239 | 151982 | 4.44 |
| 1993-94 | 10907 | 153510 | 164418 | 6.63 |
| 1994-95 | 12275 | 199286 | 211560 | 5.80 |
| 1995-96 | 9791 | 244224 | 254015 | 3.85 |
| 1996-97 | 7597 | 270805 | 278401 | 2.73 |
| 1997-98 | 12485 | 311594 | 324079 | 3.85 |
| 1998-99 | 16816 | 352021 | 368837 | 4.56 |
| 1999-00 | 25691 | 410267 | 435958 | 5.89 |
| 2000-01 | 39991 | 471443 | 511434 | 7.82 |
| 2001-02 | 53978 | 535745 | 589723 | 9.15 |
| 2002-03 | 49479 | 679736 | 729215 | 6.79 |
| 2003-04 | 35961 | 804824 | 840785 | 4.28 |
| 2004-05 | 41121 | 1059308 | 1100428 | 3.74 |
| 2005-06 | 40691 | 1466386 | 1507077 | 2.70 |
| 2006-07 | 46521 | 1884669 | 1931189 | 2.41 |
| 2007-08 | 44399 | 2317515 | 2361914 | 1.88 |
| 2008-09 | 46211 | 2729338 | 2775549 | 1.66 |
| 2009-10 | 48489 | 3196299 | 3244788 | 1.49 |

*Source*: RBI.

**Table 2:** Priority Sector Advances by Scheduled Commercial Banks

| Year | Agriculture | | SSI | | Other priority sector | | Total Priority Sector | | Non-food Gross Bank Credit Amount |
|---|---|---|---|---|---|---|---|---|---|
| | Amount | % to total credit | Amount | % to total credit | Amount | % to total credit | Amount | % to total credit | |
| 1981-82 | 4615 | 17.07 | 3901 | 14.43 | 2160 | 7.99 | 10676 | 39.49 | 27035 |
| 1982-83 | 5275 | 16.73 | 4486 | 14.23 | 2561 | 8.12 | 12322 | 39.08 | 31527 |
| 1983-84 | 6144 | 16.88 | 5447 | 14.96 | 3308 | 9.09 | 14899 | 40.93 | 36399 |
| 1984-85 | 7660 | 18.11 | 6612 | 15.63 | 4137 | 9.78 | 18409 | 43.53 | 42291 |
| 1985-86 | 9058 | 18.23 | 7816 | 15.73 | 4692 | 9.44 | 21566 | 43.41 | 49678 |
| 1986-87 | 10570 | 18.39 | 9108 | 15.85 | 5372 | 9.35 | 25050 | 43.59 | 57465 |
| 1987-88 | 12009 | 17.64 | 10820 | 15.90 | 6241 | 9.17 | 29070 | 42.71 | 68070 |
| 1988-89 | 13950 | 16.42 | 13135 | 15.46 | 7134 | 8.40 | 34219 | 40.28 | 84959 |
| 1989-90 | 16526 | 16.42 | 15543 | 15.44 | 8314 | 8.26 | 40383 | 40.12 | 100665 |
| 1990-91 | 16750 | 14.76 | 17181 | 15.14 | 8984 | 7.91 | 42915 | 37.81 | 113513 |
| 1991-92 | 18157 | 14.96 | 18150 | 14.96 | 9118 | 7.51 | 45425 | 37.44 | 121335 |
| 1992-93 | 19963 | 14.22 | 20026 | 14.26 | 9843 | 7.01 | 49832 | 35.49 | 140396 |
| 1993-94 | 21208 | 14.53 | 22617 | 15.50 | 10055 | 6.89 | 53880 | 36.92 | 145950 |
| 1994-95 | 23983 | 12.98 | 27638 | 14.96 | 12540 | 6.79 | 64161 | 34.74 | 184710 |
| 1995-96 | 27044 | 12.18 | 31884 | 14.36 | 14401 | 6.48 | 73329 | 33.02 | 222069 |
| 1996-97 | 31442 | 12.51 | 35944 | 14.30 | 17494 | 6.96 | 84880 | 33.76 | 251394 |
| 1997-98 | 34869 | 12.12 | 43508 | 15.12 | 21130 | 7.34 | 99507 | 34.58 | 287798 |

*(Contd...)*

| 1998-99 | 39634 | 12.19 | 48483 | 14.91 | 26494 | 8.15 | 114611 | 35.24 | 325196 |
|---|---|---|---|---|---|---|---|---|---|
| 1999-00 | 44381 | 11.83 | 52814 | 14.08 | 34632 | 9.23 | 131827 | 35.14 | 375127 |
| 2000-01 | 51922 | 12.10 | 56002 | 13.05 | 46490 | 10.83 | 154414 | 35.98 | 429162 |
| 2001-02 | 60761 | 12.59 | 57199 | 11.85 | 57299 | 11.87 | 175259 | 36.30 | 482749 |
| 2002-03 | 73518 | 11.86 | 60394 | 9.74 | 77697 | 12.53 | 211609 | 34.13 | 620055 |
| 2003-04 | 90541 | 12.43 | 65855 | 9.04 | 107438 | 14.75 | 263834 | 36.22 | 728422 |
| 2004-05 | 125250 | 12.53 | 74588 | 7.46 | 181638 | 18.17 | 381476 | 38.16 | 999788 |
| 2005-06 | 173972 | 12.38 | 91212 | 6.49 | 245554 | 17.48 | 510738 | 36.36 | 1404840 |
| 2006-07 | 230377 | 12.79 | 117910 | 6.55 | 287679 | 15.97 | 635966 | 35.31 | 1801240 |
| 2007-08 | 275343 | 12.49 | 132698 | 6.02 | 340032 | 15.42 | 748073 | 33.93 | 2204801 |
| 2008-09 | 338656 | 13.02 | 168997 | 6.50 | 424806 | 16.33 | 932459 | 35.84 | 2601825 |
| 2009-10 | 416133 | 13.69 | 206401 | 6.79 | 469645 | 15.45 | 1092179 | 35.93 | 3040007 |
| 2010-11 | 460333 | 12.55 | 229101 | 6.25 | 549952 | 15.00 | 1239386 | 33.80 | 3667354 |

*Source*: RBI—figures pertains to advances covered under priority sector.

## **Table 3:** Kisan Credit Cards

| Number of Kisan Credit Cards Issued: Agency-wise and Year-wise (As at end-March 2010) | | | | | | | | |
|---|---|---|---|---|---|---|---|---|
| (Amount in ₹ crores) | | | | | | | | |
| **Year** | **Cooperative Banks** | | **Regional Rural Banks** | | **Commercial Banks** | | **Total** | |
| | **Number of Cards** | **Amount** | **Number of Cards** | **Amount** | **Number of Cards** | **Amount** | **Number of Cards** | **Amount** |
| 1998-99 | 1,55,353 | 826 | 6,421 | 11 | 6,22,391 | 1,473 | 7,84,165 | 2,310 |
| 1999-00 | 35,94,869 | 3,606 | 1,73,301 | 405 | 13,65,911 | 3,537 | 51,34,081 | 7,548 |
| 2000-01 | 56,14,445 | 9,412 | 6,48,324 | 1,400 | 23,89,588 | 5,615 | 86,52,357 | 16,427 |
| 2001-02 | 54,35,859 | 15,952 | 8,33,629 | 2,382 | 30,71,046 | 7,524 | 93,40,534 | 25,858 |
| 2002-03 | 45,78,923 | 15,841 | 9,63,950 | 2,955 | 26,99,883 | 7,481 | 82,42,756 | 26,277 |
| 2003-04 | 48,78,236 | 9,855 | 12,74,289 | 2,599 | 30,94,108 | 9,331 | 92,46,633 | 21,785 |
| 2004-05 | 35,55,783 | 15,597 | 17,29,027 | 3,833 | 43,95,564 | 14,756 | 96,80,374 | 34,186 |
| 2005-06 | 25,98,226 | 20,339 | 12,49,474 | 8,483 | 41,64,551 | 18,779 | 80,12,251 | 47,601 |
| 2006-07 | 22,97,640 | 13,141 | 14,05,874 | 7,373 | 48,07,964 | 26,215 | 85,11,478 | 46,729 |
| 2007-08 | 20,91,329 | 19,991 | 17,72,498 | 8,743 | 46,05,775 | 59,530 | 84,69,602 | 88,264 |
| 2008-09 | 13,43,845 | 8,428 | 14,14,647 | 5,648 | 58,33,981 | 39,009 | 85,92,473 | 53,085 |
| 2009-10 | 17,43,253 | 7,606 | 19,49,785 | 10,132 | 53,13,085 | 39,940 | 90,06,123 | 57,678 |
| Total | 37,887,761 | 1,40,594 | 13,421,219 | 53,964 | 42,363,847 | 2,33,190 | 93,672,827 | 4,27,748 |
| % share in Total | 40.4 | 32.9 | 14.4 | 12.6 | 45.3 | 54.5 | 100.0 | 100.0 |
| *Source*: NABARD Table V.33: | | | | | | | | |

**Table 4:** Self-Help Group-Bank Linkage Programme

(Amount in ₹ crore)

| Year (end-March) | No. of SHGs Linked | | Bank Loan | | Refinance Assistance | |
|---|---|---|---|---|---|---|
| | During the year | Cumulative | During the year | Cumulative | During the year | Cumulative |
| 1993-94 | 365 | 620 | 0.36 | 0.65 | 0.19 | 0.46 |
| 1994-95 | 1502 | 2122 | 1.79 | 2.44 | 1.67 | 2.13 |
| 1995-96 | 2635 | 4757 | 3.62 | 6.06 | 3.53 | 5.66 |
| 1996-97 | 3841 | 8598 | 5.78 | 11.84 | 4.99 | 10.65 |
| 1997-98 | 5719 | 14317 | 11.92 | 23.76 | 10.74 | 21.39 |
| 1998-99 | 18678 | 32995 | 33.31 | 57.07 | 30.70 | 52.09 |
| 1999-00 | 81780 | 114775 | 135.91 | 192.98 | 98.04 | 150.13 |
| 2000-01 | 149050 | 263825 | 287.89 | 480.87 | 250.61 | 400.74 |
| 2001-02 | 197653 | 461478 | 545.47 | 1026.34 | 395.76 | 796.50 |
| 2002-03 | 255882 | 717360 | 1022.33 | 2048.67 | 622.30 | 1418.80 |
| 2003-04 | 361731 | 1079091 | 1855.53 | 3904.20 | 705.40 | 2124.20 |
| 2004-05 | 539365 | 1618456 | 2994.26 | 6898.46 | 967.80 | 3092.00 |
| 2005-06 | 620109 | 2238565 | 4499.00 | 11397.46 | 1067.70 | 4159.70 |
| 2006-07 | 1105749 | - | 6570.00 | - | 1292.86 | 5452.56 |
| 2007-08 | 1227770 | - | 8849.26 | - | 1615.50 | 7068.06 |
| 2008-09 | 1609586 | - | 12253.51 | - | 2620.03 | 9688.09 |
| 2009-10 | 1586822 | - | 14453.30 | - | 3173.56 | 12861.65 |

*Note*:
1. Data for 2009-10 are provisional.
2. Data relates to Commercial Banks, RRBs and Co-operative Banks.
3. From 2006-07 onwards, data on number of SHGs financed by banks and bank loans are inclusive of 'Swarnajayanti Gram Swarozgar Yojna' (SGSY) SHGs and existing groups receiving repeat loans. Owing to this change, NABARD discontinued the publication of data on a cumulative basis from 2006-07.

*Source*: NABARD (Table 71).

# Shift in Bank Lending

7

## Direction of Bank Lending

Lending by banks has very important role in the economy. It acts as catalyst in economic development. Generally, banks keeping in mind the safety and profit in lending, decide the lending operations. Banks are traditionally security oriented for lending purpose and look for short-term loans. As sound principle, banks should desist from lending for speculative purpose, which may jeopardise its funds. Banking when originated, the loaning decision was with the banker and it was his sweet will to decide to whom to lend. Free market concept supports this view as in a free society any type of restriction or direction is generally not acceptable.

Evolution of banking in the world has shown many variants to free market approach. In our country also, bank lending has travelled through various stages.

The importance of banks is felt gradually in a developing economy. In our own case at the time of independence in 1947, there were few banks and their deposits were meagre. They did not matter and had no great impact on the economy. Govt had no interest in banking sector except for its own treasury functions. The deposits and advances of the banks were of little consequence then. Govt was concerned about moneylenders who cheated the poor and farmers. Govt enacted usurious loans act to protect the poor against exploitation by moneylenders. Govt was also concerned about bank failures as it shook the confidence of public and made them to lose their money.

In the year 1951, commercial banks' total deposits were ₹ 822 crores and advances were ₹ 585 crores. In a way, bank loans were insignificant then. However, as the banking business developed and banking habits percolated, the resources of banks became sizeable. In the year 1969, deposits of banks were ₹ 4646 crores and advances were ₹ 3599 crores. Govt realised that bank loans have a significant influence on economy and felt that banks were not lending to agriculture and poor. Bank lending is more to traders and to unproductive sectors, which did not contribute to the development. In view of the avowed policy of the govt to create a welfare state, it was felt that some directions need to be given for bank lending so that the loans are put to developmental use. Some sort of social control on banks was felt necessary. In the year 1969, govt brought social control on banks and nationalised 14 major banks with a view to dovetail banking growth with economic growth of the country.

These momentous decisions have changed the face of banking and the economy. The success story is now history. In the year 1995, bank deposits stood at ₹ 3,86,859 crores and advances at ₹ 2,11,560 crores. Nearly 50% of bank advances were to the directed sectors. Thus, Govt achieved its goals of social control and nationalisation.

The period between 1969 and 1990 was the phase of social banking. Bank loans were directed to agriculture and small-scale industry and other priority sectors. Bank lending for uplifting the farmers and poor of the country is social lending. On their own banks would not have done this kind of lending. Nationalisation was for this purpose. RBI under its authority, made it mandatory for banks to lend 40% of loans to priority sector. Banks were forced to do it, as it was mandatory under banking rules. They had no options. Banks were also provided with many supports like subsidies and guarantee covers for these loans to make them comfortable even in case of bad loans in this sector. Thus 40% of loans were earmarked for priority sector. Besides priority sector, banks were also contributing to food credit (loan to Food Corporation of India) which was made mandatory. Banks were also directed to lend to export sector. The compulsions on banks for sanctioning loans are called 'directed lending'. Thus, about 50% of total bank loans came under the category of directed lending.

During this period, banks were also obliged to support medium and large industries for industrial growth, which banks did willingly as banks were comfortable to lend to industry. Trading sector was a traditional business for banks since the origin of banking. Banks were lending to these sectors.

During this phase RBI guidelines on credit were in keeping with national priorities. Until nineties Reserve Bank of India was insisting for loans for productive purpose and the activities directly connected with production of goods or services were given preference. This was done since bank credits are limited and it is imperative that they are better used for maximum benefit to society. The activities, which generate employment, goods and services, obviously are the first preference keeping in mind the national objectives.

Term lending to big industries was discouraged as it was in the domain of term lending institutions. Loans to real estate sector, housing loans and personal loans were discouraged. Due to pre-emption of credit to priority sectors and other areas, banks were not in a position to diversify.

However, a time came when Reserve Bank of India had to relook into this. In nineties banks became flush with funds and the same started growing at very fast pace. Banks were finding it difficult to deploy them as the demand in directed sectors had not kept pace. At times, even demand from industrial sector was also sluggish. Further, the large corporates had various finance options due to developed capital market and bond market. They were in a position to garner cheap resources directly from capital market. As the economy improved lot of foreign funds was also flowing into the country looking for investment opportunities.

Financial sector reforms were started in the year 1991. These reforms aimed at freeing the banking sector from the shackles of various controls and making them vibrant and internationally competitive. It was realised that the time of micro management of banking sector by RBI is over and banks are capable of taking care of themselves.

Govt also opened up economy in a move towards globalisation. State Monopolies and other monopolies in many areas have been broken and the sectors like telecommunication, transport, infrastructure, petroleum, aviation, banking and insurance saw entry of new players in the field.

Present thinking and understanding of the economic growth and free market concept supports demand push industrial growth rather than supply push. India in the initial stage tried to grow the economy by creating supply and asking the consumer to accept it. This is the reason why permit raj was continued for very long time. It benefited few who got permits to produce and consumers had no choice. When this gradually changed, it became apparent that the economy should work on demand push basis and the demand for product shall decide the production of any goods or services. The manufacturers have to compete to win the customer preferences for their product and services. This has made a big change in industrial scenario. Many new entrepreneurs came on the scene and old and outdated, were phased out. Production was decided by the demand for it. Customer has now variety of choices to select from. White goods and car industry is an example. Communication, aviation and insurance services are another example. Now there are many players with good products and there is huge demand from the market.

Indian banks started off in a big way in housing loans and consumer finance from the year 2000. Retail finance/credit has become a big chunk in their loan portfolio today with a never-ending demand potential to grow.

At this juncture, Reserve Bank of India decided to relook at sectors which were hitherto restricted from getting bank finance. It was felt that real estate and personal loans are the main areas where bank finance can flow. The consumer finance like home loans and personal loans were flagged off for banks. Providing home to every individual is also a welfare measure.

Infrastructure development including commercial and residential real estate projects is now identified as the key to development in other sectors. Industrial growth is not possible without infrastructure and this is the most important area, which gives boost to industrial growth. It is said that real estate and infrastructure development creates demand in more than 100 industries, mainly steel, cement, and building materials and generates employment for skilled and semi-skilled labour. This one single factor can spur the economy. Likewise, consumption pattern of public can boost industry and trade and demand picks up for white goods industry, car industry and a host of other service providers. It is important to understand that any expenditure is not wasteful in that it provides jobs and earnings to so many people connected with the activity. If we look at that even an extravagant marriage expenses considered as wasteful for the spender, is in reality not so as it supports so many service providers and creates employment.

With retrospect, it may be said that growth in resources of banks and the financial sector reforms introduced were the key factors for changes in banks' lending portfolios. Banking was ripe for the changes that were brought in with liberalisation of the economy and reforms. In a way, it is a gradual progression from scarcity management of credit to effective management of credit in the economy.

The changes witnessed after the year 1991, cannot be considered as correction in the system. It appears more like evolution and gradual movement to the next phase. The scarcity management of credit was the need of the hour then when banking was not well developed and banks had limited resources to lend. Prudent management of the economy and banking has made it possible to reach a good resource base, which made the reforms work and bring in the desired result. In fact, the prudent management has made it possible for the economy to move to the next phase of development.

### Present Trend in Deployment of Bank Credit—(Table 1)

Traditionally banks lent to trade and when industrialisation started, banks started lending to industries. In seventies banks were asked to lend to agriculture and other priority sectors and for exports. Until nineties commercial banks were lending mainly to these sectors as per requirement. After reforms and liberalisation coupled with growth in resources, banks started diversifying to other areas. The new areas of bank lending are real estate including housing loans, personal loans, infrastructure and the like.

Banks are obliged to provide food credit to FCI and non-food bank credit is given to various sectors. As prudent practice, banks are fixing exposure norms themselves to particular segment and trying to have well diversified basket of assets and are avoiding concentration of credit risk in any segment.

As on March 2010, industry sector comprising small, medium and large industries is the biggest sector accounting for 43.14% of non-food credits of commercial banks. This is mainly due to good growth in industry and the priority status given to small-scale industry and special status given to medium industry as per national objectives.

Next large sector is the service sector accounting for 23.91% of bank credit. This sector comprises of transport operators, shipping, wholesale and retail trade, commercial real estate, tourism/hotels, software, NBFCs and others. Commercial real estate, software and NBFCs are the new sectors now getting bank credit and their share is increasing.

Next sector is personal loans sector, which now accounts for 19.26% of bank credit and comprises of housing loans, vehicle loans, consumer loans, education loans and other personal loans. This sector is the new emerging sector. About 15 years back banks had hardly any exposure in these and within short span, this sector has cornered nearly 20% share. It is growing sector for banks and is quite profitable sector. This sector can see good growth in this decade also and the percentage share will go up.

Agriculture accounts for 13.69% of commercial banks credit.

Priority sector credit was 35.93% of total bank credit, as against the goal of 40%, comprising mainly of agriculture (13.69%), small enterprises (12.29%), housing (7.17%), education (1.19%) and others.

## Changes in Bank Lending from the Year 1981

The changes in trend of bank lending from the year 1981, is given in the Table 2 and the trend noticed is as under:

A priority sector advance, which was over 40% from 1981 to 1990, has come down to 37.44% in 1992 and to 35.93% in 2010. Within priority sector, share of agriculture has come down from 17.07% in 1981 to 14.76% in 1991, to 12.10% in 2001 and improved to 13.69% in 2010. Share of SSI was 14.43% in 1981 has gone up to 15.90% in 1988 has come down steeply to 9.74% in 2003 and further to 6.50% in 2010. Whereas the share of other priority sector, which was 7.99% in 1981 has gone up to 15.42% in 2010.

Fall in the share of priority sector lending is not because of any change in approach of the banks. It appears that the demand of credit from this segment is not very high and banks resources are growing at very fast pace. Further from the year 2007, targets are based on previous years outstanding. Commercial banks as a group are achieving priority sector targets from the year 2008 onwards.

Share of medium and large industry has come down from 41.26% in 1981 to 38.81% in 1991 to 32.17% 2010. Share of wholesale trade has also come down from 8.13% in 1981 to 2.83% in 2010.

Here also the reason is that industry is now having alternate finance sources in capital markets, which is well developed now. Largely the demand from industry and trade are met by banks.

The real change is in other sectors, which have gone up from 11.12% in 1981 to 18.68% in 1991 and to 23.35% in 2010. This represents shift in bank lending to real estate sector, infrastructure sector and personal loans sector.

**Table 1:** Deployment of Bank Credit by Major Sectors in 2009 and 2010

(₹ In crores)

| Sl. No. | Sector | Mar. 27, 2009 | Mar. 26, 2010 | 2009-% | 2010-% |
|---|---|---|---|---|---|
| | Non-food Credit (1 to 4) | 26,01,825 | 30,40,007 | | |
| **1** | **Agriculture & Allied Activities** | **3,38,656** | **4,16,133** | **13.02** | **13.69** |
| **2** | **Industry (Micro & Small, Medium and Large )** | **10,54,390** | **13,11,451** | **40.53** | **43.14** |
| 2.1 | Micro & Small | 1,68,997 | 2,06,401 | 6.50 | 6.79 |
| 2.2 | Medium | 1,22,155 | 1,32,636 | 4.69 | 4.36 |
| 2.3 | Large | 7,63,238 | 9,72,415 | 29.33 | 31.99 |
| **3** | **Services** | **6,46,299** | **7,26,790** | **24.84** | **23.91** |
| 3.1 | Transport Operators | 39,302 | 52,516 | 1.51 | 1.73 |
| 3.2 | Computer Software | 9,687 | 12,543 | 0.37 | 0.41 |
| 3.3 | Tourism, Hotels & Restaurants | 13,625 | 19,410 | 0.52 | 0.64 |
| 3.4 | Shipping | 9,417 | 9,200 | 0.36 | 0.30 |
| 3.5 | Professional Services | 44,257 | 43,401 | 1.70 | 1.43 |
| 3.6 | Trade | 1,44,377 | 1,64,497 | 5.55 | 5.41 |
| 3.6.1 | Wholesale Trade (other than food procurement) | 67,425 | 86,357 | 2.59 | 2.84 |
| 3.6.2 | Retail Trade | 76,952 | 78,140 | 2.96 | 2.57 |
| 3.7 | Commercial Real Estate | 92,421 | 92,128 | 3.55 | 3.03 |
| 3.8 | Non-Banking Financial Companies (NBFCs) | 98,853 | 1,13,441 | 3.80 | 3.73 |
| 3.9 | Other services | 1,94,360 | 2,19,654 | 7.47 | 7.23 |
| **4** | **Personal Loans** | **5,62,479** | **5,85,633** | **21.62** | **19.26** |
| 4.1 | Consumer Durables | 8,187 | 8,294 | 0.31 | 0.27 |
| 4.2 | Housing (Including Priority Sector Housing) | 2,79,365 | 3,00,929 | 10.74 | 9.90 |
| 4.3 | Advances against Fixed Deposits (Including FCNR (B), NRNR Deposits etc.) | 48,676 | 48,654 | 1.87 | 1.60 |
| 4.4 | Advances to Individuals against share, bonds, etc. | 2,287 | 2,863 | 0.09 | 0.09 |
| 4.5 | Credit Card Outstanding | 28,000 | 20,145 | 1.08 | 0.66 |
| 4.6 | Education | 28,579 | 36,863 | 1.10 | 1.21 |
| 4.7 | Vehicle Loans | 61,995 | 63,791 | 2.38 | 2.10 |
| 4.8 | Other Personal Loans | 1,05,390 | 1,04,095 | 4.05 | 3.42 |
| **Memo:** | | | | | |
| **5** | **Priority Sector** | **932459** | **1092179** | 35.84 | 35.93 |
| 5.1 | Agriculture & Allied Activities | 338656 | 416133 | 13.02 | 13.69 |
| 5.2 | Micro & Small Enterprises | 309195 | 373530 | 11.88 | 12.29 |
| 5.2(a) | Manufacturing | 168997 | 206401 | 6.50 | 6.79 |
| 5.2(b) | Services | 140198 | 167130 | 5.39 | 5.50 |
| 5.3 | Housing | 197110 | 217877 | 7.58 | 7.17 |

*(Contd...)*

| Sl. No. | Sector | Mar. 27, 2009 | Mar. 26, 2010 | 2009-% | 2010-% |
|---|---|---|---|---|---|
| 5.4 | Micro-Credit | 16529 | 21799 | 0.64 | 0.72 |
| 5.5 | Education Loans | 27861 | 36247 | 1.07 | 1.19 |
| 5.6 | State-Sponsored Orgs. for SC/ST | 2451 | 2749 | 0.09 | 0.09 |
| 5.7 | Weaker Sections | 139422 | 176957 | 5.36 | 5.82 |
| 5.8 | Export Credit | 25961 | 28866 | 1.00 | 0.95 |

## **Table 2:** Changing Trend in Commercial Banks' Lending Since 1981

| Year | Priority Sector | | Agriculture | | Small Scale Industries | | Other PS | Industry (Medium and Large) | | Wholesale Trade (Other than Food Procure-ment) | | Other Sectors | | Non-food Gross Bank Credit |
|---|---|---|---|---|---|---|---|---|---|---|---|---|---|---|
| | Amt. | % | Amt. | % | Amt. | % | % | Amt. | % | Amt. | % | Amt. | % | Amt. |
| 1981-82 | 10676 | 39.49 | 4615 | 17.07 | 3901 | 14.43 | 7.99 | 11155 | 41.26 | 2198 | 8.13 | 3006 | 11.12 | 27035 |
| 1982-83 | 12322 | 39.08 | 5275 | 16.73 | 4486 | 14.23 | 8.12 | 13276 | 42.11 | 2353 | 7.46 | 3576 | 11.34 | 31527 |
| 1983-84 | 14899 | 40.93 | 6144 | 16.88 | 5447 | 14.96 | 9.09 | 14621 | 40.17 | 2343 | 6.44 | 4536 | 12.46 | 36399 |
| 1984-85 | 18409 | 43.53 | 7660 | 18.11 | 6612 | 15.63 | 9.78 | 15939 | 37.69 | 2649 | 6.26 | 5294 | 12.52 | 42291 |
| 1985-86 | 21566 | 43.41 | 9058 | 18.23 | 7816 | 15.73 | 9.44 | 18422 | 37.08 | 3066 | 6.17 | 6624 | 13.33 | 49678 |
| 1986-87 | 25050 | 43.59 | 10570 | 18.39 | 9108 | 15.85 | 9.35 | 21356 | 37.16 | 3080 | 5.36 | 7979 | 13.88 | 57465 |
| 1987-88 | 29070 | 42.71 | 12009 | 17.64 | 10820 | 15.90 | 9.17 | 25153 | 36.95 | 3598 | 5.29 | 10249 | 15.06 | 68070 |
| 1988-89 | 34219 | 40.28 | 13950 | 16.42 | 13135 | 15.46 | 8.40 | 32185 | 37.88 | 4767 | 5.61 | 13788 | 16.23 | 84959 |
| 1989-90 | 40383 | 40.12 | 16526 | 16.42 | 15543 | 15.44 | 8.26 | 38262 | 38.01 | 5472 | 5.44 | 16548 | 16.44 | 100665 |
| 1990-91 | 42915 | 37.81 | 16750 | 14.76 | 17181 | 15.14 | 7.91 | 44508 | 39.21 | 5910 | 5.21 | 20180 | 17.78 | 113513 |
| 1991-92 | 45425 | 37.44 | 18157 | 14.96 | 18150 | 14.96 | 7.51 | 47090 | 38.81 | 6154 | 5.07 | 22666 | 18.68 | 121335 |
| 1992-93 | 49832 | 35.49 | 19963 | 14.22 | 20026 | 14.26 | 7.01 | 58636 | 41.76 | 6969 | 4.96 | 24959 | 17.78 | 140396 |
| 1993-94 | 53880 | 36.92 | 21208 | 14.53 | 22617 | 15.50 | 6.89 | 57865 | 39.65 | 7330 | 5.02 | 26875 | 18.41 | 145950 |
| 1994-95 | 64161 | 34.74 | 23983 | 12.98 | 27638 | 14.96 | 6.79 | 74672 | 40.43 | 9749 | 5.28 | 36128 | 19.56 | 184710 |
| 1995-96 | 73329 | 33.02 | 27044 | 12.18 | 31884 | 14.36 | 6.48 | 93053 | 41.90 | 11980 | 5.39 | 43707 | 19.68 | 222069 |
| 1996-97 | 84880 | 33.76 | 31442 | 12.51 | 35944 | 14.30 | 6.96 | 102604 | 40.81 | 12340 | 4.91 | 51570 | 20.51 | 251394 |
| 1997-98 | 99507 | 34.58 | 34869 | 12.12 | 43508 | 15.12 | 7.34 | 117530 | 40.84 | 13217 | 4.59 | 57544 | 19.99 | 287798 |
| 1998-99 | 114611 | 35.24 | 39634 | 12.19 | 48483 | 14.91 | 8.15 | 130516 | 40.13 | 13964 | 4.29 | 66105 | 20.33 | 325196 |

*(Contd...)*

| Year | Priority Sector | | Agriculture | | Small Scale Industries | | Other PS | Industry (Medium and Large) | | Wholesale Trade (Other than Food Procure-ment) | | Other Sectors | | Non-food Gross Bank Credit |
|---|---|---|---|---|---|---|---|---|---|---|---|---|---|---|
| 1999-00 | 131827 | 35.14 | 44381 | 11.83 | 52814 | 14.08 | 9.23 | 147319 | 39.27 | 16818 | 4.48 | 79163 | 21.10 | 375127 |
| 2000-01 | 154414 | 35.98 | 51922 | 12.10 | 56002 | 13.05 | 10.83 | 162837 | 37.94 | 17845 | 4.16 | 94066 | 21.92 | 429162 |
| 2001-02 | 175259 | 36.30 | 60761 | 12.59 | 57199 | 11.85 | 11.87 | 172324 | 35.70 | 20459 | 4.24 | 114707 | 23.76 | 482749 |
| 2002-03 | 211609 | 34.13 | 73518 | 11.86 | 60394 | 9.74 | 12.53 | 235168 | 37.93 | 22578 | 3.64 | 150700 | 24.30 | 620055 |
| 2003-04 | 263834 | 36.22 | 90541 | 12.43 | 65855 | 9.04 | 14.75 | 247210 | 33.94 | 24867 | 3.41 | 192511 | 26.43 | 728422 |
| 2004-05 | 381476 | 38.16 | 125250 | 12.53 | 74588 | 7.46 | 18.17 | 352304 | 35.24 | 32549 | 3.26 | 233459 | 23.35 | 999788 |
| 2005-06 | 510738 | 36.36 | 173972 | 12.38 | 91212 | 6.49 | 17.48 | 459232 | 32.69 | 39691 | 2.83 | 395179 | 28.13 | 1404840 |
| 2006-07 | 635966 | 35.31 | 230377 | 12.79 | 117910 | 6.55 | 15.97 | 579429 | 32.17 | 50143 | 2.78 | 535702 | 29.74 | 1801240 |
| 2007-08 | 748073 | 33.93 | 275343 | 12.49 | 132698 | 6.02 | 15.42 | 725646 | 32.91 | 55749 | 2.53 | 675333 | 30.63 | 2204801 |
| 2008-09 | 932459 | 35.84 | 338656 | 13.02 | 168997 | 6.50 | 16.33 | 885393 | 34.03 | 67425 | 2.59 | 716548 | 27.54 | 2601825 |
| 2009-10 | 1092179 | 35.93 | 416133 | 13.69 | 206401 | 6.79 | 15.45 | 1105051 | 36.35 | 86357 | 2.84 | 756420 | 24.88 | 3040007 |

# Bank Credit

# 8

Banking in India has evolved over last six decades. Bank credit, which was insignificant in the year 1951 at ₹ 585 crores has grown to a staggering ₹ 32,44,788 crores as at 31-3-2010. This journey of credit expansion over these six decade is remarkable and it can be said that banks in fact has built the economy. This growth was exceptional for the reason that RBI has seen to it that at no stage the growth became unmanageable and directionless. RBI has regularly guided the commercial banks and ensured that the credit expansion is in harmony with national priorities and objectives.

Section 21 of Banking Regulation Act 1949, gave powers to RBI to control advances of banks which included forming policies for bank lending and issuing directions as regards the purpose for which loans can be sanctioned or not to be sanctioned, maximum amount of loan that a bank can sanction to any one borrower and the rate of interest on loans.

When the credit was a scarce commodity, RBI has guided banks to prioritize lending to developmental activities as desired by the govt. As banks were becoming hub of economic development in 1969, the govt brought in social control on banks. For this purpose, Banking Regulation Act, 1949 was amended and provision for whole time chairman and managing director was made. The management was given to professionals. To drive social objectives of the govt, 14 major banks were nationalized in the same year 1969. At this point of time bank deposits were ₹ 4646 crores and credit was ₹ 3599 crores.

Concept of priority sector advances was introduced in the year 1974 and banks were asked to earmark 40% of total credit to this sector. Export finance was encouraged since sixties to boost the exports, as it was a national priority. Rural development programmes were introduced and lead bank scheme was launched in the year 1969.

### Credit Authorization Scheme (CAS)

#### *Credit Monitoring Arrangement (CMA)*

In fifties and sixties banks' lendable resources were limited and the loan sizes were small. As the loan sizes started getting bigger and in order to oversee that the large advances sanctioned by banks are confirming to the guidelines, RBI started credit authorization scheme (CAS) in the year 1965. Under this, banks were to seek prior approval of RBI for loans of ₹ one crore and above before conveying the sanction and disbursing the loan. This was continued for over two decades and as banks have gained sufficient appraisal skills and prudence, RBI withdrew the credit authorization scheme in the year 1988. In its place, another scheme called Credit Monitoring Arrangement (CMA) was introduced. Under this, banks were not required to take prior approval but required to report to RBI of loans sanctioned by them for over ₹ 10 crores with full details. Credit Monitoring Arrangement was finally withdrawn in the year 1997.

#### *Selective Credit Control*

In sixties, the nation was yet to become self-sufficient in food grain production and other agricultural produces. During this time, the management of food grains and its proper consumption was very important and govt had to ensure that evils like hoarding and starving of the poor due to hoarding shall not happen. RBI has ensured this and bank finance was not allowed for such purposes by introducing Selective Credit Control.

RBI introduced Selective Credit Control in the year 1956 as a tool to restrict bank finance against sensitive commodities. Identified sensitive commodities were:

(i) Food grains i.e., cereals and pulses.

(ii) Cotton textiles, which include cotton yarn, man-made fibres and yarn and fabrics made out of man-made fibres and partly out of cotton yarn and partly out of man-made fibres.

(iii) Selected major oil seeds indigenously grown viz. groundnut, rapeseed/mustard, cottonseed, linseed and castor seed, oils thereof, vanaspati and all imported oils and vegetable oils.

(iv) Sugar, Gur and Khandsari.

(v) Raw cotton and kapas.

All these commodities are of mass consumption and the purpose of control was to ensure adequate supply of these commodities in the free market. The policy was to discourage advances against these commodities as far as possible. Selective Credit Control had two different aspects as under:

(i) Minimum margin for lending against security of specified commodities is fixed.

(ii) Ceiling on the level of credit is fixed.

Reserve Bank of India also used to stipulate minimum rate of interest for lending against commodities covered under Selective Credit Control. Banks' were submitting credit proposals above ₹ 100 lakhs to Reserve Bank of India for its prior approval under Selective Credit Control. Requirement of prior approval was discontinued in the year 2000.

With liberalisation in fixing rates of interest announced by Reserve Bank, separate interest rate stipulation for loans under selective credit control was withdrawn in the year 1994. Selective credit control on all the commodities were withdrawn by RBI in the year 1996, except for stipulation of margin on stocks of sugar.

Banks in India were traditionally extending finance for financing acquisition of fixed assets by way of term loans, short-term finance for working capital requirement and bill finance by discounting bills again working capital finance. Other than this, banks also provided loan against securities like fixed deposit, LIC policy, Govt securities, shares, gold, etc. These are also basically short-term loans.

Industry and trade are financed for their fixed assets requirement by giving term loan and for working capital requirement by cash credit or bill limits.

### *Project Finance*

With industrial development taking place in the country more prominently from late sixties and seventies, the requirement of project finance was felt as new industrial units started coming up. Under project finance generally the fixed assets formed bigger component and term loan requirement was very large. In view of liquidity position of banks, Reserve Bank felt that banks are not suited to take up project finance as banks were short of funds and term loans may make them illiquid. Further, appraisal of green field projects, assessment of loan requirement was also considered as a professional job for which commercial banks had no expertise. Hence, policy decision was taken and term lending institutions/banks (development banks) were created. Thus IFCI—Industrial Finance Corporation of India (1948), ICICI—Industrial Credit & Investment Corporation of India (1955), IDBI—Industrial Development Bank of India (1964), SIDBI—Small Industries Development Bank of India (1990) and others came into existence. They were development banks and not universal banks. They are basically to extend term loans for industry and a resource base for them was created. Many states also created state financial corporation—(SFC) to promote project financing in the decade of 1950s. Thus, a different category of banks called development banks as term lending institutions were created. These development banks/FIs—(financial institutions) were initially barred from sanctioning working capital loans and only commercial banks could do that. At the same time, commercial banks were discouraged by many policy guidelines from sanctioning term loans. A balance was struck so that development banks and commercial banks did not compete as their area of operations was clearly demarcated and they had complimentary roles assigned to them to provide finance to industry. This system worked well for two decades.

However, nineties saw a big change in the scenario. Commercial banks resource base grew to great extent and they also built up good experience for assessing project finance. As they were not barred to sanction term loans, they started sanctioning project finances. Because of their closer rapport with customers, customers also preferred to take term loan from banks rather from financial institutions. Resources were no longer a constraint for commercial banks and liquidity was maintained so that there was no fear of liquidity crunch. They wanted to enter project financé in much bigger way. The development banks/FIs started to feel the competition and also the pinch for resources as their resources are drying up. They had to largely depend on govts for it. They felt that they can raise the resources from public, if allowed, and in order to grow they wanted to become universal banks as well. Reserve bank, realizing the changed scenario and the demand, accepted this and in nineties development banks were allowed to become commercial banks which many of them did. IDBI started IDBI bank in 1994 as its subsidiary and reverse merger took place when parent merged with the subsidiary. ICICI started a commercial bank—ICICI Bank, in private sector in the year 1996 and like in the case of IDBI, through reverse merger became ICICI Bank that has grown so big that it is now next to SBI in terms of business. With this, the concept of development banks and commercial banks occupying separate slots is done away with. However still some development banks like SIDBI, EXIM Bank, NHB are continuing with their original mandate. In fact, SIDBI was originally carved out of IDBI for taking up small-scale industry development. Many SFCs are also still functioning at state levels.

Term finance no longer remains with term lending institutions and banks sanction term finance based on availability of resources with them.

With starting of project finance, appraising skills have improved in banks. For sanctioning term loans bank had to look at the debt equity ratio and ensure that promoters are bringing in the necessary funds to provide margins. Generally, 3:1 ratio is the benchmark, which can be relaxed in exceptional cases of infrastructure projects. Banks are to see the projected cash flow and find out DSCR—(debt service coverage ratio), which is very important to see that the project will generate adequate cash surplus to service the loans, and for repaying the loans. Medium term loans—5-7 years are considered and long terms loans are only in case of capital incentive or infrastructure projects. Benchmark DSCR of 1.75 is generally accepted. Technical feasibility report and markets are studied to take the credit decision. Technology adopted are studied to see whether it is accepted in the industry or anywhere in the world and appears safe to bet on. Promoter's background, expertise, availability of technical people to run the project is also the important factors and looked into before sanctioning.

## Consortium Finance

### *Multiple Banking Arrangements*

The trend in financing a unit is generally by one bank only for practical and security purpose. Multiple banking was not allowed as a matter of rule. Later when the size of the projects started getting bigger, banks were finding it difficult to provide entire finance, as they cannot stretch themselves. There were fund constraints and exposure constraints also. As a prudent measure, banks are not interested to have concentrated risk. Then the consortium of banks came into picture. Reserve bank issued detailed guidelines on it in 1974 based on a committee report and revised guidelines were again issued in 1987. Under Consortium arrangement, one bank having a major share in the finance assumes the role of lead bank and other banks join the consortium as members and take up their agreed share of finance. Under consortium arrangement there is commonality of approach and common documentation and regular meeting of bankers to review the account. Generally, the lead bank takes the responsibility of assessing limits and then conveys it to member banks for taking decisions. This arrangement helped the banks to share the risk and at the same time have common control over the account.

Initially RBI wanted either that the finance shall be by one bank or, if the size is big, then by a consortium of banks.

Multiple banking was not favoured. This is because credit discipline becomes weak in such cases and no bank will be in a position to oversee the things, as there is no formal arrangement between banks under a multiple banking arrangement.

However, over a period consortium has also proved ineffective in that the decisions were delayed as each bank had to take independent decision at higher level and decisions were conveyed late. Borrowers had little say in such matter. Enhancements were unduly delayed due to different views of member banks. Though they are to go by consortium decision, it took long time. This has ultimately forced Reserve Bank to yield and agree for multiple banking arrangements. RBI allowed banks discretion to sanction loans on either consortium basis or multiple banking or syndicated loan with a view to introduce flexibility in the credit delivery system and to facilitate smooth flow of credit. RBI did not issue any guidelines for multiple banking arrangements. However, later at the instance of Chief Vigilance Commissioner, RBI advised banks in 2001 to be vigilant about the arrangements and issued some guidelines for effective sharing of information about the credit history and the conduct of the account of the borrowers among various banks.

### *Loan Syndication*

Earlier the lead bank under a consortium arrangement used to appraise and assess the limits, which was made available to member banks who generally toed the line. Now the trend is to have lead manager solely for the purpose of assessing the proposal and syndicating of loans. This is a new service provided by many banks, or through their subsidiaries. Loan syndication is becoming popular for all big projects, which help the promoter as he need not to run after banks to join the project. Loan syndicator does this job and may also join as lender. Once financial closure takes place, i.e. banks have taken up entire loan; subsequently it can be under either consortium or multiple banking.

A syndicated credit is an agreement between two or more lending institutions to provide a borrower a credit facility using common loan documentation. A prospective borrower intending to raise resources through this method awards a mandate to a bank as 'Lead Manager' to arrange credit on his behalf. The mandate spells out the commercial terms of the credit and the prerogatives of the mandated bank in resolving contentious issues in the course of the transaction. The mandated bank prepares an Information Memorandum about the borrower in consultation with the latter and distributes the same amongst the prospective lenders soliciting their participation in the credit to be extended to the borrower. The Information Memorandum provides the basis for each lending bank making its own independent economic and financial evaluation of the borrower, if necessary, by seeking additional supporting information from other source as well. Thereafter, the mandated bank convenes a meeting to discuss the syndication strategy and finalises deal timing, charges towards management expenses and cost of credit, share of each participating bank in the credit, etc. The loan agreement is signed by all the participating banks. The borrower is required to give prior notice to the 'Lead Manager' or his agent for drawing the loan amount to enable the latter to tie up disbursements with the other lending banks. Syndication is thus very similar to the system of consortium lending and is a convenient mode of raising long-term funds by borrowers.

### *Working Capital Finance*

In seventies, it was observed that though banks are financing industries for working capital requirement there was no system of appraisal uniformly followed by banks. Mostly the limits were based on bargaining powers of borrowers with their respective banks. Since bank credit is a limited resource, Reserve Bank of India was concerned about this. It was alleged that big industries cornered large bank finance without any justification. To look into this area RBI formed a committee called Tandon committee to look into the practices of banks lending to industries for working capital and suggest whether any norms can be prescribed.

### MPBF Method of Lending—Tandon Committee, Chore Committee

Tandon Committee report came in 1975 and in a way; it is path-breaking report. For the first time an attempt has been made by the committee to make an objective assessment of limits and also prescribe norms that can be followed by banks while sanctioning working capital limits. The committee went into the basic purpose of working capital finance and concluded that before financing banks shall have to make assessment of inventory required by the specific industry which shall be in line with the industries in similar business. For the first time, inventory norms have been fixed for more than 17 basic industries. Holding period for stocks and receivables were worked out and norms to be followed by the industry were fixed. After fixing the inventory norms banks were asked to assess need based limits and work out permissible bank finance. The committee recommended three methods of lending. To begin with, the first method was prescribed and then over a period to move to 2nd method and then lastly move to 3rd method of lending. Each method progressively increased networking capital requirement by the industry.

These norms were opposed by industries. Their main grouse was that how can a bank fix norms for inventory for industry. Industry shall be allowed to fix norms for themselves. It was felt that the norms are very rigid to follow. However, RBI accepted the recommendations of the Tandon committee and banks were advised to implement the same. These recommendations forced the industries for optimal holding of inventory and bank finance was available only for normal business requirement and not for holding unduly large inventory. The purpose was also to discourage hoarding of stocks by the industry. It worked and industry was forced to discipline itself to the norms. Subsequently many changes were made but the basic structure of assessment remained the same. Inventory norms came to stay as a very important tool to assess the working capital limit. Later, Chore Committee (1979) went into these recommendations and it agreed to continue with it except that it scraped the 3rd method of lending as being very stringent and not advisable for Indian industries. Under the 3rd method, the core current assets were also to be financed by net working capital, which was found not practicable.

The above assessment now is named as traditional or MPBF method and is used for all working capital loan assessments.

### *Turnover Method of Lending—Nayak Committee*

In the year 1991, Nayak committee went into assessment of working capital limits for small-scale industries and it concluded that the MPBF method is rigid and does not allow flexibility to SSI units, which are small and require special treatment. Moreover, the assessment is also very cumbersome process for them, who are basically small units and to be financed more liberally to allow them to survive and flourish. The committee recommended Turnover method as a simple and practical solution. Under this, the working capital assessment is based on projected turnover of the unit. Working capital requirement is assessed at 25% of the projected turnover and 20% of projected turnover is sanctioned as limit with the condition that 5% shall be brought in by borrower as margin. It is a simple prescription and banks need not fix any inventory norms to be followed by the borrower. This method is widely accepted and is now applicable for limits up to ₹ 5 crores.

### *Cash Budget Method of Lending*

Inventory norms were not taking into account the seasonal nature of certain industries. Though attempts have been made to make assessment as peak level and non-peak level, the problem faced by seasonal industries are not adequately addressed by banks. Then there are infrastructure projects that have irregular investment and longer gestation period. There are also software companies who do not have physical inventory, as their product is more of intellectual rights in nature.

In the year 1997 RBI permitted banks to decide on the methods of working capital finance and to take care of certain groups of borrowers discussed above, a third method of lending called as cash budget method was introduced. Under this, cash budget of the borrower is worked out taking into account the inflow and outflow. The gap is financed by the bank in the shape of working capital limit. Thus, this assessment is not based on inventory norms or turnover norms.

### *Cash Credit Facility*

Traditionally Indian banks are financing pre-sale activities and most of the time the securities are physical stocks. Banks are comfortable with security of physical stocks. However, this approach may not be correct as financing pre-sale activity is more risky as there are uncertainties about borrower's ability to manufacture and then to find buyer. Whereas if banks finance sales, then the risks attached to manufacturing and finding buyers are eliminated. The only remaining risk is non-payment by the buyer. However, here banks do not get physical security as only bills or receivables are available which are intangible. Banks are not very happy about this. Bill of exchange is not very common in the country and banks do not get the advantage of having negotiable document as security.

This is the reason why cash credit limits is the favourite with Indian banking sector. Banks feel safe in financing physical stock where they can see the securities. Until fifties and early sixties, banks were only sanctioning pledge limits and holding the stocks in their physical custody. Banks even had a list of approved commodities against the pledge of which they were prepared to lend. Then as the industry, particularly small-scale industries came on the scene and as the trade also expanded, banks slowly migrated to hypothecation limits against the stocks of trade and scrapped the approved commodities list. Since then hypothecation facility, is predominantly sanctioned. Generally, book debts are not taken as primary security as effective charge cannot be created over it. The bill culture is also absent in our economy and is seen only in organized sector. This is despite RBI starting bill rediscounting scheme to encourage it.

Hypothecation of stocks though give banks some security, in fact the security created is a myth as far as stocks are concerned. Hardly any bank can lay its hand on stocks whenever there is problem. This is due to the fact that in case of difficulty faced by the business, cash and stocks are first casualties and they are also first to disappear. By the time banks come to know about the ill health of the borrower, stock might have already disappeared. Banks are security minded, they always try to have back up security in the form of collaterals and the ultimate recovery is mostly due to these collaterals. However, banks are not yet ready for changing their views on cash credit limits, and are continuing with the practice.

In theory, working capital limits are considered as short-term loans. They are sanctioned generally for a period of one year and thereafter as per the term, bank has the option to call it back. In reality, it does not happen that way. Limits are renewed and mostly enhanced. This goes on for decades together unless something happens to the account. In most of the accounts, even the availments are not showing any regular trend in liquidation even once during the year. Most of the times, availment is more than 90% of the limit. The cash credit limit has become a permanent source of funds for the running of the business and the business cannot do without it even for a single day. Thus the cash credit limit in effect is the long-term loans of the bank and almost illiquid.

### Loan System for Credit Delivery

In nineties, it was observed that many industrial units and big borrowers had got sanctioned large working capital limits from banks and were not effectively utilising it. This created a peculiar situation as it was found that banks had sanctioned very high level of working capital limits and total limits sanctioned were far too high than the capability of banks. This anomaly crept in to the system and though limits were not utilised to full extent, it still caused concern, as banks were not in a position to meet full utilisation. Secondly, this also created problem for banks as they are committed by the sanctions and this commitment precluded them from entertaining fresh loans. Thirdly, the large undrawn limits also allowed these borrowers to use the same when it suited them may be for other than genuine requirements. Further, for the cash and liquidity management of banks, this feature was felt undesirable.

In order to contain this tendency, RBI introduced loan system for credit delivery in the year 1995.

Under this system, banks were advised to allow 80% of assessed working capital limits as loan component and only 20% of the limit sanctioned is made available as cash credit component. This was applicable to borrowers with working capital limits of ₹ 10 crores and above from the banking system. Borrowers are obliged to take the loan component first and it shall remain outstanding without changes. Only the cash credit component can fluctuate as per availment. Loan component is renewed at the time of renewal and rolled over. Borrowers are however, allowed to repay the loan component, or part of it, any time during the year in case they have liquid surplus but the limit shall not be allowed to be drawn again during the year. Limit can be restored after yearly renewal of working capital limits.

In 2001, RBI permitted some relaxations on this as under:

(a) In the case of borrowers enjoying working capital credit limits of ₹ 10 crores and above from the banking system, loan component should normally be 80%. Banks, however, have the freedom to change the composition of working capital by increasing the cash credit component beyond 20% or to increase the 'Loan Component' beyond 80% as the case may be, if they so desire. Banks are expected to appropriately price each of the two components of working capital finance, taking into account the impact of such decisions on their cash and liquidity management.

(b) In the case of borrowers enjoying working capital credit limit of less than ₹ 10 crore, banks may persuade them to go in for the 'Loan System' by offering an incentive in the form of lower rate of interest on the loan component, as compared to the cash credit component. The actual percentage of 'loan component' in these cases may be settled by the bank with its borrower clients.

(c) In respect of certain business activities, which are cyclical and seasonal in nature or have inherent volatility, the strict application of loan system may create difficulties for the borrowers. Banks may, with the approval of their respective Boards, identify such business activities, which may be exempt from the loan system of delivery.

Further export credit and bills limit are exempted as under:

**Export Credit**—The bifurcation of the working capital limit into loan and cash credit components, as stated in paragraph (1) above, would be effected after excluding the export credit limits (pre-shipment and post-shipment). Export credit limit would continue to be allowed in the form hitherto granted.

Bills limit for inland sales may be fully carved out of the 'loan' component.

The loan system was made applicable to borrowal accounts classified as 'standard' or 'sub-standard'.

## Bridge Loans

Bridge loans are a type of short-term loan typically taken from banks for a period of 2 weeks to 3 years, pending the arrangement of larger or longer-term financing. This only acts as an interim financing until permanent or the next stage of financing can be obtained. These kinds of loans are generally more expensive as interest rates are high.

Banks were sanctioning bridge loans as stopgap arrangements and sometimes it used to be without securities. In October 1995, the Reserve Bank allowed banks to grant bridge loans against an underwriting commitment of a financial institution and/or a bank in the event of the latter institution facing temporary liquidity constraints within 5% ceiling of the banks' incremental deposits of the previous year.

There were few cases when banks ran into trouble as the loan was not liquidated as expected and this led RBI to ban the sanction of such loans in the year 1995. The Reserve Bank of India (RBI) has barred banks and financial institutions from granting bridge loans to the non-banking finance companies. The RBI has also directed banks to obtain security for bridge loans.

In the year 1997, RBI allowed banks to sanction bridge loans and this time RBI has kept bridge loan outside the five per cent ceiling of the banks' incremental deposits of the previous year. The directive has also stipulated that banks must comply with individual/group exposure norms while granting bridge loans. In addition to that, banks must ensure the end-use of bridge loans. The maximum period of the loan has been pegged at one year.

At present Bridge Loans can be sanctioned by banks following the guidelines as under:

1. Banks have been permitted to sanction bridge loans to companies for a period not exceeding one year against expected equity flows/issues. Such loans should be included within the ceiling of 5% of the banks' total outstanding advances (including Commercial Paper) as on March 31 of the previous year prescribed for total exposure, including both fund-based and non-fund based exposure to capital market in all forms.
2. Banks should formulate their own internal guidelines with the approval of their Board of Directors for grant of such loans, exercising due caution and attention to security for such loans.
3. Banks may also extend bridge loans against the expected proceeds of Non-Convertible Debentures, External Commercial Borrowings, Global Depository Receipts and/or funds in the nature of Foreign Direct Investments, provided the banks are satisfied that the borrowing company has already made firm arrangements for raising the aforesaid resources/funds.

## Commercial Paper

As part of efforts to develop the money market, Commercial Paper (CP) was introduced by RBI in 1990, with a view to enable highly rated corporate borrowers to diversify their sources of short-term borrowings and also to provide an additional financial instrument to investors.

Commercial Paper (CP) is an unsecured money market instrument issued in the form of a promissory note. It is a privately placed instrument. CP can be issued in denominations of ₹ 5 lakhs or multiples thereof.

A corporate would be eligible to issue CP provided:

(a) The tangible net worth of the company, as per the latest audited balance sheet, is not less than ₹ 4 crores;

(b) Company has been sanctioned working capital limit by bank(s) or all-India financial institution(s); and

(c) The borrowal account of the company is classified as a Standard Asset by the financing bank(s) institution(s).

Banks and FIs have the flexibility to fix working capital limits duly taking into account the resource pattern of companies' financing including CPs.

Banks and FIs also have the flexibility to provide stand-by assistance, credit enhancement, etc., based on their commercial judgement, to the corporate issuing commercial paper. However, these should be within the prudential norms as applicable and subject to specific approval of the Board.

### Retail Loans

In nineties with fast expanding resource base of banks and liberalisation of credit norms by Reserve Bank of India, banks started looking for greener pastures for deploying their funds. This is the time when banks understood the importance of retail finance and consumer finance. Unlike traditional finance, retail finance is directed at a homogenous group of borrowers. Instead of individual assessments, a scheme for finance is worked out which is generally suitable for a particular segment of customers or suitable for a particular type of loan requirement. Banks realized that the country offers huge market for retail credit. Home loans, car loans, consumer loans and personal loans have excellent potential as large populace is in need of such finances. Home loans became very popular and banks started increasing their exposure to retail credit from the year 2000 onwards.

Education loans were started by banks. It started with a Supreme Court order to all public sector banks in the year 1999 to extend loans to students getting admitted in private technical colleges to help students financially. In squeal to this order and govt advice, IBA formulated a model education loan scheme for banks and almost all banks adopted the scheme. Though banks are sanctioning loans under the scheme, they do it more as a social obligation than as a commercial proposition. The hesitation is mainly due to lack of security in such loans and uncertainty about repayment. This is partly true as the student even after completing the course may not get job and had to wait indefinitely. However, it is a socially desirable scheme as in a way it is implementation of right to education for students.

Housing loan has received a very big boost now. But In sixties and seventies banks were not allowed to lend to this segment as it was considered too long a term loan and banks were not allowed to invest in such assets. There was restriction on banks for extending housing finance, which shall not exceed a small percentage of its total loans portfolio. GOI created housing and urban development corporation (HUDCO) in the year 1970 to give impetus to housing development for poor and also urban area development. Similar to the term lending institutions created for term lending to industrial units, National Housing Bank (NHB) was created by an Act of Parliament in the year 1988 as apex body for housing finance in the country. NHB is also providing refinance to banks so that they can have some exposure to this sector. Housing Development Finance Corporation (HDFC) came into existence in the year 1977 as premier housing finance company. LIC also started its housing finance company in the year 1989 to take up housing finance. Many housing finance companies were started, some were by banks. Hence till nineties banks were marginal players in housing loans. After that, the scene changed. Banks started to be aggressive in the housing loans and formulated schemes to finance housing sector.

Now banks are the major players in housing loans and housing finance companies are finding it difficult to compete. HDFC created a banking subsidiary in the year 1994 named HDFC Bank. However, HDFC is still active and is still a leader in housing finance. Many banks housing subsidiaries were later merged with parent banks.

Banks also entered consumer finance like personal loans, car loans and consumer durable loans. However, car loans are still dominated by private financiers and also subsidiary companies of car manufacturers. They are offering finance at very cheap rates in collaboration with manufacturers.

## Export Finance

Reserve Bank of India also gave separate priority status to export finance by banks and a target of 12% was fixed. This was done with the intention to boost exports, which was very much required to meet payments of imports of the country.

Export finance provided by banks is mainly into two categories. Pre-shipment and post-shipment credits. Pre-shipment credits are allowed to enable the exporter to collect and produce goods for exports. These facilities are either packing credit loans or cash credit facility. Packing credit loans are given on order-to-order basis and for the period of execution of exports and to be liquidated by export proceeds by either remittance received or bills negotiated. Hence, this facility is given on case-to-case basis, on production of firm order or letter of credit by the exporter. Subsequently to encourage large exporters, running account facility was allowed for packing credit in which the loans are released from the same running account instead of separate loans for each order. Only realisations are monitored for each export. The limit is fixed based on projection for current year looking into the previous year's performance of the exporter. Further relaxations were made and now this facility can be released on mere declaration basis without insisting for confirmed orders or LCs.

Post-shipment credits are mainly by negotiating bills under LC or without LC. Generally credit period of 180 days are allowed and in case payments are not received for some genuine reasons, the period can be extended with the approval of RBI up to 365 days and even beyond in deserving cases.

Export finance by banks is generally at concessional rate of interest as prescribed by RBI. Export Credit Guarantee Corporation was set up in the year 1957 to provide insurance cover for export business for banks and exporters. Banks can cover all eligible packing credits sanctioned by it and all bills negotiated by it, under single policy and get insurance covers varying from 60 to 90%. Likewise, banks and exporters can get buyer-wise insurance cover from ECGC to cover the risk of default in payment by any buyer. This limit is pre-determined by ECGC and approved by them.

Banks can avail Exim bank refinance for eligible advances to exporters. Exim Bank offers Rediscounting facility to commercial banks, enabling them to rediscount export bills of their SSI customers, with usance not exceeding 90 days. Exim Bank also offers Refinance of Supplier's Credit, enabling commercial banks to offer credit to Indian exporters of eligible goods, who in turn extend them credit over 180 days to importers overseas.

## Other Sectors

### *Real Estate Sector*

Real estate sector was an area of least priority for banks because of guidelines issued by RBI from time to time. RBI until nineties felt that banks should not be involved in financing real estate as it will not suit the banks and may adversely affect their liquidity and strength. It was considered as speculative area, with property prices going up disproportionately based on various factors. After nineties, there has been gradual shift in RBI stand on this sector. Real estate sector is important sector for the growth of the economy. However, real estate sector is treated as three different segments. Infrastructure is one segment under real estate, which is highly capital incentive projects and is very important for economic and industrial growth. Now this is being encouraged by RBI and banks are financing to large extent. RBI is now allowing banks to take up the projects and some reliefs in exposure norms have been allowed to encourage banks to take up infrastructure financing. Banks can now take higher exposure in case of infrastructure projects than what is permissible.

As discussed earlier, housing sector, the second segment under real estate, has now been identified as priority area for many reasons. Banks are now freely allowed to expand individual housing loans and loans to builders of housing projects as corollary to housing loans. However, in case of builders banks are not allowed to finance the acquisition of land. Banks can only finance the development cost of the housing project.

Third segment in real estate is the commercial real estate segment. RBI is not in favour of bank finance to this segment as it is considered too risky. Though banks can now sanction finance to this segment, banks were asked to fix its own exposure norms for real estate loans and for commercial real-estate loans. RBI is monitoring the growth in this sector and is making the banks aware that caution is required in this area.

### Capital Market Exposure

For obvious reasons capital market exposure for banks is a negative area. There are some statutory restrictions on the banks for lending against their own shares and for holding shares of any company either as owner or as pledge. It is subjected to double restrictions of banks own equity and the concerned company's equity. Banks are not encouraged to take position in equity market or extend finance to anyone connected with capital market like brokers and underwriters. Loans to individuals against pledge of shares are also restricted to an amount. The reason is that the finance is mostly used for speculative purpose, which is neither desirable nor good for banks to take exposures.

### Restrictions for Lending

Regulatory guidelines restricting flow of bank finance to many sectors have been prescribed from time to time and over the period they have been reviewed and suitable changes were made to keep it in line with present scenario. At present, also there are few important restrictions for banks while sanctioning credits, which are as under:

| Statutory Restrictions | | |
|---|---|---|
| **Sl. No.** | **Areas covered** | **Restrictions** |
| 1. | Limits on Banks' Exposure to Capital Markets.<br>1. Statutory limit on shareholding in companies. | In terms of Section 19(2) of the Banking Regulation Act, 1949, no banking company shall hold shares in any company, whether as pledgee, mortgagee or absolute owner, of an amount exceeding 30% of the paid-up share capital of that company or 30% of its own paid-up share capital and reserves, whichever is less, except as provided in sub-section (1) of Section 19 of the Act. Shares held in demat form should also be included for the purpose of determining the exposure limit. This is an aggregate holding limit for each company. While granting any advance against shares, underwriting any issue of shares, or acquiring any shares on investment account or even in lieu of debt of any company, these statutory provisions should be strictly observed. |
| 2. | Statutory Restrictions<br>1. Advances against bank's own shares. | In terms of Section 20(1) of the Banking Regulation Act, 1949, a bank cannot grant any loans and advances on the security of its own shares. |
| 3. | 2. Advances to bank's Directors. | 1. Section 20(1) of the Banking Regulation Act, 1949 also lays down the restrictions on loans and advances to the directors and the firms in which they hold substantial interest.<br>2. Banks are prohibited from entering into any commitment for granting any loans or advances to or on behalf of any of its directors, or any firm in which any of its directors is interested as partner, manager, employee or guarantor, or any company (not being a subsidiary of the banking company or a company registered under Section 25 of the Companies Act, 1956, or a Government company) of which, or the subsidiary or the holding company of which any of the directors of the bank is a director, managing agent, manager, employee or guarantor or in which he holds substantial interest, or any individual in respect of whom any of its directors is a partner or guarantor. |
| 4. | Exposure to Indian Joint Ventures/Wholly-owned Subsidiaries Abroad and Overseas Step-down Subsidiaries of Indian Corporates | 1. Banks are allowed to extend credit/non-credit facilities (viz. letters of credit and guarantees) to Indian Joint Ventures/Wholly-owned Subsidiaries abroad and step-down subsidiaries which are wholly owned by the overseas subsidiaries of Indian Corporates. Banks are also permitted to provide at their discretion, buyer's credit/acceptance finance to overseas parties for facilitating export of goods and services from India.<br>2. The above exposure will, however, be subject to a limit of 20% of banks' unimpaired capital funds (Tier I and Tier II capital), subject to the following conditions:<br>(i) Loan will be granted only to those joint ventures where the holding by the Indian company is more than 51%.<br>(ii) Proper systems for management of credit and interest rate risks arising out of such cross border lending are in place.<br>(iii) While extending such facilities, banks will have to comply with Section 25 of the Banking Regulation |

*(Contd...)*

| | | |
|---|---|---|
| | | Act, 1949, in terms of which the assets in India of every banking company at the close of business on the last Friday of every quarter shall not be less than 75% of its demand and time liabilities in India. In other words, aggregate assets outside India should not exceed 25% of the bank's demand and time liabilities in India. |
| 5. | Restrictions on Grant of Financial Assistance to Industries Producing / Consuming Ozone Depleting Substances (ODS) | Banks should not extend finance for setting up of new units consuming/producing the above ODS. In terms of circular No. FI/12/96-97 dated February 16, 1996 issued by the erstwhile Industrial Development Bank of India no financial assistance should be extended to small/medium scale units engaged in the manufacture of the aerosol units using CFC and no refinance would be extended to any project assisted in this sector. |
| **Regulatory Restrictions** | | |
| 6. | Credit Exposures to Individual/Group Borrowers | 1. The exposure ceiling limits would be 15% of capital funds in case of a single borrower and 40% of capital funds in the case of a borrower group. The capital funds for the purpose will comprise of Tier I and Tier II capital as defined under capital adequacy standards.<br>2. Credit exposure to a single borrower may exceed the exposure norm of 15% of the bank's capital funds by an additional 5% (i.e. upto 20 percent) provided the additional credit exposure is on account of extension of credit to infrastructure projects. Credit exposure to borrowers belonging to a group may exceed the exposure norm of 40% of the bank's capital funds by an additional 10% (i.e., up to 50 percent), provided the additional credit exposure is on account of extension of credit to infrastructure projects. As per definition of infrastructure lending and the list of items included under infrastructure sector of RBI. |
| 7. | Exposures to NBFCs | The exposure (both lending and investment, including off balance sheet exposures) of a bank to a single NBFC/NBFC-AFC (Asset Financing Companies) should not exceed 10%/15% respectively, of the bank's capital funds as per its last audited balance sheet. Banks may, however, assume exposures on a single NBFC/NBFC-AFC up to 15%/20% respectively, of their capital funds provided the exposure in excess of 10%/15% respectively, is on account of funds on-lent by the NBFC/NBFC-AFC to the infrastructure sector. Exposure of a bank to Infrastructure Finance Companies (IFCs) should not exceed 15% of its capital funds as per its last audited balance sheet, with a provision to increase it to 20% if the same is on account of funds on-lent by the IFCs to the infrastructure sector. Further, banks may also consider fixing internal limits for their aggregate to exposure to all NBFCs put together. |
| 8. | Internal Exposure Limits<br>Fixing of Sectoral Limits | Apart from limiting the exposures to an individual or a group of borrowers, as indicated above, banks may also consider fixing internal limits for |

(*Contd...*)

| | | |
|---|---|---|
| | | aggregate commitments to specific sectors, e.g. textiles, jute, tea, etc., so that the exposures are evenly spread over various sectors. These limits could be fixed by the banks having regard to the performance of different sectors and the risks perceived. The limits so fixed may be reviewed periodically and revised, as necessary.<br>2. Exposure to Real Estate—Banks should frame comprehensive prudential norms relating to the ceiling on the total amount of real estate loans, single/group exposure limits for such loans, margins, security, repayment schedule and availability of supplementary finance and the policy should be approved by the banks' Boards. |
| 9. | Limits on Banks' Exposure to Capital Markets | The aggregate exposure of a consolidated bank to capital markets (both fund based and non-fund based) should not exceed 40% of its consolidated net worth as on March 31 of the previous year. Within this overall ceiling, the aggregate direct exposure by way of the consolidated bank's investment in shares, convertible bonds / debentures, units of equity-oriented mutual funds and all exposures to Venture Capital Funds (VCFs) [both registered and unregistered] should not exceed 20% of its consolidated net worth. |
| 10. | Advances against shares to individuals | Loans against security of shares, convertible bonds, convertible debentures and units of equity oriented mutual funds to individuals from the banking system should not exceed the limit of ₹ 10 lakh per individual if the securities are held in physical form and ₹ 20 lakhs, per individual if the securities are held in demat form. Such loans are meant for genuine individual investors and banks should not support collusive action by a large group of individuals belonging to the same corporate or their inter-connected entities to take multiple loans in order to support particular scrips or stock-broking activities of the concerned firms. Such finance should be reckoned as an exposure to capital market. Banks should formulate, with the approval of their Board of Directors, a Loan Policy for granting advances to individuals against shares, debentures, and bonds keeping in view the RBI guidelines. As a prudential measure, banks may also consider laying down appropriate aggregate sub-limits of such advances. |
| 11. | Advances against shares to Stock Brokers and Market Makers | Banks are free to provide credit facilities to stockbrokers and market makers on the basis of their commercial judgment, within the policy framework approved by their Boards. However, in order to avoid any nexus emerging between inter-connected stock broking entities and banks, the Board of each bank should fix, within the overall ceiling of 40% of their net worth as on March 31 of the previous year, a sub-ceiling for total advances to—<br>(i) all the stockbrokers and market makers (both fund based and non-fund based, i.e. guarantees); and |

*(Contd...)*

| | | |
|---|---|---|
| | | (ii) to any single stockbroking entity, including its associates / inter-connected companies.<br>Further, banks should not extend credit facilities directly or indirectly to stockbrokers for arbitrage operations in Stock Exchanges. |
| 12. | Granting loans and advances to relatives of Directors | Without prior approval of the Board or without the knowledge of the Board, no loans and advances should be granted to relatives of the bank's Chairman / Managing Director or other Directors, Directors (including Chairman / Managing Director) of other banks and their relatives, Directors of Scheduled Co-operative Banks and their relatives, Directors of Subsidiaries / Trustees of Mutual Funds / Venture Capital Funds set up by the financing banks or other banks, as per details given below. |
| 13. | Advances against Bullion/Primary gold | (a) Banks should not grant any advance against bullion/ Primary gold.<br>(b) Banks should desist from granting advances to the silver bullion dealers which are likely to be utilised for speculative purposes. |
| 14. | Gold (Metal) Loans | Banks nominated to import gold as per extant instructions may extend Gold (Metal) Loans to domestic jewellery manufacturers, who are not exporters of jewellery, subject to the condition that any gold loan borrowing or other non-funded commitments taken by them for the purpose of providing gold loans to domestic jewellery manufacturers will be taken into account for the purpose of the overall ceiling (presently 25 % of Tier I capital) in respect of aggregate borrowing for non-export purposes. |

(*Source*: RBI master circular)

## Interest Rates on Loans

### *Evolution of Interest Rates on Loans from 1960*

Reserve Bank of India started prescribing the minimum rate of interest on advances granted by Scheduled Commercial Banks with effect from October 1, 1960.

RBI introduced the maximum lending rate to be charged by banks in place of minimum lending rate effective from March 2, 1968.

This was changed with effect from January 21, 1970, and the prescription of minimum lending rate was reintroduced.

RBI again introduced the ceiling rate on advances to be charged by banks effective March 15, 1976. Banks were also advised, for the first time, to charge interest on advances at quarterly rests. This practice of charging interest on quarterly rests continued thereafter and in the year 2002, with effect from April 1, 2002 the periodicity was changed to monthly rests.

From 1976, RBI administered interest rates for different types of loans. Interest rates were sector-specific, programme-specific and purpose-specific. While loans to priority sector carried lower rate of interests, other sectors were charged higher rates. Interest for export finance was generally the lowest to enable exporters to compete internationally. There used to be a big chart showing rate of interest applicable to different categories of borrowers. Bank lending rates as well as the allocation of bank credit were closely regulated by the Reserve Bank with the objective for providing credit to the productive sectors of the economy.

After financial sector reforms were introduced, deregulation of interest rates started stepwise. The changes introduced are given in the following Table 1.

**Table 1:** Evolution of Lending Rate Structure in India

| | |
|---|---|
| Sep. 1990 | The structure of lending rates was rationalized into six size-wise slabs. Of these, banks were free to set interest rates on loans of over ₹ 2 lakhs with minimum lending rates prescribed by RBI. |
| April 1992 | Slabs compressed into four. |
| April 1993 | Slabs compressed into three. |
| Oct. 1994 | Lending rates for loans with credit limits of over ₹ 2 lakhs deregulated. Banks were required to declare their Prime lending rates (PLRs). |
| Feb. 1997 | Banks allowed to prescribe separate PLRs and spreads over PLRs, both for loan and cash credit components. |
| Oct. 1997 | For term loans of 3 years and above, separate Prime Term Lending Rates (PTLRs) were required to be announced by banks. |
| April 1998 | PLR converted as a ceiling rate on loans up to ₹ 2 lakhs. |
| April 1999 | Tenor-linked Prime Lending Rates (TPLRs) introduced. |
| Oct. 1999 | Banks were given flexibility to charge interest rates without reference to the PLR in respect of certain categories of loans/credit. |
| April 2000 | Banks allowed to charge fixed/floating rate on their lending for credit limit of over ₹ 2 lakh. |
| April 2001 | The PLR ceased to be the floor rate for loans above ₹ 2 lakhs. Banks allowed to lend at sub-PLR rate for loans above ₹ 2 lakhs. |
| April 2002 | Dissemination of range of interest rates through the Reserve Bank's website was introduced. |
| April 2003 | Benchmark PLR (BPLR) system introduced and tenor-linked PLRs discontinued. |
| Feb. 2010 | Draft circular on Base Rate placed on RBI website for obtaining comments/suggestions from public/stakeholders. |
| April 2010 | Base Rate system of loan pricing introduced effective July 1, 2010. Rupee lending rate structure completely deregulated. |

*Source*: Speech by Deepak Mohanty, Executive Director, Reserve Bank of India—Perspectives on Lending Rates in India—delivered at the Bankers' Club, Kolkata on 11th June 2010.

In September 1990, a new structure of lending rates linking interest rates to the size of loan was prescribed which reduced the multiplicity and complexity of interest rates. The slabs were reduced to six and banks were allowed freedom to fix interest rates within the range for all borrowers except for loans up to ₹ 2 lakhs. Small borrowers (i.e. up to ₹ 2 lakhs) were to be charged as per guidelines. The Differential Rate of Interest Scheme under which interest rate of 4% was prescribed and Export Credit, which was subject to different rules as regards interest rates were kept out of general prescription of the lending rates.

In the year 1994, concept of Prime Lending Rate (PLR) was introduced. Prime lending rate has been explained as the rate of interest the bank would offer to its prime borrowers based on rating and security cover. Banks were not to lend below this rate except for exempted category of borrowers in priority sector and export sector. Banks were asked to fix the PLR and also fix the maximum spread above PLR. Banks were free to fix the interest rates between PLR and the maximum, to their borrowers for above ₹ 2 lakhs category. PLR acted as the floor rate. However, it was prescribed that for loans up to and inclusive of ₹ 2 lakhs, the lending rates of banks should not exceed the Prime Lending Rate of the respective banks.

Some more changes were made later in fixing PLR for different purposes. In the year 2001, RBI allowed banks to lend below PLR and it ceased as floor rate.

Subsequently it was observed that PLRs of banks turned out to be rigid and inflexible in relation to the movement of interest rates in the economy. In view of this, a BPLR system was introduced in April 2003. RBI issued guidelines for determination of Benchmark Prime Lending Rate (BPLR) as under:

> In order to enhance transparency in banks' pricing of their loan products as also to ensure that the BPLR truly reflects the actual costs, banks should be guided by the following considerations while determining their Benchmark PLR:

> Banks should take into account their (i) actual cost of funds, (ii) operating expenses and, (iii) a minimum margin to cover regulatory requirement of provisioning / capital charge and profit margin, while arriving at the benchmark PLR. Banks should announce a Benchmark PLR with the approval of their Boards.
>
> The Benchmark PLR will be the ceiling rate for credit limit up to ₹ 2 lakhs.
>
> All other lending rates can be determined with reference to the Benchmark PLR arrived at as above by taking into account term premia and/or risk premia.

Banks were advised to continue to provide information on maximum and minimum interest rates charged together with the Benchmark PLR.

However, the BPLR system also did not meet the objectives. Competition and excess liquidity had forced the banks to resort to sub-BPLR lending. BPLR lost its role as a reference rate. It was also argued that this has resulted in under-pricing of credit to corporates and over-pricing of credit to agriculture as well as small and medium enterprises.

In view of the shortcomings in the BPLR system, and after study by a committee, RBI introduced base rate concept in the year 2010.

### The Base Rate System

The base rate system has replaced the BPLR system with effect from 1st July 2010. The guidelines states—"Base rate shall include all those elements of the lending rates that are common across all categories of borrowers. Banks may choose any benchmark to arrive at the base rate for a specific tenor that may be disclosed transparently. Banks are free to use any other methodology, provided it is consistent, and is made available for supervisory review. Banks will determine their actual lending rates on loans with reference to the base rate and by including such other customer specific charges as considered appropriate."

Base rate is calculated on a formula and it takes into account followings:

(a) Cost of deposits/funds

(b) Negative carry on CRR and SLR

(c) Unallocatable overhead cost

(d) Average return on net worth

- Negative carry on CRR and SLR balances arises because the return on CRR balances is nil, while the return on SLR balances (proxied using the 364-day Treasury Bill rate) is lower than the cost of deposits. Negative carry on CRR and SLR is arrived at in three steps. In the first step, return on SLR investment was calculated using 364-day Treasury Bills. In the second step, effective cost was calculated by taking the ratio (expressed as a percentage) of cost of deposits (adjusted for return on SLR investment) and deployable deposits (total deposits less the deposits locked as CRR and SLR balances). In the third step, negative carry cost on SLR and CRR was arrived at by taking the difference between the effective cost and the cost of deposits.
- Unallocatable Overhead Cost is calculated by taking the ratio (expressed as a percentage) of unallocated overhead cost and deployable deposits.
- Average Return on Net Worth is computed as the product of net profit to net worth ratio and net worth to deployable deposits ratio expressed as a percentage.

With the introduction of the base rate system, all categories of loans to be priced only with reference to the base rate with a few exceptions. The base rate can also serve as the reference benchmark rate for floating rate loan products, apart from other external market benchmark rates.

Since the base rate will be the minimum rate for all loans, the current stipulation of BPLR as the ceiling rate for loans up to ₹ 2 lakhs is withdrawn. The interest rate on rupee export credit has also been deregulated.

Under the base rate concept banks cannot lend below the base rate. However, the following categories of loans could be priced without reference to the Base Rate:

(a) DRI advances

(b) Loans to banks' own employees

(c) Loans to banks' depositors against their own deposits.

Banks are required to review the Base Rate at least once in a quarter with the approval of the Board or the Asset Liability Management Committees (ALCOs) as per the bank's practice. Since transparency in the pricing of lending products has been a key objective, banks are required to exhibit the information on their Base Rate at all branches and also on their websites. Changes in the Base Rate should also be conveyed to the general public from time to time through appropriate channels.

## Historical Interest Rates on Advances

RBI started prescribing interest rates on advances from the year 1960. Interest rates were administered since then, and only in the year 1994-95 interest rates on advances for over ₹ 2 lakhs were freed. Banks were asked to fix Prime Lending Rates and spread over Prime Lending Rates. Hence, from the year 1995 there are no rates prescribed by RBI. During the earlier periods, either RBI was prescribing the maximum rate or sometimes, minimum rate for advances by banks. Some sectors like DRI advances, advances against bank deposits, staff loans, export credit and some advances to agriculture were having different set of guidelines.

Since interest rates are being administered by RBI, in the year 1984 a legal provision was made by amending banking regulation act and inserting a new section 21A as under:

> 21A. Rates of interest charged by banking companies not to be subject to scrutiny by courts.—Notwithstanding anything contained in the Usurious Loans Act, 1918 (10 of 1918), or any other law relating to indebtedness in force in any State, a

transaction between a banking company and its debtor shall not be re-opened by any court on the ground that the rate of interest charged by the banking company in respect of such transaction is excessive.

This section prohibited courts from disagreeing with interest rates charged by banks and banks were only to prove that the interest rate is as per RBI prescription. However, the position now is slightly different as banks are deciding the interest rates themselves.

The Table on next page gives the interest rates prescribed by RBI from 1976-77 till 1994-95. Deposit rates for deposit of 5 years and above is also shown. As stated earlier interest rates from the year 1995, were as per banks PLRs and minimum rates shown in the Table were based on PLRs of five leading banks. SBI lending rates are separately shown in the Table (SBI lending rates can be considered as benchmark rates, which were within the stipulations of RBI and reflect average/ minimum rates applicable). There was separate minimum rate stipulation for advances covered by selective credit control. This was withdrawn from the year 1995. Generally, banks maintained a minimum spread of 2.5%-3.5% over and above the PLR. Hence, maximum applicable rates can be presumed with 3% mark up on PLRs from 1995.

Loan interest rates were high in the years 1981-1983 when the maximum interest was 19.50%. It came down to 16.5% in 1988. In the year 1991, which was a crisis year, minimum interest rate went up to 19%. (Maximum was nearly 22% by adding the spread). From the year 1994 it came down and from 1995 banks fixed own PLRs.

Historically banks enjoyed high spread i.e. difference between maximum deposit rate and maximum loan rate. This can be seen from SBI advance rates and maximum deposit rates shown in the chart below and the spread is shown in the last column. It was near to 6% till the year 1994. After deregulation of interest rates from 1995, it came down to 4% and below. Spread was low in the years 1997-2001 when it was near to 2%. From 2002, it went up and now is in the range of 3 to 4%. It appears that the spread will remain in this range for some time, may be in the lower end of the range.

From the year 2011, banks have shifted to base rate and because of this, a new trend may emerge in future.

**Table: Loan Interest Rates**

| Year | Bank deposit rate above 5 years | Lending Rates | | | | Interest spread based on maximum deposit rate and SBI advance rate |
|---|---|---|---|---|---|---|
| | | Key lending rates as prescribed by RBI (All commercial banks including SBI) | | | | |
| | | SBI advance rate | Ceiling rate general | Minimum rate general | Minimum rate selective credit control | |
| 1976-77 | 10.00 | 14.00 | 16.50 | 12.50 | 14.00-15.00 | 4.00 |
| 1977-78 | 9.00 | 13.00 | 15.00 | 12.50 | 14.00-15.00 | 4.00 |
| 1978-79 | 9.00 | 13.00 | 15.00 | 12.50 | 14.00-15.00 | 4.00 |
| 1979-80 | 10.00 | 16.50 | 18.00 | 12.50 | 15.50-18.00 | 6.50 |
| 1980-81 | 10.00 | 16.50 | 19.40-19.50 | 13.50 | 16.70-19.50 | 6.50 |
| 1981-82 | 10.00 | 16.50 | 19.50 | - | 17.50-19.50 | 6.50 |
| 1982-83 | 11.00 | 16.50 | 19.50 | - | 17.50-19.50 | 5.50 |
| 1983-84 | 11.00 | 16.50 | 18.00 | - | 16.50-18.00 | 5.50 |
| 1984-85 | 11.00 | 16.50 | 18.00 | - | 16.50-18.00 | 5.50 |
| 1985-86 | 11.00 | 16.50 | 17.50 | - | 16.50-17.50 | 5.50 |
| 1986-87 | 11.00 | 16.50 | 17.50 | - | 16.50-17.50 | 5.50 |
| 1987-88 | 10.00 | 16.50 | 16.50 | - | 16.50 | 6.50 |
| 1988-89 | 10.00 | 16.50 | - | 16.00 | 16.00 | 6.50 |
| 1989-90 | 10.00 | 16.50 | - | 16.00 | 16.00 | 6.50 |
| 1990-91 | 11.00 | 16.50 | - | 16.00 | 16.00 | 5.50 |
| 1991-92 | 13.00 | 16.50 | - | 19.00 | 19.00 | 3.50 |
| 1992-93 | 11.00 | 19.00 | - | 17.00 | 17.00 | 8.00 |
| 1993-94 | 10.00 | 19.00 | - | 14.00 | 15.00 | 9.00 |

*(Contd...)*

| 1994-95 | 11.00 | 15.00 | - | 15.00 | Free | 4.00 |
|---|---|---|---|---|---|---|
| 1995-96 | 13.00 | 16.50 | - | 16.50 | Free | 3.50 |
| 1996-97 | 12.50-13.00 | 14.50 | - | 14.50-15.00 | Free | 1.50 |
| 1997-98 | 11.50-12.00 | 14.00 | - | 14.00 | Free | 2.00 |
| 1998-99 | 10.50-11.50 | 12.00-14.00 | - | 12.00-13.00 | Free | 2.50 |
| 1999-00 | 10.00-10.50 | 12.00 | - | 12.00-12.50 | Free | 1.50 |
| 2000-01 | 9.50-10.00 | 11.50 | - | 11.00-12.00 | Free | 1.50 |
| 2001-02 | 8.00-8.50 | 11.50 | - | 11.00-12.00 | Free | 3.00 |
| 2002-03 | 5.50-6.25 | 10.75 | - | 10.75-11.50 | Free | 4.50 |
| 2003-04 | 5.25-5.50 | 10.25 | - | 10.25-11.00 | Free | 4.75 |
| 2004-05 | 5.75-6.25 | 10.25 | - | 10.25-10.75 | Free | 4.00 |
| 2005-06 | 6.25-7.00 | 10.25 | - | 10.25-10.75 | Free | 3.25 |
| 2006-07 | 7.75-9.00 | 12.25 | - | 12.25-12.50 | Free | 3.25 |
| 2007-08 | 7.50-9.00 | 12.25 | - | 12.25-12.75 | Free | 3.25 |
| 2008-09 | 7.75-8.50 | 12.25 | - | 11.50-12.50 | Free | 3.75 |
| 2009-10 | 6.50-7.50 | 11.75 | - | 11.00-12.00 | Free | 4.25 |
| 2010-11 | 7.75-9.50 | 8.25 | - | 8.25-9.50 | Free | |

*Source:* for data: RBI.

# Banks Today

# 9

In our country today banks are segregated to development banks, commercial banks and cooperative banks. Under commercial banks, there are foreign banks, private sector banks and public sector banks. Banks under public sector initially started as 100% govt owned but today most of them have only majority stake of govt and rest is held by the public.

Banks in India today are trying to become financial supermarkets. In this, they are following the developments in foreign countries. Reserve Bank of India has gradually paved the way for banks to become financial supermarkets.

Besides conventional banking business, banks in India are also allowed to handle various other financial services from time to time. Important other financial services provided by banks are given under.

After an amendment to banking regulation act, in 1984, Banks were allowed to undertake merchant banking activities, through subsidiaries. Many banks accordingly set up subsidiaries for undertaking merchant banking and securities market related activities, equipment leasing, hire purchase, mutual funds, housing finance, and venture capital. Diversification of banking activities helped the banks to widen their business activities and raise their profitability through the opportunity to gain non-interest income.

Banks were allowed for acting as underwriters and bankers to capital issues floated by corporates. Banks were also allowed to create special instruments called stock invest which facilitated customers to subscribe to capital issues without actually parting with funds thereby avoiding the wait for allotment or refund. However, this instrument lost its relevance subsequently as capital market had other options available. Now Application Supported by Blocked Amount (ASBA) facility has replaced this service since 2008.

ASBA provides an alternative mode of payment in issues whereby the application money remains in the investor's account till finalization of basis of allotment in the issue. ASBA process facilitates investors to apply through Self Certified Syndicate Banks (SCSBs), in which the investors have bank accounts. SCSBs are those banks, which satisfy the conditions laid by SEBI. SCSBs would accept the applications, verify the application, block the fund to the extent of bid payment amount, upload the details in the web based bidding system of NSE, unblock once basis of allotment is finalized and transfer the amount for allotted shares, to the issuer.

Banks were allowed to become depository participants for maintaining demat accounts under CDSL and NSDL, as the bank's customers are the investors in capital market also.

Banks are permitted to enter credit card and debit card business. Today many banks are into credit card business themselves either directly, or through alliances with other credit card issuers. After ATMs came on the scene, all banks are issuing Debit-cum-ATM cards.

Banks were allowed to enter into import of gold business and also market gold to retail customers. However only selling is allowed and trading i.e. buying back from retail customers is not allowed.

Government also authorized few banks to collect direct and indirect taxes. Online tax accounting system (OLTAS) scheme was introduced in banks since the year 2001 and gradually expanded to cover different tax payments to govt. This system of tax payment on online basis has gained popularity and govt has made it mandatory now for some sections of tax-payers. This facility is based on core banking platform of banks.

Bancassurance was allowed in the year 2002. Banks were allowed to forge alliance and enter into agreement for sale of insurance products of some existing insurer. This was allowed for both life and non-life insurance. Under the model, banks are only acting as selling agents using their reach and complementary nature of business as banks are getting their loan assets insured even otherwise.

Reserve Bank of India wanted the banks to remain and concentrate on basic functions and ancillary functions and not diversify and take risk, which may jeopardize the safety of banks. This is the reason why subsequently banks were allowed to form subsidiaries to undertake many financial services. Reserve Bank of India did not want the bank to combine risks of different activities in their books. Initially subsidiaries were wholly owned by banks and subsequently they were allowed to take strategic partners for each kind of new business. Thus, many banks formed strategic alliances for various activities like insurance, capital market operations and mutual funds, etc.

### Current Status of Banking in India

In a way, banking in India has travelled a full circle. Banks were nationalized in the year 1969 and 1980 with full ownership vesting with Government. Then as the economic reforms started in nineties, banks were allowed to dilute Government equity up to 50%. Private sector banks were again encouraged to come on the scene and grow. Foreign banks were also liberally allowed to expand operations in the country. There were talks of further dilution of Government equity in banks and allow them to go into private hands. Government even considered merger route to create bigger banks in the country to be of global size. This was not enforced as stiff opposition from left parties and trade unions were encountered. However, the thinking in Government circle was that nationalisation has outlived its purpose and it is time to privatise so that banks can grow and do not demand capital from Government, which will be a drain on exchequer. Government has other priorities for its resources than giving it to banks. It appeared that these changes, which Government wanted to bring in, are a foregone conclusion and it is just a matter of time for its implementation. India has a banking system partly private and partly public and both were competing and growing at great speed. Private sector being new entrant has higher growth rate. It appeared that the western model of private sector is the better option for economic progress.

Then suddenly out of blue, things happened in USA in 2008. On 15th September 2008 the world woke up to see the collapse of Lehmann Brothers Inc. staring at it ostentatiously through the front page of every newspaper. Few more banks were in crisis, which endangered the economy of the countries. The after effects were also felt in Europe and other developed countries as bankruptcies of few major banks loomed large before them. It is financial catastrophe and Governments of those countries had to bail out the banks by infusing funds to stop them from closing the shutters. The impact was felt by the whole world and many countries were badly affected. The countries who are not directly involved are also in trouble as their system was also following the leading nations. However, India showed a remarkable resilience and withstood the tremors without much damage. Recovery from global recession was faster in India's case. The financial structure of the country and its framework stood the test. Now, amazed developed countries started looking at financial structure of our country and hailed that the model in place in our country, is the best and capable of absorbing the shock.

This clearly demonstrates that there is no purpose in simply copying things from west or any country. It is better to observe first and adopt a model most suited for our own country. The model will have to take into consideration the present status of economy of our country, the changes expected and desired with the time-frame, and changes in the model that may be required to suit our condition. All nations cannot be fitted into one size and administered same dosage for reforms.

When we consider this experience, we shall appreciate the contributions of public sector banks. They brought in green revolution and industrial revolution. They have made Indian economy strong and vibrant. They are developing work culture of private sector and accountability of public sector. They have reached out to every nook and corner of the country. Banks have brought in all the necessary changes without causing much pain, in a seamless manner, and without dislocating anything. It is quite possible that the speed was not there. However, banks are part of the nation and cannot have different speed. Of late, the Government has taken up financial inclusion. Agriculture lending and social lending is still relevant and cannot be dispensed in the near future.

Just because macroeconomic indicators are good and comparable, does not mean that microeconomic situations at grass root level has also improved fully and do not require helping hand. Country is yet to achieve large percentage of people to cross poverty line. Government is yet to achieve low unemployment percentage of eligible workers. It is known that private sector banks are not interested in this. They will enter any field only if it is economically viable for them and rightly so. When all these facts are considered the question before us—is it right time to dismantle what has been created studiously over the years? Moreover, handholding of rural poor and other poor, small enterprises is still required.

Conclusion is that the time is not right to undo any of social control on banks that means banks should remain in public sector for some more time so that Government can implement its policies for the benefit of poor. Other point is that the present model has withstood economic tremors and proved best. Then why change to something, which has failed in the west.

Banking today is so important that whether the banks are in private or public Government cannot afford to keep off and during crisis, they will have to pump in tax-payer's money to save the economy from crisis. When the modern economy has manifested itself in this fashion and made Governments an unwilling but a partner in crisis to take the brunt, then there shall be no harm in Government retaining some ownership and control on the management.

Then there is a new challenge in the form of financial inclusion. With all the developments in banking sector it is understood that only a small percentage (about 40%) of population is using banking services. Large percentage of people particularly in rural, and people unorganized in urban sector, are not using banking services. In the present day environment, with developments in communication sector, it is imperative to include each citizen so that benefits of various Government schemes and welfare measures can reach them directly. Electronic fund transfer system in place does not need any intermediaries either in public sector or private sector to reach the citizen. He can be directly plugged into the system and the funds meant for him can travel seamlessly without anybody interfering and siphoning off the money. Banking account is a must for its citizens in an advanced and welfare state. As things are changing for better, it is stupendous task to bring in everyone in the country into banking system. In next few years, banks shall have to achieve this and be instrumental for flow of prosperity to every doorstep in the country.

# Are Banks Safe

10

Are banks safe for its customers? In Indian context, it is true and the credit goes to RBI and Government. Banks are vital to the economy as they collect deposits from public and put them into productive use by giving loans. This function of banks has the multiplier effect on the economy. It is said that banks create money. Banks accepts deposits and it is accepted both in running accounts and deposit accounts. The balance in the running accounts are payable on demand without notice. By convention, banks have also maintained the liquidity for term deposits. Though as per agreement money cannot be demanded before due date, in practice banks have honored all demands for premature payments. This, banks have maintained to earn the confidence of depositors and to attract them to place deposits with bank even at lesser rate of interest compared to others who accepts term deposits at higher rates. Banks have succeeded in this and today even term deposits are paid prematurely on demand without notice. However, there is a small penalty, which is adjusted in the interest payable. Generally, one per cent penalty is imposed. Recently to help small depositors most of the banks have waived the penalty for small term deposits may be up to ₹ 5-10 lakhs. This is a customer centric approach of banks. Hence, liquidity is maintained for the depositors.

Bank lends a portion of its resources to borrowers after keeping away a percentage of deposits as CRR and SLR as prescribed by RBI. Borrowers can draw the loan amount immediately. Money gets into circulation again and borrowers also have liquidity. Thus, both depositors and borrowers are provided liquidity based on deposits alone. The liquidity created is more than the original deposit amount. Hence, it is said that banks create money.

This cycle of deposit and loan goes on as the borrower who has borrowed, deposits the loan proceeds with his bank for whom it becomes fresh deposit. This bank also then lends on the strength of the deposit. This is how the multiplier effect of the money is created by banks. In fact, RBI treats bank deposits as part of money supply along with cash lying with the public.

This multiplier function of banks continues in a developing economy and public confidence and banks image adds to the liquidity and the sentiments. Sentiments of confidence and assurance are very much required for banks to survive. The public confidence is tested on daily basis by customers in their daily dealings with the banks and they continue to feel safe with the bank as the commitments are always met by banks. However, once this sentiment of security is shaken for any reason then the result can be catastrophic for both banks and customers. When this confidence is shaken?

In the present day context, RBI acts as controller of banks and ensures that all banks follow guidelines in dealing with money. It prescribes CRR and SLR for the purpose of security in case of need. It also created few refinance windows for banks so that any emergency fund requirement can be met. It also supervises the banks' functions, particularly the asset quality to ensure that banks are liquid and asset quality is good to meet the liabilities.

Despite all this, rumours of bank getting into problem with bad loans or facing a huge loss may cause trouble for banks. Once the rumour spreads, it feeds on itself and appears as if it is authentic news. Suddenly some people may want to play safe and rush to bank to withdraw. If their demand is met immediately then the rumour may die down. If it is not met even for technical reason and delay occurs then it becomes news and damages the reputation of the bank. If the rumour makes many people to act simultaneously then there can be a run on bank. Once this news spreads, the remaining customers may also come rushing to withdraw thereby creating a crisis.

It must be understood that the liquidity of banks are managed on scientific basis, based on study, experience and past trend. Bank cannot keep all deposits as cash balance. Only a percentage is kept as cash balance and a percentage is kept in approved securities, which are near cash. Remaining is in assets of varying maturities. In normal course bank has enough liquidity to meet the demand of its customers, it also has enough fall back reserve to meet seasonal or some unexpected demands. However, once the crisis develops and everyone wants to withdraw then the bank cannot meet it.

In the past three to four decades, RBI has ensured that no major banks are closed. When few banks were in trouble, RBI merged them with stronger banks and protected the depositors. Though RBI is not legally bound to protect, in the larger interest of the economy and system it has done that. There were very few instances of small banks failing and depositors lost their money. In such cases, the DICGC had paid claims up to one lakh per account. Such instances were very few.

Whenever any bank is in problem RBI may put the bank under moratorium, means normal banking operations are suspended. Depositors are not allowed to come and withdraw. However, small payments are sometimes allowed to help depositors for their livelihood. Then RBI looks for a bank that can take over the failed bank and oversees the merger terms. Depositor's interest is protected fully and the bank is merged. Only when the status of the failed bank is irretrievable then merger may not work out and the bank may be allowed to close down.

However, there is no guarantee available to bank customers from either RBI or Government of India. In case of a bank failure, depositors of the bank are not protected. Banks can fail and depositors may lose their money. GOI created Deposit Insurance Corporation in the year 1962 which guarantees the depositors up to a limit (presently ₹ one lakh), in case of bank failures. Banks are obliged to take this insurance cover and also bear the insurance cost. This corporation was merged to form the present day DICGC in the year 1978. DICGC has so far paid claims in some 33 cases of bank failures mostly of smaller banks.

However, in case of public sector banks the situation may be different. GOI being the owner, may have to accept moral responsibility and it may be difficult for GOI to disown liability in case of bank failure in public sector. The status of public sector banks are so visualized by the public and public confidence is very high for PS banks. With GOI now becoming a majority shareholder, the equation may change little bit. However, until such time the GOI has control on PS banks and appoints CEOs for such banks, this perception of moral responsibility will continue.

### Maintaining Liquidity

How banks maintain liquidity? RBI under Banking Regulation Act has power to fix and vary CRR and SLR for banks. CRR is cash balance and balance with RBI and notified banks. SLR is approved Government securities that carry sovereign guarantee. CRR can be as high as 15% and SLR can be 40%. However, at present it is 6% and 24%. Hence, these much funds are impounded and act as security support to banks. Prudent banks always maintain little higher investments to take care of daily variations. Remaining funds can be lent by banks. At present credit deposit ratio of 70% is considered ideal. Now it is important how bank maintains its loan portfolio. It must be a mix of diversified portfolio of short-and long-term loans. Banks are advised to achieve 40% for priority sector with sub-target for agriculture at 18%. Banks are also advised to give export finance. Remaining loans can be for all other sectors including infrastructure, industry, trade, service sector and retail credit.

Refinance is also available on export credits and credits to agriculture from EXIM bank and NABARD. These refinance windows help the bank to have liquidity support and also to improve CD ratio.

Amongst its many functions, Reserve Bank of India also acts as the banker of last resort. RBI helps the banks to tide over temporary liquidity crunch by providing refinance. Since the year 2000, this is being done under Liquidity Adjustment Facility (LAF). RBI uses this as a monetary tool to suck excess liquidity in the system through repo auctions and injects liquidity to the system through reverse repo auctions. Along with bank rate, which is the rate at which RBI lends to banks, RBI also, decides repo and reverse repo rates. These rates by RBI acts as signal rates, which will affect all other money market rates.

Banks can avail refinance from RBI under the above LAF scheme in case of liquidity problem faced by them. These borrowings from RBI are backed by gilt securities.

Banks can also access Collateralised Borrowing and Lending Obligation (CBLO), an RBI approved money market instrument developed by Clearing Corporation of India Ltd. introduced in the year 2003, to help banks for borrowing and lending. This is also fully secured against collaterals. These instruments are generally for period of 7 days to three months. Banks can use this facility and the surplus govt securities held by them over and above SLR can be used for this purpose.

Banks have access to interbank market for short-term borrowing and certificate of deposit (COD) market for deposits up to one year. COD was started in the year 1989 and has become popular with banks for raising funds.

Certificate of deposits (COD) are negotiable term deposits issued by banks for fixed period at an agreed rate of interest. Certificates are issued for round amounts and only discounted value of certificates (discounted for interest accrual) is deposited with the issuing bank. As the certificate is negotiable, the payee therein can transfer the same to anyone any time during its currency to raise funds. The issuing bank will make the payment only on due date. Stamp duty as prescribed is payable on CODs.

Banks generally have some short-term loan portfolio of self-liquidating debts like bills and packing credit advances. These are short-term loans to be realized within few months. Banks sanction working capital loans on annual review basis and on paper, these loans are for one year. However, in practice these loans are renewed and remain as long-term in the books. Banks also sanction term loans with definite repayment of instalments. Pay back of instalments every month / quarter from these term loans improves the liquidity of banks. These term loans may be for short period like 3 years or long-term like 10-15-20 years. Generally, home loans and loans to infrastructure belong to long-term category.

Keeping in mind the importance of liquidity management for banks, RBI issued guidelines for Asset Liability Management (ALM) in 1998 and made it effective from the year 1999. Banks were advised to form Asset Liability Committee (ALCO) to oversee the Asset Liability Management. This means banks shall know the maturity pattern of both deposits and loans and see that as far as possible it must match, ensuring that bank can meet liability as it accrues from the matching inflow from asset held by it. Bank shall keep an eye on mismatches in the time buckets and see that the mismatches are within the tolerable limits prescribed by the board of the bank.

### Some Observations

Of late, it is observed that banks are leaning more on term loans in their portfolio of loans, which create asset liability, mismatch. This needs correction. It is also observed that banks are sanctioning loans to housing and infrastructure for 15 to 20 years whereas they have no matching liability on their books. Bank deposits are for a maximum period of 10 years only. It is also observed that banks are not encouraging long-term deposits of 5 to 10 years thinking that it increases cost and in fact, many banks have made such deposits unattractive by offering less rates than for short-term deposits. This may not be correct from asset-liability mismatch point of view.

However, banks can be considered safe in our country for a variety of reasons. They are:

1. Government ownership of many major banks.
2. RBI's proactive supervision over banks and guidance to them for practising the best standards.

3. RBI's moral stance to see that banks do not fail and depositors do not lose.
4. Creation of insurance scheme by DICGC.
5. Professional management by the banks' Boards and better compliance of standards.
6. Better asset-liability management, adequate capitalization, and better asset quality with provision coverage for bad loans.

# How Banks are Rated

# 11

How banks are rated today? Financial sector rates the bank based on its performance. Internationally banks are not recognized or rated by its ownership. Public sector has no separate status. Banks are rated based on their financial strength. Size of the bank is also not important. The strength means strong financial parameters. State ownership of banks is not common in developed economies. Most of the international banks are in private sector and are giants with their presence in all parts of the world. These are mostly Japanese banks, European banks and American banks. Even State Bank of India is a pigmy before these banks. Today a bank can get good rating by the rating agencies and the investors based broadly on following points:

1. Compliance with Basel accord for capital and risk management measures
2. Low NPA and good provision coverage ratio for NPA
3. Good NIM, better than industry average
4. Good CD ratio and exposure norms
5. Compliance to KYC/AML/CFT measures
6. Compliance of IFRS for accounting and reporting
7. Better ALM
8. Corporate governance and disclosures
9. Succession planning.

Compliance of Basel accord on capital requirement is the benchmark for any bank internationally. Basel II has prescribed minimum CRAR of 8% and it is for the Regulator of each country to fix the minimum capital requirement. Type of capital i.e. tier I or tier II or tier III are also important. Risk management policies of the bank are very important as the assessment of capital requirement is based on it. Banks shall have a sound system of risk management, which shall include risk identification, assessment, and monitoring and mitigation process.

Non-performing asset of the bank is a critical issue and bank with minimum NPA is rated the best. Besides, adequate provision coverage for bad loans is important factor to judge the strength of the bank. Ideal situation is zero net NPA but it is difficult to achieve.

Investors are very particular about the net interest margins of the bank. It is critical parameter to judge the performance of a bank. Net interest margin is the difference between the average cost of deposit and average yield on advances. Three per cent and above is considered very good. The good rated bank shall have better NIM than the industry average.

CD ratio and profile of loan portfolio is looked into. In Indian case, CD ratio of about 70% at present is considered desirable. Well-diversified loan portfolio is desirable from investor's point of view. Excessive exposure to any sector is frowned upon.

KYC has become a major issue with banks. The level of KYC compliance by banks and the measures taken against money laundering and terrorist financing is the first thing any international bank will look into before entering into any financial relationship with foreign banks. Compliance level in the bank and the country itself is checked, these days before entering into any dealings.

Accounting standards followed is critical today. IFRS has been accepted in most of the countries and unless a bank follows international standards for reporting its financial statements, the rating of the bank will suffer.

Liquidity and asset-liability management system of the bank is critical. The measures taken by the bank for its management are very important for the rating of a bank. Banks shall have a system in place to measure duration gap and interest rate sensitivity and project various future scenarios for taking management decisions.

Management functions at bank shall be capable of assessing the implementation of various policy decisions and monitoring the progress and giving directions. The management practices in this are an important issue, which reflect effectiveness of the corporate governance. Disclosure standards of the bank are very important from invertor's point of view. Though most of the disclosures are under statutory obligations, invertors watch the forthrightness of the disclosures.

Succession plan of the bank is very critical for the bank to continue and grow. It is the duty of present management to ensure that the succession is not an issue and shall be smooth with able personnel available at all levels to carry the bank forward. Grooming and training policies of the banks are looked into.

Ratings of any bank today shall be based on all these parameters.

# Bank Deposit Interest Rate

12

How the interest rates are fixed? Most markets follow a reference or benchmark rate, which is a risk neutral rate. Government security rates are ideal for the reference rate. An increase in the real interest rate in the government security market is a signal to other segments of financial market, and generally, other segments like bank deposit, debenture market and other financial companies change their rates in tandem.

Other important interest rates are the interest rates offered by govt for PPF, National Savings Certificates and interest offered by post office on term deposits. These are important rates as these deposits are also backed by govt Guarantee. However, these are administered rates by the govt. These rates do not change automatically with the market. Govt makes periodical corrections in these rates depending on govt bond rates.

Bank term deposits are considered safe and offer liquidity. In our country, RBI decided bank deposit interest rates till 1996. Deposit interest rate is freed from the year 1997 and banks now decide the rate of interest.

Hence, we have three important rates—one the interest rate on govt securities decided by govt for different maturities like treasury bills for short period and bonds for the long period. This is generally market driven. Secondly, the interest rates on deposits like PPF, NSC and post office term deposits. Lastly, the bank deposit rates for different maturities, which are also considered as, risk free investment. Then there are interest rates for company deposits, debentures, interest rates offered by NBFCs, etc. All these are considered to carry risk depending on the standings of the companies and generally carry interest more than bank deposit rates. The maxim is higher the risk, higher the interest. Risky investments shall earn more interest than the secured investments.

Interest is essentially the price people pay to have resources now rather than later and interest is conventionally expressed as a percentage for one year. The interest rate expressed is nominal interest rate, since it is without a correction for the effects of inflation. Inflation in the economy has the effect of reducing the notional interest as the purchasing power of the money comes down. Actual interest earning will be less than what is the nominal interest rate mentioned. To find out the actual interest earned the notional interest has to be adjusted by deducting the percentage impact of inflation. This adjusted interest is called the real rate of interest. Inflation is calculated based on wholesale price index (WPI).

The interest rates, rather the real interest rates are very important in an economy and the monetary authority (RBI) favours a positive real interest rate as a positive real interest rate provides incentive for savings and allocates investment more efficiently. This has been the main driving force behind the motivation of financial liberalisation in many economies.

As for the limit for real interest rates, RBI feels that the sustainability of the real interest rate is critical. Ideally, the expected real interest rate in the economy should reflect the potential rate of return on the capital stock. If an economy is operating on the maximum attainable efficiency, the rate of return on capital or the growth rate of real GDP should provide an indicator of the real interest rate in the economy. In the case of advanced economies, which are more or less operating on the best attainable efficiency level, the real growth rate sets the limit for the real interest rate in the economy. It is interesting, therefore, to observe that the typical real interest rate on government paper in some of the advanced economies vary from 3 to 4 per cent, which is close to their growth rate of GDP. In the case of developing economies, the typical real interest rates are higher than those of the developed economies, which is perhaps explained by the higher rates of growth in these economies.

(Excerpts from the Address at (FIMMDA) by Dr. Y.V. Reddy, Deputy Governor, Reserve Bank of India, on June 3, 1998 at Mumbai on—*Interest Rates in India: Status and Issues*)

This means two factors are important for determining the interest rates. First is the inflation rate to arrive at the real interest rate. Second is the real GDP growth rate or expected real GDP growth rate to determine the maximum real interest rate for benchmark interest rate i.e. govt security rates. Once the benchmark rate is fixed it will be taken as signal for other interest rates including bank deposit rates to move.

Though in theory and to maximum extent interest rates are determined by inflation rate and the real GDP growth rate there are many other factors that also affect the rates. They are liquidity position—which alters supply and demand for funds, competition, lending rates, cost of intermediation, etc. However, positive real interest rates are necessary to encourage savings and capital formation, which is crucial for development.

Bank interest rate on deposit is an important benchmark rate in the economy. It is because bank deposits are considered risk free investment and all other interest rates on other form of investment like company deposits, bonds, etc. will be marked higher depending on risk perception attached to it. Even bank lending rate is also decided by deposit interest rate, as it is the cost of funds for the bank. Whether short-term deposit rate and long-term deposit rate should have, any relationship is debatable. Historically, RBI fixed bank deposit rates earlier, progressively from short-term to long-term deposit. Even after the rate was freed, banks followed the same pattern. Today due to competition, rates tend to vary very little from bank to bank. It is also observed that sometimes the short-term deposit rate is higher than the long-term deposit rate, which is a distortion.

Bank interest rates have great importance for investors like senior citizens and customers who are risk averse. They do not want to venture into other form of investments for various reasons. Capital market is not for them due to high volatility and bull-bear phases of its market. Mutual funds though considered safe, is not widely known and understood. Government schemes like post office deposits make the deposit illiquid. Therefore, a large population of the country depends on bank deposit rate to give them reasonable return. Some even depend on it for livelihood and if the rates are low, they will have to eat away their capital over a period.

## Study of Historical Interest Rates

Important interest rates in our economy, which have bearing on each other, are given in the following table. All Rates can be compared from year 1991 to 2010. The table also gives bank deposit rates and bank rate from 1977 to 1990 and govt bond rates and bank rate from 1981 to 1990.

| Year | Interest rates on | | | | | Bank rate/ Repo rate from 2006 |
|---|---|---|---|---|---|---|
| | Bank term deposits Maximum/ range | Central Govt securities range | Post office term deposit | National Savings Certificate | PPF | |
| Early 1970s | 6.5- 7 | | | | | 6 |
| Mid 1970s | 9 | | | | | 7 -9 |
| 1977 | 10.00 | | | | | 9 |
| 1978 | 9.00 | | | | | 9 |
| 1979 | 9.00 | | | | | 9 |
| 1980 | 10.00 | | | | | 9 |
| 1981 | 10.00 | 5.98 -7.50 | | | | 9 |
| 1982 | 10.00 | 6.00 -8.00 | | | | 10 |
| 1983 | 11.00 | 6.25- 9.00 | | | | 10 |
| 1984 | 11.00 | 7.75 -10.00 | | | | 10 |
| 1985 | 11.00 | 7.75 -10.50 | | | | 10 |
| 1986 | 11.00 | 9.00 -11.50 | | | | 10 |
| 1987 | 11.00 | 10.00 -11.50 | | | | 10 |
| 1988 | 10.00 | 10.50 -11.50 | | | | 10 |
| 1989 | 10.00 | 10.00 -11.50 | | | | 10 |
| 1990 | 10.00 | 10.50 -11.50 | | | | 10 |
| Mar-91 | 9.00 -11.00 | 10.50 -11.50 | 12.00 -13.50 | | 12 | 10.0 |
| Mar-92 | 12.00 -13.00 | 10.50 -12.50 | 12.00 -13.50 | | 12 | 12.0 |
| Mar-93 | 11.00 -11.00 | 12.00 -12.75 | 12.00 -13.50 | 12 | 12 | 12.0 |

*(Contd...)*

| | | | | | | |
|---|---|---|---|---|---|---|
| Mar-94 | 10.00 -10.00 | 12.00 -13.40 | 10.50 -12.50 | 12 | 12 | 12.0 |
| Mar-95 | 11.00 -11.00 | 11.00 -12.71 | 10.50- 12.50 | 12 | 12 | 12.0 |
| Mar-96 | 12.00 -13.00 | 13.25 -14.00 | 10.50 -12.50 | 12 | 12 | 12.0 |
| Mar-97 | 11.00 -13.00 | 13.40 -13.85 | 10.50 -12.50 | 12 | 12 | 12.0 |
| Mar-98 | 10.50 -12.00 | 10.85 -13.05 | 10.50 -12.50 | 12 | 12 | 10.5 |
| Mar-99 | 9.00 -11.50 | 11.10 -12.60 | 9.00 -11.50 | 11.50 | 12 | 8.0 |
| Mar-00 | 8.50 -10.50 | 10.73 -12.45 | 8.00 -10.50 | 11 | 11 | 8.0 |
| Mar-01 | 8.50 -10.00 | 9.47 -11.70 | 7.50 -9.00 | 9.50 | 9 | 7.0 |
| Mar-02 | 7.50 -8.50 | 6.98 -11.00 | 7.25 -8.50 | 9 | 9 | 6.5 |
| Mar-03 | 4.30 -6.30 | 6.57 -8.62 | 6.25 -7.50 | 8 | 8 | 6.25 |
| Mar-04 | 4.00 -5.50 | 4.62 -6.35 | 6.25 -7.50 | 8 | 8 | 6 |
| Mar-05 | 5.30 -6.30 | 4.49 -8.24 | 6.25 -7.50 | 8 | 8 | 6 |
| Mar-06 | 6.00 -7.00 | 6.70 -7.79 | 6.25 -7.50 | 8 | 8 | 6.50 |
| Mar-07 | 7.50 -9.00 | 7.69 -8.75 | 6.25 -7.50 | 8 | 8 | 7.75 |
| Mar-08 | 7.50 -9.00 | 7.55 -8.64 | 6.25 -7.50 | 8 | 8 | 6.0 |
| Mar-09 | 7.80 -8.80 | 5.44 -10.03 | 6.25 -7.50 | 8 | 8 | 5.0 |
| Mar-10 | 6.00 -7.50 | 6.09 -8.43 | 6.25 -7.50 | 8 | 8 | 5.0 |

*Source*: RBI.

While comparing the rates we will have to keep in mind that bank deposits have a maximum tenure of 10 years whereas govt securities are for 15-20 years period. PPF is also for over 15 years. NSCs are for maximum 5-6 years. The trend reveals that bank deposits are priced at lower than the govt security rates. However, the spread is narrowing. The rates for other govt Deposit schemes are administered and generally get fixed after the govt security and bank deposit rates are fixed and generally with a time lag.

Another important comparison is between bank rate fixed by RBI and bank deposit rates. They are closely related within one per cent range except after 2007 when the difference has increased. This means that banks are definitely following the bank rate while fixing their deposit rates. Bank rate is a lending rate but as banks can borrow from RBI at that rate, from banks point view, it becomes an important indicator for fixing deposit rates.

## Study of Deposit Rate in Relation to Inflation Rate

The Table on next page shows bank deposit rates and inflation rates based on WPI and CPI from period 1977 to 2010. Real GDP growth rates from 1981 to 2010 are also shown.

Inflation rate is worked out based on WPI. Inflation rate based on CPI is shown for comparison purpose, as there is a demand that the inflation rate based on CPI is more relevant. It can be seen that inflation rate based on CPI is generally higher than WPI.

Bank interest is seen moving in tandem with inflation rate. Maximum deposit rates were 9% in 1978 and 1979 when inflation was comparatively low. Inflation increased from the year 1980 to double digit. Deposit interest increased to 10% and then to 11%. It remained high till 1987. It came down by one percentage for next three years. Deposit interest again went up to 11% from 1991 and to 13% in 1992 as inflation rate had crossed 10% in 1991 and over 13.7% in 1992. Deposit interest remained high up to 13% till the year 1997 as inflation rate was in double digit in the years between 1991 and 1995. Inflation started coming down from 1997 and till 2005 it remained low at average of 5%. As inflation was low, deposit rates started coming down in 1998 to 12% and to 10% in 2001 and further to 8.5% in 2002. Deposit rates further came down to a low of 5.5% in 2004. The period of year 2003 to 2005 was the period when the interest rates were the lowest. Deposit interest increased in 2007 and 2008 to 9% and again came down in 2009 and 2010 to 7.5%. Largely bank deposit rate is moving in line with changes in inflation.

The year 1991-92 was the crisis year for the economy when inflation was at over 13% and GDP growth was just 1.4%. This was the year when the country faced balance of payment crisis.

| Year | Bank term deposit interest rates % | Wholesale price index (WPI) inflation rate % | Consumer price index(CPI) inflation rate % | Real GDP growth % |
|---|---|---|---|---|
| 1977 | 10.00 | 2.1 (base 1970-71) | -3.8 (base 1959-60) | |
| 1978 | 9.00 | 5.2 | 7.6 | |
| 1979 | 9.00 | 0 | 2.2 | |
| 1980 | 10.00 | 17.1 | 8.8 | |
| 1981 | 10.00 | 18.2 | 11.4 | Average 5.6 |
| 1982 | 10.00 | 9.3 | 12.5 | |
| 1983 | 11.00 | 4.9 (base 1981-82) | 7.8 | |

*(Contd...)*

| 1984 | 11.00 | 7.5 | 12.6 | |
|---|---|---|---|---|
| 1985 | 11.00 | 6.5 | 6.3 (base 1984-85) | |
| 1986 | 11.00 | 4.4 | 6.8 | |
| 1987 | 11.00 | 5.8 | 8.7 | |
| 1988 | 10.00 | 8.1 | 8.8 | |
| 1989 | 10.00 | 7.5 | 9.4 | |
| 1990 | 10.00 | 7.5 | 6.1 | |
| Mar-91 | 9.00 -11.00 | 10.3 | 11.6 | |
| Mar-92 | 12.00 -13.00 | 13.7 | 13.5 | 1.4 |
| Mar-93 | 11.00 -11.00 | 10.1 | 9.6 | Average 7.6 |
| Mar-94 | 10.00 -10.00 | 8.4 | 7.5 | |
| Mar-95 | 11.00 -11.00 | 12.6 (base 1993-94) | 10.1 | |
| Mar-96 | 12.00 -13.00 | 8 | 10.2 | |
| Mar-97 | 11.00 -13.00 | 4.6 | 9.4 (base 1986-87) | |
| Mar-98 | 10.50 -12.00 | 4.4 | 6.8 | 4.8 |
| Mar-99 | 9.00 -11.50 | 5.9 | 13.1 | 6.5 |
| Mar-00 | 8.50 -10.50 | 3.3 | 3.4 | 6.1 |
| Mar-01 | 8.50 -10.00 | 7.2 | 3.8 | 4.4 |
| Mar-02 | 7.50 -8.50 | 3.6 | 4.3 | 5.8 |
| Mar-03 | 4.30 -6.30 | 3.4 | 4 | 3.8 |
| Mar-04 | 4.00 -5.50 | 5.5 | 3.9 | 8.5 |
| Mar-05 | 5.30 -6.30 | 6.5 | 3.8 | 7.5 |
| Mar-06 | 6.00 -7.00 | 4.4 | 4.4 | 9.4 |
| Mar-07 | 7.50 -9.00 | 6.6 | 6.7 | 9.6 |
| Mar-08 | 7.50 -9.00 | 4.7 | 6.2 | 9.0 |
| Mar-09 | 7.80 -8.80 | 8.1 | 9.1 | 6.7 |
| Mar-10 | 6.00 -7.50 | 3.8 | 12.4 | 7.4 |

*Source*: RBI.

However, bank interest rates appear low from 2002 onwards till 2010. Between periods 2002 - 2005, average inflation has been 4.7% and average GDP growth was 6.4%. Interest rates of banks have come down drastically to 6.3% and 5.5%, which in comparison is very low.

Similarly, from period 2006 to 2010, average inflation was 5.5% and average GDP growth was high at 8.5%. However, bank interest was maximum 9%, which came down to 7.5% in 2010. During this period also, bank interest rates seem to have been lower.

# Banker Customer Relationship

# 13

Banker customer relationship is a special relationship. It is a relationship between creditor and debtor and much more. By tradition, confidentiality of the relationship was established and is accepted by the law. Though law accepted the practice, there was no written provision in any of the earlier laws about the secrecy clause. The secrecy clause about customer information is reiterated for the first time in the banking companies' acquisition and transfer of undertaking act 1970.

Sec. 13 of Banking Companies' Acquisition and Transfer of Undertaking Act 1970:

(1) Every corresponding new bank shall observe, except as otherwise required by law, the practices and usages customary among bankers, and, in particular, it shall not divulge any information relating to or to the affairs of its constituents except in circumstances in which it is, in accordance with law or practices and usages customary among bankers, necessary or appropriate for the corresponding new bank to divulge such information.

Under this clause, bank is supposed to maintain confidentiality of dealings of the customer. This bank cannot break, as it is the cornerstone of the relationship. In some countries, the secrecy is almost absolute like in Switzerland and others. In our own country, law recognizes the confidentiality and bank is obliged to follow it except as per practices, in very few instances as under:

1. When it is in public interest to disclose the affairs.
2. To safeguard bank's own interest.
3. When bank is compelled by the law under due process to disclose.
4. When the customer authorises the bank to do so.

In practice, banks maintain secrecy and do not break it. Banks divulge information only on compulsion by law or when the customer authorises it. Banks hardly invoke the first two provisions, as they are fraught with risk and may lead to litigation with customers. There could be a few exceptions.

Bank customers are deposit account holders in which case the bank becomes debtor and the customer is creditor. In case of borrowers, bank is the creditor and the customer is the debtor.

RBI has issued KYC guidelines in the year 2004 and these guidelines provides as under:

For the purpose of KYC policy, a 'Customer' may be defined as:

- "a person or entity that maintains an account and/or has a business relationship with the bank;
- one on whose behalf the account is maintained (i.e. the beneficial owner);
- beneficiaries of transactions conducted by professional intermediaries, such as Stock Brokers, Chartered Accountants, Solicitors, etc. as permitted under the law;
- and any person or entity connected with a financial transaction which can pose significant reputational or other risks to the bank, say, a wire transfer or issue of a high value demand draft as a single transaction."

Hence, besides deposit account holders and borrowers, there are other category of customers now identified by the KYC policy as bank customers. They are beneficial owners on whose behalf accounts are maintained, beneficiaries of transactions conducted by professional intermediaries and persons who may use bank's services particularly remittance facilities or any other financial services. All these people are treated as bank customers even if they do not maintain any accounts with the bank.

While Indian laws permit disclosure of customer account details as provided in the specific acts on certain grounds, at the same time invoking this right by the Law or Law Enforcing Agencies is made very stringent. Law cannot make general inquiry into customer's affairs and bank cannot give it. Law has to compel the bank under requisite provisions of any Act of the Government wherein specific authority has been defined and names of the officials empowered to make such demand is given. Only judiciary has full authority. Others will have to issue summons to the bank under relevant section of specific Act they are empowered to do so and quote their authority under the Act. Police however during investigation of any crime will have authority to call for information on parties connected and banks shall provide the same. Hence, the position is that only when the bank is served with summons to produce, the bank shall divulge information on customers. This means bank can divulge information only under duress and the threat of disobeying has penal consequences.

Various Government authorities like Income Tax dept., Excise, Sales Tax, Enforcement Directorate, and Customs under the respective acts governing them have provisions for calling customer information. At one time, it is accepted that except judiciary and police others will have no authority to make general kind of enquiry from banks. They will have to be specific about the customer and his accounts, which are subject matter of some proceedings before the said authorities.

However, the provisions for disclosure by banks came for test when income tax dept. started making general type of enquiries and initially counsels advised banks that they need not reply to such queries. Then Government had to take more holistic view of the issues involved. Under tax laws, income tax dept. has to check transactions to ensure that there is no evasion of tax. They cannot do this unless they get the information from banks. There are requirements under tax laws for such verification even before any formal proceedings have been started against any individual. There are provisions in income tax that deposits over ₹ 20000/- cannot be repaid in cash and shall be credited to accounts only. Demand drafts for over ₹ 50000, if issued against cash then full details shall be maintained by banks. Banks are also obliged to call for PAN details and keep record of it. Looking into all these provisions of law, it is now accepted that income tax dept. can make transaction specific enquiries from banks and banks are bound to provide the same so that the authorities can check and supervise the compliance of rules under income tax act. Therefore, we can say that in today's context, confidence of customer account though maintained is subject to demands by Government under economic laws of the country.

Government passed an Act called PMLA—(Prevention of Money Laundering Act) in the year 2002 in line with international best practices and passed another law for combating finance to terrorist activities. RBI also issued guidelines on *Know Your Customer*. Government has set up an authority to oversee and coordinate financial information and the authority is called Financial Intelligence Unit of India (FIU-IND). Under the PML act, banks are duty bound to submit Cash Transaction Reports, Suspicious Transactions Reports, and Counterfeit Currency Reports to FIU-IND. These disclosures are confidential, customers need not know about it, and in fact, banks are barred from informing to customers on such reporting. These guidelines are in line with international best practices to fight money laundering and terrorist financing, as they are threats to the sovereignty of the nations.

Traditionally bank is accepting new customer based on identification by itself or based on an introduction provided by an existing customer of the bank. Once an account is opened on this basis, it is deemed that the bank has taken due care in opening the account. The concept of 'properly introduced account' is in vogue, and the law recognizes it. Banks are getting protection and indemnity for financial transactions they put through in these accounts. It was realized that many launder their ill gotten or tax evaded money by misusing this liberal system and lately even to finance terrorism in the country. This could happen because banks were depending on one introduction and were not duty bound to make any inquiry into the real purpose of the account and transactions happening in it. The identity can be bogus and can be manipulated. Banks do not even have correct addresses of parties, as the addresses provided are also bogus. There was no check on this. At the same time, it was argued that banks could not do this job, as logistics involved is costly and prohibitive.

Computers and telecommunication have been a lethal combination and internet has changed the entire gamut of communication and fund transfer. It is so quick, like lightening, and nobody can do anything to stop it. Governments and others are grappling with the problem as to how to trace the origin of either funds or information as the entire globe is interconnected. While these things are making life easier for people it also protects and hides the criminals as they are camouflaged for their nefarious activities. Hence, changes in legal provisions and the practices were necessary to make it possible for law enforcing agencies to catch up with the culprits.

On this background lot of studies were made and it was decided that some changes are required while a bank opens an account for anyone. It was decided that the identification of the customer is necessary and it cannot be left to chance or mere declaration and/or introduction. This is now applicable in case of some other services providers also like telephones and mobiles.

Under KYC rules, now banks are responsible for correct identification of their customers. They must know the places of residence and the activities they are engaged. Banks have no unrestricted license to carry on financial transactions without being accountable. Banks are expected to know their customers, their financial dealings, and their worth. It is now incumbent on banks to understand the purpose behind the transactions they are putting through for their customers and be observant about it. In case they find that, the transactions cannot be explained or understood, or apparently there is no underlying economic purpose, then they are now duty bound to inform the details of these transactions to FIU-IND. As discussed earlier, banks are responsible for any wrong collection of instruments in the account without carrying out due diligence into the affairs of their customers.

Hence, today the relationship between bank and customer is seen in new perspective where bank is expected to know its customers and their dealings. The shelter that was available to banks under the 'properly introduced account' concept no longer holds good. The role and responsibility of bank in the relationship between customer and bank has been enhanced. It is a special type of relationship and confidentiality shall be maintained as per the practices and law subject to provisions of the law for disclosure.

# Cheques

14

A cheque is a document/instrument (usually a piece of paper) that orders payment of money from a bank account. The person writing the cheque, the drawer, usually has a current account or savings account where the money is previously deposited. The drawer writes the various details including the amount, date, and the name of a payee on the cheque and signs it, ordering his bank, known as the drawee, to pay to the named person or company the amount of money stated.

The ancient Romans are believed to have used an early form of cheque known as 'praescriptiones' in the 1st century BC.

In India, during the Mauryan period (from 321 to 185 BC), a commercial instrument called 'adesha' was in use, which was an order on a banker desiring him to pay the money of the note to a third person, which corresponds to the definition of a cheque.

A class of credit Instruments, termed as *Hundis* were widely used since 12th century and even now in our country. They are: *Darshani Hundi*: (this corresponded to a demand bill of exchange) and *Muddati Hundi*: (this corresponded to a usance bill). Mainly four types of *Darshani Hundi* were in use. They were called *Sah-jog, Dhanni-jog, Firman-jog* and *Dekhavanhar* hundies. The *Dekhavanhar* hundi was a bearer demand bill of exchange payable to the person presenting it to the drawee. It corresponded to a bearer cheque.

In modern era, cheques were said to be in use since 9th century by customers of banks. The Bank of England pioneered the first use of a pre-printed form in 1717. These forms were printed on cheque paper in a numbered form to prevent fraud, and customers had to come to bank and collect it personally.

It is informed that the Bank of Hindoostan, the first joint stock bank established in 1770 in our country, introduced cheques. Subsequently Negotiable Instrument Act was passed in the year 1881, which act gave legal framework for usage of cheques and other negotiable instruments like bill of exchange and promissory notes.

Cheque is a negotiable instrument and negotiable instrument is a wonderful concept developed by practice and customs, and it helped the commerce. Negotiation of an instrument came to be recognized which is slightly different from transfer. The basic difference is that the transferee under transfer gets the same title of transferor i.e. if the title of the transferor is defective then the same deficiency will attach to the transferee. Whereas, when a negotiable instrument is negotiated then the transferee gets a valid title devoid of any defect, if he has acted in good faith and as per the law. Clearly, there is an advantage in accepting a negotiable instrument.

There are three types of negotiable instruments—cheques, bills and promissory notes. They are defined in the Negotiable Instruments Act 1881 (NI Act 1881). There are semi-negotiable instruments also like transport receipts, railway receipts, bill of lading, warehouse receipts—all title to goods, which by practice and customs have attained this status. Negotiation means transferring the title to the property shown in the instrument by endorsing and delivering it to other parties. This will pass the title to other party and is legally enforceable in their own name.

Bank pay orders and bank drafts are treated as cheques for this purpose and hence are negotiable instruments.

Bills of exchanges and promissory notes attract stamp duty under the Indian Stamp Act whereas the cheques are exempted from any stamp duty. This exemption was granted in the year 1927 to encourage the use of cheques for settling the payments.

## Cheque-Legal Provisions

Usage of cheques was common in the country and every bank or indigenous banker used cheques for withdrawal by their customers. The Negotiable Instrument Act came in 1881, which legalised the use of cheques, made rules for it, and defined the respective responsibilities of parties to a cheque. It is an elaborate Act on the subject of negotiable instruments, which goes to prove that the cheques and their features were in regular use by banks.

NI Act section 6 defined a cheque as under:

[6. "Cheque"

A "cheque" is a bill of exchange drawn on a specified banker and not expressed to be payable otherwise than on demand and it includes the electronic image of a truncated cheque and a cheque in the electronic form.

*Explanation I.*—For the purposes of this section, the expressions—

(a) "A cheque in the electronic form" means a cheque which contains the exact mirror image of a paper cheque, and is generated, written and signed in a secure system ensuring the minimum safety standards with the use of digital signature (with or without biometrics signature) and asymmetric crypto system;

(b) "A truncated cheque" means a cheque which is truncated during the course of a clearing cycle, either by the clearing house or by the bank whether paying or receiving payment, immediately on generation of an electronic image for transmission, substituting the further physical movement of the cheque in writing.

*Explanation II.*—For the purposes of this section, the expression "clearing house" means the clearing house managed by the Reserve Bank of India or a clearing house recognised as such by the Reserve Bank of India.]

The words "and it includes the electronic image of a truncated cheque and a cheque in the electronic form" and the explanations I and II are inserted as amendment in the year

2002. This was effected for enabling the cheque truncation process to be introduced for clearing purposes.

As per definition, cheque is a bill of exchange drawn on specified banker and is payable on demand. It also includes cheque in electronic form and an image of the truncated cheque transmitted to paying bank.

As per Section 26 of the NI Act, every person capable of contracting may make and draw a cheque. Hence, there is no restriction for using cheques by anyone.

The NI Act defined 'banker' in section 3 as under:

**3. Interpretation** ***clause***

In this Act-

"Banker": ["banker" includes any person acting as a banker and any post office savings bank.]

NI Act recognizes any person acting as banker is to be a banker and post office is also recognized as banker. As per NI Act, anyone in banking business as banker can allow the use of cheque by his customers for payment purpose as per provisions of the act.

This position remained till the year 1959. All the banks and also the indigenous bankers in the country were issuing their own cheques to customers for use.

Authority to use cheques by indigenous bankers was withdrawn in the year 1959 when new section 49A was inserted in Banking Regulation Act 1949 as under:

*"Section 49A. Restriction on acceptance of deposits withdrawable by cheque*

No person other than a banking company, the Reserve Bank, the State Bank of India or any other banking institution, firm or other person notified by the Central Government in this behalf on the recommendation of the Reserve Bank shall accept from the public deposits of money withdrawable by cheque:

Provided that nothing contained in this section shall apply to any savings bank scheme run by the Government."

This section was introduced in the year 1959 reserved the use of cheques exclusively by banking companies. The exception provided in this section is for post office savings accounts conducted by the government (though post offices are already authorised to use cheques under NI Act). Only govt on the recommendations from RBI, can allow any others for using cheques for withdrawals. This section prohibited other entities (indigenous bankers) in banking business to issue cheque books.

One reason for this could be that RBI wanted only banks in corporate sector to continue and debar others from banking business. Other reason could be that with the usage cheques becoming popular in trade, clearing operations were necessary to collect payment of cheques. Clearing houses were established and some sort of discipline was necessary for its smooth functioning. As all indigenous bankers were using their cheques and if these cheques were to be collected through clearing houses, then allowing membership of clearing house to indigenous bankers would become necessary. Clearing house operations called for stable banks to participate in the clearing process and large number of banks and bankers in a centre would have created logistic and settlement problems. There was also the issue of financial soundness of indigenous bankers.

Hence, from the year 1959 only banking companies were allowed the use of cheques in the country.

### Features of a Cheque

Cheque is a written order of the account holder to his bank to make the payment of the amount specified to some person as per other stipulations on the cheque. Hence, cheque has three parties involved. The account holder who issues the cheque, the bank on whom it is drawn and the person named therein called the payee who is to get the payment. The account holder is the drawer and the bank is the drawee. Usage of cheques is subject to various provisions of negotiable instrument act and the customs of the banks. Even the customs and practices of the banks in handling cheques have legal sanctity as the law now recognises it.

## Crossing of Cheque

There is a provision under NI Act 1881 for crossing of cheques. Crossing means two parallel lines drawn across the face of the cheque at any place. It can be placed diagonally or horizontally or in any other manner. It may contain the word "& co" or "& company" or without such letters. A bank's name can also be inserted in between these two lines.

Crossing of the cheque prohibits its payment in cash at its counters to anyone other than another bank. It means that crossed cheques will have to be collected by another bank. This makes the payee to deposit such cheques with his bank who will collect the payment from the drawee bank and credit it to his account. Thus, the account holder ensures by crossing the cheque that the payment is made to the bank of the payee only. This leaves the trail of payment, which can be traced, if found necessary for any reason subsequently.

NI Act 1881 also recognizes special crossing which means name of a bank has been written between the two lines. When name of any bank appears like this, the cheque is said to have been specially crossed to that bank. This means only the bank named therein can collect the payment from the drawee bank. Drawee bank cannot make payment to any bank other than the bank named therein. This provides extra safety in that the payment goes to the intended bank only.

There is a practice with banks to stamp all cheques coming into their possession with a crossing stamp. This stamp has two lines and the name of the bank and branch written between these lines. This is treated as special cross. Banks do it so that once instruments passes through their hand, it shall not be misused by anyone and find its way to another bank.

## Not Negotiable Cheques

Sometimes the cheques are issued and either in the crossing or at any other place the word "not negotiable" is written. It is mandatory that such writing shall remove the negotiability of the instrument. However, transferability of it is not restricted. Then, what is the significance? The payee must accept such cheques with care as his title can be affected by any existing defect of the person issuing or endorsing it.

### Alterations Permitted by Others

Law permits any bonafide holder of the cheque, other than the maker of the cheque, to make it order if it is originally drawn as bearer. This can be achieved by simply cutting the word bearer or by cutting the word bearer and writing order near it. Thereafter the instrument will be treated as order and subsequently cannot be made bearer. Likewise, any holder of the cheque can cross it, if it is not crossed, and also make crossing a special crossing by inserting banks name and it is permitted. However, only the maker of the cheque can cancel the crossing. Others cannot do it.

### Protection to Banks in Dealing with Crossed Cheques

Crossing of the cheques made it obligatory for banks to accept cheques issued in favour of their customers, then collect, and credit the amount to the accounts. This is a burden on banking system. Subsequently tax laws also insisted on this as it leaves the trail of fund transfer, which is necessary for enforcement agencies for verification. Since banks were burdened with this activity, law gave them certain privileges and exemptions by way of some protections from the rigours of the law. They are paying bank's protections and collecting bank's protections as enshrined in The Negotiable Instruments Act 1881 under its sections as under:

*Sec. 128. Payment in due course of crossed cheque*

> Where the banker on whom a crossed cheque is drawn has paid the same in due course, the banker paying the cheque, and (in case such cheque has come to the hands of the payee) the drawer thereof, shall respectively be entitled to the same rights, and be placed in the same position in all respect, as they would respectively be entitled to and placed in if the amount of the cheque had been paid to and received by the true owner thereof.

This section provides protection to paying bank for payment of a crossed cheque in due course. Under this section, paying bank is entitled to debit the account of the customer for the cheque paid by them.

*Sec. 131. Non-liability of banker receiving payment of cheque*

A banker who has in good faith and without negligence received payment for a customer of a cheque crossed generally or specially to himself shall not, in case the title to the cheque proves defective, incur any liability to the true owner of the cheque by reason only of having received such payment.

[*Explanation I*—A banker receives payment of a crossed cheque for a customer within the meaning of this section notwithstanding that he credits his customer's accounts with the amount of the cheque before receiving payment thereof].

["Explanation II—It shall be the duty of the banker who receives payment based on an electronic image of a truncated cheque held with him, to verify the *prima facie* genuineness of the cheque to be truncated and any fraud, forgery or tampering apparent on the face of the instrument that can be verified with due diligence and ordinary care.]

This section provides protection to collecting bank who has acted in good faith and without negligence. Explanation I of the section allows the banks to credit the amount even before receiving the payment, as is the practice of banks to credit the account for cheques in course of clearing and collection.

Explanation II has been inserted by an amendment after cheque truncation was permitted and this explanation casts a responsibility on collecting bank who is collecting payment of cheque based on electronic image transmitted through cheque truncation system.

## Validity of Cheque

Cheques are generally issued on current dates and bear current date of issue on it. As per practice of banks accepted by law, cheque is valid for six months from the date of issue for payment. Banks do not honour the cheque beyond this period and return it as stale cheque. Such cheques can be paid only when the drawer revalidates the date.

There is a practice to reduce the validity to lesser period by expressly writing it on the cheque. Most of interest warrants and dividend warrants are made current for three months only and this restriction is accepted.

However, under the provisions of limitation act, suit can be filed for recovery of amount till three years from the date of issue. Hence, stale cheque is not time barred and the payee has a right to demand for its revalidation by the drawer or file suit in the court of law.

RBI recently changed validity period of the cheque i.e. 6 months, to three months effective from 1-4-2012. Hence, the present practice shall be changed from this date.

### Post-Dated Cheques

The law does not debar anyone issuing a post-dated cheque. However, the legal status of the post-dated cheque is not defined and is not clear. As per practice, banks cannot make payment of post-dated cheques and debit it to the account of the customer. Cheques can be paid only on the date shown on the cheque or thereafter within six months. It is informed that in few countries there is legal bar to issue post-dated cheques and the cheque even though bears a future date shall be treated as current date only.

In our country, post-dated cheques became popular in usage even by banks as banks and finance companies collect post-dated cheques for repayment of loan instalments. However, no action can lie before the date of the cheque.

### Issuing Blank Cheque

It is possible and is in practice to issue blank cheque, which may not contain some vital information like amount, date or name of the payee. In such case, the holder of the cheque has a right to complete the cheque and then present it for payment. The drawer is bound by such additions made by the holder (section 20).

Payment of the cheque after the death of account holder.

Cheque is a mandate of the account holder and is in force during his lifetime. When death occurs, all the mandate gets automatically cancelled as per law. Even a power of attorney gets cancelled. In view of this legal position, cheque cannot be paid after the death of the accountholder. However, for protection of banks, this cancellation of mandate is applicable only when the notice of death reaches banks or bank learns about it. Hence if the bank is unaware of the death then the cheque paid by it is good payment in law.

### Certified Cheque

There was a practice of getting the cheque certified by the bank, which use to stamp the cheque with words "good for payment". This practice was used to satisfy the payee of the cheque as regards the payment of the cheque. Since the bank is certifying it as good, it gives guarantee to the payee. Generally, banks after issuing the certificate use to mark lien on the account for the balance so that the cheque can be honoured on presentation. This practice was there till seventies and eighties. However, this practice did not find favour with RBI who advised the banks to discontinue with it and instead issue pay orders for the amount.

### At Par Cheques

Generally the cheques are payable at the branch on whom they are drawn. Hence, the cheque needs to be sent to the branch by others who demand payment. In case the drawee branch is in another station then the cheque will have to be sent for collection. There is a practice with banks and for important customers they allow the payment of the cheques at any branch of the bank. This facility is extended to select customers at their request and such cheques are called "payable at par cheques" this feature of the cheque is imprinted on the face of cheque for public notice. Sometimes cheques are also allowed payment at selected few places mentioned in the cheque. This feature is more used in case of dividend/interest warrants.

After core banking, *payable at par* feature of the cheque is gaining importance and under the speed clearing system introduced by RBI it has become mandatory now.

### Instruments Similar to Cheques

Besides the cheques, some more instruments are in use which are treated by law as cheques. They are:

### Demand Drafts

Demand draft is a cheque issued by a bank on its own branch or correspondent bank in the name of a payee. It is always an order instrument and shall be paid on identification only. As a bank is issuing the draft, it is safest mode of payment. Banks issue drafts after collecting the payment for it and the draft always mentions the fact—'value received' on the instrument.

### Pay Orders

This is also issued by banks but unlike the draft, it is payable at the office issuing it. Otherwise, it is similar to bank draft. This is generally used for local payments when the payee also resides in the same centre.

### Interest/Dividend Warrants

These are cheques issued generally by corporates for payment of either dividend or interest on deposits taken by them. Generally, these instruments are issued with a currency of three months only. Normally the company opens an account with the bank for the purpose and deposits the total amount payable in it.

### Travellers' Cheques

Travellers' cheques are issued by the banks for different denominated amounts enabling a traveller to encash it at any centre. The purchaser of travellers' cheques puts his signature on the instrument at the time of purchase. This acts as identification and he can approach any branch and encash the travellers cheques and at the time of encashing, he is required to sign again on the instrument. These are extensively used for foreign travels. In fact, foreign travellers can carry only a limited foreign currency with them and can carry travellers cheques for the expenses during their foreign tour. Travellers cheques are also paid instruments and the purchaser either can get these encashed or cancelled subsequently.

### Gift Cheques

Gift cheques are issued by banks as order instruments for gift purposes and generally in a fixed amount series. Name of the payee is left blank which can be filled subsequently and presented for payment.

### Return of Cheques by Banks

As it is known banks return the cheque if the account does not have sufficient balance to honour it. A cheque has to be paid in full and there is no provision to make part payment by banks. Even in case of a very small shortfall in balance to meet the cheque, it shall be returned. Banks generally return the cheques, which is unpaid and attach with it a memo stating the details of the cheque and giving reason for return. The payee has a right to receive this memo for the dishonour, as it is the legal proof of dishonour accepted by everyone. Cheque can be returned by the bank for variety of reasons besides no balance in the account to honour it. There are over 30 reasons now in use by banks for returning a cheque. There can be defect in the cheque, improper endorsements, presentation of cheque for payment in contradiction to the tenor of the cheque, etc. Banks are cautious in returning the cheques and the reason for return is carefully given. This is because banks have a responsibility and in case of wrongful dishonour of the cheque, it may face action from both customer and payee.

Banks generally give the correct reasons for return like 'insufficient funds', 'uncleared effects', 'not arranged for', 'full cover not received', 'payments countermanded by drawer', type of defect in the cheque or endorsements, etc. The purpose is to inform the payee the correct reason for dishonour. When banks cannot give a proper reason for return due to any reason then they simply write 'refer to drawer' meaning thereby that the payee shall approach the drawer and find out the reason for dishonour. However, in practice in our country, this reason—'refer to drawer' became commonly used when there is no balance in the account to honour the cheque. This practice claims that writing 'insufficient funds' means bank is disclosing the status of the account of the customer and hence objectionable as banks are bound by confidentiality of accounts. Banks should not disclose the status of the account as it is derogatory. Because of the practice the reason—'refer to drawer' is extensively used by banks in the country and most of the time it means that there is no balance in the account.

Banks also give reason for return as—'unclear effects' and ask the payee to represent the cheque. Banks generally write 'effects not clear, present again'. Some banks also write—'funds expected—present again'. Sometimes banks use to write-'present again tomorrow'. 'Effects not clear—present again' means the drawer has some collection pending credit to his account like uncleared cheques in the process of clearing. 'Funds expected—present again' means some funds are expected to the credit of the account being in the pipeline at present. Generally, these reasons are given for good accounts where the banker is aware that the payments can be made as arranged by the customer. The purpose is to call back the cheque from the presenting bank immediately so that the cheques can be paid at the earliest. Otherwise, if the cheque is returned to the payee by collecting bank then lot of time is wasted for its re-presentment and payment. In fact, banks are helping businessmen to settle account knowing that the problem is a temporary one and it is in the interest of parties to do so. However, at times such practice creates problems in the sense that it may tantamount to bank's promise to pay the cheque on re-presentment. If such cheque is dishonoured again bank's position becomes vulnerable and bank invites trouble unnecessarily on itself. However, Banks are still following this practice.

### Bouncing of Cheques—An Offense

Cheques are widely used by trade and individuals for making payments. However, the cheques can be paid only when sufficient balance is held in the account. Otherwise, the bank shall dishonour the cheque and the settlement of payment does not happen. Extensive use of cheques by businessmen for settlements between them has increased the volume of cheque usage. Tax laws also made certain prescription for payment through cheques so that the origin of funds can be traced. Hence while the use of cheques has become a necessity for parties, there is however no guarantee for payment. In case the cheque is dishonoured the payees remedy is in filing a civil suit, which is time-consuming exercise. Hence, many a time, bank demand draft is insisted for payment.

Fraudsters cheated people by issuing cheques without having balance to make the payment. Payees, many a time tried to initiate criminal action against the persons for cheating them. Sometimes police registered such cases and took action. However, the legal provision under criminal law was not clear. There was no law, which made bouncing of cheque a criminal offence. Cheating cases are tried under the provisions of Indian penal code and generally, it depended on the circumstances. For example, when a person makes the other to believe in him, gives him cheque for payment, and induces the other person to part with valuables like goods, etc. then a case of cheating can be made. On the other hand, when two parties deal with each other for long time knowing each other well and settling payments by cheques regularly and if one of the cheque is dishonoured it becomes difficult to treat the same as a case of cheating. Based on facts of the case the police and courts gave different interpretations on criminal action. This necessitated specific provision in law to deal with cheque bouncing particularly in view of certain compulsions for using cheques to settle payments. Sanctity of cheques must be preserved for economic reasons so that financial transactions can take place smoothly. In the year, 1988 a new chapter VII was added to Negotiable Instrument Act by an amendment act and the provisions of new sections 138 to 142 were made effective from the year 1989.

*Sec. 138. Dishonour of cheque for insufficiency, etc., of funds in the account*

Where any cheque drawn by a person on an account maintained by him with a banker for payment of any amount of money to another person from out of that account for the discharge, in whole or in part, of any debt or other liability, is returned by the bank unpaid, either because of the amount of money standing to the credit of that account is insufficient to honour the cheque or that it exceeds the amount arranged to be paid from that account by an agreement made with that bank, such person shall be deemed to have committed an offence and shall, without prejudice to any other provision of this Act, be punished with imprisonment for a term which may extend to one year, or with fine which may extend to twice the amount of the cheque, or with both:

Provided that nothing contained in this section shall apply unless—

(a) the cheque has been, presented to the bank within a period of six months from the date on which it is drawn or within the period of its validity, whichever is earlier;

(b) the payee or the holder in due course, of the cheque as the case may be, makes a demand for the payment of the said amount of money by giving a notice, in writing, to the drawer of the cheque, within fifteen days of the receipt of information by him from the bank regarding the return of the cheque as unpaid; and

(c) the drawer of such cheque fails to make the payment of the said amount of money to the payee or, as the case may be, to the holder in due course of the cheque, within fifteen days of the receipt of the said notice.

*Explanation*—For the purposes of this section, "debt or other liability" means a legally enforceable debt or other liability.

Dishonour of cheque for insufficiency of funds is now made an offense punishable with imprisonment and/or fine. Though the intention was to treat issuing of cheque without provision for payment as a criminal offense and bring discipline in such matters, the subsequent experiences are not encouraging. It is observed that the implementation of the provisions of the act is proving cumbersome and is not helping the payee.

Usage of cheques continued to grow as it was the only mode of payments between parties till late 1980. After the electronic modes of payments like credit cards, debit cards, ATM cards and internet banking with RTGS and NEFT fund transfer systems were introduced the usage of cheques as payment mode is coming down.

### Bankers Clearing Houses

The activity of issuing cheques by parties necessitated the banks to find some solution to make the payments of cheques and collection of cheques. Every Bank is bound to act as paying bank in some cases and collecting bank in other cases. Banks in the same centres will have claims and cross claims on other banks at the centre for the cheques deposited by their customers and for cheques drawn on them issued by its customers. To overcome the numerous individual claims and cross claims, banks created clearing house mechanism to take care of this. Clearing house is an association of banks and a meeting place for banks where they exchange cheques drawn on each other and then arrive at settlement figure. Usually all banks maintain accounts with one bank acting as clearing manager bank and through the accounts with this bank settle the claims between themselves.

### Origin of Cheque Clearing Function

Origin of clearing system and clearing house is traced to England. It is informed that the daily cheque clearings began around the year 1770 in England when the bank clerks met at the Five Bells, a tavern in Lombard Street in the City of London, to exchange all their cheques in one place and settle the balances in cash.

Origin of bankers clearing house is in England. The first organisation for clearing cheques was the "Bankers Clearing House" established in London in the early 19th century. It was founded by Lubbock's Bank on Lombard Street in a single room where clerks of London banks met each day to exchange cheques and settle accounts.

In fact, it is learnt that the special crossing of cheques originated from this activity in United Kingdom. There the banks started witting their names on the cheques coming into their possession so that the cheques can be clearly identified as to which bank it belongs to. Law subsequently duly recognized this practice and legal provision was made to this effect.

In our country, the first Clearing associations were formed by the banks in the Presidency towns and the final settlement between member banks was effected by means of cheques drawn upon the Presidency Banks. The first clearing house was established at Calcutta followed by Bombay and Madras. After RBI came in the year 1935, it started managing clearinghouses at centres it had offices and at other centres, the imperial bank of India continued managing.

## Clearing Houses

Clearing houses were established at every centre where there is more number of banks to facilitate collection of cheques. Each bank sorts out cheques bank-wise, prepares a list with total of amounts of all cheques drawn on the said bank and hands it over to the representative of the said bank at the Clearing house at appointed time. Likewise, every bank delivers cheques of other banks and receives cheques drawn on it. Thereafter settlement is arrived by working out net figures with each bank and then as against all banks. This final net figure for each bank is taken by the clearing manager bank and it passes necessary credits and debits to the accounts of member banks maintained with it. Maintaining sufficient funds in the account to meet the settlement amount on daily basis is the responsibility of individual banks.

As all the cheques presented in the Clearing house may not be paid for want of funds in some customer's accounts or for any other valid reason, the clearing house conducts another clearing for the purpose of returning of the cheques which were not paid and same procedure is followed for settlement. Generally, return clearing is held on the same day or next day.

As per practice, banks credit customers' accounts for the cheques being collected and presented in clearing house on the same date. However, this credit is subject to realisation of cheque and bank reserves the right to debit the cheque if it is returned unpaid by the paying bank. These credits are provisional credits and considered as clear credits only after the return cheque clearing is held at clearing house and the cheque is not received back.

It is interesting to note that there will be no confirmation of payment immediately available to banks. Cheque shall be treated as paid unless it is received back unpaid in the designated return clearing house. Of course, subsequent enquiry can be made in case of need and the banks are obliged to give information and also confirmation if required by other banks.

Clearing houses were managed by RBI at centres where it has branches and at other centres, SBI managed the same. This is the tradition and any other bank also can manage the clearing house since it is a local arrangement with mutual consent of local banks. There were 501 clearing houses in the year 1978 and more centres were added and by the year 2010 their number grew up to 1139 in the country. In the year 2009-10, number of cheques processed through clearing houses were 13793 lakhs for a staggering amount of ₹ 1,04,03,988 crores.

Hence clearing house is an important institution for fund transfers between customer accounts at various banks.

### MICR Technology

In the year 1959, MICR technology was patented in the United States for use with cheques clearing. This opened the way for the first automated reader/sorting machines for clearing cheques.

RBI started Clearing houses using the advanced MICR (Magnetic Ink Character Recognition) technology in the year 1984 beginning with Bombay and then added more centres. By the year 2010, 66 major centres in the country are under MICR clearing. This advance technology helped the banks to mechanise the process and speed up the clearing. For this purpose, MICR cheques were introduced. Magnetic Ink Character Recognition cheques are similar to earlier cheques used by banks except that the paper quality is better and the cheque has a clear band of area along the full length of cheque at the bottom. Here the cheque number bank/Branch code, instrument type code and finally the amount has to be encoded from an encoder machine with a special ink called magnetic ink. In practice, all the relevant information except the amount is pre-printed along with the cheque printing. After the cheque is deposited with a bank, that bank using an encoder machine encodes the amount of the cheque at the relevant space and then sends it to clearing house. The quality of paper and the ink used makes the magnetic strip readable by the reader sorter machine installed at clearing house. This avoids manual work and that the meeting of bank representatives face to face is also not required. Banks are required to deliver the cheques in batches to the Clearing house and the reader sorter machine does the job of reading the cheque as it passes through it and also sorts the cheque bank-wise and branch wise and prepares list containing details. Sorting takes place automatically and the banks are only required to collect the inward clearing at the appointed time.

### Cheque Truncation

Technology has further brought in some more changes. In the mid nineties cheque truncation technology was introduced in many countries. Truncation means a physical cheque is converted into electronic form for transmission to the paying bank or clearing house. The physical movement of the cheques from collecting bank, clearing house and then to paying bank is stopped. Cheque is truncated at some point, generally at the hands of collecting bank being the first entry point to banking system for clearing and thereafter only electronic image of the cheque travels. Truncation also means that the cheque is held in the physical custody at this point and thereafter, only an electronic image of the cheques is sent to paying bank via clearing house. This is done electronically and lot of time in physical movement is saved. Safekeeping of the cheque is the responsibility of truncating point office. The paying bank makes the payment only by seeing electronic image of the cheque, which is as good as the physical cheque in all respects. The whole idea of this is to quicken the process of clearing and make it less time consuming and fast.

However, to bring in this change, banking law was to be amended. It is because till then the paying bank was to make payment only when the original physical cheque is presented to it at its counters and hold the cheque in custody. They cannot make payment otherwise. Therefore, the law had to permit the payment based on the electronic image of the cheque. Then there are clearly defined roles of paying bank and collecting bank and their responsibilities against each other and customers. Payment shall be Payment in due course and as per the tenor of the instrument. Collecting bank has the protection for collecting the instruments in good faith without negligence. Since the actual cheques are not seen by paying bank the role of collecting bank, needs to be redefined. Since KYC regime has been introduced in the banking system, the collecting bank needs to own more responsibility for collection. NI Act 1881 has been suitably amended in the year 2002 to take care of this requirement.

*Explanation II on Sec. 131 of NI Act*—It shall be the duty of the banker who receives payment based on an electronic image of a truncated cheque held with him, to verify the *prima facie* genuineness of the cheque to be truncated and any fraud, forgery or tampering apparent on the face of the instrument that can be verified with due diligence and ordinary care.

Onus is on the collecting bank and it is now responsible to verify the *prima facie* genuineness of the cheque.

Cheque truncation system has been started at NCR Delhi on test basis from February 2008 and gradually it will be spread to other centres. This will be a vast improvement and reduce the burden on banking system in handling physical cheques and moving them across the banks in the process of collection and payment.

# Customer Service

15

Customer service area for banks has undergone lot of changes. Though the concept—customer is king is not new to Indian banking, lot of things were lacking. Customer friendliness was there in serving them when they came to branch but mostly customers are not aware of rules and regulations applicable to them. They have to simply believe whatever bank officials say. Lot of things have happened in this direction now—mainly in the area of customer education.

RBI had set up committees, R.K. Talwar Committee in 1975 and Goiporia Committee in 1986 to look into customer service area and give recommendations. RBI accepted most of the recommendations of these two committees and these were implemented. These recommendations covered all routine banking services.

## Creating Awareness

Time norms for different services at the counters of banks were introduced to make the staff accountable to attend and the time norms were made to be displayed at the bank.

Service charges for different types of services were now standardized and displayed at the branches for the information of customers. Banks are now required to be transparent in their charges and no hidden charges are to be levied.

Banks were advised to bring out 'citizen' charters' wherein the rights of the customer and duties of the bank are defined and made known to customers. Most of the banks created and issued this document around the year 1997. In the year 2000, Indian

Bankers Association (IBA) had reviewed the charters of different banks and brought out a *Model Citizen Charter* explaining to the customers what they could expect from the banks as a matter of right. Banks are now periodically updating this document and making it available to customers and public.

IBA brought out its *Bankers' Fair Practice* code in July 2004 and all member banks had adopted it voluntarily. IBA also came out separately with *Fair Practice Code for Credit Card Operations* and *Model Code for Collection of Dues and Repossession of Security* to address specific concerns voiced by customers about banking practices in these areas. These have been implemented by member banks.

Subsequently, Banking Codes & Standards Board of India (BCSBI) was formed in the year 2005, as a voluntary organisation and banks became members of the Board. The board brought out standard code for banks, for implementation in July 2006 and revised code in August 2009 and the copies of these standards are supplied to every customer of the bank for information.

Reserve bank is keen to ensure that the bank customers are fairly treated by banks. Information sharing is one area where banks shall have to make the customers aware of products and services. Banks shall have to be transparent in levying service charges and there shall not be any hidden charges. The rate of interest should be clearly informed and banks shall not mislead customers on yield based on compounding of interest. Banks shall observe time norms for services and stick to it. RBI frowns upon teaser rates on advances where the customers are told that the loans will be cheaper but only for a short period thereby misleading the customer.

Banks are to have time norms for disposal of loan applications and dispose them as per norms. Banks shall also provide copies of loan agreements to the borrowers for reference.

### Customer Facilities

Bank deposits were without nomination facility earlier. Because of this, in case of death of a customer, claim settlement was unduly delayed as the procedure followed by banks was cumbersome and legal issues were involved. Banks were insisting for succession certificate in many cases. Only in case of death of one of the joint holder, the amount was paid to the other joint holder as per mandate obtained at the time of opening the account. To address this problem, Govt approved nomination rules for bank deposits and bank lockers in the year 1985. The Banking Regulation Act 1949 was amended and new sections were inserted to enable nomination facility for bank deposits and bank safe deposit lockers. This has helped customers. Banks were also advised to review the death claim settlement procedures and simplify it. Banks have now reframed the rules for settlement of death claim cases liberally without insisting for succession certificates in most of the cases and some powers are also delegated to field staff to dispose the claims.

Nomination facility for bank accounts is being promoted and to ensure that customers are made aware of it, banks are now asked to offer it at the time of opening the account and record refusal, in case the customer does not want the same.

Collection of upcountry instruments was taking long time and there were no rules. RBI prescribed time norms for collection for different centres and made it mandatory for banks to stick to it. Penalty was imposed on banks as banks were asked to pay interest for the delayed period. RBI also advised banks to give immediate credit for small value cheques to help small customers. Banks are now giving immediate credit up to ₹ 15,000 for outstation cheques under collection with some minimum rules about the conduct of the account.

RBI has made it compulsory for banks to share ATM network to benefit customers of all banks. In a way, ATMs are treated as national property for the benefit of public. RBI initiated National Financial Switch (NFS) is an interbank network managed by Euronet India Pvt. Ltd. It was conceived and run by the Institute for Development & Research in Banking Technology—IDRBT (an arm of the Reserve Bank of India) and was launched on 27 August 2004. National Payments Corporation of India is the settlement agency for this network. The number of ATMs linked to the National

Financial Switch (NFS) has increased to 75,178 as of March 31, 2011.

Failed ATM transactions were causing inordinate delay in settling the claims and now RBI has fixed 14 days as the limit beyond which banks shall have to pay ₹ 100 per day for the delay.

Banks have now become customer centric. The competition and the technological developments over the period have changed the outlook of banks towards its customers. Customers cannot be taken for granted. They know their rights and have choice for doing business.

Ambience of branches have undergone sea change now. Banks in fifties had a standard set up with high counters and customer area clearly demarcated. Customers could not go anywhere else in the branch. This has given way to low counters and broken counters. Area dedicated to customers in banking hall is increased. Adequate seating arrangements are made. Basic amenities like drinking water and washroom facilities are provided. Branches are now neat and clean and many of them are air-conditioned. May I help you counter is provided at bigger branches. Arrangements for receiving handicapped customers are now available at branches. Senior citizens are given privileges to do their transactions. Banking hall has displays on almost all important matters for the information of customers.

### Redressal of Grievances

Consumer Protection Act 1986 was passed by GOI and bank customers are covered under the act. Banking services have been brought under the purview of consumer act as customers avail banking services and pay for it. Customer can approach consumer forums for redressal of any breach or deficiency in service. Banks will have to defend themselves before the consumer forums.

Internal complaint redressal system has been started by banks and a senior officer of the bank is nominated as designated officer for looking into complaints. His name and address is displayed at all branches for the notice of customers.

Reserve Bank of India has also started Banking Ombudsman Scheme in the year 1995 under which complaints can be referred to Banking Ombudsman who shall decide the matter. At present, he can try cases up to a compensation of ₹ 10 lakhs and banks are bound by the order. Deputy Governor of RBI is the appellate authority under the scheme. The Banking Ombudsman Scheme was revised during the years 2002 and 2006. The Banking Ombudsman Scheme (BOS) 2006 covers all Commercial Banks, Regional Rural Banks and Scheduled Primary Co-operative Banks under its scope.

Public sector banks are also accountable under RTI Act 2005 and Public Grievance Redressal System of Govt of India.

Banks are advised to have a compensation policy in place under which banks shall acknowledge liability and compensate for certain deficiencies identified while extending the services to customers. Under this policy, even cases of wrongful debits to customer's accounts shall be dealt and they are compensated at the earliest.

### Areas of Dissatisfaction

Still there is lot of areas of dissatisfaction. One area is intimation of due dates of deposits. Though banks are supposed to remind the customer in time, the same is not regularly being done. Things have improved after core banking, as the system is capable of generating such reminder letters. Other area is about TDS. Tax laws make it compulsory for depositors to give declarations every year to be eligible for exemption. Banks are supposed to collect it every year by reminding customer before deducting TDS. However, this does not happen regularly with the result lot of complaints emanate.

### Bank Services and Income Tax Rules

There are certain income tax rules applicable on services provided by banks. Important of them are as under:

1. Rule 114B of Income Tax Rules: Under this rule Quoting of PAN is mandatory for opening bank accounts, placing fixed deposits in excess of ₹ 50,000 depositing ₹ 50,000 or more in cash to a bank account

on any day, issue of demand drafts against payment of cash of ₹ 50,000 or more, issue of credit cards, etc.

Banks are required to verify the PAN quoted by the customers. Income Tax Dept. has started providing facility, for verification of PAN, for organisational users to query their PAN database in batch mode on their website http://incometaxindiaefiling.gov.in. The authorised users including banks, after registering with the IT authorities, can enter the PAN and will be able to view Name, Date of Birth and Address as available against that PAN in their database.

2. As per present income tax guidelines, banks are required to tax deduct at source (TDS) on deposits if the total interest earned by a person on all fixed deposits in a bank is more than ₹ 10,000 in a financial year. Even minor's fixed deposit is also subject to these rules.

   Depositors can claim the credit for such TDS in their income tax returns. However, if the depositor furnishes form 15G or 15H, Bank will not deduct any TDS from the interest earned by the depositor. This form has to be submitted separately for every financial year by the depositors. A person who is below 65 years can file the Form 15 G. However, only a person of 65 years or more is eligible to file Form 15 H.

   TDS is not applicable for interest paid on savings accounts, recurring deposit accounts and NRE/FCNR deposit accounts.

3. Under section 269T of Income Tax Act 1961, payment of maturity proceeds of deposits with banks, in case the deposit amount with interest exceeds ₹ 20,000, shall be made by the bank by an account payee cheque or by credit to SB or current account of the depositor.

## Banking Cash Transaction Tax (BCTT)

GOI introduced BCTT in the year 2005 as a new tax under which all banking transactions involving cash withdrawals were taxed. It was applicable to individuals withdrawing more than 25,000 and others more than one lakh rupees. The tax was levied at 0.1% and the purpose was to move the financial transactions to use cheques and other facilities and to discourage money laundering. However, this did not find favour with public and created lot of problems for banks and tax authorities to implement the tax regime. Finally, GOI withdrew this tax in the year 2009.

# Know Your Customer Guidelines

# 16

International community is concerned with money laundering and terrorist activities since long. After the 9/11 terrorist attacks on US in 2001, the issues were brought to focus and all the nations took notice of the seriousness of these maladies. It was felt that there is a nexus between money laundering and terrorist financing. Though banks were used for these purposes by criminal elements, banks were not in a position to either identify or curb such activities. It was in this background, Financial Action Task Force (FATF) an International Body of Nations made certain recommendations to control such menace by better control on banking operations and by legal provisions to bring the culprits to books. The Basel Committee on Banking Supervision issued a paper on Customer Due Diligence (CDD) for banks, with indicative suggestions. Banks have been advised to ensure that a proper policy framework on 'Know Your Customer' and Anti-Money Laundering measures is formulated and put in place.

In view of the above, GOI enacted Prevention of Money Laundering Act 2002 (PMLA 2002), a new legislation to fight against money laundering and created FIU-IND (Financial Intelligence Unit of India), a statutory body under Ministry of Finance to implement the provisions of PMLA. RBI issued guidelines to banks on 'Know Your Customer' (KYC) in 2002 and issued detailed guidelines in the year 2004 advising banks to have 'Know Your Customer Policy' based on guidelines. RBI has stated the objectives of the guidelines as under:

> "The objective of KYC guidelines is to prevent banks from being used, intentionally or unintentionally, by criminal elements for money laundering activities. KYC procedures also enable banks to know/ understand their customers and their financial dealings better which in turn help them manage their risks prudently."

RBI has issued KYC guidelines in the year 2004 and these guidelines gave a new definition for 'customers' as under:

For the purpose of KYC policy, a 'Customer' may be defined as:

- "a person or entity that maintains an account and/or has a business relationship with the bank;
- one on whose behalf the account is maintained (i.e. the beneficial owner);
- beneficiaries of transactions conducted by professional intermediaries, such as Stock Brokers, Chartered Accountants, Solicitors, etc. as permitted under the law;
- and any person or entity connected with a financial transaction which can pose significant reputational or other risks to the bank, say, a wire transfer or issue of a high value demand draft as a single transaction."

RBI guidelines on KYC policy now identified besides deposit account holders and borrowers, other category of customers as bank customers for the first time. They are beneficial owners on whose behalf accounts are maintained, beneficiaries of transactions conducted by professional intermediaries and persons who may use bank's services particularly remittance facilities or any other financial services. All these people are now bank customers even if they do not maintain any accounts with the bank and KYC guidelines are applicable in their cases also.

RBI advised banks to incorporate the following four key elements in the KYC policy:

- Customer Acceptance Policy;
- Customer Identification Procedures;

- Monitoring of Transactions; and
- Risk Management.

Banks are advised to prepare a profile for each new customer based on risk categorisation. The customer profile is required to contain information relating to customer's identity, social/financial status, nature of business activity, information about his clients' business and their location, etc. The nature and extent of due diligence will depend on the risk perceived by the bank.

KYC compliance is now taken seriously by banks. Since the year 2005, banks are also obliged to report cash transactions of ₹ 10 lakhs and above, suspicious transactions as described, and transactions involving counterfeit currency notes to FIU-IND.

KYC guidelines are now mandatory for opening new accounts by the bank and banks are advised to cover all the existing accounts under the guidelines in a phased manner. Banks cannot now open accounts without complying with the guidelines.

Though KYC guidelines are an elaborate document giving detailed instructions and defining many things in new perspective, the essence is not different from what banks were practicing all these years.

In olden days banker was a very careful person, weighed his acts, and judged the value and worth of customer. He was opening accounts for known persons or for persons who are properly introduced by existing customers. If we consider the area of operations of a bank branch, we will realise that this system is sufficient to take care of identity of the customer and there can be no wrong identification unless the introducer has tricked the banker by falsely testifying about the new customer. No manager worth his salt in olden days would fail to meet the new customer and find out his status and activity. It is convention to know the customer. Financial transactions happening at the branch have to be in the knowledge of the manager and he has his own system of keeping track. The transactions are monitored for various purposes. It is not feasible that any transaction misses the radar of the Branch Manager as he is in charge of operations. Manager used his discretion not to open accounts, if he had knowledge about undesirable feature of an individual. Banks' manuals described the procedural part for accounting purpose and due diligence on the new customer was a convention those days.

However, it was observed that with fast expansion of bank branches, the level of due diligence has come down at banks. Opening of new accounts have become mere rituals and generally are not overseen by senior officers. Once the due diligence is not done at the time of opening the account and if the Branch Manager does not keep track of financial transactions happening in the account, then the sanctity of customer banker relationship is diluted and becomes meaningless. This is what has happened over the years. Banks do not know their customers. They have no information about the financial dealings and activities of their customers. Due to increase in workload, this position was accepted and the only precaution exercised is by way of introduction obtained at the time of opening the account. Even the quality of introduction is not given due importance. It was observed that due to secrecy clause available many people are using banks to keep their ill gotten or tax evaded money, some times in benami accounts. Banks were also encouraging them due to pressure to increase deposits.

Subsequently tax laws were made stringent and benami accounts were made illegal. Obtaining photographs of account holders was prescribed in the year 1993 and tax declaration was made applicable for many cases. After these changes, banks started discouraging benami accounts as it involved fair amount of risk for them. TDS and restriction on cash payment of deposit proceeds (₹ 20,000 and above) made it very difficult for people to use bank account for hiding black money.

Now the KYC guidelines have made it more stringent and codified all the unwritten conventions and best practices of banks into a policy.

What are the guidelines and what is the purpose behind it? As discussed above, the practice followed by banks for opening accounts for customers is not foolproof. In fact, the existing procedure of banks depended on introduction route to identify the new customer and bank can argue that an existing customer of the bank has properly introduced that new customer. Bank does not make any verification on its own and does not even collect basic information on the customer. This is the reason for the KYC guidelines to be brought in. As the name denotes, banks are now obliged to know their customers. This is their duty and it is now incumbent on banks that they carry out due diligence on the customers before accepting them. Under the KYC guidelines banks are asked to identify their customer by conducting due diligence. This means banks must identify the customers and establish the identity by satisfying themselves and by calling for necessary documents for the purpose. Customer due diligence means bank must check and record the identification of customer, his status, his occupation, place of his residence and his financial dealings.

Banks are advised to collect and verify the identity proof and residence proof of the customer. Banks shall have to compile a profile of the customer containing relevant information about the status, business and financial standing. Banks are also required to assign a risk rating to the customer. All this information is to be used for monitoring transactions in the account.

Under the KYC guidelines, banks are also required to know the transactions that they are handling on behalf of customers. Banks cannot plead ignorance about the transactions, as they are responsible for it. This is where the risk perception comes in. Banks are exposed to risks while handling customer transactions and may face third party claims for wrongful transactions. Banks may incur financial loss besides reputational loss.

### Identity Proof of Customers

For establishing the identity, banks are now calling for photo identity proofs and generally, following type of identity proofs are accepted:

- Valid Passport
- Valid PAN Card
- Valid Driving License
- Valid Voters ID Card
- Valid Armed Forces ID Card
- Valid Ration Card with Photograph of Primary Holder in whose name the account is being opened
- Valid Identity Card of any accredited institution

Banks shall collect copies of identity proofs and retain it after verifying the original. Banks shall satisfy themselves about the authenticity of the original identity proofs.

Getting identity proof is generally not a problem because mostly people have different types of identification documents, which can be accepted. But the question is—how banks will satisfy themselves about the genuineness of the identity papers? Except PAN enquiry, there is no way of knowing immediately the authenticity of documents produced. Even subsequent checking may not be possible in all cases as many authorities simply may not reply or entertain queries.

However, identification of the account holder is very important for bank because customer relationship has to run for long time and many transactions are likely to take place in the account. Banks responsibility will continue till the end. Here the system of introduction can help. If a known person is giving reference and identifying the customer then the task of the bank becomes easier. In case the introduction is waived then something else may have to be done to establish the identity.

### Residence Proof

Besides identification, banks shall know the current address of the customer where he can be found. This is also a mandatory requirement and banks generally call for proofs. These proofs are:

- Current Utility Bills—Electricity Bill or Telephone Bill (only Landline Bill) with name and address of the customer.

- Valid Ration Card with or without Photograph, with Customer mentioned as one of the family members.
- Current Bank Statements with address
- Current Credit Card Statements with address
- Form 16—Tax Deducted at Source Certificate
- Certified Birth Certificate
- Certified Marriage Certificate
- Registered Lease Deed
- Professional License with Photograph
- Trade License with Photograph
- Any other documentary evidence in support of the person's residential address to bank's satisfaction.
- Letter from the head of the family with whom the account holder resides (applicable for members of the family).

Documents to be accepted as residence proof must contain the residential address that shall be the current address.

In fact residence proof is the new concept which was never given due importance by banks earlier. Any person can open account anywhere in country, as law does not prohibit it. However, the correct residential address for communication and to locate the customer is necessary. Now it is a legal requirement. Here again it is important to have the current residential address of the account holder where he can be reached and not any past or native address. Strictly speaking, the status of the account holder in relation to his place of residence is immaterial. It is not material whether he owns it, rents it, or simply stays with some relatives or friends or stays in some campus of employer, institution where he is associated, etc. The proof called for is not to establish ownership or other status but to know whether in fact he is residing there currently. If the purpose is to know where the account holder resides then absence of a particular type of documents is not a hindrance to open account. It is matter of due diligence and satisfaction of bank about the correctness of the present address.

Visits to check the correctness of the address are generally not possible by banks and not made mandatory. However, some banks have outsourced this function.

### Purpose of Collecting Identity Proof and Residence Proof

Is it sufficient if the copies of identity and residence proofs of prospective customer have been obtained for opening an account? Whether the account so opened can be treated as KYC compliant? Though it appears so, but in reality it is not enough. We must understand that we cannot identify the person solely on the basis of some identity paper. Who is confirming the authenticity of the identity paper? Is there any way of knowing the authenticity of it? How the identity can be established? Collecting papers should not be mistaken for identifying. Identifying is an act of due diligence which the bank shall undertake. Collection of papers is only a process. Connecting the papers to the individual is important.

Strictly speaking due diligence is required to open an account and not mere collection of papers. In this, meeting the customer and interviewing him is very important. The manager or senior official must meet the customer and during the interview, find out about the intended transactions. Once the type of account, the purpose, the status and financial standing are known, it becomes easier to understand. Interview and collection of all relevant customer information gives an insight to understand and know the customer. Once this is done and recorded, monitoring can be taken care at back end and during transaction processing.

### Risk Perception and Risk Category Under KYC

KYC policy requires customers to be categorised based on risk perception. As banks are exposed to many risks in handling the transactions in customers' accounts, risk categorisation is very crucial. Risk category will decide the extent of monitoring required to handle the accounts.

From the banks point of view risk perception is based on the volume of transactions and its frequency. It is also based on sources of funds and purpose of transactions. Any transaction or movement of funds that is definitely identified as to the source of funds and the underlying economic purpose for the transaction is known, the risk factor for banks becomes low. On the other hand, when the sources of the funds are not known or cannot be easily identified and/or the purpose of transactions is not understood, the risk factor for the bank goes up.

While transactions in individual savings accounts will be personal transactions, the same in case of entities and current accounts are complex and for high values. Risk involved in savings accounts is far less than those in other accounts are. Accounts of non-residents and high net worth individuals necessarily carry more risk as bank may not know all their sources. Accounts of trusts, associations, accounts managed by intermediaries also pose higher risk for banks.

Policy puts customers generally in four categories on the basis of risk perception. They are low risk, medium risk, high risk and very high-risk categories. The level of due diligence required for each category of customers will be different.

When the customer is of small means like salaried, small business or rural poor, the risk level in handling the account is quite low. Total turnover is not expected to exceed few lakhs of rupees. These accounts will call for minimum supervision that also when the turnover exceeds threshold limit. Enquiry can be made to find out the facts and reasons when the limit is breached.

All the accounts of Government and semi-Government, local authorities, public sector undertakings are assigned low risk as these accounts carry no risk, even though may have large volume transactions. Banks need not worry about the genuineness of transactions, as these accounts are Government owned.

Generally, the percentage of low risk customers is very large and can be as high as 90% for banks, as large chunk of savings accounts of individuals and small business accounts in current accounts, accounts from govt and public sector undertakings fall under this category. This reduces the overall burden of supervision for banks.

As discussed earlier, perception of the risk for banks goes up if any customer has large volume of transactions and if the sources are uncertain and activity is diversified. Accordingly, risk category of medium, high or very high shall have to be assigned.

Medium risk category can be large volume but with definite source of funds and identifiable ownership and management. These can cover all corporate and business firms, etc. where the activity is clearly known and the management is clearly identified. On this basis, all large corporate accounts fall under this category, if they are public limited companies with identified ownership and majority stake is widely held.

The sources of funds cannot be clearly identified in case of non-residents and high net worth individuals, as they may have large and different sources. Bank cannot estimate their likely turnover. These type of customers fall under high-risk category. Business firms or companies who are not considered as medium risk are also considered high risk.

Very high-risk customers are those carrying highest risk for banks due to their dealings. They are, politically exposed persons of foreign origin, customers with dubious reputation, trusts, societies, associations, etc. Here bank is in dark as to the sources of funds and its use. Except individual accounts, the real ownership is not clearly identifiable and makes it very difficult for the bank to satisfy itself about the transactions in these accounts. These accounts are to be handled extremely carefully as there is every possibility of shady transactions happening in these accounts.

## Customer Due Diligence

Correct risk classification is necessary for applying appropriate due diligence at the time of opening the account and then subsequently monitoring the transactions.

Low risk customers are salaried class, poor people, small business people and the Government sector, etc. It is because except Government sector, all others are of small means and/or definite means as salaried class. Once their status is known, due diligence is limited to examining the documents for the purpose of identification only. Detailed information of the person is not necessary as his account is not going to have large value transactions and sources are few. Bank can conveniently fix some threshold limit in his account, and keep minimum watch on the account. Only when the threshold is breached or large value transaction is put through in the account, facts may be inquired.

In case of medium and high-risk customers, more due diligence and more information about the activity and sources of funds will be required. Information about their customers/suppliers will be required, which will enable the bank to understand transactions in the account. Reason is that these accounts may have high volume transactions and understanding these transactions is necessary for the bank for handling it.

Very high-risk customers are generally to be handled with care and intensive due diligence will be required in their case.

## Customer Profile and Threshold Limits

Based on information collected from customers banks shall prepare a profile of the customer. The profile will contain all the basic information and other details as applicable. After compiling the profile, the risk category assigned will also be noted on the profile. Banks can have only a short profile for low risk customers with minimum basic information. For other categories of customers, banks need to compile a detailed profile and include all relevant information on status, financial standing, details of clients/suppliers, etc.

For the purpose of monitoring the accounts banks are required to fix some threshold limits for each account. The purpose is to know the likely annual turnover in the account. This is important because otherwise bank will not know whether the turnover in the account is commensurate with the known profile and resources of the customer or unreasonably high. By fixing threshold limit bank can ensure that the turnover is as per projections and in case of deviation or breach, bank may inquire into the same to satisfy that account is in order. As banks are to watch for suspicious transactions, this becomes an important tool to identify accounts for verification.

Generally, banks fix a default threshold limit or minimum limit to take care of all low risk accounts of individuals. This will avoid them spending time on small value accounts, which is very large in number, and allows them to concentrate on other accounts for monitoring. Banks may fix any threshold limit as they deem fit for other categories after studying the information collected at the time of opening the account. This limit can be reviewed and re-fixed as required. However to avoid frequent reviews proper fixing of threshold limit is necessary.

### Monitoring the Transactions

RBI Guidelines prescribed Monitoring of Transactions in the accounts by banks as under:

> "Ongoing monitoring is an essential element of effective KYC procedures. Banks can effectively control and reduce their risk only if they have an understanding of the normal and reasonable activity of the customer so that they have the means of identifying transactions that fall outside the regular pattern of activity. However, the extent of monitoring will depend on the risk sensitivity of the account. Banks should pay special attention to all complex, unusually large transactions and all unusual patterns which have no apparent economic or visible lawful purpose. The bank may prescribe threshold limits for a particular category of accounts and pay particular attention to the transactions which exceed these limits. Transactions that involve large amounts of cash inconsistent with the normal and expected activity of the customer should particularly attract the attention of the bank. Very high account turnover inconsistent with the size of the balance maintained may indicate that funds are being 'washed' through the account. High-risk accounts have to be subjected to intensified monitoring. Every bank should set key indicators for such accounts, taking note of the background of the customer, such as the country of origin, sources of funds, the type of

transactions involved and other risk factors. Banks should put in place a system of periodical review of risk categorization of accounts and the need for applying enhanced due diligence measures. Banks should ensure that a record of transactions in the accounts is preserved and maintained as required in terms of section 12 of the PML Act, 2002. It may also be ensured that transactions of suspicious nature and/or any other type of transaction notified under section 12 of the PML Act, 2002, is reported to the appropriate law enforcement authority."

As per RBI guidelines, Monitoring means understanding of the normal and reasonable activity of the customer so that banks can identify transactions that fall outside the regular pattern of activity. Banks should pay special attention to all complex, unusually large transactions and all unusual patterns, which have no apparent economic or visible lawful purpose. Banks may prescribe threshold limits for a particular category of accounts and pay particular attention to the transactions, which exceed these limits. Transactions that involve large amounts of cash inconsistent with the normal and expected activity of the customer should particularly attract the attention of the bank. Very high account turnover inconsistent with the size of the balance maintained may indicate that funds are being 'washed' through the account. These are the basic purpose of monitoring which banks are required to do now.

Under KYC guidelines, monitoring the transactions in the accounts is the responsibility of banks. They will have to monitor the transactions for identifying money laundering and also to identify financing of terrorist activities. Under the provisions of PMLA, banks are duty bound to identify suspicious transactions and report the same to FIU-IND.

As most of the banks are now under core banking and offers anywhere banking facilities to its customers, banks now have no branch control on the accounts as in the earlier period. Under core banking, accounts are operated at any point and the parent branch has no knowledge and the system runs without the knowledge of banks. Bank can only know about it subsequently, if it looks for it.

Once the account is opened, bank has a responsibility to make banking services available to those customers. It is not possible for banks to hold the transaction and seek information. Most of the transactions happening in the accounts are system driven and have to be completed within time norms. In view of this, the risk i.e. operational risk is very high. It is quite possible that culprits use banking services under the very nose of banks, without the knowledge of banks. Stopping any transaction is risky, even if there is an opportunity available to the bank, because there will be repercussions and liability arising out of such decisions. Moreover, bank may risk its reputation if it does such things. It is very unusual to stop anything merely on some suspicion and there is no legal protection available. Bank has to fight its own battle in such matters.

On the other hand, PMLA 2002 enacted by the Government puts the responsibility to report suspicious transactions to FIU-IND. It is now a mandatory duty of banks. At the same time, it can be said that the law recognizes and accepts that banks cannot stop transactions based on suspicion. Banks are bound by banking laws and practices to complete the transactions as per rules applicable, and then report such transactions to FIU-IND who will decide and coordinate with law enforcement agencies. Hence, it is a big relief for banks, as their action in conducting the transactions will not be questioned, if it is as per practices of banking and if bank has submitted STR (suspicious transaction report). Bank's responsibility is to give clue and lead to law enforcement agencies through FIU-IND. However any deficiency in due diligence at the time of opening the account may put bank into problems.

Volume of banking transactions is so high it is humanly impossible for banks to monitor every transactions. Still as they are accountable and responsible, banks have to create a system of control to monitor transactions and to identify suspicious transactions. The control can be by looking at exceptions. This is good enough because there is no purpose in looking at genuine transactions and wasting time on it.

Exceptions are transactions, which are not in usual pattern of transactions in relation to customers profile, his activity and the amount being unusual given the background of the customer. The purpose is to bring out exceptions that may lead to suspicion so that they can be studied.

This is possible by software programmes now available to generate such exceptions. These are called AML software. Programmes can be designed by banks using their experience and the legal requirements. Threshold limits can be fixed for each account so that whenever breach occurs, the system can generate exceptions (alerts) and throw it up for verification. Banks are now using AML software to generate alerts on different parameters to enable them to identify suspicious transactions.

To make threshold limit an important tool to identify exceptions, threshold limit in the account will have to be realistic and futuristic. Then only the real exceptions can be brought out. When there is a breach, bank has to call for additional information and may be bank has to revise the limit based on additional information gathered. In view of this, the exercise can become unwieldy and cumbersome if large number of alerts is generated. Only when exceptions are generated carefully, it will be meaningful and give correct warning signals to the bank.

## Suspicious Transactions—Examples

Besides generating alerts based on threshold limit, AML software can generate many other predesigned alerts, which banks will have to verify in order to identify suspicious transactions. A suspicious transaction has been defined under PMLA 2002 and the definition is given under head 'Money laundering' below. Few examples of suspicious transactions may be:

- Accounts where deposits or withdrawals are primarily in cash. Substantial cash deposits composed of many high denomination notes.
- Accounts where deposits and withdrawals are received from/made to sources apparently unconnected with the business activity/dealings.

- Unusual purchase of DD / TT / PO against cash.
- Accounts with large volume of credits whereas the nature of business is not known or does not justify such credits.
- Deposit of large number of cheques for small amounts but rare withdrawals. Accounts where apparently money is collected as donations from public but the activity/purpose is not disclosed. Accounts receiving foreign donations or contributions.
- Account of a customer who does not reside/have office near the branch but lives at far off place or another city.
- Funds coming from foreign countries/centers, which are known for money laundering.
- Customer who has no record of past or present employment but makes frequent large transactions.
- Sending or receiving frequent or large volumes of cross border remittances.
- Receiving large TT/DD remittances from various centers and remitting the consolidated amount to a different account/center on the same day leaving minimum balance in the account.
- Multiple accounts under the same name or different names and frequent inter transfers of funds in these accounts.
- Regular deposits of Cheques, Drafts of third parties in the account.

### Updation of Customer Profile and Information

Ironically, there was no system of updating customer profile by the banks earlier. Even when the account has run for over a decade, banks had the same information collected at the time of opening the account and also the same old photograph of account holder. With passage of time, documents lose its relevance/importance. KYC now prescribes that periodical updation of customer data is required and periodicity has been fixed depending on risk perception. Banks are advised to obtain latest photographs also periodically.

As per RBI guidelines, the periodicity of such updation of customer data should not be less than once in 5 years in case of low risk category customers and not less than once in 2 years in case of high and medium risk categories. Banks are required to collect fresh documents and photographs as the earlier obtained papers may be redundant due to any change in the status of the account holder.

RBI has also advised banks to put in place a system of periodical review of risk categorisation. In case of higher risk perception on a customer such review of risk categorisation of customers should be carried out at a periodicity of not less than once in six months.

### KYC and Role of Introduction

Another important issue after the implementation of KYC policy is about the role of introduction. Prior to KYC, the general practice of banks was to obtain an introduction from existing account holder for opening new account. It served the purpose of identification of the new account holder and also acted as a reference. Further, depending on the quality of introduction bank can take consolation about the new account. Introduction though carried no legal liability on introducer acted as moral restraint and helped the banks in many ways. Identification of the account holder is considered established based on introduction. This position was upheld by courts of law also.

KYC policy is silent about the role of introduction. RBI has made a mention about the role of introduction in banks as per practice and IBA guidance to banks. However, KYC policy makes it compulsory for banks to identify the customer on the basis of identity proofs and no role is ascribed for introduction for this purpose. Whether banks should continue to take introduction or dispense with this practice is left to banks to decide.

### Simplified KYC Procedure

After the KYC policy had been introduced it was found that many persons, particularly poor cannot fulfil the KYC requirement for opening banking account as many a time they do not have a proper identity paper acceptable to banks and also may not be in position to produce residence proof. As they will be precluded from banking services, RBI allowed banks to open basic banking account or no frill account for them by following a simplified procedure. This procedure is now called simplified KYC.

Under this, bank can open a basic banking account for a person and such basic banking account will be limited to a balance not exceeding ₹ 50,000 in all accounts and the total credit in the accounts for the year not to exceed ₹ 1 lakh.

In case where a person who wants to open an account is not able to produce the prescribed documents banks may open accounts of such persons by following a simplified KYC procedure as under:

(a) Introduction from another account holder who has been subjected to full KYC procedure. The introducer's account with the branch should be at least six months old and should show satisfactory transactions. Photograph of the person who proposes to open the account and his address should be certified by the introducer.

(b) Any other evidence as to his identity and address of the customer to the satisfaction of Branch In charge.

If at any point of time, the balance in all accounts with the bank (taken together) exceeds ₹ 50,000 or total credit in the accounts taken together exceeds ₹ 1,00,000 no further transactions would be permitted until full KYC procedure is completed.

These types of accounts are now encouraged under 'Financial Inclusion' as it is now the national goal where every individual in the country is to be linked to banking system.

### Money Laundering PMLA, 2002

Criminal activities, such as drug trafficking, smuggling, human trafficking, corruption and others, tend to generate large amounts of profits for the individuals or groups carrying out the criminal act. However, by using funds from such illicit sources, criminals risk drawing the authorities' attention to the underlying criminal activity and exposing themselves to criminal prosecution. In order to benefit freely from the proceeds of their crime, they must therefore conceal the illicit origin of these funds.

Money laundering is the process by which illegal funds and assets are converted into legitimate funds and assets. Generally, the following are the steps in the process:

1. Placement: Illegal funds or assets are first brought into the financial system.
2. Layering: Use of multiple accounts, banks, intermediaries, corporations, trusts, countries to disguise the origin.
3. Integration: Laundered funds are made available as apparently legitimate funds.

However, all money laundering transactions may not go through layering process and the same may be skipped.

PML Act 2002 defines money laundering offense as under:

> **Offence of Money Laundering**—Whosoever directly or indirectly attempts to indulge or knowingly assists or knowingly is a party or is actually involved in any process or activity connected with the proceeds of crime and projecting it as untainted property shall be guilty of offence of money laundering.

As discussed earlier, PMLA 2002 is enacted to curb money laundering and Financial Intelligence Unit of India (FIU-IND) is created to oversee the implementation of this act. FIU-IND is the coordinating agency for financial information, which it collects from banks and others. The information collected is decimated by it and in case it is felt that the transactions shall have to be looked into, then FIU-IND passes on the information to Enforcement Agencies for investigation. Under the act and the rules, banks and others are duty bound to report certain transactions to FIU-IND on regular basis.

### *Reporting to FIU-IND under PML Act 2002*

Section 12 of the act prescribes maintenance of records of transactions and reporting requirement.

*"Section 12. Banking companies, financial institutions and intermediaries to maintain records—*

(1) Every banking company, financial institution and intermediary shall—

(a) maintain a record of all transactions, the nature and value of which may be prescribed, whether such transactions comprise of a single transaction or a series of transactions integrally connected to each other, and where such series of transactions take place within a month;

(b) furnish information of transactions referred to in clause (a) to the Director within such time as may be prescribed;

(c) verify and maintain the records of the identity of all its clients, in such manner as may be prescribed:

Provided that where the principal officer of a banking company or financial institution or intermediary, as the case may be, has reason to believe that a single transaction or series of transactions integrally connected to each other have been valued below the prescribed value so as to defeat the provisions of this section, such officer shall furnish information in respect of such transactions to the Director within the prescribed time.

(2) The records referred to in sub-section (1) shall be maintained for a period of ten years from the date of cessation of the transactions between the clients and the banking company or financial institution or intermediary, as the case may be.

Detailed rules under the act have been framed for banks to submit above information and the disclosure of such information is mandatory. The act also provides immunity to banks for this disclosure against any legal action. Hence, this act is another exception to the banking secrecy laws of the country.

Under provisions of PML Act, banks have to submit following reports:

1. Cash transaction reports—for cash transactions of ₹ 10 lakhs and above either single or number of transactions integrally connected.

2. Suspicious transactions report.
3. Counterfeit currency reports—reports where counterfeit currencies have been detected by banks.

Suspicious transactions have been explained as under:

> Suspicions transaction means a transaction whether or not made in cash which, to a person acting in good faith—gives rise to a reasonable ground of suspicion that it may involve the proceeds of crime; or appears to be made in circumstances of unusual or unjustified complexity; or appears to have no economic rationale or bonafide purpose.

However, the exception for disclosure provided in this act is different as under the rules, banks are prohibited from informing the customers about the disclosure of information on the account. Rules framed under the act states as under:

> However a banking company, financial institution or intermediary, as the case may be, and its employees shall keep the fact of furnishing information in respect of transactions referred to in clause (D) of sub-rule (1) of rule 3 strictly confidential [proviso inserted to Rule 8(3) vide notification 13/2009 dated 12-11-2009].

This means that banks cannot inform the customers about the reporting as such information to the customer may hamper the investigation process by legal authorities, if desired by them based on information provided by banks.

### Combating Financing of Terrorism

According to the International Convention for the Suppression of the Financing of Terrorism, a person commits the crime of financing of terrorism "if that person by any means, directly or indirectly, unlawfully and wilfully, provides or collects funds with the intention that they should be used or in the knowledge that they are to be used, in full or in part, in order to carry out" an offense within the scope of the Convention.

The primary goal of individuals or entities involved in the financing of terrorism is therefore not necessarily to conceal the sources of the money but to conceal both the financing and the nature of the financed activity.

In our country, terrorist activities comes under the purview of UAPA 1967 [Unlawful Activities (Prevention) Act, 1967]. In view of increased threats of terrorist activities around the globe and in view of many resolutions passed by Security Council of United Nations, The Unlawful Activities (Prevention) Act, 1967 (UAPA) has been amended by the Unlawful Activities (Prevention) Amendment Act, 2008. Government has since issued an Order dated August 27, 2009 detailing the procedure for implementation of Section 51A of the Unlawful Activities (Prevention) Act, 1967 relating to the purposes of prevention of, and for coping with terrorist activities.

UAPA deals with terrorist activities, financing of terrorist activities and provides for punishment and also seizure of terrorist proceeds or assets.

### Unlawful Activities (Prevention) Act, 1967–*Obligation of Banks*

**1.** Banks should scan all existing accounts to ensure that no account is held by or linked to any of the entities or individuals included in the consolidated list of individuals/entities connected with terrorist activities as circulated by Reserve Bank. Banks shall have to provide full details of accounts bearing resemblance with any of the individuals/entities in the list immediately to RBI and FIU-IND.

**2.** Reserve Bank circulates the list to all banks and financial institutions as and when list of individuals and entities, approved by Security Council Committee [established pursuant to various United Nations' Security Council Resolutions (UNSCRs)], are received from Government of India. Banks/Financial Institutions are required to update the consolidated list of individuals/entities as circulated by Reserve Bank.

Before opening any new account, it should be ensured that the name/s of the proposed customer does not appear in the list and account shall not be opened for such individuals or entities.

**3.** On receipt of the list of individuals and entities, subject to UN sanctions (referred to as designated lists) from RBI, Banks should follow the procedure prescribed under Section 51A of UAPA, in regard to freezing/unfreezing of financial assets of the designated individuals/entities enlisted in the UNSCRs held in the form of bank accounts as under:

(i) Maintain updated designated lists in electronic form and run a check on the given parameters on a regular basis to verify whether individuals or entities listed in the schedule to the Order (referred to as designated individuals/entities) are holding any funds, financial assets or economic resources or related services held in the form of bank accounts with them.

(ii) In case, the particulars of any of their customers match with the particulars of designated individuals/ entities, the banks shall immediately, inform full particulars of the of bank accounts, held by such customer on their books to the Joint Secretary (IS-I), Ministry of Home Affairs.

(iii) Banks shall also send by post a copy of the communication to the UAPA nodal officer of RBI, Chief General Manager, Department of Banking Operations and Development, Anti Money Laundering Division, World Trade Centre, Centre-1, Cuffe Parade, Colaba, Mumbai-400005. Banks shall also send a copy of the communication to the UAPA nodal officer of the state/UT where the account is held as the case may be, and to FIU-India.

(iv) In case, the match of any of the customers with the particulars of designated individuals/entities is beyond doubt, the banks would prevent designated persons from conducting financial transactions, under intimation to Joint Secretary (IS-I), Ministry of Home Affairs, at Fax and convey over telephone.

(v) Banks shall also file a Suspicious Transaction Report (STR) with FIU-IND covering all transactions in the accounts carried through or attempted, as per the prescribed format.

**4. Freezing of Financial Assets.** In terms of Section 51A, the Central Government is empowered to freeze, seize, or attach funds and other financial assets or economic resources held by, on behalf of or at the direction of the individuals or entities connected with terrorist activity.

In case, the verification indicates that the properties are owned by or held for the benefit of the designated individuals/entities, an order to freeze these assets under section 51A of the UAPA would be issued within 24 hours of such verification and conveyed electronically to the concerned bank branch under intimation to Reserve Bank of India and FIU-IND. The order shall take place without prior notice to the designated individuals/entities.

**5. Implementation of requests received from foreign countries under U.N. Security Council Resolution 1373 of 2001.** U.N. Security Council Resolution 1373, obligates countries to freeze without delay the funds or other assets of persons who commit or attempt to commit, terrorist acts or participate in or facilitate the commission of terrorist acts; of entities or controlled directly or indirectly by such persons; and of persons and entities acting on behalf of, or at the direction of such persons and entities, including funds or other assets derived or generated from property owned or controlled, directly or indirectly, by such persons and associated persons and entities.

To give effect to the requests of foreign countries under U.N. Security Council Resolution 1373, the Ministry of External Affairs shall examine the requests made by the foreign countries and forward it electronically, with their comments, to the UAPA nodal officer for IS-I Division for freezing of funds or other assets.

The UAPA nodal officer of IS-I Division of MHA, shall cause the request to be examined, and upon satisfaction, the request would be electronically forwarded to the nodal officers in RBI. The proposed designee as mentioned above would be treated as designated individuals/entities. RBI then sends the list to banks for action under the act.

**6. Communication of Orders under section 51A of Unlawful Activities (Prevention) Act.** All Orders under section 51A of Unlawful Activities (Prevention) Act, relating to funds, financial assets or economic resources or related services, would be communicated to all banks through RBI.

# Bank Deposit Accounts

17

## Bank Term Deposits

Banks accept deposits from public and pays interest on it. Deposits are accepted from 7 days period to 10 years and bank pays varying interest rates. Maximum period of deposit is 10 years as per RBI guidelines. The deposit period can be more than 10 years in case courts directs for specific cases. Generally, it happens in case of minor's deposits. Since the year 1997, the rate of interest is decided by the banks depending on market trend and competition.

Bank deposits are generally accepted for any number of days and month as per customers' choice. Hence, customer can decide the due date as per his requirement and place the deposit.

## Interest and Tax

Interest on deposit cannot be changed by the bank during the currency of deposit. Bank shall have to honour the contract.

Bank pays interest on quarterly basis. However, customer can also opt for monthly interest as all banks have the scheme for it. However, the interest calculated on monthly basis will be little less as it is discounted value of quarterly interest.

Banks also have reinvestment deposit schemes wherein the quarterly interest shall be automatically reinvested. This gives benefit of cumulative interest and payable only on maturity. However, the basic rate of interest is same, because of cumulating factor customer gets good yield at the end.

Bank interest income is taxable and rules of TDS is applicable. If the interest paid or credited is more than ₹ 10,000 in a year TDS is deducted at specified rate and paid to treasury. Customers have an option to give declaration—form 15G or 15H to banks each year in case they are not taxable or they have specific exemptions from IT dept in which case bank will not deduct TDS. Bank is responsible to deposit TDS with the government and issue TDS certificate to the customer.

### Joint Deposits

Fixed deposits can be held in joint names also. Usually bank accepts three joint holders but also can accept more names. Deposits can be placed by individuals or any entity in its name. Banks will take constitutional documents from the entities.

In case of joint deposits, the depositors have the option of giving mandate for its payment informing the bank who will give discharge to the bank. Joint deposits can be placed on 'either or survivor', 'former or survivor', 'later or survivor' basis. 'Either or survivor' means that on maturity either of joint holders can collect payment from bank by surrendering the deposit receipt or in case of death of one or more joint depositors, the survivor can collect the payment. In other two cases, person named i.e. former/later is authorised to collect and only on his death, the survivor can collect payment. Joint accounts can be of any persons either related or not related. When bank deposits are accepted on these terms, the legal heirs will not have any recourse against the bank in case of death of their elder but they can have recourse against the person receiving the payment from the bank. This is because bank honours the agreement with the customers and by doing so it does not confer any right or title to the person receiving the payment. The payment by bank is as per mandate only. Hence, the person receiving the payment may have to account for it to legal heirs of the deceased joint account holder.

Joint depositors can change the mandate anytime during the currency of deposit and bank is bound to accept the change and act accordingly. However, original mandate can be changed only when all the joint holders agree and sign the new mandate.

### Minor's Deposit

Bank can also accept deposits in minor's names either singly or jointly with another minor or guardian. Only natural guardian or court appointed guardian can open account for minor. The provisions of personal law applicable to the depositor decide who the natural guardian is. Banks cannot accept anyone else as guardian and open account. This is because natural guardian has the authority to deal with minor's affairs and bank may face litigation on the matter. However, as per practice accepted by banks, mother can act as guardian for a minor for the purpose of placing deposit and father's consent is not necessary. It is important to note that persons cannot be accepted as guardians even if they are close relatives like grandparent, uncle, etc. unless either court has appointed them as guardian or by virtue of personal law applicable they have become guardians in the absence of natural guardian.

Bank shall record the date of birth of the minor and keep track of minors attaining majority. If the minor has become major at maturity date then bank shall have to take his discharge for making the payment. Guardian can be asked to introduce and identify the minor who is now major.

### Nomination Facility

Nomination facility is also available to customers. They can nominate one person only as their nominee to receive payment in case of death of sole or all depositors. Nomination can also be made of a deposit held in joint names and nominee will come in the picture only after the death of every joint account holder.

Minor can also be made nominee in which case a guardian shall have to be named to act on behalf of minor. Nomination rules allow depositors to name a guardian for minor and no restrictions were placed whether the guardian shall be natural guardian or legally appointed guardian. Hence, it can be inferred that for the purpose of nomination for a bank deposit, anyone can be named as guardian for the minor.

Nominee can be a relative or anybody else. There is no restriction. No consideration or declaration for the reason of nomination is required. Nomination can be changed any number of times. There is no need to identify the nominee by the bank or inform him about the nomination. Depositor can keep it as a close secret and change it as per his wishes. Bank will ask for identity proof when it is called to make payment to nominee.

### Payment, Renewal and Premature Payment

Payment of deposits is made only when the deposit receipt is surrendered to the bank and not otherwise. In case of renewal bank may issue a new receipt or merely endorse the renewal on the original receipt itself and return it to customer. Bank allows renewal of deposits even if due dates have passed. At present if the deposit is renewed within 14 days of due date, the deposit is renewed with original due date i.e. backdated. In case the deposit has remained overdue for more than 14 days from due date then bank renews the deposit from the current date but pays interest for the overdue period so that customer does not loose.

Income tax rules prescribes that bank deposit with interest, if exceeds ₹ 20,000 then the payment shall have to be either by credit to account or by account payee cheque. This is mandatory with penal provision for breach. The purpose is to have trail of deposits and make it available to investigating agencies and to stop tax evasion. Now the question is whether bank can make payment to third parties at the request of the depositor instead to depositor. Though it appears as acceptable since mandate from customer is available, it cannot be done in view of tax rules. Tax law makes it obligatory to credit to account if the bank has the account or pay by account payee cheque so that the amount goes to the account of the depositor only. Hence, payment of deposit must find its way to depositors account first and only then, depositor can divert it, as he likes. So payment of deposit cannot be made to third parties. However, deposit can be paid to one of the joint depositor based on the existing mandate or new mandate by all joint depositors. Bank need not split the amount amongst joint depositors. Rather bank should not split the amount arbitrarily as bank is not aware of individual stakes of joint depositors and shall be guided by the mandate.

In case the deposit receipt is lost by the depositor, bank will issue duplicate receipt after taking indemnity from the depositor. Duplicate receipt will be paid on maturity. Bank may insist deposit receipt to be discharged on revenue stamp, if cash payment of deposit receipt is sought. In case the deposit is in joint names bank shall not know with whom the receipt is kept. If such deposit receipt is reported lost, it is better to take application signed by all joint depositors before issuing duplicate receipt. After maturity of the deposit, it is safe to accept the indemnity from anyone of the depositor, who is mandated to collect payment for issuing duplicate receipt.

Bank deposit can be prematurely withdrawn and as per practice, it is a right of the customer. If the bank wants to reserve the right, to reject the request then bank shall have to inform the customer at the time of accepting the deposit. Bank shall have to declare its rules for such withdrawals and the penalty it imposes for such things.

Customer has also the option to renew the deposit prematurely i.e. even before the deposit has fallen due, for further period and renew the deposit at the current rate of interest of the bank. This is a customer friendly provision to enable customer to get better interest rate in case the rates have moved up.

### Loan Against Deposit

Customer can also avail loan from the bank on security of deposit. Bank also allows loan to any third party at the request of the depositor and the rate of interest on loans shall be as per declared policies of the bank. Margin requirement for loan is also as per declared policy of the bank.

Deposit receipts cannot be given to third parties as security or lien without the consent of the bank as it does not recognize third party rights. Bank deposit receipt is not transferable and not negotiable. If third parties are taking position then they do so at their risk.

Likewise, the rule applicable for payment of deposit need not be applied while giving loan against the deposit. However, when the loan is liquidated on maturity then the balance amount shall be credited to depositors account even if the balance amount is less than ₹ 20,000 but the deposit in question with interest exceeds ₹ 20,000.

## Death Claims

Banks allows either nominees or survivors to withdraw deposits even before maturity in case of death of the depositor. If the deposit is in single name without nomination and the depositor dies then bank makes payment to legal heirs on the basis of death claim submitted. For death claims banks are guided by the personal laws governing the depositor or Indian succession act whichever is applicable. Succession certificates are not insisted unless it is very huge deposit and payment is claimed by other than class I legal heirs. The same rule applies to joint deposits with no nomination and all the depositors die. Bank also pays the interest at contracted rate till maturity if the deposit remains with it and claimed only on maturity. If the claim is delayed or made only after due date then also bank pays interest for the extra period the deposit has remained with the bank till its payment.

## Other Provisions

There is no restriction for depositing cash for placing the deposit. Any amount of cash can be deposited but in case it exceeds ₹ 50,000 then PAN details must be taken by the bank.

Bank deposit is also an account with the bank and KYC compliance of the depositor is necessary and bank has to obtain photos, identity proof and residence proof and profile as per requirement. Deposit can be accepted even when savings or current account is not with the bank as KYC is applicable to deposit account also. If cash is deposited for placing the deposit it will also come under the ambit of reporting to FIU-IND as per cash transaction reporting requirement.

Bank deposit is not guaranteed by Govt or Reserve Bank of India. However, Deposit Insurance and Credit Guarantee

Corporation of India guarantees rupees one lakh per account in case of bank failure.

### Savings Bank Accounts

Banks open running account for individuals as savings bank account. Customer can use this running account to deposit and withdraw for all his personal transactions. Banks pay interest @ 3.5% as prescribed by RBI since the year 2003, on minimum balance maintained in this account between 10th and last day of the month. Interest is paid on half-yearly basis. In 2011, banks have started paying interest on daily product basis, which is benefiting customers. Rate of interest is also increased to 4%. RBI freed the savings interest from October 2011 and banks are now free to fix any interest rates.

Savings accounts can be opened for individuals, minors and physically handicapped. Banks have been asked to encourage physically handicapped, blind persons and senior citizens to open accounts and banks are advised to make special arrangements for their convenience. Banks shall extend all help to these people to operate their accounts at banks.

Under savings bank account rules of Banks, non-profit making organisations like trusts, clubs, societies, and associations can open savings accounts. Banks also open savings account for professionals, for Govt and semi Govt Depts./organisations and Local Authorities. However, RBI has stipulated that Govt organisations who receive grants from Govt shall not be eligible to open savings accounts.

Bank interest income on savings bank does not attract TDS provisions of income tax. Banks are not deducting any tax.

For SB account with the bank, KYC compliance on the customer is necessary and bank has to obtain photos, identity proof and residence proof and profile as per requirement.

### Joint Accounts

SB accounts can be held in individual name or joint names. Technically bank can allow any number of individuals as joint account holders. However, presently banks restrict the numbers to maximum three mainly due to operational reasons.

In case of joint account, the joint account holders have the option of giving mandate for its operation informing the bank who will authorise withdrawals from the account.

Joint accounts can be opened on 'either or survivor', 'former or survivor', 'later or survivor' basis. 'Either or survivor' means that in case of death of one or more joint account holders, the survivor can operate the account and withdraw the amount. In other two cases, only on the death of former/later, the surviving joint holder can operate and withdraw the amount.

Joint accounts can be of any persons either related or not related. When SB account is opened on these terms, the legal heirs will not have any recourse against the bank in case of death of their elder but they can have recourse against the survivor. This is because bank honours the agreement with customers and by doing it does not confer any right or title to the survivor. The payment by bank is as per mandate only. Hence, the person receiving the payment may have to account for it to legal heirs of the deceased joint account holder.

### Minors Account

Bank shall record the date of birth of the minor and keep track of minors attaining majority. When the minor has become major bank shall have to take his signature and thereafter allow operations under his signature only.

Bank can also open account in minor's names either singly or jointly with another minor or guardian. Only natural guardian or court appointed guardian can open the account for minor. The provisions of personal law applicable to the depositor generally decide who is the natural guardian. Banks cannot accept anyone else as guardian and open account. This is because natural guardian has the authority to deal with minors accounts and bank may face litigation in the matter. However, as per practice accepted by banks, mother can act as guardian for a minor for the purpose of opening SB account and father's consent is not necessary. It is important to note that persons cannot be accepted as guardian even if they are close relatives like grandparent, uncle, etc. unless either court has appointed them as guardian or by virtue of personal law applicable they have become guardians in the absence of natural guardian.

### Nomination Facility

Nomination facility is also available to account holders. They can nominate one person only as their nominee to receive payment in case of death of sole or all account holders. Nomination can be made of account held in joint names also and nominee will come in the picture only after the death of all joint account holders.

Minor can also be nominated in which case a guardian shall have to be named to manage the things. Nomination rules allow account holders to name a guardian for minor and no restrictions were placed whether the guardian shall be natural guardian or legally appointed guardian. Hence, it can be inferred that for the purpose of nomination any one can be named as guardian.

Nominee can be a relative or anybody else. There is no restriction. No consideration or declaration for the reason of nomination is required. Here also while bank may make payment to the nominee as per mandate. The nominee may be accountable to the legal heirs.

Nomination can be changed any number of times. There is no need to identify the nominee by the bank or inform about the nomination. Account holder/s can keep it as a close secret and change it as per wishes. Bank will ask for identity proof when it is called to make payment to nominee.

### Operations in the Account

Security or lien cannot be created in favour of third parties on SB account without the consent of the bank, as it does not recognize third party rights. Banks generally do not encourage it.

Loan facility against the security of SB account is also not favoured by banks and as a special case banks may allow after taking back the chequebook from the customer and marking lien on the account.

Bank issues a passbook, which it will update on request. Customers can also opt for statement of account in place of passbook.

Bank issues cheque book for the use of account holder. Account holders can also use loose cheque or withdrawal form to withdraw the amount personally at the bank. Pass book is generally insisted for such transactions.

Savings accounts are meant for personal transactions of account holders and if business transactions are observed bank can ask the customer to change the account to current account.

Any number of credit transactions is allowed. But generally withdrawals are restricted to 100 per year.

Bank may charge minimum balance charges for account with cheque book facility if the balance in the account is below the minimum. Inoperative charges are also levied in case the account becomes inoperative i.e. if there are no operations in the account for more than six months. Bank will also charge for duplicate passbook if requested.

There is no restriction for depositing cash in the account. Any amount of cash can be deposited but in case it exceeds ₹ 50,000 then PAN details must be taken by the bank.

Banks generally do not allow credit of third party cheques/drafts in savings account as the account is meant for personal transactions only.

Banks now offer ATM cards and debit cards to account holders free of cost. Any Branch banking facility is also given to customers. Free internet banking facility is extended. SMS services are also extended free of cost.

Free at par immediate credit of outstation cheques up to ₹ 15,000 is allowed to customers. Standing instructions are accepted for execution without charge. Account holders can also avail RTGS and NEFT remittance facilities and EFT credit and debit facility.

### Death Claims

Banks allows either nominees or survivors to withdraw amount in case of death of the account holder. If the account is in single name without nomination and the customer dies then bank makes payment to heirs based on death claim submitted. For death claims banks are guided by the personal laws governing the depositor or Indian succession act, whichever is applicable. Succession certificates are not insisted unless it is very huge amount and payment is claimed by other than class I legal heirs. The same rule applies to joint accounts with no nomination and all the account holders die. Bank also pays the interest till payment.

### SB Accounts for Non-Residents

Savings accounts can be opened for Non-Resident Indians (NRI) under Non-Resident External (NRE) account scheme. However, such accounts shall be funded only by foreign remittance or from another NRE account. Local funds are not allowed to be credited in this account. The balance and the interest earned in this account are freely repatriable. There is no income tax liability on such accounts.

For local funds of non-resident Indians, savings account under Non-Resident Ordinary (NRO) account scheme can be opened and local funds can be credited freely. However, no repatriation without RBI approval can be allowed. Funds in this account can be used freely by NRI for any local payments. Now the interest earned on this type of account has been made repatriable as an incentive to NRIs.

Banks can also open savings accounts for foreign nationals staying in India for their personal use just like resident Indians. However, repatriation of balance will require RBI permission.

### Basic Banking Account

Banks are now opening savings accounts for poor as basic banking account/no frill account as part of financial inclusion. This is done with a view to achieve financial inclusion of poor and there are no charges on these accounts. However, the balance in this account shall not exceed ₹ 50,000 and annual turnover shall be less than ₹ 1 lakh. Otherwise, normal savings account will have to be opened/converted. Even KYC norms have been simplified to help the poor. Banks are now offering ATM cards to this type of accounts.

## Current Deposit Accounts

Current deposit accounts are meant for business transactions. Banks allow anyone to open current account. Individuals singly or jointly can open current account if they require to transact large number of transactions. Unlike savings accounts, there is no restriction for anyone to open a current account whether individuals or entities.

Current accounts are meant for business and all business firms, corporate and other entities can open current account.

Bank does not pay any interest on current accounts. However, banks levy service charges on the account depending on number of transactions in the account. To attract good balance in the current accounts, banks offer many incentives to account holders like concessional service charges or free services.

There is no restriction on number of credits or debits in a current account. In fact most of the bank services are availed by them like deposit and withdrawal of cash, collection of cheques, issue of cheques, remittances, etc.

Third party instruments are also accepted in current accounts for collection and credit.

Generally banks issue statement of accounts on monthly periodicity or oftener as required by the customer. Sometimes passbooks are also issued.

KYC compliance is must to open current accounts. Besides identity proofs and residence proofs of the persons authorised to operate the account, banks also collect constitutional documents in case of entities. Depending on the constitution of the entities, other papers like registration certificate, memorandum, byelaws, deeds, etc. will be called for.

## Recurring Deposit Accounts

Banks also open recurring deposit accounts and under this depositor can deposit a fixed amount each month for period from six months to ten years. This is suitable for regular savings by individuals or others and the total amount deposited with interest is payable after the period fixed.

This is a very good deposit scheme from the point of view of customer. Customer earns higher interest rates on the deposit than the savings bank interest rate. Bank pays interest rate as applicable to term deposit of similar period. As the deposit is made each month and the period of investment for each instalment deposit is progressively coming down, still the depositor get the rate applicable for the entire period. This allows depositor to earn better return on his savings. Customer is expected to deposit on a fixed date every month and the maturity amount including interest amount is shown in the passbook.

Recurring deposit account also has tax benefit, as the interest earned is not subject to deduction of TDS under income tax rules.

Generally, bank issues a passbook for the account and monthly deposits are recorded in the passbook. Individuals or entities can open such accounts and accounts in joint names, minors name can also be opened. Nomination rules as applicable to bank deposits are also applicable to these deposits. These deposits can also be pledged to get loans like term deposits. Customer is expected to deposit the amount every month on a fixed date and he has option to deposit advance instalments. In case of delay in paying the monthly deposit amount, bank may charge a small penalty for the delayed period. In case few instalments are missed then the customer has an option to extend the period of deposit and the maturity.

Many banks are also offering some variants of this deposit scheme to attract the depositors. One type of variant is flexibility in monthly deposit amount where the depositor has the option of depositing higher amount than the fixed instalment deposit.

## Sweep Accounts

A new type of deposit product has been developed by banks in nineties after they have shifted to core banking. It is a combination of running account and term deposit account. This product is enabled by the technology and is quite beneficial to depositors.

Banks call this product by different names as sweep accounts or flexi deposit accounts. In this, the customer who is having a savings or current account is given an option to have this facility. A minimum balance is agreed and any amount in excess of the minimum balance is swept to a deposit account on daily basis. The amount so transferred is generally in an agreed slab of amount or in multiples of it. The period for deposit is also agreed and hence the surplus balance in the running account is automatically shifted and invested as term deposit.

This type of account also ensures the liquidity, the account holder is free to issue cheques, and any shortfall in the running account will be automatically adjusted by crediting the required amount from the deposit account by a reverse sweep operation. All these transactions are system enabled and automatically carried out without any human intervention. Thus, the customer enjoys the liquidity and at the same time better returns on his deposits.

Though banks have started this deposit product, it has its implications. It will make the deposit cost for banks to go up. However, this product is yet to catch the attention of customers and once it is widely used, the banking system will see a change in the composition of its CASA and the cost of deposits.

## Types of Bank Customers

Who are banks' customers for whom the banks open and maintain accounts? Normally bank customers are recognized as two types. They are individuals and other than individuals. Individuals are natural persons and other than individuals may belong to various types. Some of them may be legal persons. Legal persons are entities who have legal recognition and are created as per provisions of any existing law like Companies act and Societies act. There can also be entities though recognized by the law, do not have status of legal person. They are partnerships, HUFs etc.

The test for the legal person is that whether it is treated as separate and distinct from the persons who have promoted it. Legal person can act like a natural person and sue or be sued in its own name in the court of law. Legal person is a person in perpetuity and can remain and continue forever. Other entities though recognized, are not treated as separate and distinct from the creators or promoters, and will not be able to sue or be sued in its own name.

## Bank Account—A Contract

Opening a bank account is a contract between the customer and the bank under the Indian Contract Act. Hence, it will be governed by the said act. For creating a contract, proposal from one party and acceptance from the other party is necessary. The account opening form, which is suitably worded, is the proposal from the prospective customer and acceptance of the bank is by way of opening an account in its books. Thereafter both parties are bound by the relationship (contract) they have entered.

Under the Indian Contract Act, the contract can be entered into between two consenting individuals or entities. Then only it is enforceable in the court of law. In case of natural persons, they are required to be majors, as minors cannot enter into any contracts. There needs to be free consent and hence persons who are mentally unfit (lunatics) or who are temporarily unfit (persons under the influence of alcohol, etc.) are incapable of entering into contracts. Requirement of free consent is also a damper to open accounts for illiterates.

Banks do not open accounts for lunatics. Banks open accounts for minors under the guardianship of natural guardian or court appointed guardian. However, banking practice is now accepting mother as guardian for opening the account of the minor. Banks also have started the practice of opening accounts for literate minors under minor's signatures. As regards illiterates, banks are opening accounts for them as a practice, if they are mature adults. Banks allow them to operate the account through thumb impressions placed before the bank. Chequebook facilities are generally not extended to them.

Banks open accounts for all types of physically challenged persons (excluding mental disability) and in fact help them to have bank account by providing additional facilities. Banks also encourage senior citizens to have accounts and help them.

## Entities Opening Accounts

Following are the types of entities that are dealing with banks.

| Sl. No. | Type of Entity | Constitutional Documents required besides identity and residence proofs |
|---|---|---|
| 1. | **Hindu Undivided Family (HUF)**<br>HUF is recognized under the Hindu Succession Act, 1956 but is not a legal entity. This act was amended in 2005 and daughters are also made co-parceners now. However, income tax laws recognizes it as separate entity for taxation purpose. The head of the family is called Karta and other members are called co-parceners. Only Karta is authorised to act on behalf of the HUF. HUF is generally recognized by a family name. HUF not being a legal entity cannot enter into partnership with anyone. Only the Karta can become the partner in his individual capacity. | • Name of the karta and list of all major and minor co-parceners required.<br>• Banks allow only Karta to operate the account. |
| 2. | **Proprietary concern**<br>Proprietary concern is owned by an individual. The concern may have a trade name. In law, the proprietor and the firm are one only. Firm does not have separate legal status. | • Declaration of Proprietorship is obtained.<br>• Account is opened in the trade name of the firm with the owner as the proprietor. |
| 3. | **Partnership firm**<br>Partnership is association of individuals for carrying on business. Partnerships are governed by Indian Partnership Act 1932. Partnership agreement can be oral or a deed may be created. If the deed is created, Partnership can be registered but registration is not compulsory. Partnership can have minimum 2 partners and maximum 20 partners.<br>Partnerships are not legal entities separate from the partners. However, income tax law recognizes it as separate entity for taxation purpose. Partner's liability is unlimited.<br>Minor cannot become a partner but can be admitted to the benefits of partnership. Hence minor is not responsible for firm's act.<br>HUF cannot become partner and only Karta in his personal capacity may become partner. | • Partnership Deed or Declaration of Partnership by all the Partners if the partnership deed has not been executed.<br>• Registration Certificate of firm if registered. |

*(Contd...)*

| | | |
|---|---|---|
| 4. | **Private Limited Company**<br>Companies are incorporated under the Companies Act 1956. Owners are the shareholders of the company and the shareholders liability is limited to their share capital in the company. Companies are legal entities and are separate from the shareholders. Companies are run by board of directors elected by the shareholders. Private limited companies can have minimum 2 shareholders and maximum 20. Companies are considered as born after the certificate of incorporation is issued by the Registrar of Companies (ROC). Company's management is governed by the memorandum and articles of association. The name of the private limited company shall contain the words "private limited". | • Certificate of incorporation.<br>• Memorandum and Articles of Association duly certified by a Director/Secretary.<br>• Duly certified Resolution passed by the Board of Directors.<br>• List of Directors. |
| | **Public Limited Company**<br>It is similar to private limited company. A public limited company has minimum 7 shareholders. It also requires to obtain certificate of commencement of business from ROC before commencing the business activity. (This requirement is not applicable to private limited companies). The name shall contain the word "limited". | • Certificate of incorporation.<br>• Certificate of commencement of business.<br>• Memorandum and Articles of Association duly certified by a Director/Secretary.<br>• Duly certified Resolution passed by the Board of Directors.<br>• List of Directors. |
| 6. | **Section 25 Companies**<br>When an association—<br>(a) is about to be formed as a limited company for promoting commerce, art, science, religion, charity or any other useful object, and<br>(b) intends to apply its profits, if any, or other income in promoting its objects, and to prohibit the payment of any dividend to its members,<br>It can approach Central Govt, and Central Govt, on satisfaction may issue licence, and direct that the association may be registered as a company with limited liability, without the addition to its name of the word "Limited" or the words "Private Limited".<br>Such companies are called section 25 companies and the name need not contain the word "Limited" or the words "Private Limited". | Same as above. |

| | | |
|---|---|---|
| 7. | **Coop Societies**<br>Cooperatives is a state subject and every state has its own State Coop Societies Act in place. Co-operative society is formed with the objective of promotion of the economic interests or general welfare of its members, or of the public, in accordance with co-operative principles, may be registered under this Act. Generally, minimum 10 members are required to form a society.<br>There are different types of coop societies depending on its purpose. Coop banks are also registered as coop society. Societies are governed by the byelaws that they adopt and register at the time of formation. | • Duly certified copies of constitution and bye-Laws/Rules.<br>• Certified copy of Registration Certificate issue by Registrar of Societies.<br>• List of Members/Members of the Managing Committee.<br>• Resolution passed by the Managing Body authorizing opening of account including mandate for operation of the account. |
| 8. | **Societies**<br>**(Clubs, Associations)**<br>Societies may be formed under The Societies Registration Act, 1860 by any seven or more persons associated for any literary, scientific, or charitable purpose, or for any such purpose as is described in section 20 of this Act, by subscribing their names to a memorandum of association, and filing the same with Registrar of Joint-stock Companies.<br>The following societies may be registered under section 20 of the Act—<br>Charitable societies, the military orphans funds or societies established at the several presidencies of India, societies established for the promotion of science, literature, or the fine arts for instruction, the diffusion of useful knowledge, the diffusion of political education, the foundation or maintenance of libraries or reading-rooms for general use among the members or open to the public or public museums and galleries or paintings and other works of art, collections of natural history, mechanical and philosophical inventions, instruments, or designs. | • Duly certified copies of constitution and Memorandum and Articles of Association.<br>• Certified copy of Registration Certificate.<br>• List of Members/Members of the Managing Committee.<br>• Resolution passed by the Managing Body authorising opening of account including mandate for operation of the account. |
| 9. | **Trusts**<br>Trusts are created by a donor (settler) who donates an amount for the cause or for the benefit of beneficiaries named in the trust deed. Trusts are managed by trustees appcinted as per provisions of the trust deed. Trust deed generally | • Certificate of registration.<br>• Certified copy of the Trust Deed.<br>• Names and addresses of Trustees.<br>• Resolution passed by the trustees to open Account with the Bank. |

(*Contd...*)

| | | |
|---|---|---|
| | mentions the purpose and the guidelines for running the trust<br>Trusts are governed by Indian Trusts Act 1882. Public and charitable trusts are governed by Charitable and Religious Trusts Act, 1920.<br>Besides, many States also have trust acts applicable within the state.<br>Some trusts are also registered as societies under societies registration act. | |
| 10. | **Statutory Corporations/Bodies**<br>Statutory corporations/bodies are created by the act of Central or State govt. It is separate from the government owned companies registered as companies under the companies act. Statutory corporations/bodies are created by the relevant act, which governs its management and functions. | • Copy of the notification of Act by virtue of which the corporation has come into existence.<br>• Memorandum and Articles of incorporation/relevant. Rules/Regulations/Schemes, if any.<br>• Resolution of the governing body authorising the corporation to open an account with the bank and naming the persons authorised to operate it. |
| 11. | **Govt—Both central and states,**<br>**Govt Departments**<br>**Constitutional bodies**<br>**Local authorities**<br>Accounts of government departments, Judiciary, Parliament and State Legislatures, Autonomous bodies, Local governments like Municipal Corporations, Panchayats, etc. | • Relevant govt Notifications.<br>• Govt orders regarding maintaining and operating bank accounts. |

# Foreign Exchange Business

# 18

Economic reforms ushered in by the Government have changed the status of the economy and have proved successful. Probably all started when the nation was facing foreign exchange crunch in 1991 when the nation came close to default to pay for its imports and had to pledge gold to get liquidity. A host of economic policy decisions were taken thereafter, and these changes brought back the economy on even keel and foreign exchange reserve position became comfortable.

## Non-Resident Accounts

In seventies Government had realised that non-resident Indians are a good source for foreign exchange as they generally remit to their families in India and also are interested to maintain their roots in the country. Then existing exchange control rules provided that NRIs can have Non-Resident Ordinary accounts (NRO) with banks which are similar to domestic accounts. However, NRIs could not take back the balance in those accounts. Govt then started to woo the non-residents to remit their savings into the country by giving tax breaks and repatriation options. Banks started luring them with many attractive schemes.

Besides NRIs, Persons of Indian Origin and Overseas Corporate Bodies predominantly owned by NRIs were also allowed to open accounts under various schemes. These three categories are identified as under:

### *Non-Resident Indian (NRI)*

An Indian citizen who stays abroad for employment/carrying on business or vocation outside India or stays abroad under circumstances indicating an intention for an uncertain duration of stay abroad is a non-resident. (Persons posted in UN organisations and officials deputed abroad by Central/State Governments and Public Sector undertakings on temporary assignments are also treated as non-residents.)

### *Person of Indian Origin (PIO)*

For the purposes of availing of the facilities of opening and maintenance of bank accounts and investments in shares/securities in India: a foreign citizen (other than a citizen of Pakistan or Bangladesh) is deemed to be of Indian origin, if,

1. he, at any time, held an Indian passport, or
2. he or either of his parents or any of his grandparents was a citizen of India by virtue of the Constitution of India or Citizenship Act, 1955 (57 of 1955).

*Note*: A spouse (not being a citizen of Pakistan or Bangladesh) of an Indian citizen or of a person of Indian origin is also treated as a person of Indian origin for the above purposes provided the bank accounts are opened or investments in shares/securities in India are made by such persons only jointly with their NRI spouses. Non-resident foreign citizens of Indian origin are treated on par with non-resident Indian citizens (NRIs).

### *Overseas Corporate Body (OCB)*

Overseas Corporate Body (OCB) means a company, partnership firm, society and other corporate body owned directly or indirectly to the extent of at least sixty per cent by Non-Resident Indians and includes overseas trust in which not less than sixty per cent beneficial interest is held by Non-resident Indians directly or indirectly but irrevocably, which was in existence as on September 16, 2003 and was eligible to undertake transactions pursuant to the general permission granted under Foreign Exchange Management Regulations.

### NRE Deposit Scheme

Non-resident external accounts (NRE) scheme was introduced in the year 1970, wherein the repatriation of the balance was guaranteed without seeking any permission from Reserve Bank of India. Non-residents were allowed to open savings, current as well as fixed deposit accounts. Interest earned was also repatriable and tax-free. However, there was exchange risk for the non-residents. Interest rates on NRE deposits were as prescribed by RBI and were almost similar to domestic deposits. Hence, NRE account though carried exchange risk on repatriation, it earned higher interest than it could have at other countries.

This special status continued for many years and when domestic deposit interest rate was freed, RBI allowed the banks to decide on NRE deposit rates also. In April 1996, RBI freed interest rates on NRE term deposits of over 2 years to be decided by banks. Again, from September 1997, banks were allowed to fix their own interest rates on NRE term deposits of 6 months and over. Finally, in the year 2003, RBI prescribed Interest rate ceilings on NRE deposits and linked it to LIBOR / SWAP rates. Thus, after the year 2003, NRE deposits do not enjoy better interest yield.

### FCNR Deposit Scheme

Reserve Bank of India came out with foreign currency non-resident deposit scheme (FCNR) in the year 1975 under which deposits of the non-residents were held in either US dollar or Pound Sterling. Subsequently two more currencies were added. Thus, the exchange risk was eliminated for NRIs. For banks, Reserve Bank of India asked them to surrender the same to Reserve Bank of India and get local funds and on maturity, banks can draw from Reserve Bank of India the original currency at the same rate. Thus, banks were insulated against exchange risks and the country got foreign exchange. The interest rates for FCNR were attractive as it was better by at least 2% over what non-residents would have got in their countries. Loans were also allowed against these deposits. This scheme attracted lot of deposits and inflow of foreign exchange improved.

In the year 1993, RBI discontinued FCNR deposit scheme and in its place allowed FCNR- Bank scheme on similar line. This was done as the forex reserves have improved and RBI felt that henceforth the exchange risk could be borne by banks themselves without support. Banks were allowed to retain FCNR-B deposits, hold foreign exchange assets and use the same as per their requirement and as per guidelines of RBI for the same. Banks were also allowed to lend foreign currency to its customers mainly exporters to bring down the cost of exports and to make them globally competitive.

### NRNR Scheme

At the height of foreign exchange crunch in the year 1991, RBI introduced another deposit scheme for non-residents called non-resident non-repatriable rupee deposit scheme (NRNR). The Scheme came into effect from 15th June, 1992. Under this, banks accepted term deposits from 6 months to 3 years and the rate of interest was very attractive. Interest rates were to be decided by banks and banks were given incentives in that these deposits were made free from CRR requirements, thereby inducing the banks to pay higher interest. It was on non-repatriable basis. There was tremendous response to this deposit scheme and under the scheme, only fresh remittances were allowed to be deposited. It was successful and foreign exchange inflow became sizeable.

Later when forex reserve position has improved substantially, RBI withdrew the scheme w.e.f. 1st April 2002.

Though the deposits were accepted on non-repatriable basis, RBI allowed the maturity proceeds of these deposits to be credited to NRE account after 1st April 2002 and hence made it repatriable for the non-residents.

### NRSR Scheme

RBI introduced with effect from 15th April 1999, a new type of account viz., Non-Resident (Special) Rupee (NRSR) Account for NRIs and PIOs who would voluntarily undertake not to seek repatriation of funds held in these accounts. The purpose is to simplify the procedures applicable to operation of bank accounts and financial transactions in India by non-resident individuals of Indian nationality/persons of Indian origin. This facility was not available to overseas corporate bodies.

The non-resident individuals of Indian nationality/persons of Indian origin maintaining Non-Resident (Ordinary) Account have the option of converting these accounts into Non-Resident (Special) Rupee Accounts. Similarly, when a resident becomes a non-resident by virtue of going abroad on emigration/employment, etc. he will also have an option of designating his account as Non-Resident Ordinary Account or Non-Resident (Special) Rupee Account.

NRSR accounts may be current, savings, recurring or fixed deposits accounts. Requirements in regard to resident accounts, including nomination facility, shall apply to NRSR accounts.

As RBI is intending providing full convertibility on non-resident deposit schemes, non-resident special rupee (NRSR) account schemes were discontinued with effect from April 1, 2002 along with NRNR scheme. Balances in these accounts were allowed to be credited to NRO account.

At present though NRE & FCNR schemes are continuing, the rate of interest has come down in line with rates overseas.

Opening up of the economy also witnessed loosening of controls on foreign exchange. Foreign Exchange Regulation Act 1947 (FERA) was replaced in the year 1999 by Foreign Exchange Management Act (FEMA) which was quite a liberal law. Country achieved current account convertibility in the year 1994, under which any current account payment like for import of goods and services are totally freed with minimum formalities for remitting funds abroad. As the Government wants to achieve capital account convertibility, many other changes have been made and Non-residents are benefitted. Interest earned on Non-resident ordinary accounts (NRO) became eligible for repatriation and are freely permitted to be remitted. Further relaxations have been allowed and now balance in NRO account can be repatriated up to one million dollars per year.

## NRI Deposits

NRI deposits have grown over the years and the status of these deposits from 1993 to 2011 is given in the following Table. Despite competitive rate of interest at present, NRI deposits are a source of regular forex inflow for the country as is evident from the Table.

### NRI Deposits Outstanding—Rupees

| Year (end-March) | NR(E) RA | FCNR (A) | FCNR (B) | NR(NR) RD | NRO | FC (B&O)D | FC (O)N | Total |
|---|---|---|---|---|---|---|---|---|
| 1993 | 8616 | 33163 | - | 1952 | - | 3261 | - | **46992** |
| 1994 | 11053 | 29176 | 3476 | 5501 | - | 1672 | 38 | **50916** |
| 1995 | 14348 | 22207 | 9648 | 7831 | - | - | 32 | **54066** |
| 1996 | 13452 | 14616 | 19648 | 12166 | - | - | 45 | **59927** |
| 1997 | 17886 | 8282 | 26906 | 20116 | - | - | 14 | **73204** |
| 1998 | 22267 | 4 | 33445 | 24735 | - | - | 9 | **80460** |
| 1999 | 25629 | - | 33222 | 28058 | - | - | - | **86909** |
| 2000 | 29465 | - | 35632 | 29447 | - | - | - | **94544** |
| 2001 | 33357 | - | 42357 | 31966 | - | - | - | **107680** |
| 2002 | 41205 | - | 47175 | 34392 | - | - | - | **122772** |
| 2003 | 71184 | - | 48651 | 16253 | - | - | - | **136088** |
| 2004 | 92977 | - | 49572 | 7895 | - | - | - | **150444** |
| 2005 | 93159 | - | 50108 | 1015 | - | - | - | **144282** |
| 2006 | 98443 | - | 58272 | - | 5119 | - | - | **161834** |
| 2007 | 106786 | - | 65955 | - | 7047 | - | - | **179788** |
| 2008 | 106824 | - | 56651 | - | 11148 | - | - | **174623** |
| 2009 | 119181 | - | 66803 | - | 24134 | - | - | **210118** |
| 2010 | 124473 | - | 67607 | - | 34998 | - | - | **227078** |
| 2011 | 117802 | - | 69658 | - | 43352 | - | - | **230812** |

*Source*: RBI -Table 152 ( crore)

FCNR(A) : Foreign currency non-resident (accounts)

FCNR(B) : Foreign currency non-resident (banks)

FC(B&O)D : Foreign currency (bank and other) deposits

NRO : Non-Resident Ordinary Rupee Accounts

NR(E)RA : Non-Resident (external) Rupee accounts

NR(NR)RD : Non-Resident (non-repatriable) Rupee deposits

FC(O)N : Foreign currency (ordinary) non-repatriable deposits

At present only three schemes i.e. NRE, FCNR and NRO are in operation. As the country is moving towards capital account convertibility, NRO accounts may also gain full repatriation soon.

## Share of NRI Deposits

NRI deposits have helped the country during its critical years and became a major component in bank deposits as can be seen from the Table below.

(₹ In crores)

| Year (end-March) | Total deposits of scheduled commercial banks | Total NRI deposits | % age of NRI deposits to Sch. Commercial banks deposits |
|---|---|---|---|
| 1993 | 268572 | 46992 | 17.50 |
| 1994 | 315132 | 50916 | 16.16 |
| 1995 | 386859 | 54066 | 13.98 |
| 1996 | 433819 | 59927 | 13.81 |
| 1997 | 505599 | 73204 | 14.48 |
| 1998 | 598485 | 80460 | 13.44 |
| 1999 | 714025 | 86909 | 12.17 |
| 2000 | 813345 | 94544 | 11.62 |
| 2001 | 962618 | 107680 | 11.19 |
| 2002 | 1103360 | 122772 | 11.13 |
| 2003 | 1280853 | 136088 | 10.62 |
| 2004 | 1504416 | 150444 | 10.00 |
| 2005 | 1700198 | 144282 | 8.49 |
| 2006 | 2109049 | 161834 | 7.67 |
| 2007 | 2611933 | 179788 | 6.88 |
| 2008 | 3196939 | 174623 | 5.46 |
| 2009 | 3834110 | 210118 | 5.48 |
| 2010 | 4492826 | 227078 | 5.05 |

(*Note*: NRI deposits figures is for all banks including coop banks whereas total deposits of scheduled commercial banks are only taken for arriving the share of NRI deposits in total deposits)

The share of NRI deposits in total deposits of banks is sizeable as can be seen from the Table above. In early nineties, NRI deposits were pursued to ease balance of payment shortfall and in 1993; share of NRI deposits was highest at 17.50% of total deposits of scheduled commercial banks. The share remained above 10% until the year 2004 and thereafter it came down to 5.05% in 2010. It is pertinent to note that NRNR scheme was withdrawn from the year 2002 and interest on NRE scheme was pegged to LIBOR in the year 2003. Even though NRI deposits have grown quantum-wise even after this period, its share in total deposits has come down.

**Foreign Exchange Business**

As earlier mentioned in this book, foreign exchange business was under the exclusive domain of *exchange banks* until the year 1935. This was changed only after the RBI came on the scene in 1935. Indian banks were then allowed to handle foreign exchange business. Foreign Exchange Regulation Act 1947 (FERA) was passed and RBI monitored banks on the compliance of it. Banks were issued licenses as 'authorized dealers' to handle this business. This act has been replaced by Foreign Exchange Management Act 1999 (FEMA). Foreign exchange dealings are now governed by the FEMA 1999.

Export and Import business with other countries requires foreign exchange, as the payment for imports can be made in a currency acceptable to the seller in the foreign country. Generally, the payments of exports and imports are accepted in free currencies like sterling, dollar, euro and few other currencies. These currencies are accepted in the international trade, as the respective governments do not put any restrictions for movement of the currency across the world. Currencies, which are not convertible, are generally not accepted by other nations. Our rupee is not a free currency it is not yet accepted as a currency for international trade. Hence, for imports, the importer has to pay in the currency desired by the seller. Importer can get the necessary currency from an authorised dealer. RBI authorises banks in the country as authorised dealers for foreign exchange, based on certain norms fixed by it. This means these banks can trade in foreign currencies—buy and sell as per requirement.

RBI also issues 'money changer' licenses to parties who are authorised to purchase foreign currencies from tourists or locals in some cases. However, they cannot sell foreign exchange. Most of the hotels and businesses dealing with foreign tourists obtain this license to do business with tourists. These money changers will have to handover the foreign currencies to authorised dealers only.

Similarly, for exports by our country, the exporter cannot insist for rupee payment as rupee is not a freely converted currency and the buyers abroad will find it difficult to make payment in rupee. Hence, the exporter is permitted to get the payment in international currencies like Pound, Dollar, Euro or Yen and many others.

Hence, both for imports and exports, authorised dealers are required to trade in few international currencies. Authorised dealers buy and sell these currencies as per demand from importers and exporters. Authorised dealers also handle other foreign exchange business like inward remittances by NRIs, FIIs and outward remittances by locals for various approved purposes.

### Nostro Accounts

In order to handle payments and receipts of foreign exchange, authorised dealers maintain accounts at foreign centres with foreign banks through which these transactions are routed on behalf of the customers. These accounts of Indian banks with foreign banks at foreign centres are called NOSTRO accounts. Foreign exchange transactions by banks will convert rupees to foreign currency and *vice versa*. As our country has attained current account convertibility, all payments for imports and other current account transactions are freely permitted by banks as authorised by RBI. At present, transactions of capital nature are under certain restrictions.

Banks are handling these transactions through its international banking depts. and for this purpose, banks have 'dealing rooms' for foreign exchange. Dealers in this dealing room undertake buying and selling of foreign currencies as per the needs of customers and banks. Deals are entered into with foreign banks or local banks.

Bank maintains NOSTRO account separately for each currency at the concerned centres. The transactions undertaken by banks on ongoing basis generally result in their having balance in these NOSTRO accounts. Buying and selling are at current market rates for the respective currencies, which changes almost daily depending on demand and supply, on short-term basis and stability of the currency and the economy of the country concerned, on long-term basis. In view of this, there is an element of risk in holding foreign currency in NOSTRO accounts as their exchange valuation keeps changing daily for better or worse. This is the currency risk for banks and since long, as per RBI directives, banks are managing risk by squaring off their position on almost daily basis.

### Forward Contracts

Imports and exports business are generally on credit basis. Though the contracts are drawn and due dates for payments are fixed, importers and exporters are exposed to exchange risk as the rates fluctuate on daily basis. They are not in a position to know their rupee liability or receipt on due date. However, they can cover these risks by entering into forward rate contracts with authorised dealers. This means they can enter into agreement with banks, which will fix the exchange rate for the future transaction, now itself. This will protect the customers, as their liability or income gets fixed and exchange risk is mitigated. These types of contracts are called forward contracts, a derivative product of foreign exchange. In fact, importers and exporters are always advised to cover their risk on this basis. However, this is not compulsory and the parties may choose to carry the risk and face the same. Forward bookings are also undertaken by the dealing rooms.

### Currency Premium

While booking forward contracts, it can be observed that most of the international currencies are quoted at a premium for future date. This means the future rate for the currency in terms of rupee is more than what it is on current date. This rate difference is called the premium of the currency. Likewise, there can be discount for a currency also. In fact, if currency A is at premium against currency B, then the currency B is at discount as against the currency A. The premium or discount of currencies is based on the relative position of currencies and the status of their country's economy. Economies are not same and interest rate structures are not same in any two given countries. For example, dollar is at premium as against the rupee. This is because the interest rates in US are low and in India, they are high. This is again the result of status of the economies as US economy is more stable with low inflation as compared to Indian economy. These are the fundamentals, but market is also influenced by other factors like demand and supply, new economic or political events, etc.

Premium is mainly based on interest rate differentials of two currencies as otherwise arbitrage takes place to take the advantage of interest rate differentials. For example if interest is higher in India then people may convert other currency and keep it as rupee deposit in India, earn higher interest and then convert back to the original currency thereby earning more than what they could have earned. As there is exchange risk and if they want the forward cover to hedge against the risk, then the premium of that currency nullifies the higher interest earnings. This acts as a deterrent for arbitrage.

## Managing Currency Risk

Banks are managing the currency risk by daily squaring off their position in foreign currencies as mentioned earlier. For the purpose, banks take on their trading book all spot transactions and forward transactions and enter into matching reverse transactions with other banks. Thus if a bank has surplus dollars with it then it sells the same in forex market to attain near zero position. If the surplus is on cash basis, it enters into spot selling so that the cash is disposed. If the surplus is because of forward contracts then it sells forward so that the balance is disposed off on its due date of receipt. There can be simultaneous spot sales and forward purchase for the same amount. This can happen when dollar balance held is surplus now, but will be required after certain date, as some liability will accrue on that certain date. Likewise, bank may purchase dollar on spot basis, if it is short of dollar now, but at the same time sell it forward as it is expecting dollar inflow on a particular future date.

## Handling Imports and Exports by Banks

Foreign exchange is precious for the nation to meet its import bill. Balance of payment position has to be monitored to ensure that, all current account transactions are paid from the receipts. Since current account convertibility is already in place, such payments either for import of goods and services or other purposes are allowed by banks under the guidelines. To keep track of forex transactions, all authorized dealers shall have to submit R-Returns to RBI on fortnightly basis. This statement consists of all credit and debit transactions effected by the dealer. For imports, banks are allowed to make payment as per terms of import. However, banks shall have to collect bill of entry certified by customs dept for the entry of goods into the country. This information they have to submit to RBI under BEF statement periodically. Banks shall have to get the same certified by internal/external auditors also. This is the precaution to ensure that bogus imports are not taking place and foreign exchange is released for the right purpose.

Banks also handle export bills both for collection and negotiate the bills. Once export has taken place, it must be ensured that the proceeds are received in time, as it represents nation's forex earnings. Monitoring is important to ensure that the proceeds are not delayed unnecessarily or siphoned off. Banks are duty bound to follow up and report to RBI, all the pending bills for payment in XOS statement periodically.

Exports are very vital for the country, as foreign exchange earned is required to make payments for the imports. Though imports appear to be controllable and can be reduced, in practice it does not happen. Country is dependant for crude oil from other countries and crude oil import is the major item under imports for our country. Besides, many other imports are required for industries and other users in the country. Under the General Agreement for Trade and Tariff (GATT) between the countries, govt cannot put restrictions for payment of imports and should not restrict imports just to protect local industries. Govt should not also levy import duties on imports, which is excessive and has the effect of restricting imports.

These compulsions are on the basis to allow free trade between the countries, which is now accepted as requirement for international trade. Every country shall try to export as much it can, the goods and services produced economically in the country. Hence, under the present dispensing of international trade, every country will try to export to the maximum so that it need not put any restriction for imports.

This is what the govt and the RBI has been doing over the years. The liberalisation and replacement of FERA with FEMA is a step in this direction.

## Exports

Historically India is known for its exports of cotton and many produces under British regime. In fact, colonisation of our country by the British was mainly with the purpose to control this trade. In the beginning of East India Company rule, it was opium, which was exported from the subcontinent and British wanted to control opium trade.

With the intention to boost exports, Reserve Bank of India gave separate priority status to export finance by banks and advised public sector banks to achieve 12% of its credit. Foreign banks are given a target of 12% for finance to exports as in their case all export finance is treated as priority sector advance. Govt created Exim Bank to finance exporters and to provide refinance to banks. Export Credit Guarantee Corporation was created to provide guarantee cover to exporters. Govt also started interest subvention scheme for banks so that the credit is allowed to exporters at low interest rate to make them internationally competitive.

Exports are foreign exchange earner and are classified into two categories—merchandise exports and invisible exports.

Commodities exported from our country are mainly agriculture and allied products, ores and minerals, manufactured goods from leather, chemicals, engineering, textiles, gems and jewellery and handicrafts. Invisible exports are services exported. Services comprise service related to travel, transportation, insurance, software services, business services and financial services, etc.

Total exports of the country for the year 2008-09 and 2009-10 is given in the following Table. It can be seen that software services have become a major foreign exchange earner for the country now.

| Exports (₹ in crores) | 2008-2009 | 2009-2010 |
|---|---|---|
| 1. Merchandise | 857960 | 862333 |
| 2. Services | 488010 | 453246 |
| *of which:* Software services | 212242 | 235161 |

*Source*: RBI.

## Export Finance by Banks

Export finance of commercial banks have grown from ₹ 40,460 crores in the year 2000 to ₹ 1,38,143 crores in the year 2010 (see Table below). However, the percentage-wise export credit has come down from 10.79% to 4.54% of total bank credit of commercial banks during the same period.

₹ in crore

| Year-March | Total non-food credit of Commercial Banks | Export credit | % |
|---|---|---|---|
| 2000 | 375127 | 40460 | 10.79 |
| 2001 | 429162 | 45387 | 10.58 |
| 2002 | 482749 | 43123 | 8.93 |
| 2003 | 620055 | 50248 | 8.10 |
| 2004 | 728422 | 59744 | 8.20 |
| 2005 | 999788 | 69059 | 6.91 |
| 2006 | 1404840 | 86207 | 6.14 |
| 2007 | 1801240 | 104926 | 5.83 |
| 2008 | 2204801 | 129983 | 5.90 |
| 2009 | 2601825 | 128940 | 4.96 |
| 2010 | 3040007 | 138143 | 4.54 |

*Note*: Data for export credit also includes three co-operative banks.

*Sources*: RBI.

It appears that export finance has not kept pace with credit expansion in the country. One reason may be that the credit expansion of banks was much faster than the growth in exports. Export finance is being encouraged by banks and there is no demand for credit from this segment, which is not considered by banks. There are other reasons for this. Export growth is not dependant on bank credit alone as there is host of other reasons for it mainly the demand in international market.

## Derivatives

Derivatives are comparatively new financial products now permitted by RBI for banks and public to deal in. Forward exchange cover, which has been in use as permitted by RBI under exchange control rules, is also a derivative product by definition.

For regulatory purposes, derivatives have been defined in the Reserve Bank of India Act, as follows:

> "derivative" means an instrument, to be settled at a future date, whose value is derived from change in interest rate, foreign exchange rate, credit rating or credit index, price of securities (also called "underlying"), or a combination of more than one of them and includes interest rate swaps, forward rate agreements, foreign currency swaps, foreign currency-rupee swaps, foreign currency options, foreign currency-rupee options or such other instruments as may be specified by the Bank from time to time.

Derivatives are present in many areas like securities market, commodity market and financial market. In India, different derivative instruments are permitted and regulated by various regulators, like Reserve Bank of India (RBI), Securities and Exchange Board of India (SEBI) and Forward Markets Commission (FMC). RBI is empowered to regulate the interest rate derivatives, foreign currency derivatives and credit derivatives.

Futures contracts, forward contracts, options and swaps are the most common types of derivatives. Derivatives are contracts and can be used as an underlying asset.

Some derivative products are used as hedge against a specific risk as part of sound risk management policy. The most commonly used derivative is forward contracts for foreign exchange business. Here the importer or the exporter enters into forward contracts with their banks for their exposure in foreign currency due to their business. This forward contract helps them in hedging the risk of future currency fluctuation. Derivatives like forward covers, interest rate swaps, currency swaps are for hedging the risks for the concerned parties. Further, the derivative products, like futures and options though have an element of speculation in them, are permitted as these products expand and deepen the respective markets, making it more vibrant and competitive for the participants.

At present, RBI permits following types of derivative instruments, subject to certain conditions:

Rupee interest rate derivatives:

1. Forward Rate Agreement (FRA),
2. Interest Rate Swap (IRS),
3. Interest Rate Futures (IRF).

Foreign Currency derivatives:

1. Foreign Exchange Forward,
2. Currency Swap,
3. Currency Option.

Definitions of these generic derivatives are as under:

### *Forward Rate Agreement (FRA)*

A Forward Rate Agreement is a financial contract between two parties to exchange interest payments for a 'notional principal' amount on settlement date, for a specified period from start date to maturity date. Accordingly, on the settlement date, cash payments based on contract (fixed) and the settlement rate, are made by the parties to one another. The settlement rate is the agreed bench-mark/reference rate prevailing on the settlement date.

### *Interest Rate Swap (IRS)*

An Interest Rate Swap is a financial contract between two parties exchanging or swapping a stream of interest payments for a 'notional principal' amount on multiple occasions during a specified period. Such contracts generally involve exchange of a 'fixed to floating' or 'floating to floating' rates of interest. Accordingly, on each payment date—that occurs during the swap period—cash payments based on fixed/floating and floating rates, are made by the parties to one another.

### *Interest Rate Futures (IRF)*

Interest Rate Future is a standardised, exchange-traded contract with an actual or notional interest-bearing instrument(s) as the underlying asset.

In 1998, Reserve Bank of India permitted scheduled commercial banks (excluding Regional Rural Banks), primary dealers, and all-India financial institutions to undertake Forward Rate Agreements/Interest Rate Swaps (FRAs/IRS) as a product for their own balance sheet management and for market making purposes.

In 2003, the Securities and Exchange Board of India (SEBI) permitted these derivatives to be traded on The Bombay Stock Exchange, Mumbai (BSE) and National Stock Exchange (NSE).

In the first phase, banks and FIs can transact only in interest rate futures on notional bonds and T-Bills for the limited purpose of hedging the risk in their underlying investment portfolio. Allowing transactions in a wider range of products, as also market making will be taken up in the next stage based on the experience gained.

Derivatives offer immense opportunity for mitigating the market risks inherent in the balance sheet, but it can also expose one to substantial losses on account of inadequate understanding of the product, absence of proper monitoring, poor risk control measures, etc. As these products are new, banks are cautious in their approach.

### *Foreign Exchange Forward*

"A foreign exchange forward is an over-the-counter contract under which a purchaser agrees to buy from the seller, and the seller agrees to sell to the purchaser, a specified amount of a specified currency on a specified date in the future—beyond the spot settlement date—at a known price denominated in another currency (known as the forward price) that is specified at the time the contract is entered into."

A person resident in India may enter into a forward contract with an Authorised Dealer Category-I bank (AD Category I bank) in India to hedge an exposure to exchange risk in respect of a transaction for which sale and/or purchase of foreign exchange is permitted under the Foreign Exchange Management Act, 1999 and rules. This product is useful to importers and exporters of goods and services to hedge against exchange risk.

***Currency Swaps***

"A currency swap is an interest rate swap where the two legs to the swap are denominated in different currencies. Additionally the parties may agree to exchange the two currencies normally at the prevailing spot exchange rate with an agreement to reverse the exchange of currencies, at the same spot exchange rate, at a fixed date in the future, generally at the maturity of the swap."

***Currency Options***

"A currency option is a contract where the purchaser of the option has the right but not the obligation to either purchase (call option) or sell (put option) and the seller (or writer) of the option agrees to sell (call option) or purchase (put option) an agreed amount of a specified currency at a price agreed in advance and denominated in another currency (known as the strike price) on a specified date (European option) or by an agreed date (American option) in the future."

The above two derivatives are useful to Residents in India who have borrowed in foreign markets in accordance with the provisions of Foreign Exchange Management (Borrowing and Lending in Foreign Exchange) Regulations, 2000. They may use this product and enter into an Interest Rate Swap or Currency Swap or Foreign Currency Option contract with an authorised bank for hedging their loan exposure and unwinding from such hedges.

As a part of further developing the derivatives market in India and adding to the existing menu of foreign exchange hedging tools available to the residents, currency futures contracts have been permitted to be traded in recognized stock exchanges or new exchanges, recognized by the Securities and Exchange Board of India (SEBI) in the country. The currency futures market would function subject to the directions, guidelines, instructions issued by the Reserve Bank and the SEBI, from time to time.

Persons resident in India are permitted to participate in the currency futures market in India subject to directions contained in the Currency Futures (Reserve Bank) Directions, 2008.

# LCs and BGs

19

Letters of Credits and Bank Guarantees are part of bank business. They appear as contingent liability in the bank's balance sheet. For Indian banks, it is good source of income and there is good demand for these products. In fact, these facilities known as non-fund facilities play a crucial role in trade and commerce. Banks facilitate trade and commerce, by lending their name and credit to enable parties' to do business with each other.

## Letters of Credit

Letters of credits are undertaking by the bank in writing issued in favour of the beneficiary at the behest of opener of LC, wherein bank undertakes that bills drawn in conformity with terms specified therein shall be honoured by the bank on presentation. Banks in India only deal with documentary letters of credit, which means the requirement of LC is to facilitate trade and movement of goods from seller to buyer. The requirement arises when the seller and buyers are not well known to each other and do not want to take risk unnecessarily. For example, the seller has to be paid as soon as he sends out the goods. However, buyer wants to pay only when he is assured of the arrival of goods and the quality of the goods. Generally, trade happens when the parties develop mutual trust. It takes a long time to develop. With new parties, it becomes difficult for the other parties to accept and take risk. Herein the bank steps in. It lends its name and credit to the buyer and issues LC in favour of the seller. Now the seller has a bank undertaking which is far safer for him. He can get to know about the bank issuing credit in no time from his own bank. Hence, the letter of credit brings parties together and the trade takes place.

LCs business is non-fund business for the bank in which only their commitment is involved and funds are not involved. The opener of LC has to provide funds on due dates for payment of the bills. Only when he fails, it devolves on bank and bank has to make payment, and facility becomes funded one for the bank.

LC are issued both for local and international trade. In fact, it is more relevant in international trade as besides the party risk, there is other kind of risks attached to international trade. Risks like country risk, payment risk, etc.

LCs are governed by uniform customs and procedures for documentary credit (UCPDC) rules, which have been accepted internationally.

### Uniform Customs and Practice for Documentary Credit (UCPDC)

Uniform Customs and Practice for Documentary Credit (UCPDC) is a set of predefined rules established by the International Chamber of Commerce (ICC) on Letters of Credit. The UCPDC is accepted by bankers and commercial parties in more than 200 countries, including India, to facilitate trade and payment through LC.

UCPDC was first published in 1933 and subsequently updated over the years. The Banking Commission of the ICC approved the latest revision in October 2006. This latest version, called the UCPDC 600, formally commenced on 1 July 2007. It contains about 39 articles extensively dealing with various issues pertaining to LCs.

The International Chamber of Commerce (ICC) in the Uniform Custom and Practice for Documentary Credit (UCPDC) defines L/C as:

> An arrangement, however named or described, whereby a bank (the Issuing bank) acting at the request and on the instructions of a customer (the Applicant) or on its own behalf is to make a payment

to or to the order third party (the beneficiary) or is to accept bills of exchange (drafts) drawn by the beneficiary authorises another bank to effect such payments or to accept and pay such bills of exchange (draft), authorised another bank to negotiate against stipulated documents provided that the terms are complied with.

A key principle underlying letter of credit (L/C) is that banks deal only in documents and not in goods. The decision to pay under a letter of credit will be based entirely on whether the documents presented to the bank appear on their face to be in accordance with the terms and conditions of the letter of credit.

**LC Terms**

The bank issuing LC is called issuing bank. The party on whose behalf and request it is issued is the opener of LC. To whom the LC has been issued, is the beneficiary under LC. LC issuing bank, if not in the same place as the beneficiary, sends the LC to its own branch or another bank requesting that branch or bank to convey it to the beneficiary. The bank conveying the LC is called advising bank. There is a provision, if required; the advising bank can also confirm the LC by adding its confirmation. Then the advising bank becomes confirming bank also. By confirming the LC, the bank takes the responsibility to honour the commitment as per LC terms. These are generally used in foreign trade as the seller of the goods may insist for confirmation of LC advising bank locally, so that he has the commitment of a bank in his city, which is very safe for him.

The beneficiary then can submit bills strictly as per the terms of LC to his own bank or any other bank or even advising bank for negotiating the bill. Such bank will be called as negotiating bank. However, the LC can contain a condition to restrict negotiation by a particular bank in which case, only that bank can negotiate the bill and make payment to beneficiary and claim reimbursement for the LC from issuing bank. If no condition is stipulated for negotiation, it is open for any bank to negotiate and LC opening bank is bound by it.

Now the LC can be issued as demand LC, in which case the payment has to be made on presentation of the bills. LC can be issued on usance basis and it is called DA LC. The usance period can be any period and it may start from LC date or shipment date. The LC can be issued as revocable, and in this case, the LC can be revoked by the issuing bank before the actual negotiation of bills any time. This type of LC is generally not accepted as it is risky and normally irrevocable LC is only accepted. Here the LC issuing bank or the opener cannot revoke the LC, once issued.

Normally the LC will contain mandatory clauses like what are the documents to be submitted, latest date for shipment and negotiation. There can also be additional clauses like inspection, certificates, packing list, etc. The negotiating bank has to check every document submitted and ensure that the LC terms are fully complied with. A small mistake anywhere may give chance to opening bank to reject the document and refuse the payment. However, there are time norms within which the opening bank has to do that.

Though it is said that the LC is documentary, means it accompanies proof of shipment of goods, banks have no responsibility whether the goods of right quality and quantity have been shipped. This is because banks deal with documents only and not the actual goods. Their checking is limited to prescribed documents under LC and compliance of terms and conditions. In the normal course, all these precautions ensure that the goods as desired are shipped. However, if some clever manipulation takes place or the goods do not reach, then one cannot hold banks responsible for it. In case of shipping documents, LC will prescribe the type shipping document to be submitted. It can be FOB—free on board—shipping bill in which case ali expenses for loading the goods is on sellers account. Price to be shown on invoice can be CIF value, means the cost of goods, the insurance cost, and freight cost has to be borne by the seller. The LC condition may also stipulate that insurance or freight cost may be on buyer's account in which case the buyer will have to arrange for insurance and pay the freight charges. There can be stipulation for clean bill of lading, which means that the bill of lading should not contain any remarks by the shipping company about the condition of goods or its packaging.

LC may also contain terms about the type of shipping company to be used for shipping and whether transhipment is allowed. These terms shall be complied with.

LC can be issued as transferable letter of credit. Under this LC, the first beneficiary who is usually an intermediary may request the nominated bank to transfer credit in whole or in part to the second beneficiary. In the transferable LC, there is a right to substitute the invoice and the whole value can be transferred to a second beneficiary.

Generally LC issuing bank specify the arrangement for reimbursement and the negotiating banks shall follow it.

### Back to Back LC

Sometimes the beneficiary of the LC after receiving the LC may approach his bank or any bank to open a LC in favour of his supplier to enable him to procure the goods for shipment. Banks may accept this request since there is a LC and payment is guaranteed once the goods are shipped. To facilitate the same they issue LCs at liberal terms or may be even without insisting for security for the facility. They only keep the original LC in their possession. These type of LCs opened are called back to back LC.

### Standby Letters of Credit

Of late international banks also started issuing standby letters of credit, which is purely a guarantee of the bank. It is not documentary credit and goods are not involved. Instead of issuing guarantees, they are issuing standby LCs for various purposes.

### Buyers Credit

In case of imports besides normal credit from the supplier the buyer can also look for credit from some other source abroad and get extension of due dates on the LC. Opening bank generally obliges by extending the due date. This is a form of import financing resorted to get cheaper credit as the interest rates abroad is far less than in our country. This is also called the buyers credit.

### SWIFT

Earlier for foreign LCs issued, telex messages were being sent to the advising banks and the banks had check ciphers known to each other to check the genuineness of telex messages. Since 1991, SWIFT communication system is available to banks for sending messages in a safe mode. Banks are now extensively using this facility.

SWIFT is the Society for Worldwide Interbank Financial Telecommunication, a member-owned cooperative with its headquarters in Belgium through which the financial world conducts its business operations with speed, certainty and confidence. More than 9000 banking organisations, securities institutions, and corporate customers in 209 countries use this facility to exchange standardised financial messages.

### Bank Guarantees

BGs have also become very useful in trade and commerce. It is used to secure oneself against contingencies while doing business. The requirement and purpose for bank guarantees are varied. However, since bank's credit and name is involved, parties feel safe. Bank guarantee is treated differently than a guarantee under Contract Act. While basic responsibility is same and coextensive with the principal party, unlike other guarantees, bank guarantee is payable on demand. It is to be paid on the day it is revoked and as per customs and practices there is no grace period for a bank to make payment under the invoked bank guarantee. Reserve Bank of India and Courts have recognized this as something sacrosanct and in the interest of commerce, they view that the sanctity shall be maintained. Litigations are not acceptable and bank, unless prohibited by law, cannot withhold payment. Even the Courts are not interfering now, making it clear to banks that payment shall be made on revocation.

Bank guarantee business is a lucrative business for banks as they charge commission for the guarantee amount and get some margin deposits.

**Types of Bank Guarantees**

BGs are of two types. Financial guarantees, and Performance guarantees. Financial guarantees are simple money guarantees for financial obligation of the party, like standing as surety for the loan taken or money owed. Generally, these types of guarantees are not encouraged and some restrictions have been placed on banks for issuing it.

On other hand, performance guarantee is very desirable to promote trade and commerce. Here the bank is issuing guarantee on behalf of its customers for the due performance of some job or assignment or contract. One type of need arises when contractors are required to keep security deposits with the principals for whom they are working. It is insurance for the principal party that the contactor shall perform as per contract. Though security deposits can be accepted in cash and kept by the principals themselves, they prefer to have bank guarantee instead for various administrative and accounting reasons. Secondly, the principal party also asks contractor to provide bank guarantee for certain amount as performance guarantee for the due performance of the contract or supply. Generally, bank guarantees are in lieu of cash deposit and if the party deposits cash for these purposes then their working funds are blocked. To avoid that banks sanction bank guarantee limits. As per practice, banks take some cash margin and also some other security to secure the exposure.

Sometimes, govt tax depts and courts also ask for bank guarantees in lieu of cash deposit. It is now a normal practice by tax departments like income tax, customs, excise, etc. to insist for bank guarantee in case of disputed assessments under appeals. However, in such cases banks are advised to issue the guarantee against full cash margin. Courts also, when hearing a money suit for recovery, prescribe the amount or part of it to be given as bank guarantee.

Share brokers also need to submit bank guarantees in favour of stock exchanges for their trading limits with the exchanges. RBI has advised banks to obtain minimum 50% cash margin for such guarantees as the exposure is considered risky and that it is exposure to capital market.

Bank guarantees are issued always with an expiry date. For the convenience of beneficiary to file claim under the guarantee, generally a notice period of three to six months are built in the guarantee. However, the guarantee does not extend for the notice period and it only enables beneficiary to file claim pertaining to guarantee period only.

Banks also do not issue bank guarantee with onerous clauses. Onerous clauses may be like beneficiary getting a right to extend the guarantee period/automatic renewal clause, expand the coverage of guarantee, or increase the guarantee amount. Such like clauses are not accepted by banks and banks generally make the clauses to be simple and definite as to the amount and the period. Normally banks insert a standard clause at the end of bank guarantee that stipulates, "Notwithstanding anything contained in the guarantee the guarantee is for the specified amount only and is valid till the expiry date shown in the guarantee."

### Invocation of Bank Guarantee

Once bank guarantee is invoked, bank shall verify the clause enabling the beneficiary to invoke the guarantee and whether the authority invoking the guarantee is authorised in terms of the guarantee to do so. If found in order bank shall make the payment.

Bank has no obligation to inform the party on whose behalf guarantee is issued before making the payment. It also does not require approval or consent of the party for it. Only after the payment bank shall inform the party and demand the amount, if guarantee has devolved on the bank. Banks cannot consider any request of the party for time to enable them to approach courts or other authorities. Bank cannot take cognizance of any dispute between the parties and their individual stand on the matter. This is because the guarantee condition stipulates, "that bank shall make the payment on demand and without demur".

Bank has a right to demand presentation of bank guarantee before making payment and take back the original guarantee bond. Bank also has a right to demand for a receipt from the beneficiary for satisfaction of claims against the bank. Generally, the claim can be made for total claim at one time and partial claims are not allowed unless it is clearly spelt out in the bond. The beneficiary shall be careful to find out the total claim and demand the same from the bank. Even when the claim is less than the guaranteed amount, further claims at a later date, shall not be entertained by the bank and the guarantee bond expires immediately. Bank also has a right to insist for the invocation of guarantee to specify the date of breach and a certificate to the effect that the claim has arisen during the guarantee period only.

Some govt depts have claimed that the guarantee issued in their favour is valid for twenty years or more as per some provisions in the Acts governing them. This has created a peculiar situation and banks are in dilemma. The obligation under bank guarantee is contractual one and provisions of any other law are generally not applicable. However, the govt authority is at different footing. In view of this, banks insist for return of original bonds or a discharge by the govt depts., for deleting bank guarantee issued in favour of govt authorities from their books.

## Co-Acceptances

Co-acceptance of bill of exchange by a bank also is a form of bank guarantee. RBI has allowed banks to do it with a view to encourage bills market. Bill of exchange being a negotiable instrument can be used to raise finance for business. Co-acceptance of bills makes such bills backed by bank guarantee, and the bill will become prime security for any lender. Generally, these bills are drawn by machinery suppliers on the buyers of these machines and are relatively for long maturities. For the buyer of the machinery it will be suppliers credit based on co-acceptance by a bank, otherwise he has to arrange for loan from bank to buy the machineries.

## Issuing LCs and BGs—Precautions

LC and BG are sometimes, misused by unscrupulous parties and many frauds have taken place. Frauds have also taken place where the staff has connived. Due to increase in such frauds, IBA has advised banks to issue LC and BG under dual signatures and to follow an authentication process to check the genuineness of documents by referring the same to controlling authorities of issuing banks. Now a practice has been created and banks, before acting on these documents seek confirmation from the controlling offices of the banks.

# How Banks Create Securities

20

Banks are giving loans and in order to safeguard the banks interest and also to ensure that the borrowers stick to their commitments, banks create securities for the loan lent. These securities are fallbacks in case of need and by creating security; the bank gets specific rights over the assets under its charge and can claim the asset for liquidation of loan in preference to any other general creditor of the borrowers.

In the ordinary course of business, securities are generally moveable assets, immovable assets, and actionable claims. Depending on the type of security offered, bank creates charge on the asset as appropriate and recognized by law. These charges can be created as per provision of a particular Act, then only it becomes enforceable legally through court of law. There are many laws applicable to different kind of assets. Immovable property is covered by Transfer of Property Act. Goods are covered by Sale of Goods Act and also Indian Contract Act. Assignments are recognized under various acts. Before accepting any security bank shall have to ensure that the asset can be legally charged under some provision of the relevant act. Then only a legally enforceable charge can be created and bank is said to have secured the loan.

The word lien and charge are also used as general terms sometime to explain the right of the bank against the particular asset. However, it is important for the bank to create charge on the security in an appropriate manner.

Different types of charges commonly in use are:

### Banker's Lien

Lien is defined as:

> A right given to another by the owner of property to secure a debt, or one created by law in favour of certain creditors.

The right of lien generally arises by operation of law, but in some cases, it is created by express contract.

Lien is a right of a third party against goods or assets coming into his possession in the course of business and it entitles him to hold back the asset against the owner till such time his dues are paid. Lien has general application in most of the trade and services. Unpaid seller has a lien on the goods sold as given in the Sale of Goods Act. Likewise, any professional or service provider can hold back the goods or items in possession till such time his charges are paid by the owner.

Lien recognized by the law is of two types. One is specific and the other is general. Under specific lien the goods can be held back only for the specific performance of the owner in relation to the goods in the custody of the third party. Third party cannot continue to keep the goods once charges in respect of those goods have been paid, irrespective of any other claims against the owner.

Under general lien, the third party is entitled to hold back the goods and items of the owner for any claims against the owner in general. Very few persons are allowed to have this type of lien and bank is one of them.

*The Indian Contract Act, 1872, Section 171.—General lien of bankers, factors, wharfingers, attorneys and policy brokers—*

Bankers, factors, wharfingers, attorneys of a High Court and policy brokers may, in the absence of a contract to the contrary, retain as a security for a general balance of account, any goods bailed to them; but no other persons have a right to retain, as a security for which balance, goods, bailed to them, unless there is an express contract to that effect.

Further, the lien does not entitle the person exercising lien to dispose of the goods. He can merely hold it as security till he is paid and if not paid; he has to seek legal remedies against the owner.

However, bankers have general lien on the assets of the customers in their custody and it is more than general lien. It is bankers lien and in practice/law it is equivalent to pledge. It is known as implied pledge. This entitles the bank to dispose it and realise its dues after giving notice to the customer.

When a bank accepts the security of the deposit accounts it is generally by way of marking lien in these deposit accounts. In case of term deposit, the receipts are taken back duly discharged by the parties and lien is noted in the deposit ledger folio. Some time, it is called as pledge of deposit. But, basically the security created is lien on deposit accounts.

## Assignment of Actionable Claims

Way of creating security on actionable claims is by assignment. Actionable claims are those claims wherein the person who has to receive certain amount from another person can transfer his right to receive the payment to some third party. The person who has to pay generally has no say in the matter and he is bound by the assignment and has to accept it.

The term 'Actionable Claim' has been defined in Section 3 of the Transfer of Property Act, 1882. As per this section, actionable claim means a claim to any debt, other than a debt secured by mortgage of immovable property or by hypothecation or pledge of movable property, or of any beneficial interest in movable property not in the possession, either actual or constructive, of the claimant, which the Civil Courts recognize as affording grounds for relief, whether such debt or beneficial interest be existing, accruing, conditional or contingent.

Simply stated, an actionable claim means a claim to any *unsecured* debt or a claim to any beneficial interest in movable property, not in the possession of the claimant. The debt or beneficial interest may be existing, accruing, conditional or contingent.

LIC policies fall under this category. So also the book debts of business firms. The correct way of transferring the title in these cases, are by assignment. In case of LIC policy the assignment is noted on the policy and signed by the policy holder and then it is submitted to LIC for recording the assignment. Once assigned, the amount therein, is payable to the assignee only. The person making the payment is duty bound to do it. Assignment of book debts also takes place in similar way and a notice is then sent to the debtor. He is bound to accept the assignment. Factoring business is created on this basis.

## Pledge

*The Indian Contract Act, 1872, section 172. "Pledge", "Pawnor", and "Pawnee" defined—*

The bailment of goods as security for payment of a debt or performance of a promise is called "pledge". The bailor is in this case called "pawnor". The bailee is called "pawnee".

Pledge is a way of creating security on moveable assets and the essential feature of the pledge is the physical possession of the asset is given to creditor/bank. Thereafter the asset remains in the custody of bank till such time the loan is repaid. Pledge is a fixed charge on specific assets and in case of bank; bank has the authority to dispose the asset after giving notice to the party. All moveable assets can be pledged and also securities like bonds, shares, deposit receipts, warehouse receipts, transport or railway receipts, etc. In case of paper securities, besides handing over the possession the borrower shall also have to complete some other formalities like endorsing or signing transfer deeds, assigning, etc. In case of physical assets, the pledge shall have physical possession of the assets and in case of paper securities; the pledge gives constructive possession of assets represented in the paper security. Both types of possession are acceptable to create pledge.

## Hypothecation

Moveable assets can also be charged by hypothecation charge and in this unlike pledge, the possession remains with the borrower. It is a hovering charge over the asset and normally banks have a right to convert the same to pledge by giving notice and taking possession.

A hypothecation is a mortgage of movables, unlike a pledge, there is no possession, and there is 'constructive possession'. Hence, both in pledge and hypothecation, legal possession is given.

Until enactment of the Securitisation and Reconstruction of Financial Assets and Enforcement of Security Interest Act in the year 2002 (SARFAESI Act or Securitisation Act), hypothecation charge was not defined by any of the existing acts and it was as per the practice of banks and commerce duly recognized by law. Hypothecation charge was defined for the first time by securitisation act.

The Securitisation and Reconstruction of Financial Assets and Enforcement of Security Interest Act, 2002 defines "Hypothecation means a charge in or upon any movable property, existing or future, created by a borrower in favour of a secured creditor without delivery of possession of the movable property to such creditor, as a security for financial assistance, and includes floating charge and crystallization into fixed charge on movable property."

Stock in trade, machinery and equipments, any other fixed assets of the business other than immovable property can be hypothecated. Even the vehicles can be hypothecated.

In case of stock in trade, the charge is truly hovering as the borrower has the authority to sell the stock and convert it into other current assets and again purchase fresh stock. Bank charge is hovering over the goods that are lying at borrowers premises and if the hovering charge is crystallised then whatever stock lying at that particular point of time becomes the charged property for the bank and bank can take it into possession. However, at the same time bank cannot lay its hand on stock that has already moved out of business.

In case of fixed assets hypothecated though it remains in the custody of borrower, he cannot dispose it without bank's permission. The charge of the bank is specific to that particular asset and it cannot even be replaced with similar assets without bank's consent. In case of vehicles the charge is hypothecation and as per transport vehicle act, it is compulsory for the bank to register the charge with the vehicle registering authority—RTO. Similarly, when the hypothecation charge is created on moveable assets of a company, under the companies act, the charge shall have to be registered with registrar of companies—ROC. Banks are also covering book debts under hypothecation charge but the right procedure to charge book debts is assignment. However, due to practical difficulties it is not done as the business may be having large book debts consisting of large number of debtors. Hypothecation agreement on book debt will bind the borrower whereas it will not bind the debtor of the borrower.

SARFAESI Act 2002 has provided for setting up of Central Registry for recording all security interest created in favour of secured creditors and makes it obligatory for secured creditors including banks to register charges with it. This is similar to charge registration by ROC in case of companies. However, central registry is yet to become operational.

## Mortgages

*Under the Indian Transfer of Property Act, 1982 the term "mortgage" is defined under Section 58(a) as follows:*

"A mortgage is a transfer of interest in specific immovable property for the purpose of securing the payment of money advanced or to be advanced by way of loan, an existing or future debt or the performance of an engagement which may give rise to a pecuniary liability."

The TP act also provides for the charge on immovable property, which is different from mortgage. However, the consequences and redemption is similar for both charge and mortgage.

*Under the Indian Transfer of Property Act, 1982 the term "charge" is defined under Section 100 as follows:*

"Where immovable property of one person is by act of parties or operation of law made security for the payment of money to another, and the transaction does not amount to a mortgage, the latter person is said to have a charge on the property and all the provisions hereinbefore contained which apply to a simple mortgage shall, so far as may be, apply to such charge."

Charge is also an encumbrance on the property. The remedies available to charge holder are same as in case of a mortgage holder. Hence, it is possible that a document created as mortgage deed, if fails the test of the mortgage for some reason, still it may hold good as charge on the property. This is an important point in favour of any creditor including banks.

Mortgage is a charge created over immovable property by the owner for securing pecuniary obligations. The TP Act defines different types of mortgages recognized by the law. Under the law, mortgages are to be reduced to writing as a deed and to be registered. It is compulsory. The only exception is creating equitable mortgage. Stamp duty is also levied on the mortgage deed. Different types of mortgages are:

#### *1. Simple Mortgage*

Commonly used mortgages are simple mortgages and they are also called registered mortgages. In this the property remains with the owner and only a charge has been created in favour of creditor. This mortgage shall have to be registered and stamp duty is also applicable. In case of default, the mortgage can be foreclosed by approaching civil court, which may order the sale of property for discharging the debt. Properties mortgaged can only be brought to sale through courts.

#### *2. Mortgage by Conditional Sale*

In a mortgage by conditional sale, there is ostensibly a sale with the condition that on default in payment of the mortgage money by a certain date, the sale would become absolute and on such payment being made, the sale can be avoided. From a banker's perspective, this form is rarely used.

#### *3. Usufructuary Mortgage*

Under this, the property is given to the creditor for enjoying the benefit during the debt period. On redemption of debt, the property shall be returned to the owner. In case of foreclosure, the procedure is same as in case of simple/registered mortgage. This too is rarely used in banking security creation.

### 4. English Mortgage

An English mortgage (or as is popularly known "legal mortgage") is a transaction by which a mortgagor binds himself to repay the mortgage money on a certain date, and transfers the mortgage property absolutely to the mortgagee subject only to a condition that the mortgagee will retransfer it to the mortgager upon payment of the mortgage money as agreed. The three essentials of an English mortgage are:

(a) the undertaking to pay

(b) the property is absolutely transferred, and

(c) the transfer is subject to provision that the property would be reconveyed on redemption of the debt due.

The operative words are the same as those of an absolute conveyance. A characteristic feature of an English mortgage is that a right of sale without intervention of court is generally included as a covenant in the mortgage deed in order to enable the mortgagee to realise the mortgage money. The Transfer of Property Act recognizes this right of an English mortgagee. This form of mortgage has a high stamp duty incidence in most states in India.

### 5. Anomalous Mortgage

Anomalous mortgage is basically a residual category. In India, several kinds of mortgages based on local practices and moulded by custom or the whim of the creditor are in existence. Mortgage, which does not fall within any of the other five categories described, is anomalous. These forms of mortgage are also rarely used in banking transactions.

### 6. Mortgage by Deposit of Title Deeds (Equitable Mortgage)

Another type of mortgage generally preferred by banks is equitable mortgage. In this, mortgage is created by mere deposit of title deeds of the property by the owner with the creditor within the notified area. There will be no agreement and deed for the same. If the deed is created, then the option is to have simple mortgage by registering it. Hence, equitable mortgage is not required to be registered.

It is informed that this type of mortgage is in existence in our country only. When British wanted to codify the transfer of property act, they observed that in metro towns, traders are using this kind of transaction for borrowing and it was very simple and effective system. British were impressed by this practice and made a provision for it in the law. To start with, equitable mortgages could be created in three presidency towns only. However, the property could be situated at any part of the country. Only condition was that the mortgage shall take place in presidency towns. Thereafter the state govts who are authorised to notify towns for this purpose have expanded the list of towns and today almost all bigger towns are notified for this purpose.

As no agreement existed for creating equitable mortgage, banks as abundant precaution started maintaining mortgage register in which the bank noted the mortgage transaction under the signature of the manager and it was also witnessed to give it veracity. This became to be called as title deed register. Banks also started taking confirmation from the borrower at a subsequent date for having deposited the title deed at the bank for the purpose of creating mortgage. This is only confirmation and it is not treated as agreement and hence conditions of registration did not apply to it. Only it has to be dated subsequent to mortgage date. This confirmation became to be known as memorandum of deposit of title deed. As the possession of original title deed is the proof of mortgage, bank shall not part with the title deed for any purpose and if parted, the borrower can misuse the same and misguide others to believe that no mortgage exists. Hence, the title deed never went out of the bank and even when required by law, the bank officer carries the same to the authority and brings it back. The effective possession of title deed shall not be broken or else question of priority in charge may arise and the bank may lose its mortgage.

Banks prefer equitable mortgage because it is simple, time saving, and also effective. It gives some benefit to the borrower also as the mortgage is not disclosed to public and stamp duty for creating simple mortgage is also saved. However at present stamp duty on equitable mortgages are levied by many state govts.

### Equitable Mortgages—Title Deeds

The transfer of property act gives out the procedure for creating equitable mortgage and it mentions about the deposit of title deeds for creating it. However, the act does not define what is title deed. In view of this, some confusion is created. Title deed is a document showing the ownership and interest of the party to a property. There were many case laws when courts have accepted even tax receipts and revenue record copy as title deed. Hence, title deed can be any document. However commonly seen and accepted title deeds are sale deeds, partition deeds and the court orders. These are considered as good documents establishing title of the owner. However, in their absence any other document can take the place of title deed for the purpose. For example, agreement for sale can be accepted as title deed so also the share certificate of housing society.

For creation of the mortgage, what is important is that there shall be consideration and there shall be an intention to create mortgage and the owner of the property shall create the mortgage. These three points are important and essential ingredients of a mortgage and not the nature of title deed. If these three points are complied then any paper or document with the owner can be accepted as title deed in the absence of any other better paper/document. Hence, mortgage is valid with any type of document depicting title to the property. This is the reason we can recognize documents under different circumstances, which will constitute title deed for the purpose of creating mortgage.

In case of an equitable mortgage, deposit of title deed is required and as stated earlier, the law does not prescribe what constitutes a title deed and it is decided by the facts of the case. If it is learnt that the owner has a registered sale deed in his possession, banks shall have to ask for it and not accept any other document as title deed. This is because the original sale deed can be misused, if not taken into possession. Absence of original sale deed, which has been created, will give rise to doubts and banks do not accept explanation of the owner about its loss or misplacement. Generally, in such cases banks insist for registered mortgage as it is safe, and absence of original sale deed shall not make any material difference and the encumbrance is noted on the records of the sub-registrar.

Banks shall have to be careful in accepting any document as title deed and shall have to ensure that it is the original document and that there exists no better document than the one produced by the borrower. Bank mortgage charge may not fail in the court, as the important ingredient for mortgage always exists i.e. intention, consideration, and ownership. Some minor lapse in the documents may not jeopardise the charge but the thing will be different if there are other claimants for charge on the same property in which case courts shall have to decide priority of charges and also the effective creation of charge. Here sometimes a bank may lose the case.

### Stamp Duty for Equitable Mortgage

To start with, no stamp duty was prescribed on equitable mortgage as no deed is created and the mortgage takes place only by deposit of title deed. This transaction has to take place in notified towns only as notified by state governments.

Many states like Maharashtra and others started levying stamp duty on equitable mortgages also to generate revenue. Then the question arose as to how the stamp duty shall be paid as no deed is created. The clarification was given that it can be affixed either on the title deed register page of the bank or on the memorandum of deposits that banks take. Banks started stamping MODs with the stamp duty. Stamp duty is made payable on the property value and later on changed to loan amount.

Since separate stamp duty has been prescribed for equitable mortgage, whether the memorandum of deposit of title deed which is confirmation by the borrower needs to be subsequently dated as is the practice or it can be of same date of deposit of title deed by the borrower? This needs to be clarified. At present, the language used in the memorandum is same as before. In a way, the date difference has now lost relevance as MOD is now treated as document witnessing equitable mortgage and stamped. Further, it is now known that some states like Gujarat have even prescribed procedure for registration of equitable mortgage. It appears that the significance of equitable mortgage is lost and State governments in their zeal to collect revenue through stamp duty have dismantled the excellent and unique provision of law and negated the prerogative given for such type of mortgage.

### Mortgage for Housing Loans

Banks are sanctioning housing loans in a big way now, the security is the house being financed, and mortgage is created. Banks generally make the disbursement of loan directly to the seller in case of ready built house or seller of land on which house is being constructed. Loan for construction is released in instalments as per progress of construction ensuring the end use of funds disbursed. Besides, ready flats are also financed by making payment to the builder/society/house development authority. In case of flats under construction loan is released again in instalments.

In case of ready built house/flat or sale of land, sale deed is created and registered. Banks after releasing the loan create mortgage on the property by taking the sale deeds/sale agreements. In case of partly constructed house/flat bank creates mortgage on the basis of agreement to sell/allotment letter along with consent letter from the seller.

Maharashtra Government had made rules for registration of builder's agreement for sale of flats and also resale agreement of the flat in a society and brought them under the purview of stamp duty as applicable to sale of property and also compulsory registration of such agreements. This was done to plug the loophole in the law when registration and stamp duty is postponed creating interim agreements, instead of sale agreements and the period became indefinite. Many a time final sale agreement is never executed and Government was losing stamp duty.

Now in view of these rules, a builder if he books a flat, which is not even ready or existing then also the agreement he enters into with the buyer shall have to be registered and stamp duty paid. Under the law, a right and charge is created in favour of the buyer on a share of immovable property and it is enforceable in the court of law. In some southern states, the agreement for a flat shall also specify the undivided share of land of the flat owner. Other states do not insist on such inclusion in the agreement for sale.

## Mortgage of Agriculture Property

Banks are actively financing farmers for agriculture and as security for the loan; the land owned by the farmer is mortgaged. Historically the farmers inherited the land for generations and no documents could be found. Sale deed is available in very few cases where the sale has taken place say during last 50 years. The ownership record of the land is difficult to get. However, in all such cases, the revenue record of the govt is up-to-date and by convention, the revenue record has assumed the role of primary proof of ownership. It is accepted for all subsequent sales. As most of the farmers are not in a position to produce any title document, it became customary to get copies of revenue record duly certified by tehsildar or any revenue authority and treat them as title proof and deed. It is called by different names in different parts of the country like *7/12 extract, khasra khatauni, firz jamabandi*, etc. Further, as farmers are an exploited lot, state governments passed legislations to protect them. The law in almost all states is that farmer cannot create mortgage over agriculture property for any purpose other than borrowing for agriculture. Hence, creditor or moneylender cannot cause mortgage for money lent, and then deprive the farmer of his land.

Many state govts have remitted stamp duty payable by farmers for creating mortgages in favour of banks for availing loan for agriculture purpose. Separate rules have been formulated for creating mortgage and forms have been prescribed. The crux is that the revenue authority is the competent authority to receive and acknowledge mortgage of agriculture properties. Here the mortgage created is similar to simple mortgage and is under the provision of state act. It is quite safe for banks.

However, there is some discussion and argument whether owner can create equitable mortgage on agriculture property by depositing registered sale deed for securing loan taken by him for non-farm purpose. Some opinion is that it is possible and there is no bar. However, it is a tricky situation and the relevant state laws shall have to be studied before deciding on it.

### Bank Loan Recovery by Revenue Authorities

It is also noteworthy that many states have laws making bank loan recovery at par in status as that of land revenue recovery and the revenue authority i.e. Collector has jurisdiction to recover, if the bank makes an application to him. The effect of this law is that instead of civil suit in civil courts, banks have the option to file application in revenue court presided by district collector. Civil courts will not have jurisdiction in such matters.

### Personal Guarantees

Banks generally obtain personal guarantees to secure the loans. The borrower is liable and the obligation to repay the loan is personal. Hence, borrower is not executing any separate personal guarantee agreement. Banks generally take personal guarantees of third parties to secure the loan collaterally. Normally banks prefer tangible collaterals to secure the loan and when tangible collateral are not available then banks may accept personal guarantees.

Guarantees are governed by the Indian Contract Act 1872 and guarantor is called surety. The chapter VII of the said act defines the rights and liabilities of surety.

*Indian Contract Act 1872 defines contract of guarantee as under:*

*Section 126. "Contract of Guarantee", "Surety", "Principal Debtor" and "Creditor"*—A "contract of guarantee" is a contract to perform the promise, or discharge the liability, of a third person in case of his default. The person who gives the guarantee is called the "surety", the person in respect of whose default the guarantee is given is called the "principal debtor", and the person to whom the guarantee is given is called the "creditor". A guarantee may be either oral or written.

Banks accept continuing guarantee to cover series of transactions in the borrowers account. Section 129 of the act defines continuing guarantee as under:

*Section 129. Continuing Guarantee*

A guarantee which extends to a series of transaction, is called, a "continuing guarantee".

*Section 127. Consideration for Guarantee*

Anything done, or any promise made, for the benefit of the principal debtor, may be a sufficient consideration to the surety for giving the guarantee.

There is no bar for accepting guarantee from anyone either related or otherwise and the contract of guarantee need not have any monetary consideration for binding oneself. It is presumed that the promise made for the benefit of principal debtor is sufficient consideration as per section 127 of the act. It is very difficult for the guarantor to escape liability due to this.

*Section 128. Surety's Liability*

Liability of the surety is co-extensive with that of the principal debtor, unless it is otherwise provided by the contract.

Liability of the surety is co-extensive with the principal debtor. This means the surety is liable for anything owed by the principal debtor and to the same extent. Whatever the principal debtor is liable the surety is also liable.

Personal guarantees are also obtained when borrower is other than individual or partnership firm. Like companies or trusts, etc. This is because these are being legal entities, their action will not make the individual director or trustees legally liable for the loan in their personal capacities. In order to make the directors or trustees legally liable for the loan, banks take their personal guarantees to secure the loans. Generally, in case of private limited company personal guarantees of directors are always taken as a rule. In case of public limited companies or other entities, it is taken as per requirement of individual case.

The limitation act prescribes limitation for an action under personal guarantee as three years from the date of demand made on the guarantor.

Agreement of guarantee involves three parties i.e. the bank, the guarantor and the debtor. However, it is signed between the bank and the guarantor only. The terms of the agreement cannot be changed once it is signed. The guarantor has a right to know his liability at any time and bank is bound to provide the same. Bank cannot also alter the terms of agreement with the borrower for the loan or any securities without the consent of the guarantor. If the terms are changed without consent then the guarantor can get the relief (section 133).

Personal guarantee once signed is irrevocable means it cannot be withdrawn by the guarantor. However, he can revoke the guarantee as to the future by giving notice to the bank (section 130). Such notice will make him free from future liability and he shall be liable for the balance outstanding as on the date of his revocation. Normally in such cases where the guarantor has withdrawn the guarantee banks crystallise the account and then make the demand on the guarantor and debtor. Operations in the borrowal account are not allowed so as to keep the liability of the guarantor alive. If this is not done then any subsequent credit to loan account will reduce the liability of the guarantor to the extent and over a period bank may lose its recourse against the guarantor. In case of death of the guarantor, also, the same situation arises and the guarantee is determined till the date of the death and thereafter estate of the guarantor is not liable (section 131).

Bank can start action against the borrower and guarantor simultaneously or separately against each. Bank can also proceed against the guarantor only and there is no requirement to proceed against the debtor or to exhaust all remedies against the borrower before suing the guarantor for recovery. This is because the guarantee agreement is an independent agreement between bank and the guarantor and the provisions of Indian contract act govern the liability.

There can be more than one guarantor under the common guarantee agreement or separate agreement. Here though the several guarantors are individually and jointly liable and can be proceeded against individually. Generally banks proceed against all the guarantors at a time and get judgement against them. However, the guarantor has a right as against other guarantors to limit his liability to the extent of share of his liability under the joint responsibility of all guarantors (section 146).

*Guarantor's rights after discharging debt*

Guarantors after discharging the debt to the bank steps in to the shoes of the bank (section 140, 141). Guarantor has a right to recover the amount from the principal debtor and also has right on the securities held by the bank in the account. This means that the kind of charge on securities that existed in favour of the bank is transferred in favour of guarantor. Banks are bound to transfer their rights in favour of guarantors.

*Corporate guarantees*

Besides individuals, all legal entities can also execute contract of guarantees. Generally, banks are taking corporate guarantees from corporates to secure loans sanctioned to other corporate borrowers. Examples are when bank accepts corporate guarantee of the holding company for sanctioning loan to a group company. Similarly, banks also accept corporate guarantee from a company to secure loan sanctioned to its associate or group company.

# Non-Performing Assets and Recovery

21

Concept of non-performing assets was introduced in banking sector in nineties when prudential norms were introduced. Earlier to this, banks were also not following the income recognition norms. It was a common practice to keep on debiting interest to loans even if the loan accounts are irregular and no repayment has been received. Income recognition norms changed this practice, as under it, income can be booked only when it is actually recovered. Now interest on NPAs is not debited to the account, but is kept in a memorandum.

Simply stated an asset becomes NPA when it ceases to generate income for the bank. RBI has laid down various criteria for classification of various types of advances as NPA. The basic rule is if either interest or instalment is overdue for more than 90 days then the account would become NPA. (Norms for asset classification and provisioning are given under chapter financial sector reforms.)

## Health Code System of Asset Classification

However, a different method of asset identification as prescribed by RBI in the year 1985 was followed earlier. It was known as health code system. Health code system in fact was the forerunner to NPA recognition. Health code No. 1 to 8 was given to accounts as shown under, depending on the status of the account and the irregularities in them.

| Description | Health code |
|---|---|
| Satisfactory | 1 |
| Irregular | 2 |
| Stick: Viable-under nursing | 3 |
| Stick: Non-viable/sticky | 4 |
| Advances recalled | 5 |
| Suit file accounts | 6 |
| Decreed accounts | 7 |
| Bad and doubtful debts | 8 |

Earlier, unless recalled, the loan continued in the regular ledger of the bank. Only when the recall was made and the loan remained unpaid, then the account used to be shifted to 'protested bill' category. After the suits for recovery has been filed, the account is moved from 'protested bill' to 'suit filed account'. When the suit is decreed, the account is moved to 'decreed accounts'. Interest was not charged to the account only after it is moved to protested bill account category and above.

Prudential norms were introduced in the year 1992, which included asset classification norms, income recognition norms and provisioning norms. As the concept of NPA was new, RBI initially allowed banks to recognize one year default as NPA to begin with and then the default period was gradually brought down to 90 days.

## Why NPAs are Created

NPAs are very critical issue for banks. Banks are into lending business. However, banks are not moneylenders. This means banks are not like proverbial moneylenders who adopt any method and ensure that they recover their loans. Moneylenders at times, are also employing strong-arm methods, for recovery and can go to any extent. They may even cross the line and do illegal acts. However, banks are different. It is an institution. It has to act like an institution. It has to employ legal method for recovery. There can be no enmity or bad intention.

It is said in lighter vein that 100% recovery is not banking. It is money lending. A closer look at this statement is really revealing. It brings out the fine difference between money lending and banking. Any credit extending has an element of inbuilt risk. Whether it is trading or banking. Once the credit is extended, then there is always the possibility of defaults due to any reason and the funds remain blocked. Sometimes it is delayed beyond the period. Sometimes it can only be recovered in bits and pieces, after lot of persuasion and efforts. Sometimes it may become irrevocable for various reasons. A creditor or a bank is fully aware of this and still extends credit or gives loan. Business depends on extending of credit. Though there may be few segments of business where credit is not allowed, majority of trade takes place on credit.

Banks are in the business of giving loans, as they can only earn by deploying the deposit that they have collected. For them there is no other good option to deploy funds. Besides the compulsions of banks to give loans, the economy can progress fast only when loans are made available to those who can profitably deploy it in business and increase business. In case of manufacturer, he takes loans and produces goods and services required for the society. It is a very useful activity as it spurs the economy, creates employment, and creates wealth. So giving loans by banks is a requirement of the economy for faster growth. Banks are acting as mediators between depositors who have money and persons who have ideas for business but no money. It is an organised system of transfer of resources for best utilisation of it and puts the economy on growth track.

For banks, NPAs are occupational hazards and unavoidable. They have to live with it and make profit and grow. Since non-performing assets and bad loans are bound to be there, banks shall have to manage the same. Their endeavour is to keep it to the minimum so that it does not hurt. Banks will have to absorb the loan loss and make it good by making more profits. In fact, the interest charged by banks from borrowers has an element of loading for the default rates.

## Why NPAs are Critical

In today's world, economic stability of a country is the real issue and the government is much concerned about this. Economic stability will depend on the performance of financial sector in the country. Banks play a very crucial function in the financial system as they act as intermediaries. Health of banking sector is important for the economy and a major bank failure can be catastrophic. Banks health is dependent on the level of NPAs. In fact, level of NPAs is also a barometer for the financial health of the country as it reflects the status of business and industry. In view of this, govt and RBI are much concerned about the level of NPA. After the financial sector reforms were introduced, govt has made many changes in the existing laws to help banks to recover the bad loans quickly.

Rise in NPA of banks necessitates additional provisions and this will affect the profitability of the banks. In case of very high NPAs, the financial strength of the bank becomes weak and there can be a threat to its existence. NPA level of the banks, fiscal deficit of the govt and the rate of inflation in the economy are the three major issues identified for financial sector consolidation, for the country to achieve capital account convertibility.

## Management of Assets

Health of the banks is judged by the quality of its assets and the capital base. For banks, liquidity is very important from short/medium term perspective, but in the long-term perspective, it is the quality of assets that matters. Theoretically a bank may be illiquid but with good assets. Likewise Bank may be liquid but with weak assets. Stability of the banks is very important for the economy. Failure of bank in today's context can be catastrophic for the nation, depending on the size of the bank and its after-effects and ripple effects on the economy.

Financial sector reforms have recognized this area as an important factor to be kept in mind. Banking sector shall be stable if NPAs are within a reasonable limit and managed properly. Even bad loans of few per cent are also a matter of serious concern. In fact rising of bad loans in an economy reflects that things are not in good shape. It is a pointer to the fact that the economy is going down. If the economy is picking up then loan default will be minimum.

Besides checking the growth in bad loans, banks shall have to provide for probable loan losses and make adequate provision as cushion. Prudential norms to be followed by banks in asset classification, income recognition and provisioning is for the purpose that banks make sufficient provisions for future losses on continuing basis so that they shall not get sudden shocks due to losses. Narasimham Committee in its report has prescribed control on bank's NPA as one of the goal posts to be achieved before the country allows capital account convertibility of rupee.

### NPA Management

Asset management is very crucial for banks. NPA management starts at identifying potential NPAs and analyzing the reason for it and take steps for plugging it. For NPAs bank shall have specific mechanism to follow up and either bring them back to standard assets or take immediate recovery action and recover.

Why NPAs are created? We have stated that NPAs are bound to be there. There can be no zero position for any bank. However, why an individual loan has become NPA is important to learn so that corrective action can be undertaken and lesson is learnt. For this purpose, we may have to find out various reasons for default.

Why default occurs? Is it natural phenomena or man made? Why a borrower after agreeing to repay at particular time defaults? Are intentions had to do anything or is it out of control of the borrower?

To answer all these we must first understand the loaning functions of the bank. To whom bank gives loans, purpose of the loans, and how repayment is visualised.

Banks gives loans to manufacturing units for manufacturing of goods or services. The idea is that the manufacturer shall use bank loan, expand manufacturing, sell the goods or services, make money, and then return the loan. Bank also gives loans to traders for similar purpose except that it is only for trading, which has a smaller cycle. Bank gives loans to small business, self-employed and professional, transporters and many who are into providing various services. All these are for the business activity, money is used for business growth and from the earnings, loan has to be repaid. Bank also provides loans to farmers for their crop and for financing farm equipments. Here also the loan shall be repaid from the farm income generated. Banks give loans to exporters who after exporting and earning, return bank loans. Then banks finance consumption and personal needs. Like personal loans, housing loans, car loans, consumer loans, etc. Here the loan is spent for consumption and the asset even if created is not giving any income. Therefore, this loan has to be repaid from the existing income stream of the borrowers. Of late, banks are also giving educational loans. Banks are also giving loans against some selected securities like deposits, gold, investments, etc. Here either the loan has to be repaid out of existing income or by liquidating the asset charged to the bank.

Therefore, management of NPA goes back to the stage of selection of borrower. If the selection is wrong and assumptions are erroneous, there is more likelihood of loan default.

### Selection of Borrowers

If the loan is given for business development, then assessment of the business and its prospect has a bearing on loan default. If the perception about the business is erroneous then expected income generation will not be there. It becomes difficult for borrower and bank to get back the money. Money put in business, if not successful, there is every chance that money is lost in the process as business loss. In such case, loan default is certain and the question is how the loan can be recovered, as the amount is lost in the business.

Next important issue is the intentions of the borrower. What happens when the borrower is successful and made money but instead of returning the loan, he is finding some other avenues for the money and not returning it or delaying the repayment with intention to use the loan for some more time and make more profits?

Then there is the bad intention of the borrower who is not interested to return the loan. He is trying to avoid the liability, initially by postponing it and finally the intention is to cheat.

Firstly the bank has to be selective while giving loans (based on reasonable study), to avoid bad borrowers whose integrity is doubtful and avoid future problems with them. This is where the identification of borrowers and checking credentials assumes importance. Market report, cross-references, bank confidential report, and interview with the prospective borrower allow the bank to screen borrowers and eliminate undesirable ones. Elimination of borrowers who are patently out for cheating is the first precaution and an experienced banker will identify and avoid such borrowers.

After this come the three "C's" of the prospective borrowers, Character, Capacity, and Capital in that order. This is an age old and tested proposition in selection of borrowers. While patent cheaters are avoided in the first instance as above, the character of the borrower particularly with reference to his financial commitments is very important to decide the sanction. Financial discipline, fear of law and fear for bad reputation are essential characters to look for in the borrower. To some extent, this will depend on the moral character also. However, financial discipline can be separate from moral ethics in personal life. While criminals or people with criminal bent of mind are to be avoided, many of society's moral codes can be overlooked in selection as having no bearings on the financial matters.

The capacity of the borrower is very important. Whether he is capable of delivering, what he is undertaking to do? Whether he has adequate knowledge and feel of the market for the business activity he is undertaking. Whether he is sincere and hardworking and has commitment and a mission to succeed? These are essential traits to be identified in the borrower who is embarking on new business or expanding his business. If the borrower is capable, he will manage the business successfully and the repayment is reasonably assured.

The capital and the net worth of the borrower instills confidence as his stake in the business gives comfort to the bank. Person will definitely take care of his own capital in the business. Loan is safe in his hands and return of loan can be presumed. Capital also acts as cushion to bank loan and in case of some loss, the capital of the borrower will absorb the loss and loan amount can still be retrieved.

### Default Due to Business Difficulties

Borrowers' psychology is same as any other individuals in general. No one wants to be a defaulter. Everyone will be honest till it makes no difference to them or hurt them. Morals and ethics of the society are generally followed. Interpersonal relationship is important for individuals and reputation is very important. Everyone would like to be known as reputable and trustworthy. However, his ethics will be tested in adverse conditions only. The test is when the conditions are adverse and the individual will have to face inconveniences. How will he react? Whether he still thinks about his reputation? What he feels about the default?

The reactions of individuals are different under testing conditions. Some borrowers are still sticking to ethics, undergo small discomfort, and maintain the commitment. Other borrowers may not react in this way. They will first think about themselves, postpone the commitments to banks and only when things improve may fulfil the commitments. There may be yet other borrowers who may not bother about commitments now or in the near future. They make no effort to retrieve the situation and leave it to fate.

### Restructuring/Nursing

Banks will have to analyze the reason for default and the reaction of the borrower. Banks need to assess whether it is business related problem or otherwise. If it is business related then bank will have to work out some solution. Mostly it will involve restructuring of loans. If the market condition for the borrower is bad and is likely to improve over a period, then some sort of nursing is required. If the problem is for short time then restructuring of loan by postponing few instalments may do the trick. If the problem is for little longer period say couple of years to improve business conditions and liquidity then nursing will have to be done. If the unit has become sick but viable otherwise, rehabilitation programme may have to be drawn.

RBI has issued guidelines and advice for such assistance for SSI units, SMEs, etc. The purpose is to revive the units and not to kill them, if they can be turned around. In all such cases banks make sacrifices by allowing concessional interest rates and/or by providing additional funding, if required. Even for larger industries which have become sick, reference will have to be made to board for industrial and financial reconstruction—BIFR (established in the year 1987) to see whether any rehabilitation package can be worked out. There is also Corporate Debt Restructuring (CDR) mechanism, introduced by RBI in the year 2001 for large corporate borrowers who are unable to meet the liabilities. This is a voluntary scheme and borrower may opt for it.

For all other smaller loans to farmers and the business, depending on the problem faced by borrowers in their business, banks will have to offer some help and restructure or rehabilitate them. For personal loans also in case of temporary cash crunch, banks' may have to rephase the repayments looking at the cash flows and bring the accounts back to normal.

Rephasement/Nursing/Rehabilitation is necessary since bank loans are mostly given for development purpose and it is the moral duty of banks to support business when it is going through rough patch. This is the difference between banking and moneylending. Banks cannot act like moneylender. Even the society cannot afford to liquidate businesses built over a period just because of some temporary difficult situations. Business will have to be supported and nursed in the larger interest of the economy and employment. A small sacrifice by banks and others like Govt is a small price paid for a good cause.

Even though banks are obliged to turn on to nursing mode for such loans, banks problem with NPA, still remains. Bank has to classify the loan as NPA depending on the default and make provision for it. There is no immediate relief for banks.

However, over a period, the rules permit the banks to upgrade the asset based on actual performance after rephasement of loans. At that time, it benefits banks, as they are able to write back the provisions.

## Handling Default

Hence, whenever an account slips to NPA the first decision for bank is to decide whether it is a case for nursing or recall. If the problem is self-created by the borrower wilfully diverting the funds or due to dishonesty or the business has suffered loss and the damage is not repairable, then bank shall have to take hard decision to recall the advance and proceed for recovery.

NPA management hence involves selection of borrowers, regular follow up of loan accounts and review, getting early alerts on irregularities in the account and taking action on that, identifying NPAs, deciding the course of action for identified NPA,—legal action or nursing programme, follow up of legal action for recovery, and settlements wherever possible. All these steps shall have to be taken at appropriate time so that there is no delay at any stage.

Handling of NPA and difficult accounts requires skill and experience. Banker shall meet the borrower and understand the problem. If bank is rigid and unyielding in its approach, it may put off the borrower and free and frank interaction will be difficult. Banker-customer, including borrower, relationship is based on mutual trust. It must be there between the parties. Bank shall not, in the first instance, intimidate the borrower of the legal consequences for the default. Bank shall try to find out and understand the real problem. Borrower must have confidence in his bank that it will keep his interest in mind while dealing. He will require support at his difficult time. Proverb says that banks are known "to hold umbrella during fair weather and withdraw it when the weather becomes rough or it rains". There is a lesson in this proverb for the banks. You cannot hold umbrella over customers head during fair weather and withdraw it during rains. The purpose of umbrella holding is defeated. It is during the rains customer need the umbrella more. Thus, it is during the rough patch the customer needs the bank to support him and help him.

Bank shall be quick in analysing the reason for default and discuss the same with the borrower. How fast the thing can be remedied and what help the borrower expects from the bank must be found out. Little handholding and little space for manoeuvre will go a long way in solving the problem.

Any credit requirement of the borrower should be immediately looked into and it should not be viewed as 'throwing good money after bad money'. Bank shall know for certain that the situation is hopeless and beyond redemption before rejecting the request for additional credit. Otherwise, bank must provide additional dose of finance so that the recovery can be quicker. Under financing means slowly killing the business as it cannot survive due to lack of adequate finance.

### Recovery through Legal Process

When the loan becomes NPA and all the efforts to regularise the loan fails, bank is left with no alternative but to proceed legally for recovering the amount.

### Civil Courts

Banks will have to file civil suits for recovery of loans with civil courts. Bank cases are also called money suits as it is for recovery of money. Civil Courts are at every taluka places and District Civil Court at district levels. Bank has to file the suit in appropriate court having jurisdiction. Jurisdiction is generally based on the location of the bank branch and the suit amount. Suits can be filed in lower courts up to a monetary limit and if it is above the limit, then with the District Civil Court. The District Civil Courts have unlimited jurisdiction irrespective of the amount involved in the suit. High Courts and the Supreme Court have appellate jurisdictions over the cases decided by lower courts.

However, there are some aberrations to this general rule. As legacy of British Rule, the High Courts in the three presidency towns i.e. Mumbai, Kolkata and Chennai are still having original jurisdiction to try money suits above a particular limit and even now, cases will have to be filed in High Courts, in these three cities for cases above the limit.

### Debt Recovery Tribunals

Debt Recovery Tribunal Act was passed in the year 1993 and many DRTs were established. Under this act, the jurisdiction of trying bank/FI loan cases of rupees 10 lakhs and above was transferred to tribunals from the civil courts. Appellate Tribunal at national level was also formed. Hence, appeals cannot be filed with High Courts or Supreme Court. This was done in view of large number of pending cases at civil courts and the delay that is taking place to the detriment of banks/FIs. DRTs are dedicated for trying bank cases and to quicken the legal process, DRTs were allowed to create their own procedures to dispose the cases. The rules and procedures of civil courts are not binding on DRTs.

### Securitisation Act

To further help banks in recovery, Govt also passed another legislation called Securitisation Act in 2002. The purpose was to overcome the existing legal hurdles for recovering by disposing off the assets charged to banks. Under the existing laws, mortgaged immovable properties could be sold only on court orders. This was also applicable for hypothecation charge on moveable assets. Only pledged goods could be sold without court intervention. Due to this, inordinate delays were taking place for selling the assets. Under this act, banks were empowered to dispose the properties in their custody by following certain guidelines but without the intervention of courts. Courts are also barred from taking up appeals as DRTs have been named as appellate authority.

Act provides for taking physical possession of property through the help of Collector/Chief Metropolitan Magistrate and then auction it to recover dues. The provision of the act for enforcement of securities is now used by banks to auction properties and recovering dues.

### Revenue Recovery Acts

To help banks for recovery in priority sector loans particularly agriculture loans, many States made Revenue Recovery Acts of the state applicable for bank loans to agriculture and other priority sector loans. Under this act, the District Collector is the authority to recover, once the application is filed by banks and civil courts have no jurisdiction over the matter. Collector has appointed Tehsildars to recover the dues by following rules for recovery of revenue.

Banks can chose the course to either file case under state revenue act or file civil suit with Civil Courts.

### Negotiated Settlements

Legal process of recovery is lengthy and time consuming. Though Debt Recovery Tribunals (DRTs) are formed to help the banks and Securitisation Act has been passed to help the banks in recovery without the intervention of courts, the actual experience is that these measures are not enough. Banks cannot recover in time and borrowers play all sorts of games to delay the action.

This despondency has forced the banks to look for negotiated settlements. Banks are now actively pursuing this course and enter into dialogues with borrowers for settlements. In order to bring the borrowers to discussion table, banks have to sacrifice something and offer incentives to borrowers. Ethically and morally, it appears wrong, as it is rewarding default and enriching the defaulter. It is same as amnesty schemes for income tax. Law-abiding citizens are in a disadvantageous position as against defaulters. It is argued that these things will make the honest people also dishonest in the end. There is disincentive to be honest. However, despite all these arguments banks shall have to take very practical view in their own interest and see that the blocked funds are released and recycled to generate income. From this point of view the action for settlements are justified. Even judiciary also encourages out-of-court settlement and Legal Services Authorities Act 1987 made rules and provisions for Lok Adalats at various courts for quicker disposal of cases.

Today every bank has a settlement policy in place, which prescribes the rules for such settlements.

### Recovery Agents

Historically bank staff were doing follow up for recovery of loans. Of late, in late nineties some banks particularly foreign banks started outsourcing loan recovery functions by appointing recovery agents. Though it is a legitimate action, at times, the overzealous approach of recovery agents caused embarrassments to these banks. There was also public outrage as it was informed that the recovery agents have at times stooped low and used strong-arm tactics. This became contentious issue and RBI had to intervene. It was accepted that outsourcing of this function is a natural corollary to the expansion in business and is bound to be there. At the same time, it was felt that the recovery agents are representatives of banks and bank has to own up the responsibility for their deeds. Strong arm tactics have no place in a civilized society and banks can only act as per provisions of the law of the country. Law prescribes the recovery proceedings and banks are bound by it. RBI has now advised banks to be careful about such things and function in a transparent manner. Banks shall properly screen the agents before appointment, maintain record of such appointments, and display the names of recovery agents appointed by it on the website for public knowledge. Banks are also advised to observe some norms for visits and follow up and such visits shall not take place at odd and unacceptable hours.

### Defaulters' List and Wilful Default

In the year 1994, RBI has initiated a system of reporting of defaulters with ₹ 1 crore and above and making the list of defaulters available to banks for due diligence purpose. Caution list of defaulters in whose accounts claims have been paid by guarantee organisations like ECGC and DICGC are also made available to banks.

In the year 1999, RBI has also initiated to identify wilful defaulters with ₹ 25 lakhs, and above, based on certain criteria, and issued guidelines in the matter. Banks were advised to report such wilful defaulters to RBI for enlisting them and advising all banks on them. The purpose was to bring pressure on such borrowers as their credit history and rating was affected, and as a deterrent they shall not be able to access banks or institutional credits. Issuing public information on such borrowers was also allowed to embarrass them and to create pressure on them. In view of this, banks were advised to be careful for declaring the borrower as wilful defaulter and banks were also asked to give notices to the borrowers about the bank's intention to declare them as wilful defaulters and give them opportunity of hearing.

### Credit Information Bureau (India) Ltd. (CIBIL)

It was felt that information/data on borrowers is crucial for sound credit decisions. This necessitated the establishment of credit information bureau/s to obtain and share information. The Union Budget 2000-01, announced the establishment of Credit Information Bureau (India) Ltd. (CIBIL). Further, with a view to strengthening the legal mechanism and facilitating credit information bureaus to collect process and share credit information on borrowers of bank/FIs, the Credit Information Act was enacted in May 2005, and rules and regulations thereunder were also notified. The Act empowered the Credit Information Companies to collect information relating to all borrowers. The act also empowered the Reserve Bank to determine policy in relation to the functioning of credit information companies and give directions to such companies.

### Asset Reconstruction Companies (ARC)

Financial sector reforms introduced included enactment of Securitisation Act 2002. This act also provided for starting of asset reconstruction companies for taking over impaired assets from banks.

The Securitisation Act mainly provided for the following:

- enforcement of Security Interests by secured creditors;
- transfer of NPLs to asset reconstruction companies (ARCs), which can then take measures for recovery as prescribed under the Securitisation Act, 2002;
- a legal framework for securitisation of assets.

This paved the way for creating asset reconstruction companies and the first was ARCIL, which came into existence in the same year 2002. Three major players in Indian banking system, namely, State Bank of India, ICICI Bank Limited and

IDBI Bank Limited took the lead and came together to set-up the first ARC, named ARCIL.

Banks can now sell their impaired assets to these ARCs under negotiated settlement, and ARC shall take over the account from the bank and then proceed to recover the dues. As ARCs paid banks on taking over the accounts, this enabled banks to clean its books by getting rid of impaired assets. Besides immediate realisation of the asset, it also enables the bank to bring down its gross and net NPA position.

### NPAs of Scheduled Commercial Banks

Position of NPAs of scheduled commercial banks in the country since the year 1999 to 2010 is given in the table below.

**Gross and Net NPAs of Scheduled Commercial Banks**

(Amount in ₹ crores)

| Year (end-March) | Advances | | Non-Performing Assets (NPAs) | | | | | |
|---|---|---|---|---|---|---|---|---|
| | Gross | Net | Gross | | | Net | | |
| | | | Amount | As Percentage of Gross Advances | As Percentage of Total Assets | Amount | As Percentage of Net Advances | As Percentage of Total Assets |
| **Scheduled Commercial Banks** | | | | | | | | |
| 1998-99 | 399436 | 367012 | 58722 | 14.7 | 6.2 | 28020 | 7.6 | 2.9 |
| 1999-00 | 475113 | 444292 | 60408 | 12.7 | 5.5 | 30073 | 6.8 | 2.7 |
| 2000-01 | 558766 | 526328 | 63741 | 11.4 | 4.9 | 32461 | 6.2 | 2.5 |
| 2001-02 | 680958 | 645859 | 70861 | 10.4 | 4.6 | 35554 | 5.5 | 2.3 |
| 2002-03 | 778043 | 740473 | 68717 | 8.8 | 4.1 | 29692 | 4.0 | 1.8 |
| 2003-04 | 902026 | 862643 | 64812 | 7.2 | 3.3 | 24396 | 2.8 | 1.2 |
| 2004-05 | 1152682 | 1115663 | 59373 | 5.2 | 2.5 | 21754 | 2.0 | 0.9 |
| 2005-06 | 1551378 | 1516811 | 51097 | 3.3 | 1.8 | 18543 | 1.2 | 0.7 |
| 2006-07 | 2012510 | 1981237 | 50486 | 2.5 | 1.5 | 20101 | 1.0 | 0.6 |
| 2007-08 | 2507885 | 2476936 | 56309 | 2.3 | 1.3 | 24730 | 1.0 | 0.6 |
| 2008-09 | 3038254 | 2999924 | 68328 | 2.3 | 1.3 | 31564 | 1.1 | 0.6 |
| 2009-10 | 3544965 | 3497092 | 84747 | 2.4 | 1.4 | 39126 | 1.1 | 0.7 |

Gross NPA of Scheduled Commercial banks were ₹ 58,722 crores in 1999, which was high at 14.7% of advances. In a period of about 10 years, banks have tried to control this and gross NPA was ₹ 84,747 crores in 2010, which was 2.4% of advances. On percentage basis this is very good achievement and is now within tolerable levels. Having reduced the gross

NPA, banks have tried to build up provisions against them. Net NPA, which was at 6.2% of total advances in 1999, has come down to 1.1% in the year 2010.

**Banks and Limitation Act 1963**

Banks are in financial business like accepting deposits and giving loans. All these involve financial dealings and contracts. At times, in case of dispute with anyone bank has to take recourse to the laws of the land. Financial dealing are governed by some relevant law and remedies are available. In case the disputes are not resolved between the parties, legal recourse is the remedy. Banks like any other have to approach courts for redressal and enforcement of its rights. All financial matters are civil matters and bank shall have to approach civil court.

Law provides that the financial dealings shall be brought before the courts within some specific time limit on occurrence of breach. It is for the reason that cases cannot be filed after very long time or after indefinite delay. It is logical that these issues cannot be taken up after considerable lapse of time as conducting such case becomes difficult and meaningless. Hence, law enjoins that the litigant must be vigilant, approach the court within reasonable time for disposal of it and he shall not have the right in perpetuity to decide about the time to approach the court for such matter.

In view of such prescription by the law, bank or any party loses its recourse and help from the court, in case the suit is not filed within the prescribed time limit for such matters. This is called as 'limitation in law' and the limitation act prescribes limitation for each type of actions to be filed before the court. If anyone wants to enforce his right under the provisions of any civil law involving financial obligations, he has to act within the time limit.

For banks, money suit is an important issue. In case the borrower fails to repay the loan as agreed, bank has to enforce its right with the help of courts for recovery of the amount.

Indian Limitation Act 1963, deals with these issues. Basic rule is that the money suit is maintainable within 3 years from the date the money becomes payable as per agreement. Hence, limitation for money suit is 3 years. However, the period of three years is counted from the date on which the money becomes payable under the contract or agreement.

In many cases, Demand promissory notes secure bank loans and in such case, the limitation starts from date of promissory note. In case of term loan agreement where instalments are fixed for repayment, limitation for each instalment shall start from its respective due dates.

Limitation in respect of surety agreement shall start from the date of invocation of the guarantee.

Limitation for mortgages is 12 years under the provisions of the act hence where mortgage is the security, the limitation for such loan is 12 years.

### Extending Limitation

Limitation can be extended as per the act on following basis:

1. Written confirmation of the debt by borrower shall extend the limitation from the date of written confirmation.
2. Part payment of the debt by the borrower shall also extend the limitation from the date of part payment.

In view of this, banks have a practice of obtaining balance confirmation from the borrowers on half yearly/yearly basis. Banks can continue with chain of balance confirmations obtained from time to time and keep the limitation alive. However, every subsequent balance confirmation should be signed within the limitation of previous one or else the chain will be broken and debt shall become time barred.

### Obtaining Fresh Loaning Documents

Banks generally obtain fresh loaning documents periodically or at the time of renewal of limits. Banks also take fresh loaning documents when the facilities are enhanced or reduced. This way banks ensure that the limitation of three years is extended from time to time. Sometimes fresh documents are necessitated due to change in constitution of borrowers.

Fresh loaning documents can be obtained even in case a debt becomes time barred but the borrower is willing to execute fresh loaning documents. Fresh limitation will start from the date of fresh documents. Fresh loan document executed for a time barred debt is a legal document and is enforceable.

### Letter of Revival

Banks generally obtain letter of revival from corporate borrowers instead of fresh loaning documents. Banks take supplemental agreements instead fresh loaning documents whenever there is change in limit sanctioned to corporate borrowers. This is for the reason that generally, assets of the company are charged to the bank and the charge is registered with ROC. If bank obtains fresh loaning documents then the original charge shall have to be vacated and new charge has to be filed. Though in the normal course there is not much difference, fresh charge in place of original charge may work against bank's interest in case priority of charges are to be decided by competent courts. Banks as abundant caution would like to retain the original charge with ROC in their favour and prefer only modifications in the charge for the changes. For this reason, banks obtain letter of revival from companies confirming the credit limits and the securities created in favour of bank in the shape of board resolution of the company.

### Bankers Book Evidence Act 1891

This is an important legislation protecting banks from having to part with their books, ledgers, etc. for any litigation before courts and authorities. This is because banks deal with money and their books are very essential for them to carry on their day-to-day affairs. If banks are made to handover the ledgers, even for a brief period the banking business will be affected and the customers will be put to inconvenience, as they cannot transact due to the ledgers being not with the bank. In order to avoid this problem, law has bestowed a special privilege on banks and exempted them from producing their books before courts or authorities. These privileges are provided in the Bankers Book Evidence Act 1891, in the following sections of the act:

*Section 4. Mode of proof of entries in Bankers' Books—*

Subject to the provisions of this Act, a certified copy of any entry in a Banker's book shall in all legal proceedings be received as *prima facie* evidence of the existence of such entry, and shall be admitted as evidence of the matters, transactions and accounts therein recorded in every case where, and to the same extent as, the original entry itself is now by law admissible, but not further or otherwise.

*Section 5. Case in which officer of bank not compellable to produce books—*

No officer of a bank shall in any legal proceeding to which the bank is not a party be compellable to produce any banker book the contents of which can be proved under this act, or to appear as a witness to prove the matters, transactions and accounts therein recorded, unless by order of the Court or a Judge made for special cause.

Section 4 of the act makes it mandatory on all to accept certified copies of entry in the banker's book in all legal proceedings to be treated as evidence of existence of such entry. Hence, the original record of the bank cannot be insisted upon to be produced. This rule applies to all legal authorities including courts and also all govt authorities who have the power to call for evidence from banks.

Section 5 of the act also prohibits compelling bank officers to attend any court proceedings to produce bankers' books unless the bank is a party in such legal proceedings. This protection exempts banks from appearances in legal proceedings between third parties and where bank is not a party and the only exception is provided by an order of the court to do so. Hence, third parties cannot drag the bank to give evidence or produce books in support of their litigations.

Only certified copy of entries in banks book's can be called for in evidence and Section 2 of the act defines certified copy under clause 8 as under:

[*(8) "Certified copy" means when the books of a bank,—*

(a) Are maintained in written form, a copy of any entry in such books together with a certificate written at the foot of such copy that it is a true copy of such entry, that such entry is contained in one of the ordinary books of the bank and was made in the usual and ordinary course of business and that such book is still in the custody of the bank, and where the copy was obtained by a mechanical or other process which in itself ensured the accuracy of the copy, a further certificate to that effect, but where the book from which such copy was prepared has been destroyed in the usual course of the bank's business after the date on which the copy had been so prepared, a further certificate to that effect, each such certificate being dated and subscribed by the principal accountant or manager of the bank with his name and official title; and

(b) Consist of printouts of data stored in a floppy, disc, tape or any other electromagnetic data storage device, a printout of such entry or a copy of such printout together with such statements certified in accordance with the provisions of Section 2A.]

[(c) A printout of any entry in the books of a bank stored in a micro film, magnetic tape or in any other form of mechanical or electronic data retrieval mechanism obtained by a mechanical or other process which in itself ensures the accuracy of such printout as a copy of such entry and such printout contains the certificate in accordance with the provisions of Section 2A.]

The explanation given in the section specifies what constitutes a certified copy and it shall contain a certificate at the foot. Certified copy now includes computer printouts as per the amended definition as above.

# Financial Sector Reforms

# 22

Around 1990, Indian economy faced a serious balance of payments crisis and India had to airlift gold to International Monetary Fund (IMF) to get loan to meet its financial obligations. This event called for introspection on the financial sector in the country by the Govt. Banking sector was the important constituent of financial sector and most of the banking was in public sector. There was urgent need for reforms to ensure that the crisis do not repeat again.

It was felt that rigidities and weaknesses had made serious inroads into the Indian banking system, and after the crisis, the Government of India (GOI) took several steps to remodel the country's financial system. The banking sector, handling 80% of the flow of money in the economy, needed serious reforms to make it internationally reputable. GOI wanted to accelerate the pace of reforms and develop the economy of the country, as an efficient, vibrant, and competitive economy to adequately support the country's financial needs.

In the light of these requirements, an Expert Committee was set up in 1990 under the chairmanship of M. Narasimham (an ex-RBI governor) which is widely credited for spearheading the financial sector reforms in India.

The Narsimham Committee was set up in order to study the problems of the Indian financial system and to suggest some recommendations for improvement in the efficiency and productivity of the financial institutions. The first Narasimham Committee (*Committee on the Financial System—CFS*) submitted its report in 1991.

The committee made the following major recommendations:

- *Reduction in the SLR and CRR*: The committee recommended the reduction of the higher proportion of the Statutory Liquidity Ratio 'SLR' and the Cash Reserve Ratio 'CRR'. Both of these ratios were very high at that time. The SLR then was 38.5% and CRR was 15%. This high ratio of SLR and CRR meant locking the bank resources for government uses. It was hindrance in the productivity of the bank thus the committee recommended their gradual reduction. SLR was recommended to reduce from 38.5% to 25% and CRR from 15% to 3 to 5%.
- *Phasing out Directed Credit Programme*: In India, since nationalisation, directed credit programmes were adopted by the government. The committee recommended phasing out of this programme. This programme compelled banks to earmark their financial resources for the needy and poor sectors at confessional rates of interest. It was reducing the profitability of banks and thus the committee recommended the stopping of this programme.
- *Interest Rate Determination*: The committee felt that the interest rates in India are regulated and controlled by the authorities. The determination of the interest rate should be on the grounds of market forces such as the demand for and the supply of fund. Hence, the committee recommended eliminating government controls on interest rate and phasing out the concessional interest rates for the priority sector.
- *Structural Reorganisations of the Banking Sector*: The committee recommended that the actual numbers of public sector banks need to be reduced. Three to four big banks including SBI should be developed as international banks. Eight to Ten Banks having nationwide presence should concentrate on the national and universal banking services. Local banks should concentrate on region specific banking. Regarding the RRBs (Regional Rural Banks), it

recommended that they should focus on agriculture and rural financing. They recommended that the government should assure that henceforth there will not be any nationalisation and private and foreign banks should be allowed liberal entry in India.

- *Establishment of the ARF Tribunal*: The proportion of bad debts and Non-performing asset (NPA) of the public sector Banks and Development Financial Institute was very alarming in those days. The committee recommended the establishment of an Asset Reconstruction Fund (ARF). This fund will take over the proportion of the bad and doubtful debts from the banks and financial institutes. It would help banks to get rid of bad debts.
- *Removal of Dual Control*: Those days banks were under the dual control of the Reserve Bank of India (RBI) and the Banking Division of the Ministry of Finance (Government of India). The committee recommended the stepping of this system. It considered and recommended that the RBI should be the only main agency to regulate banking in India.
- *Banking Autonomy*: The committee recommended that the public sector banks should be made free and autonomous. In order to pursue competitiveness and efficiency, banks must enjoy autonomy so that they can reform the work culture and banking technology upgradation will thus be easy.

Some of these recommendations were accepted by the Government of India and were implemented. These became the banking reforms in the country.

In 1997, the government appointed yet another committee under the chairmanship of same Mr. Narsimham. It is also known as the Banking Sector Committee. It was told to review the banking reform progress and design a programme for further strengthening the financial system of India. The committee focused on various areas such as capital adequacy, bank mergers, bank legislation, etc. The committee submitted its report in 1998, called Narasimham committee report II.

It submitted its report to the Government in April 1998 with the following recommendations:

- *Strengthening Banks in India*: The committee considered the stronger banking system in the context of the Current Account Convertibility 'CAC'. It thought that Indian banks must be capable of handling problems regarding domestic liquidity and exchange rate management in the light of CAC. Thus, it recommended the merger of strong banks which will have 'multiplier effect' on the industry.
- *Narrow Banking*: Those days many public sector banks were facing a problem of the Non-performing assets (NPAs). Some of them had NPAs as high as 20% of their assets. Thus for successful rehabilitation of these banks it recommended 'Narrow Banking Concept' where weak banks will be allowed to place their funds only in short-term and risk free assets.
- *Capital Adequacy Ratio*: In order to improve the inherent strength of the Indian banking system the committee recommended that the Government should raise the prescribed capital adequacy norms. This will further improve their absorption capacity also. Currently the capital adequacy ratio for Indian banks is at 9%.
- *Bank Ownership*: As it had earlier mentioned the freedom for banks in its working and bank autonomy, it felt that the government control over the banks in the form of management and ownership and bank autonomy does not go hand in hand and thus it recommended a review of functions of boards and enabled them to adopt professional corporate strategy.
- *Review of Banking Laws*: The committee considered that there was an urgent need for reviewing and amending main laws governing Indian Banking Industry like RBI Act, Banking Regulation Act, State Bank of India Act, Bank Nationalisation Act, etc. This upgradation will bring them in line with the present needs of the banking sector in India.

- Apart from these major recommendations, the committee has also recommended faster computerisation, technology upgradation, training of staff, de-politicising of banks, professionalism in banking, reviewing bank recruitment, etc.

Financial sector reforms that were introduced as a part of structural reforms initiated in 1991. The purpose of the reform process in the financial sector was to have a strong and resilient banking system.

## Reform Phase

The macro-economic crisis faced by the country in 1991 paved the way for extensive financial sector reforms, which brought sea changes in banking in the country. It included deregulation of interest rates, creating competition, technological changes, prudential guidelines on asset classification and income recognition, capital adequacy, autonomy to banks, etc.

The Reserve Bank made sustained efforts towards adoption of international benchmarks in a gradual manner, as appropriate to the Indian conditions, in various areas such as prudential norms, risk management, supervision, corporate governance and transparency and disclosures. The reform process helped in taking the management of the banking sector to the level, where the Reserve Bank ceased to micro-manage commercial banks and focused largely on the macro goals. The focus on deregulation and liberalisation coupled with enhanced responsibilities for banks made the banking sector resilient and capable of facing several newer global challenges.

Financial sector reforms were initiated from the year 1991. Prudential norms (IRAC norms) pertaining to income recognition, asset classification and provisioning for banks were introduced for the first time by Reserve Bank of India during financial year1992-93 i.e. year ended 31st March 1993 in line with the international practices. Government also wanted banks to be Basel I compliant for capital. Internationally banks are recognized by the intrinsic strength of the banks in terms of capitalization and observance of prudential norms. Basel 1(1988) prescribed capital adequacy ratio of 8% for banks and Reserve Bank of India prescribed it at 9%.

Banks were advised to switchover to prudential norms. These norms included identifying non-performing assets, non booking of interest on NPAs, provision for NPAs and loan losses before arriving at net profit, norms for income recognition- so that income is not inflated and asset classification norms which made it obligatory to indentify loan losses i.e. irrecoverable loans. As this was entirely new concept, Reserve Bank of India allowed almost 5 years for banks to comply with it in a phased manner. Many banks went in to red because of new norms. Capital base of many banks were very low. Government had to provide additional capital by issuing special bonds so that nationalized banks could achieve minimum capital requirement. The total capital contribution by the Government to nationalised banks from 1993 up to March 1998 aggregated ₹ 20,046 crores. Asset classification norms brought the quality of the assets of the bank in to sharp focus and banks were obliged to focus on this area and improve asset quality by either close monitoring of NPAs or recovering, entering in to settlements, etc.

The RBI guidelines on prudential norms for banks as updated and applicable as at March 2011 are as under:

### Capital Adequacy for Banks

The basic approach of capital adequacy framework is that a bank should have sufficient capital to provide a stable resource to absorb any losses arising from the risks in its business. Capital is divided into tiers according to the characteristics/qualities of each qualifying instrument. For supervisory purposes capital is split into two categories: Tier I and Tier II. These categories represent different instruments' quality as capital. Tier I capital consists mainly of share capital and disclosed reserves and it is a bank's highest quality capital because it is fully available to cover losses. Tier II capital on the other hand consists of certain reserves and certain types of subordinated debt. The loss absorption capacity of Tier II capital is lower than that of Tier I capital.

Banks were advised to have minimum of 9% capital adequacy ratio from the year 2000 on their risk-weighted assets.

### Income Recognition Norms

Income from NPA is not recognised on accrual basis but is booked as income only when it is actually received. Therefore, interest on any NPA should not be recognized unless realized.

Once the account is identified as NPA, the interest on such account is kept in a memorandum as recorded interest and not credited to income head. Even the unrecovered interest of preceding period from the date of NPA is also reversed.

### Asset Classification Norms

Simply stated an asset becomes NPA when it ceases to generate income for the bank. RBI has laid down various criteria for classification of various types of advances as NPA. The basic rule is if either interest or instalment is overdue for more than 90 days then the account would become NPA.

Having identified assets as NPA, banks are required to classify them further into:

(a) **Sub-standard Assets**—A sub-standard asset is one, which has remained NPA for a period of less than or equal to 12 months.

(b) **Doubtful Assets**—An asset is classified as doubtful if it has remained in the sub-standard category for a period of 12 months.

(c) **Loss Assets**—A loss asset is one where loss has been identified by the bank or internal or external auditors or the RBI inspection but the amount has not been written off wholly. In other words, such an asset is considered uncollectible and of such little value that its continuance as a bankable asset is not warranted although there may be some salvage or recovery value.

## Prudential Norms

Banks are required to make adequate provisions for any diminution in the value of loan assets, investment or other assets.

In conformity with the prudential norms, provisions should be made on the non-performing assets based on classification of assets into prescribed categories taking into account the time lag between an account becoming doubtful of recovery, and the realisation of the security, the erosion in the value of security charged to the bank over the time.

Provision requirement as advised by RBI is as under:

**Loss assets.** Loss assets should be written off. If loss assets are permitted to remain in the books for any reason, 100% of the outstanding should be provided for.

## Doubtful Assets

(i) 100% of the extent to which the advance is not covered by the realisable value of the security to which the bank has a valid recourse and the realisable value is estimated on a realistic basis.

(ii) In regard to the secured portion, provision may be made on the following basis, at the rates ranging from 25% to 100% of the secured portion depending upon the period for which the asset has remained doubtful:

| Period for which the advance has remained in 'doubtful' category | Provision requirement (%) |
|---|---|
| Up to one year | 25 |
| One to three years | 40 |
| More than three years | 100 |

## Substandard Assets

(i) A general provision of 15% on total outstanding should be made without making any allowance for ECGC guarantee cover and securities available.

(ii) The 'unsecured exposures' which are identified as 'substandard' would attract additional provision of 10 per cent, i.e., a total of 25% on the outstanding balance.

### Standard Assets

Provisioning for standard assets has been introduced in the year 1999. The provisioning requirements for all types of standard assets stand as below. Banks should make general provision for standard assets at the following rates for the funded outstanding on global loan portfolio basis:

(a) Direct advances to agricultural and Small and Micro Enterprises (SMEs) sectors at 0.25%.

(b) Advances to Commercial Real Estate (CRE) Sector at 1.00%.

(c) Housing loans extended at teaser rates and restructured advances at 2%. (Housing loans extended at teaser rates has been increased from 0.40% to 2.00%. The provisioning on these assets would revert to 0.40% after 1 year from the date on which the rates are reset at higher rates if the accounts remain 'standard'. Restructured accounts classified as standard advances will attract a provision of 2% in the first two years from the date of restructuring.)

(d) All other loans and advances not included in (a), (b) and (c) above at 0.40%.

### Provisioning Coverage Ratio

Provisioning Coverage Ratio (PCR) is the ratio of provisioning to gross non-performing assets and indicates the extent of funds a bank has kept aside to cover loan losses.

RBI advised banks to build up provisioning and capital buffers in good times i.e. when the profits are good, which can be used for absorbing losses in a downturn. The purpose is to enhance the soundness of individual banks, as also the stability of the financial sector. Banks were advised to augment their provisioning cushions consisting of specific provisions against NPAs as well as floating provisions, and ensure that their total provisioning coverage ratio, including floating provisions, is not less than 70%. Banks were advised to achieve this norm not later than end-September 2010.

**Measures for Loan Recovery**

It was observed that banks are finding it difficult to recover loans through legal process as it took very long time in courts to decide the matter. Pendency of cases at courts also added to the delay making the system ineffective. This favoured defaulters as they get plenty of time to defer their liabilities to the detriment of banks. To improve the system Govt decided to have dedicated tribunals to try bank cases. Debt Recovery Tribunal Act was passed and DRTs were established in the year 1993. The jurisdiction of trying bank loan cases of rupees 10 lakhs and above was transferred to tribunals from the civil courts. Appellate tribunal at national level was also formed. This has helped banks to some extent. However, of late tribunals are also overburdened with cases and the cases are pending for more than 5 years, which is against the spirit of their formations.

Govt also passed another legislation called Securitisation Act in 2002 to help banks. Under this act, banks were empowered to dispose the properties in their custody by following certain guidelines but without the intervention of courts. Courts are also barred from taking up appeals. However, DRT has been named as appellate authority to give natural justice to aggrieved parties. Act provides for taking physical possession of property through the help of collector/chief metropolitan magistrate and then auction it to recover dues. The act also provided for setting up of Central Registry where all charges are to be registered under the act. However, this is yet to start. The provision of the act for enforcement of securities is now in force and banks are using it to auction properties and recovering dues.

Securitisation Act 2002 also enabled creation of Asset Reconstruction Companies who can take over assets from banks so that bank can get rid of bad asset and clean its books. ARCIL, the first such company came into existence in the same year 2002.

Legal Services Authorities Act 1987 made rules and provisions for promoting Lok Adalats at various courts for quicker disposal of cases. Under this, banks and borrowers in litigation before the court can arrive at mutual settlement and submit the same to court for approval. Once approved, it will form the order of court for disposal of the case.

At many States, revenue recovery acts were made applicable for bank loans to agriculture and other priority sector loans. Under this act, the District Collector is the authority to recover and such authority cannot be challenged in courts. Collector has appointed Tehsildars to recover the dues in the similar way the revenue of the Govt is recovered. This has helped banks at many places but is not very effective as such actions by the collector is a politically sensitive issue and also the borrowers are poor people and hence Collector need to be circumvent in dealing such cases.

**Other Changes**

In early nineties Government decided to dilute its 100% stake in banks, many banks went public and issued fresh shares to the public successfully. SBI and Oriental Bank of Commerce are the first to enter capital market with issues in the year 1994. Many banks followed suit thereafter.

Government also opened up the economy and new generation private sector banks were encouraged to come on scene with minimum ₹ 100 crores capital. Many banks were started in private sector from the year 1994. At the same time, RBI also allowed few financial institutions to convert themselves into universal banks or float subsidiaries to undertake universal banking business.

Foreign banks were allowed to expand their network in the country with the result foreign banks expanded and many new foreign banks came into the country.

Interest rates were made free except for savings bank accounts. Banks are now deciding interest rates both for deposits and advances themselves. (*Savings interest was freed in October 2011.*)

Keeping in line with the recommendations, RBI has lowered SLR and CRR and at present SLR is prescribed at 25%, as recommended and CRR has been brought down to 5%.

GOI has provided capital support to all weak nationalised banks to enable them to achieve CRAR of 9% and has allowed nationalised banks to dilute govt stake and take capital from public.

Role and functions of RBI has been identified as monetary authority and many of its functions, which either created conflict of interest or inconsistent with its role have been removed. RBI ownership of SBI was transferred to GOI. RBI has now freed of micro management of banks and is concentrating on macro management of banking.

## Technology Developments

Along with these changes, technology upgradation and computerisation in banking also took place. Computerisation in banking started with stand-alone machines to handle customer accounts in savings and current deposit accounts around the year 1985. These machines were called AELPMs (Advanced Electronic Ledger Posting Machines). TBA (total branch automation) branches started in the early part of nineties. Under this all the functions of a branch were brought under an integrated branch software so that total computerisation of the branch was achieved. Gradually number of branches under this was increased. Banks started installing automated teller machines—ATMs around the year 1996. Banks introduced core banking solution (CBS) around the year 2000. In next 5 years' time many of the banks achieved 100% core banking. With core banking in place, banks went for massive expansion of ATMs with the result ATMs are everywhere today. ATM sharing was started in the year 2004, to benefit customers so that they can use any ATMs close to their place.

Core banking has ushered in 'anywhere banking' and 'Any Branch Banking'. Customer now is not the customer of one branch. He is now the customer of the bank and can walk into any outlet to do his banking transactions.

Internet banking has been introduced as sequel to core banking. In a way computers and telecommunication has rewritten banking services and banking services are now available at the click of button at any place. Mobile banking is also introduced.

The fund transfer system has undergone changes with introduction of real time gross settlement—RTGS (2004) and national electronic fund transfer—NEFT (2005) by Reserve Bank of India. This electronic fund transfer system has now made it possible for transfer of funds from one bank account to any bank account across the country seamlessly through the system.

MICR technology for clearing operations was introduced by RBI in 1984 and in 2008; cheque truncation was introduced in Delhi.

Speed Clearing was introduced in the year 2008 and banks with core banking in place, banks are advised to make payment of cheques at the same centre where it is presented irrespective of on which centre the cheque is drawn, using core banking facilities available to them. This will stop the unnecessary physical movement of cheques from different centres. Credits are now instantaneous.

## Banks After Financial Sector Reforms

Indian banking has changed and has come up of age. After 20 years of reforms phase, banks have emerged much stronger. Here again the credit goes to RBI for its masterly handling the reform phase and painlessly transforming Indian banking to global standard. Indian banks are now adequately capitalised, their NPAs are well under control with adequate provisions. Indian banking has upgraded technology and is now working with contemporary technologies. Risk management standards have vastly improved which is being continuously upgraded.

Indian banking is now capable of managing own affairs and no longer require micro management from RBI. Banks have handled successfully the transformation from regulated banking to open and competitive banking.

In fact the Indian banking proved to the world that the structure of Indian banks is the best to absorb financial shocks by weathering the recent global financial crisis and coming out almost unscathed.

# Risk Management and Basel Accord

# 23

Banking and financial sector is very important for any country's economy to develop and prosper. Stability of these sectors is of paramount importance. Any instability in these sectors can be catastrophic for the economy and put it back significantly. Banks play a vital role in the economy and the faith of depositors in the bank is the cornerstone of this whole edifice. It is dependent on how banks deploy their funds and how well they manage the liquidity position. While risk management is vital, equally vital is the risk absorbing capacity of the banks. This risk absorbing capacity will come from the capital of the bank. Since there were many instances of dis-stability of banks internationally, it was decided to look into this area and prescribe and set up some standards for banks. This is how Basel Accord came into picture.

Formerly, the Basel Committee on Banking Supervision consisted of representatives from Central Banks and Regulatory Authorities of the Group of Ten countries plus Luxembourg and Spain. Since 2009, all of the other G-20 major economies are represented in the committee, as well as some other major banking locales such as Hong Kong and Singapore.

**Basel Accord I** (1988) as it is now known, has attempted to take into account the credit risk and market risk faced by the banks and it was decided that banks shall have minimum of 8% capital to their risk weighted assets. This minimum was given as the benchmark to be considered as internationally acceptable level.

**Basel II** is the second of the Basel Accords, which are recommendations on banking laws and regulations issued by the Basel Committee on Banking Supervision. The purpose of Basel II, which was initially published in June 2004, is to create an international standard that Banking Regulators can use when creating regulations about how much capital banks need to put aside to guard against the types of financial and operational risks banks face. Under this new accord besides credit and market risk, it was identified that operational risk is also very important and banks shall have to make provision in its capital for this risk also. This accord was to be complied by 2015 by all countries. This new international standard intends to protect the international financial system from the types of problems that might arise should a major bank or a series of banks collapse. Basel II attempted to accomplish this by setting up risk and capital management requirements designed to ensure that a bank holds capital reserves appropriate to the risk the bank exposes itself through its lending and investment practices.

Basel II has spelt out its approach for bank strengthening as three pillars requirement. Under the first pillar, capital requirement for credit risk, market risk, and operational risk is to be provided. To begin with, standardised approach for credit risk and basic indicator approach for operational risk is to be adopted. However, banks are advised to progress to other sophisticated approaches based on internal management assessment of individual bank and then decide the level of capital requirement. In essence, uniform standard for all banks is not prescribed, rather banks are asked to develop capabilities to assess the risks and also decide on the level of capital requirement for themselves.

Under second pillar, supervisory review and internal control of banks are given due recognition. Controllers and management are advised to review the adequacy of systems and control and decide on the level of capital requirement for the bank. Controller can demand higher level of capital for a bank based on review, if considered necessary.

Under the third pillar, enhanced disclosure of more relevant areas and also observance of market discipline was prescribed for the banks. Transparency is very essential and banks shall have to follow internationally accepted accounting standards and make it available to public. This will make the bank management more responsible and open for appraisal and criticism by public.

Hence, Basel II is complete package of norms for banks to follow. Important developments after implementation of Basel Accord is risk management. Risk management will involve following stages:

- Risk identification
- Assessing the magnitude of the risk
- Monitoring the risk
- Controlling and mitigating the risk
- Setting aside capital for probable loss.

For banks, important risk factors are credit risk, market risk, earning risk and operational risk. The capital requirement for banks is to be worked out on the basis of risk perceived in these areas. To start with, some standard prescriptions are made. The accord visualizes that there shall not be uniform requirement for all. Rather it must be based on individual banks strength and perception.

In view of this, entire management perspective has to be changed. Risk perception in every facet of banking needs to be developed. Every activity of banks like credit, operation, earning, etc. will have to be evaluated on the basis of risk perception. This means the steps will be identification of risks in each area, assessing the magnitude of risk involved, regular monitoring of the risk, taking corrective actions to control and mitigate the risks and finally to provide capital support to absorb probable loss on account of such risks materialising and crystallising.

**Credit Risk**

This is crucial area for banks as the main activity of the bank is credit. Banks are advised by RBI to have minimum 9% capital adequacy ratio of its risk weighted assets. Loan assets are to be segregated on the basis of default risk perception and actual tangible security available. Each loan asset shall have to be given a particular risk weightage from 0 to 100% or even more than 100%. For example fully secured loan secured by tangible liquid securities like bank deposits, govt bonds, etc. can be assigned zero risk. Loans to govt or loans to others but backed by govt guarantee can be considered as zero risk as they carry sovereign guarantee. All other loans shall be placed under different %age of risk weightage category based on a formula prescribed for this purpose. RBI has been changing the risk weigtage to a particular type of loans depending on whether it has to be encouraged or discouraged. For example, real estate loans, loans to capital market exposure may be made to carry higher risk weightage, in excess of even 100% to discourage banks as it means banks shall have to carry higher capital for them. Likewise, priority sector loans can be assigned lesser risk weightage as it will encourage banks to increase loans to this sector, as banks need lesser capital for it.

Banks were also advised to have internal credit rating for all loans so that banks can assess and understand the risk involved in each loan account. To ensure that banks comply with it, the risk weightage for rated loans and unrated loans are made different. Rated loans can have lesser risk weightage based on credit rating. RBI has also advised banks to fix interest rates based on credit rating. As the risk weightage is less for better rated loans, banks can quote finer interest rate to them. Since last three years, RBI has also advised banks to have the loans rated by external agencies like CRISIL, ICRA, etc. so that the ratings are impartial and hence can be more dependable. Borrowers are now encouraged to get themselves rated by these rating agencies by giving sops like better interest rates and quicker disposal. External ratings are now compulsory for loans over ₹ 25 crores and this limit may be gradually decreased to cover maximum loans. Credit ratings, particularly by outside agencies will afford sanctity as well as dependability for credit risk assessment by banks.

### Market Risk

Market risk for banks is mainly in the area of investments it holds. Banks were advised to categorise investments in to HTM-(held to maturity), HFT-(held for trading) and AFS-(available for sale). Permanent investments held till maturity by banks can be held at book value and no depreciation needs to be provided for them. For all other investments, banks shall have to provide for depreciation in case the market rate of the security held comes down. Market rate for a security may appreciate or depreciate based on its coupon rate and movement of interest rate for securities in the market. It can be observed that whenever fresh securities with higher coupon rates hit the market, the earlier securities carrying lesser coupon rate depreciate and *vice versa*.

### Operational Risk

Operational risks for the banks are of various types. Normal banking operations involving financial transactions involve many risks. There is risk of delay in transactions, negligence by staff in handling transactions, loss due to frauds by staff and outsiders. In view of this, internal controls, systems, and procedures in place, play a vital role in controlling and mitigating these risks. Hitherto these were controlled by internal inspections and audit and also by periodical external inspections by authorities. Banks were undertaking inspection/audit of all its functions since long and a full-fledged set up exists in each bank for this purpose. However, in the context of risk perception envisaged in Basel accord, it was felt that the present system of inspection and audit by banks are not bringing out risk factors and also not reflecting truly the risk factors in operational areas of the bank. It was felt by RBI, that the inspection function in banks needs to be reoriented to reflect the risk factors faced by the bank. It was felt that the inspection and audit of banks should be risk based. However, the inspection reports developed and used by the banks were not suitable for binging out risk factors. NIBM was then involved to develop a risk-based inspection model and this model with some changes were adopted by banks.

Under the model presently in use by banks all functions of banks are examined on two parameters of inherent business risk and control risk. Each of these risk categories carries equal weightage. Level of compliance and extent of breaches, as against the procedures/targets set for such activities are examined to find out the level of overall compliance and the risk factor emerging for the bank in handling such activities. Scoring is given and finally total scores under business risk and control risk are arrived at. Based on scores, risk ratings are given from low to very high category. A risk matrix is drawn for business risk and control risk to arrive at a composite risk rating for the office under inspection.

The main advantage under this system is that the rating given is not arbitrary or subjective. Since level of compliance and breaches are actually measured on either 100% coverage basis, or wherever it is not possible, on sample basis, the scores and ratings given are truly reflective of risk factors involved and gives better information and feedback to the management.

Banks are now required to make provision for operational risk based on basic indicator approach. Under this, banks are assessing the past trend in losses sustained in operational areas and making a provision, which is now calculated at a percentage of actual profits of the bank.

**Basel III** is a new global regulatory standard on bank capital adequacy and liquidity agreed by the members of the *Basel Committee on Banking Supervision*. The third of the *Basel Accords* was developed in a response to the deficiencies in financial regulation revealed by the global financial crisis. Basel III strengthens bank capital requirements and introduces new regulatory requirements on bank liquidity and bank leverage. The G20 leaders officially endorsed the Basel III framework on 11-12th of November 2010.

Basel III proposes many newer capital, leverage and liquidity standards to strengthen the regulation, supervision and risk management of the banking sector. The capital standards and new capital buffers will require banks to hold more capital and higher quality of capital than under current Basel II rules. The new leverage and liquidity ratios introduce a non-risk based measure to supplement the risk-based minimum capital requirements and measures to ensure that adequate funding is maintained in case of crisis.

***Summary of Proposed Changes***

First, the quality, consistency, and transparency of the capital base will be raised.

*Tier 1 capital*: the predominant form of Tier 1 capital must be common shares and retained earnings.

*Tier 2 capital* instruments will be harmonised.

*Tier 3 capital* will be eliminated.

Second, the risk coverage of the capital framework will be strengthened.

Third, the Committee will introduce a leverage ratio as a supplementary measure to the Basel II risk-based framework.

Fourth, the Committee is introducing a series of measures to promote the build up of capital buffers in good times that can be drawn upon in periods of stress ("Reducing procyclicality and promoting countercyclical buffers").

Fifth, the Committee is introducing a global minimum liquidity standard for internationally active banks that includes a 30-day liquidity coverage ratio requirement underpinned by a longer-term structural liquidity ratio called the *Net Stable Funding Ratio*.

The Committee also is reviewing the need for additional capital, liquidity or other supervisory measures to reduce the *externalities* created by *systemically important* institutions.

Bank for International Settlements (BIS) has stated that:

"Basel III" is a comprehensive set of reform measures, developed by the Basel Committee on Banking Supervision, to strengthen the regulation, supervision and risk management of the banking sector. These measures aim to:

- improve the banking sector's ability to absorb shocks arising from financial and economic stress, whatever the source.

- improve risk management and governance.
- strengthen banks' transparency and disclosures.

The reforms target:

- bank-level, or micro prudential, regulation, which will help raise the resilience of individual banking institutions to periods of stress.
- macro prudential, system wide risks that can build up across the banking sector as well as the procyclical amplification of these risks over time.

These two approaches to supervision are complementary as greater resilience at the individual bank level reduces the risk of system wide shocks.

The new framework is expected to be translated into national laws and regulations by member countries, and will be implemented starting on January 1, 2013 and fully phased in by January 1, 2019.

Basel II accord in already under implementation and RBI wanted the banks to comply with the requirements and create systems for implementation. The supervisory review both by central bank and bank management is being strengthened for effective control on banking system. As Basel III recommendations are now received, it means the present decade shall be for strengthening of banks and financial systems to guard against the repetition of recent crisis in financial sector witnessed in the world.

# Asset Liability Management

# 24

Basel Accord on capital requirement for banks has identified various risks faced by banks and prescribed capital requirement for them. Further deregulation of interest rates and foreign exchange market has exposed banks in the country to interest risk and currency risk. It became necessary that the banks be geared up to face the changed environment. Financial sector reforms and Liberalisation called for better risk management capabilities with banks to identify, quantify, and mitigate the risks and to make capital provision for it. In this backdrop, asset-liability management assumed importance for banks. RBI wanted the banks to have necessary changes in management functions to oversee the risk perception and effectively manage it. Asset liability management (ALM) function has been identified as crucial for the banks to prepare themselves to face the new challenges.

The scope of ALM function is described as follows:

- Liquidity risk management
- Management of market risks
- Trading risk management
- Funding and capital planning
- Profit planning and growth projection.

RBI issued draft guidelines in 1998, for Asset Liability Management system (ALM) and made it operative from the year 1999. The guidelines also advised banks to form Asset Liability Committees (ALCO) to look into the liquidity position of the bank on regular—almost daily basis. Asset Liability Management assumed great importance for banks.

Broad guidelines were issued in respect of interest rate and liquidity risks, management systems in banks, which form part of the Asset-Liability Management function. The initial focus of the ALM function was to enforce the risk management discipline viz. managing business after assessing the risks involved.

Banks were advised to form Asset Liability Committee and the role of ALCO is defined as a decision-making unit responsible for balance sheet planning from risk-return perspective including the strategic management of interest rate and liquidity risks. Banks were advised to start with assessment of liquidity risk and interest rate risk.

ALCO has to look into the business issues and consider, product pricing for deposits and advances, desired maturity profile of the incremental assets and liabilities, and to monitor the risk levels of the bank. The ALCO should also review the results of and progress in implementation of the decisions made in the previous meetings in respect of the funding policy.

## Liquidity Risk

Banks deal with public deposits and the faith of the depositors is very important for them to function and continue. After providing for SLR and CRR, the remaining funds with the banks are available for lending. In fact, banks major profit comes from lending operations. Maintaining liquidity is of utmost importance to the bank as a major portion of deposits is in demand deposit category like savings and current deposits. Account holders can withdraw these anytime. Fixed deposits accepted by the banks have also by convention and practice, become payable on demand. Depositor can opt for premature payment of deposits and banks are bound to honour the demand. As technically speaking the entire deposit portfolio has become payable on demand, it is very important for banks to maintain sufficient liquidity to meet any sudden demand by depositors.

CRR and SLR are not for the purpose of meeting the day-to-day demand as banks shall have to maintain it at all times. This means banks shall have adequate cushion in cash or liquid securities to fall back to meet urgent demands. Maintaining huge cash is a losing proposition and hence banks shall have to invest in liquid assets or near liquid assets. Loan portfolio is somewhat illiquid as most of the exposure is in working capital limits, which never are repaid. Only term loan instalments are received every month/quarter/half year/year. Banks are now sanctioning term loans for even 20 years in case of infrastructure and housing loans. Whereas banks liabilities are short-term and even the fixed deposits accepted is for maximum 10 years period.

Hence, managing liquidity is a serious issue.

Measuring and managing liquidity needs are vital activities for commercial banks. A model of assessing liquidity position and maturity pattern of both assets and liabilities was put in use. This model requires segregation of assets and liabilities into definite time buckets starting from 14 days to 5 years duration as under:

(i) 1 to 14 days
(ii) 15 to 28 days
(iii) 29 days and upto 3 months
(iv) Over 3 months and upto 6 months
(v) Over 6 months and upto 12 months
(vi) Over 1 year and upto 2 years
(vii) Over 2 years and upto 5 years
(viii) Over 5 years

Wherever the assets and liabilities have a definite contractual due date the same are placed in the time bucket based on their residual maturity period. A portion of demand deposits as per a given formula, actual experience of the behaviour of demand deposits, are placed in short-term bucket, and remaining portion is distributed to medium term bucket. Likewise, every asset and liability is considered due on a period either based on actual date or based on accepted formula and placed in the corresponding time bucket. After this, totals of each bucket are drawn. The endeavour is to see whether under any time bucket the assets are more or matching the liabilities of the same time bucket. If the liability is more in any time bucket, then it is a potential danger signal for the management to be taken up and remedial measures to be initiated.

The mismatch during 1-14 days and 15-28 days should not in any case exceed 20% of the cash outflows in each time bucket as a benchmark.

The Statement of Structural Liquidity shall be prepared by placing all cash inflows and outflows in the maturity ladder according to the expected timing of cash flows. A maturing liability will be a cash outflow while a maturing asset will be a cash inflow. It would be necessary to take into account the rupee inflows and outflows on account of forex operations including the readily available forex resources [FCNR (B) funds, etc.], which can be deployed for augmenting rupee resources.

This study also enables the bank management to monitor and control growth of asset or liability in a particular time bucket and take management decisions for immediate actions. For example, if bank finds that the term loans are disproportionately increasing which has the impact on assets being pushed to medium and long-term buckets, serious mismatch can be visualised and management can take decision to curb sanction of term loans for longer duration and shift to working capital loans or bill advances. Management will also know the type of deposits to be encouraged either by increasing rate or by adding benefits in order to remove the mismatch in the particular bucket.

This study shall have to be taken seriously now as infrastructure lending and housing loans are shifting the loans to longer maturity buckets. Discouraging long-term deposits (as costly and without re-pricing) is placing the liabilities in short-term buckets. Hence, mismatch in long-term buckets have become prominent. Banks shall have to address these issues on ongoing basis to maintain the liquidity.

### Interest Rate Risk (IRR)

Interest rate risk for the banks arises due to changes in interest rates. Earlier RBI prescribed interest rates for both deposits and advances and banks enjoyed a protected Net Interest Margin (NIM) in their favour. This allowed banks to earn profits and they were not unduly worried about the interest rates, or its movement either way. Once the interest rates are deregulated in phased manner and banks are asked to decide themselves, banks will no longer have a protected NIM. Now it is dependent on market conditions and is difficult to predict. This has exposed banks to interest rate risk on both sides of their balance sheet.

To measure this risk it is necessary to understand the impact of interest movement on each type of asset and liability of the banks. Interest rate changes may have different impact on assets and liabilities. Some assets/liabilities may be interest rate non-sensitive. Examples are capital and current account deposits on liability side and cash and fixed assets on asset side. Other assets and liabilities are interest rate sensitive to varying degrees. For example, a term deposit is non-sensitive till its maturity but becomes sensitive after maturity as it will be repriced. Loans carrying fixed rate of interest is non-sensitive whereas the loan with floating interest rate is sensitive as the interest changes with change in PLR. In view of this, banks are required to segregate rate sensitive assets (RSA) and rate sensitive liabilities (RSL) according to the maturity of their becoming rate sensitive. This means most of the assets and liabilities remain without change in interest rate until due dates or maturity and thereafter shall be repriced as per market movements of rates.

An asset or liability is normally classified as rate sensitive if:

(i) within the time interval under consideration, there is a cash flow;

(ii) the interest rate resets/reprices contractually during the interval;

(iii) RBI changes the interest rates (i.e. interest rates on Savings Bank Deposits, DRI advances, Export credit,

Refinance, CRR balance, etc.) in cases where interest rates are administered; and

(iv) it is contractually pre-payable or withdrawable before the stated maturities.

All the rate sensitive assets and liabilities are to be segregated and placed in the time buckets based on their residual maturity or due dates (as they shall be repriced thereafter) on the following table. Difference in each bucket is called Gap and Gaps are arrived for each time bucket. Non-sensitive assets and liabilities are also shown as a separate bucket. The likely date of future change in PLR is also considered to place the PLR linked advances in the appropriate time bucket. RBI has advised the banks on classification of various items of rate sensitive assets and liabilities in the Balance Sheet, which shall be followed.

(i) Up to one month

(ii) Over one month and upto 3 months

(iii) Over 3 months and upto 6 months

(iv) Over 6 months and upto 12 months

(v) Over 1 year and upto 3 years

(vi) Over 3 years and upto 5 years

(vii) Over 5 years

(viii) Non-sensitive

As stated earlier the Gap is the difference between Rate Sensitive Assets (RSA) and Rate Sensitive Liabilities (RSL) in each time bucket. The positive Gap indicates that it has more RSAs than RSLs whereas the negative Gap indicates that it has more RSLs. Now based on this it is possible to simulate interest rate changes and study the impact on the earnings of the bank. For example, bank can have simulation study to find out the impact of say one per cent increase in deposit rates and see how much the bank is losing in its earnings. Likewise, bank can also study the impact of decline in interest rates on deposits and similarly increase or decline in interest rates on advances. Bank can also know whether positive gap (RSA > RSL) or negative gap (RSL > RSA) in the time buckets is working in their favour or against them, in the scenario of interest rates increasing or declining. The Gap can therefore, be used as a measure of interest rate sensitivity. The simulation study with changed interest rate can also measure the likely changes in the Net Interest Income (NII) or Net Interest Margin (NIM).

Banks are advised to set prudential limits on individual Gaps with the approval of the Board/Management Committee. The banks shall work out earnings at risk, based on their views on interest rate movements and fix a prudent level with the approval of the Board/Management Committee.

In view of poor MIS, slow pace of computerisation in banks, and the absence of total deregulation, initially RBI prescribed the Traditional Gap Analysis (TGA) as a suitable method to measure the Interest Rate Risk for banks.

Now banks have moved to modern techniques of Interest Rate Risk measurement like Duration Gap Analysis, simulation and Value at Risk, etc.

### Currency Risk

Foreign exchange rates were decontrolled in mid nineties and floating rates came into existence. This added a new dimension to the risk profile of banks. Banks were required to look into their position in individual currencies they are dealing and holding assets and liabilities. Any mismatch in assets and liabilities in any individual currency exposes the bank to currency risk as the exchange rate for the currency may go up or down in future.

Banks generally undertake operations in foreign exchange like accepting deposits, making loans and advances and buy/sell foreign currency and sometimes trading in the currency. This activity is bound to create mismatches in assets and liabilities in the particular currency.

The simplest way to avoid currency risk is to ensure that mismatches are reduced to zero or near zero. Mismatched currency position also exposes banks to country risk and settlement risk. Managing Currency Risk is one more dimension of Asset-Liability Management.

However, currency risk management is not a new subject. Banks were doing it. In the year 1978, RBI had introduced the concept of "end of the day near square position" and advised banks to set up overnight limits. Banks have been following it and the currency risk is thus mitigated to the maximum extent. From the year 1981, RBI advised banks to control even maturity mismatches. Maturity mismatches (Gaps) occur due to forward contracts and usance bills negotiated and even collection of bills and instruments as these transactions are at future dates. Subsequently RBI advised banks to make capital provision for overnight limits set up for currencies.

# Banks and IFRS

# 25

One of the requirement under third pillar (Basel II) is market discipline and the aim is for sharing information with others including investors, analysts, customers, other banks and rating agencies. Financial statements form important information for everyone. Generally, the financial statements are prepared and presented as per the requirements of provisions of law applicable and as per the accounting standards prescribed by authorities. In our country, the financial statements of bank are subjected to disclosure norms prescribed by RBI after adoption of prudential norms. The Institute of Chartered Accountants of India (ICAI) also has prescribed standards for bank financial statements.

Generally, every country in the world has its own accounting standards developed over the years. With globalisation of trade, now the financial statements are also seen and studied by international players for various purposes. As the financial statements were based on different standards, it becomes difficult for others to understand the financials and it requires comparison and conversion to other standards of accounting. This is a big challenge for international community.

Earlier in late nineties US-GAAP standard was used by others to make comparison as US was a leading economy in the world and also that the accounting standards there are considered better. Few of our banks were even getting their financial statements audited as per US-GAAP and publishing the same in addition to Indian standard. Since the different accounting standards followed by countries are posing serious problems for international players, a need for common standard was acutely felt and this has given birth to International Financial Reporting Standards (IFRS).

## IFRS Foundation and the IASB

The IFRS Foundation is an independent, not-for-profit private sector organisation working in the public interest based in London, U.K. The International Accounting Standards Board (IASB) is the independent standard-setting body of the IFRS Foundation. Its members are responsible for the development and publication of IFRSs, including the IFRS for SMEs and for approving Interpretations of IFRSs. The origin of IFRS can be traced to International Accounting Standards (IAS) issued between 1973 and 2001 by the Board of the International Accounting Standards Committee (IASC). The new IASB took over from the IASC the responsibility for setting International Accounting Standards from 1st April 2001.

IFRS are considered a "principles based" set of standards in that they establish broad rules as well as dictating specific treatments. Principal objectives of IFRS are:

- to develop a single set of high quality, understandable, enforceable and globally accepted international financial reporting standards (IFRSs) through its standard-setting body, the IASB;
- to promote the use and rigorous application of those standards;
- to take account of the financial reporting needs of emerging economies and small and medium-sized entities (SMEs); and
- to bring about convergence of national accounting standards and IFRSs to high quality solutions.

It is reported that IFRS are used in more than 113 countries around the world, including all of Europe, currently require, or permit IFRS reporting. Approximately 85 of those countries require IFRS reporting for all domestic listed companies. It is said that the US is also gearing towards IFRS.

IASB is said to follow a thorough, open, and transparent due process and brings out publication of consultative documents, such as discussion papers and exposure drafts, for public comment before finalising the standards. The IASB also engages closely with stakeholders around the world, including investors, analysts, regulators, business leaders, accounting standard-setters and the accountancy profession.

Worldwide adoption of IFRS will be beneficial to investors and other users of financial statements. It reduces the costs of comparing alternative investments and increases the quality of information. Companies will benefit, as investors will be more willing to invest. IFRS is useful to everyone due to its following qualitative characteristics of financial statements:

- Understandability
- Reliability
- Comparability
- Relevance
- True and Fair View/Fair Presentation.

Our country has decided to adopt IFRS and the Indian Accounting Standards will be convergent with IFRS.

The Institute of Chartered Accountants of India (ICAI) has announced that IFRS will be mandatory in India for financial statements for the periods beginning on or after 1st April 2011. This will be done by revising existing accounting standards to make them compatible with IFRS. The ICAI has also stated that IFRS will be applied to companies above ₹ 1000 crores from April 2011.

On January 22, 2010, the Ministry of Corporate Affairs issued the road map for transition to IFRS. In the first phase, companies included in Nifty 50 or BSE Sensex, and companies whose securities are listed on stock exchanges outside India and all other companies having net worth of ₹ 1000 crores will prepare and present financial statements using Indian Accounting Standards converged with IFRS. According to the press note issued by the government, those companies will convert their first balance sheet as at April 1, 2011, applying accounting standards convergent with IFRS, if the accounting year ends on March 31. This implies that the transition date will be April 1, 2011.

Reserve Bank of India has stated that financial statements of banks need to be IFRS-compliant for periods beginning on or after 1st April 2011.

# Rupee Convertibility

26

To begin with, our country was a closed economy in the sense citizens were not free to trade or do business with outside world. There were all sorts of restrictions on such transactions. Every country would like to be self-sufficient and not to depend on other countries for its existence or sustenance. While this is good in theory, but in practice it is not possible. A nation cannot live in isolation. Likewise, the country's economy cannot remain isolated. Every country is not self-sufficient in natural resources. Like in our case, oil is imported, as sufficient supply is not available in the country. Oil being the best source of energy known, is in short supply necessitating it to be imported. Initially until the green revolution was achieved by the year 1980, even food grains were to be imported. Lot of other products and services were to be imported as economy was growing and these were needed to make the country strong. However, every nation has to pay for its imports by equivalent exports of goods and services it can produce. In a way, it is barter system, and this is how the international trade takes place.

So nation's capacity to import is limited by its capacity to export. Due to oil imports, which formed major chunk and limited export base, all sorts of restrictions were placed for imports. In the beginning, one needed license to import anything. Payment for imports will have to be approved by RBI. To manage foreign exchange, Foreign Exchange Regulation Act 1947—FERA was enacted. Nation was in perennial shortage of foreign exchange, payments were becoming difficult, and prospects of default were looming large. FERA was a strict act and violation of it attracted severe penalties. RBI was also monitoring receipt of payments on exports to ensure that the proceeds are not diverted or siphoned, thereby denying the nation its benefit.

RBI monitors the inflow and outflow of foreign exchange. Inflow and outflow takes place mainly due to imports and exports of goods and services and capital inflow or outflow and financial charges and some other payments or receipts. Net difference of import and export of goods and services is called balance of trade. To this, other receipts and payments of capital and other nature during the year are added and balance of payment is arrived. These figures are worked out on annual basis. Balance of payment is critical for the country as it is the obligation of govt to see that no default takes place and every payment whether for imports or repayment of loans or servicing of interest on loans or other commitments are met on due date during the year. In case of shortfall, govt has to manage to borrow from international organisations like IMF, World Bank etc. In practice, govt is obliged to maintain foreign exchange reserves for this purpose and ensure that the reserves are adequate to take care of sudden demands. RBI manages foreign exchange reserves for the govt.

### NRI Deposits

In order to bridge the gap in *balance of payment*, RBI introduced schemes to attract Non-Resident Indians (NRI) deposits in the year 1970 as it provided inflow of foreign exchange. NRIs were wooed with tax exemptions, attractive schemes paying higher interest and promise of repatriation on automatic basis without having to seek prior approval. Rupee deposits were paid higher than domestic rate of interest. Non-resident external (NRE) accounts were opened for them in which the deposit is held in rupee but repatriation was immediately allowed by banks. This became popular with NRIs and lot of funds flowed into the country.

Foreign Currency Non-Resident (FCNR) deposit scheme was introduced in the year 1975. Under this, NRIs could place their deposits in foreign currency, initially with dollar and sterling, earn better return and avoid exchange risk on repatriation. Initially for FCNR deposits, RBI on behalf of Govt bore the exchange risk by purchasing such deposits from banks with a promise to release the same on maturity at the same exchange rate thereby protecting the banks. In the year 1993, RBI allowed banks to retain the FCNR deposits with them under FCNR-Bank (FCNR-B) scheme, and deploy themselves and bear the exchange risk. Banks were also allowed to give forex loans to its customers out of such funds. Such loans were given mainly to exporters who could borrow foreign currency at cheaper rate and be competitive in their business internationally.

Non-Resident ordinary (NRO) accounts, which are the accounts for local funds of NRIs, are subject to approval for repatriation and local income tax. NRE and FCNR are free from income tax liabilities. In late nineties RBI further relaxed and allowed income/interest earned from NRO accounts to be repatriable. Further relaxations have been allowed and now balance in NRO account can be repatriated up to one million dollars per year.

(Also see chapter on foreign exchange.)

## Convertibility

Rupee was not a convertible currency and everyone who received foreign exchange was bound to surrender it to Govt. Under the rules of FERA, no resident can retain foreign exchange with him. RBI is handling the foreign exchange reserves for Govt. The RBI fixed the exchange rates and there was no market rate of exchange. RBI changed the exchange rates from time to time. Historically Indian rupee was linked to pound sterling and RBI used to fix the exchange rates between rupee and sterling. Later in the year 1975, this linkage was shifted to a basket of currencies. RBI was fixing the exchange rates in relation to this basket of currencies. Mostly the exchange rates were rigid and unchanging. The official rates were not reflecting the true exchange rates based on current market conditions. This has created problem and under this sort of arrangement the only way out was devaluation of rupee, which had to be resorted to many times by RBI. A major devaluation of rupee took place in the year 1966 when rupee was devalued by 36.5%.

In the year, 1991 foreign exchange reserves plunged to very low level, which forced the government to pledge its gold to tide over the situation. Then came the financial sector reforms with wide ranging changes. FERA was replaced by FEMA, which is a friendly legislation.

Turnaround was a gradual process due to financial sector reforms introduced in the year 1991. These reforms made it possible and mainly the exports picked up. Non-resident inflows also increased. Due to liberalisation, inflow of foreign investments were encouraged and the country witnessed large inflow. Companies were also allowed to enter foreign capital markets for their capital raising through GDR issues. All these favourable changes improved the foreign exchange reserves of the country to a large extent and the position became clearly comfortable within couple of years.

Then for the first time in the year 1992, RBI introduced dual exchange rate system and allowed partial convertibility of rupee. Under this, 40% of remittance received was to be exchanged at official rate of RBI and 60% was allowed to be converted at market rate. Within a year i.e. in the year 1993, RBI scraped the dual exchange rate system and introduced uniformly market determined rates. In the year 1994, Govt announced move to current account convertibility and official exchange rate was abolished. Exchange was allowed at market rate.

With this, RBI no longer controlled exchange rates and allowed it to be determined by market forces. In the beginning, RBI had entered the market to give signal or stop the rupee from sliding. However, this was temporary measure to stabilize the market and not to direct or dictate the exchange rates. Slowly the intervention became less and less and now the exchange rates are truly market driven.

Restrictions on imports were gradually reduced and most of the items were kept on open general license (OGL) category for actual user industries or business. Very few items were kept under restrictive list requiring prior approval for imports. Banks were freely allowed to make payment for imports. As all the trade payments are freed from approval and banks are allowed to make payments, the rupee attained current account convertibility and status of the currency enhanced in the international market. It became one of the reliable currencies internationally.

Export was encouraged right from sixties by giving many incentives. Banks were asked to support exporters by extending loans on easy and cheap terms. Banks were advised to lend 12% of their loan funds to exports.

Govt is obliged to liberalise imports and exports rules and levy of taxes like customs duty, etc. in terms of GATT and World Bank agreements. For availing mutual trade benefits from other countries, it is essential for the Govt to avoid protection of local trade making it unattractive for other countries. As no nation can operate in isolation, and to derive benefits of technology and competitive prices for goods and services, opening up of economy in line with other countries became essential.

### Full Convertibility

Now as the economy is growing stronger, Govt is thinking in terms of making rupee a fully convertible currency. This means besides current account convertibility, capital account convertibility will also be permitted. Capital account convertibility (CAC) is defined as "the freedom to convert local financial assets into foreign financial assets and *vice versa* at market determined rates of exchange". In simple language, this means that CAC allows anyone to freely move from local currency into foreign currency and back. It means that the citizens will be free to move their assets anywhere in the world without permission. This is the cherished highest status for a currency to achieve, Even though, it will enhance the status of the country and attract large funds from abroad for investment, at the same time fear of locals fleeing country with their assets is also there. Balance of Payment position may become adverse and nation may end up as a defaulter.

A committee on capital account convertibility was setup by the Reserve Bank of India (RBI) under the chairmanship of former RBI deputy governor S.S. Tarapore to "lay the road map" to capital account convertibility. In 1997, the Tarapore Committee had indicated the preconditions for Capital Account Convertibility. The five-member committee has recommended a three-year time frame for complete convertibility by 1999-2000. The committee recommended that some preparation for the same would be required. Before allowing full convertibility, nation shall ensure that macro-economic conditions are in good shape and the economy achieves certain goal posts as preparatory steps. They are, Govt deficit to be controlled within 3.5%, inflation to be brought down below 3-5%, banks are strengthened by adequate capital and their NPAs to be under 5%, and CRR for the banking system to be at 3%. In committee's views when these goal posts are reached, then it will be the right time to allow full convertibility.

Though these steps were initiated by RBI final decision was delayed, as Govt and RBI were cautious and did not want the decision to be hurried.

In 2006, The Reserve Bank of India has again appointed a committee to set out the framework for fuller Capital Account Convertibility. The Committee, chaired again by S.S. Tarapore, was set up by the Reserve Bank of India in consultation with the Government of India to revisit the subject of fuller capital account convertibility in the context of the progress in economic reforms, the stability of the external and financial sectors, accelerated growth and global integration.

Tarapore committee II, has made its recommendations for steps to be taken for achieving full convertibility.

The committee has recommended a five-year roadmap, to be implemented over three phases, to relax regulations on capital account convertibility.

The Committee report, said the phase I should start from the fiscal (2006) while phase II should be implemented in the next two financial years (2007-09) and the last phase in the following two fiscals (2009-11).

Following are the main issues to be addressed as preparatory and necessary steps for attaining fuller capital account convertibility as per committee report:

Committee made recommendations for further reforms in banking sector like encouraging setting up of new banks in private sector, encouraging foreign banks, strengthening of capital ratios for banks and compliance of Basel II recommendations. It also recommended that all commercial banks should be subject to a single banking legislation and all banks, including public sector banks, should be incorporated under the Companies Act. Committee made some recommendations on the role of investments by FIIs, non-resident corporate, non-residents. It further recommended that non-resident corporate should be allowed to invest in the Indian stock markets through SEBI registered entities, including MFs and PMSs. Committee recommended for moderation in public sector borrowings and that the office of public debt should be set up to function independently outside the RBI.

The Govt is cautious in its approach to the issue of CAC and though it is committed to achieve fuller capital account convertibility, at the same time it will not be committed without adequate preparation. Govt is moving in this direction. Banks have been strengthened and their NPAs are under control. RBI has allowed foreign investments up to some limit to create confidence in the minds of international players. Foreign funds are allowed to invest in the country on certain terms. Govt deficit and inflation are being monitored and controlled. Though no time limit is now set, it can be expected that rupee convertibility will happen at an appropriate time in future.

# Technology Developments in Banks

# 27

Till seventies banks were functioning on manual basis and entire work of record keeping and transaction processing was handled by staff manually.

In seventies banks started using ledger posting machines supplied by Bluestar (Calstar) and other companies which had the facility to calculate the balance after credit and debit. This machine was mainly used for maintaining current accounts and served very limited purpose. Account Statement was printed as a copy of the ledger sheet.

Technology upgradation in banks started very late. This was mainly due to opposition of labour force who thought that computerisation would kill jobs in the industry. Introduction of computers started in eighties but not much progress was made. Even the technology was not developed and reliable power supply and communication network were not available then. In the beginning, the driving force for computerisation was increase in volume of transactions and banks wanted computerisation to take care of error free housekeeping. Manual system was not capable of keeping pace with the requirement. Those days even banking software was not developed and was not available in the country.

When computers made entry to banking, it was the hardware companies, who drove the market by supplying hardware, and to make the hardware sell, they provided some rudimentary accounting software along with it. This is how the computerisation in banking started. Computers were called as advanced electronic ledger posting machines (AELPM), may be just to pacify the labour who are against computerisation. However, the name was very apt as these computers were only doing this function. Savings and current accounts were maintained in the computers and software took care of credits and debits, balances, balancing of accounts, statement of accounts and calculation of interest and its posting.

This was the level of computerisation until late eighties and beginning of nineties. No other software was available. Special posts were created, named AELPM operators, by giving special allowances. However, this partial computerisation effort was appreciated as it took load off the staff.

It was during the same time RBI made changes to introduce MICR technology for clearing operation of cheques. Reader Sorter machine was first installed at Mumbai in the year 1984 and banks were asked to switch over. This required banks to bring in MICR cheque books which were otherwise not available in the country. Printers were identified and approved who can print MICR cheques. Encoder machines were introduced by few companies and MICR clearing was started. With all the initial teething problems, the technology has stabilised and it was spread all over the country. By the year 2010, 66 major centres in the country were under MICR clearing. Till date this technology is being used at many centres for clearing. In the year 2008, RBI has moved to Cheque Truncation and introduced it at Delhi. It is yet to be started at other centres.

Another important development was in collection of cheques drawn on upcountry stations. As the cheques are to be paid at the bank branch it is drawn on, the physical presentation of cheques is required and it necessitated sending the cheques either to the drawee bank or to another bank in the centre for collection. Once the paying bank makes payment, the fund is transferred back to the bank that has sent the cheque for collection by either using internal transfer mechanism of only sending advice, in case of same bank, or by a demand draft in favour of the collecting bank. This process took unduly long time, as banks were to depend on postal department for sending the instruments. This prompted RBI to prescribe time norms for collection for different centres and banks were advised to stick to the norms. RBI has further introduced an immediate credit system pending collection so that customers can get immediate credit for out station cheques.

RBI introduced national clearing for important centres and managed it, which worked on a set time norm and delays are avoided. RBI coordinated the function to ensure that credit is allowed on predetermined time schedule.

After the banks have migrated to core banking, RBI has introduced Speed Clearing in the year 2008 at select centres and banks with core banking in place are advised to make payment of cheques at the same centre where it is presented irrespective of on which centre the cheque is drawn, using core banking facilities available to them. This will stop the unnecessary physical movement of cheques from different centres. Credits are now instantaneous.

It was in the nineties that things started happening. Financial sector reforms ushered in by the Govt made it necessary for automation of bank functions as manual system cannot support the reforms. Slowly more software to computerise other modules of bank operations like deposits, loans, etc. was introduced. Still this is partial computerisation as the system was not integrated and each segment of banking operation was handled on separate PCs on stand-alone basis.

The new generation private sector banks started computerisation from day one in nineties after the year 1994 and the foreign banks have introduced it by then as they are supported by their parents. ATMs were introduced in nineties by private sector banks and public sector banks were under pressure to compete and retain business. It became imperative that banks adopt technology and upgrade their operations in order to remain in the market.

Banks started with total Branch automation, a package offered by companies like Tata Consultancy Services and others. This was necessary to start ATM facility. Banks were in haste to computerise and start ATMs in order to retain customer base.

Then in twenties, Core-banking software was introduced as a complete package for bank operations. This Core banking has added advantage of any Branch banking as the entire bank is brought under a central computer system and all branches of a bank are interconnected. Core banking technology found support as the telecommunication infrastructure in the country was also upgraded and connectivity, which was the bane of networking, was made to support. Banks went for core banking solution, as it was the ultimate as on date, and brought the banks at par with international standards. By taking up core banking, banks leapfrogged into today's technology and are now at par with the best. By the year 2005, many banks have achieved sizeable progress and it is expected that it will be complete in this decade.

Core banking has enabled banks to get into internet banking and make available host of other related services to customers. SMS facility and mobile banking has also been introduced and the next development in banking technology is the mobile banking.

After financial sector reforms have been introduced, computerization gained momentum in all spheres of economy. Time is money and telecommunication and computers have the capabilities to reduce transaction time and make things happen almost instantaneously. Delay is a cuss word in new environment. Transaction processing must be fast and accurate and at real time. Technology and telecommunication has enabled financial services to be redesigned and made them more reliable.

### Dematerialisation (Demat) of Securities

India had a vibrant capital market which is more than a century old, and the trading was taking place on the paper-based settlement of trades. This caused problems like bad delivery and delayed transfer of title till recently. The enactment of Depositories Act in August 1996 paved the way for establishment of depository in the country. Dematerialisation of physical scrip is a step to reduce paper work in capital market operations. It started in nineties and today holding shares and securities in physical form is a cumbersome as trading in such securities takes very long time.

### National Securities Depository Limited

NSDL, is the first and largest depository in India, established in August 1996 and promoted by institutions like banks and others responsible for economic development of the country for moving to holding of securities in dematerialised form. It has established a national infrastructure of international standards that handles most of the securities held by individual investors in demat account and facilitates trading and settlement in securities. Investors are no longer required to hold on to paper securities.

### Central Depository Services (India) Limited

CDSL was another depository established by Bombay stock exchange and few banks was set up in the year 1999 with the objective of providing convenient, dependable and secure depository services at affordable cost to all market participants. Settlement of trades in the demat mode is through BOI Shareholding Limited, the clearing house of BSE.

Under demat mechanism investors are required to maintain their investment account in securities with a Depository Participant (DP) who are authorised by the depository. Many banks have become depository participants with NSDL and CDSL and maintain demat accounts for customers. Demat accounts also help the investors as they receive the dividend and other payments directly to the credit of their link bank account.

Telecommunication and internment has made it now possible to trade in securities at the click of the button with automatic settlements. Online trading in securities is now a reality for Indian investors. This facility requires the investor to have demat account with a DP, trading account with a broker and a running account with a bank. The investor can enter into trading transactions in securities through internet and as his DP account, trading account and bank account are interconnected by an arrangement between banks and brokers, the trading and settlement takes place instantly.

## Technology and Fund Transfer

An important benefit derived from technology by banking is in fund transfer activity.

Requirement of fund transfer is manifold:

1. There is need to transfer money from one account to another account in the same bank or another bank.
2. Cheques are issued in settlement of transactions with one another.
3. Funds are required to be sent to beneficiaries in another city.
4. Funds required to be carried by the person while travelling.

As we know, hundis were in use in olden days by indigenous bankers, which acted as a solution for transfer of funds from one centre to another centre. Later, banks started issuing bank drafts. Thereafter traveller's cheques came on the scene. Post offices also provided the service of money orders, a simple and effective way to remit money to another station. Hence, cheques, drafts, travellers cheques and postal money orders became the instruments of fund transfer.

After computerisation of banks, many more avenues were opened up for fund transfers. Electronic fund transfer system is one. Electronic clearing system is another, which has both credit and debit clearing.

RBI introduced NEFT—national electronic fund transfer through its system, which allowed any bank to remit funds to any account with other banks at any centre. As this was done through network which joins the banks and RBI, funds are transferred and automatically credited to beneficiary account without any paper work or movement of papers. This system worked on batch mode at fixed time intervals. Further RBI introduced RTGS—real time gross settlement system, which processes individual fund transfers between banks on real time basis. This is almost instantaneous credit.

Electronic clearing system both credit and debit helps the bulk payment requirement like dividend and interest payments by companies or any large number of payments required to be effected by anyone. Similarly, the debit clearing enables utility providers to collect utility bills of large numbers without any paper work.

Core banking has also allowed banks to transfer funds between its own branches through its internal network instantly and this enabled any branch and anywhere banking for customers.

## Evolution of Payment and Settlement Systems

Payment and settlement systems became a focal point to modern banking. As cash has been replaced by cheques and later electronic modes of payment, it became important that a reliable and fast payment and settlement system is put in place to settle claims arising out of financial transactions.

Cash is replaced by bank account where everyone held their funds, in view of this, any payment settlement system necessarily shall have to involve the banks as ultimately they are making payment of either cheques issued by the customers or other types of mandate issued by customers. Hence, for any payment system banks necessarily shall be involved.

Banks themselves created clearing house mechanism to clear cheques drawn on them. Clearing house mechanism is a voluntary association of banks, now of course has become a necessity for them to operate in the market. This involved all banks to maintain accounts with one bank—managing bank, and settle accounts between them through this managing bank. This managing function was first undertaken by presidency banks and then by Reserve Bank of India. Though it is voluntary system, intervention of central bank became necessary and subsequently it was recognized as one of the exclusive function of RBI to create and oversee the payments and settlements systems of various types. RBI prescribed uniform rules for clearing houses and managed clearing houses at centres where it has offices. For other centres, the function of managing is looked after by State Bank of India and at few places by other banks.

Largely the cheques played an important role in payment settlement in the economy. Clearing house mechanism is relevant even today and it is now mechanised with MICR technology brought in. Cheque truncation is also introduced. However, the basic settlement system is same. The clearing house managing bank acts as final settlement platform for all member banks.

In 2008, RBI also pushed electronic clearing services—credits and debits. Electronic clearing of debits and credits are for the purpose of instant bulk payments and receipts. This reduces the work and time particularly for dividend and interest payments by corporates. It also facilitates collection of payments by utility service providers like telephones, electricity, etc.

Remittance and fund transfer through electronic media has changed business for banks. Hitherto remittances were made by mail transfers, telegraphic transfers and drafts. Now these are things of past. RBI has introduced RTGS (real time gross settlement) in 2004 and funds can be transferred from an account with a bank to an account with any other bank within the country. This takes place within one to two hours. NEFT (national electronic fund transfer) was introduced in the year 2005 and is also used for the same purpose. Under RTGS, individual large value transactions are processed independently whereas under NEFT transactions are processed in batches. For remittances within the bank, core banking allows the facility instantly.

RBI also acts as settlement bank and oversees the payments and settlements for national clearing, electronic credit and debit clearing, NEFT and RTGS. All these settlements between banks are through their accounts with RBI.

### Credit Cards

Another important development in payment system is the introduction of credit cards and debit cards. Probably Diners Club International, founded as Diners Club was the first independent credit card company in the world to start a charge card in the year 1950. Bank of America issued its credit card in 1956. Other banks like Citi Bank and American Express Bank also started their credit cards around the same time.

In India, Diners card was introduced in seventies and became popular with elite people. Later the Indian operation of this was taken over by Citi Bank credit card.

Credit cards are basically a credit limit allowed by the issuing body to the customer for using the credit card to make payment to merchant establishments, hotels and other service providers. The cards are instantly accepted by these shops by raising a charge slip on the credit card organisation. The charge slip is signed by the customer. Card holder can use the card to the extent of credit limit fixed for individual transactions. Credit card organisation makes the payment to the shops through its merchant acquirers, generally banks, who will reimburse the shops on production of charge slips signed by credit card holders. Credit card organisation raises monthly bills on the credit card holder to make payment. Credit card helped in two ways. Cardholder need not to carry cash for shopping. He also gets credit to an extent fixed.

With introduction of electronic cards and plastic money like credit cards and debit cards, transactions started happening through electronic media. But the settlement of payments was through banking channels. Then came the international cards which enabled customers to use the cards for both domestic and foreign payments. This called for a different system of settlement. Then there was also the issue of acceptability of cards issued by an issuer worldwide. This gave birth to two major settlement agencies for plastic cards i.e. Masters (since 1966) and Visa (since 1976) who are the biggest and worldwide organisations who provide settlement services for card use. Both these organisations were started by international banks to create a reliable system of acceptance of cards and to facilitate payment system. Under this, the parties to transactions in plastic cards are linked to these organisations who are responsible and facilitate payment and settlement between the participants (acquirers and card issuers).

Debit cards are issued by banks and it is a charge card in the sense that the cardholder can use it in the same way as credit card provided he has balance in the account. There is no credit available on these cards. Generally, banks combine ATM and debit cards together.

Other important payment settlement system was needed for stock exchanges, commodity exchanges, etc. However, these markets were controlled by respective exchanges and these exchanges used the services of banks for achieving settlement amongst the traders and members of these markets. Normally a bank functioned as settlement bank for the exchanges.

Payment settlements regarding imports and exports with other countries were managed by banks with RBI at the control. RBI is also the manager of foreign exchange reserves of the country for GOI. Bank for International Settlement (BIS) at Basel, established in the year 1930 acts as banker to central banks of the countries and facilitates settlements between central banks.

### The Clearing Corporation of India Ltd. (CCIL)

At the initiative of RBI, The Clearing Corporation of India Ltd. (CCIL) was set up in April, 2001 for providing exclusive clearing and settlement for transactions in Money market, GSecs market and Foreign Exchange market. It was promoted by six 'core promoters'—State Bank of India, IDBI Bank Ltd., (formerly Industrial Development Bank of India), ICICI Bank Ltd, Life Insurance Corporation of India (LIC), Bank of Baroda and HDFC Bank Ltd. The objective is to improve efficiency in the transaction settlement process, and to insulate the financial system from shocks emanating from operations related issues. The company commenced operations on February 15, 2002 when the Negotiated Dealing System (NDS) of RBI went live. CCIL started providing the settlement of forex transactions since November 2002. CCIL is thus providing the settlement services for bulk transactions of banks and other institutions relating to money market operations, forex transactions and trading in govt securities. CCIL launched a new money market product based on Gilts as collaterals called the Collateralised Borrowing and Lending Obligation (CBLO) in January 2003.

With the advent of ATMs and till such time the ATMs were for captive use of the bank's customers, settlement of payment was not an issue as it was purely internal accounting for the bank carried out on networked system. But when the sharing of ATMs started it called for a settlement system for transactions initiated by ATM cards of other banks.

ATM and debit cards gained momentum since the year 2000 when banks started migrating to core banking. RBI took major initiative for ATM sharing and in the year 2004, The National Financial Switch (NFS) was launched. It is an interbank network managed by Euronet India Pvt. Ltd., conceived and run by IDRBT (an arm of the Reserve Bank of India). The NFS Network connected 49,880 ATMs of 37 banks in the year 2004. Total number of shared ATMs increased to 75,178, as of March 31, 2011. National Payments Corporation of India (NPCI) is the settlement agency for banks connected to NFS.

### The Payment and Settlement Systems Act 2007

In view of the importance assumed by a reliable payment system in the modern economy and the crucial function of it which called for financial discipline and reliability of the authority managing settlement system, GOI passed an act in the year 2007, called The Payment and Settlement Systems Act 2007. This act empowers RBI to be the authority for creating the system needed in the interest of commerce and has the power to approve any authority to undertake the payment settlement system in any area.

RBI set up the Board for Payment and Settlement Systems in 2005, the board approved a proposal to set up an umbrella institution for all the Retail Payment Systems in the country. The core objective was to consolidate and integrate the multiple systems with varying service levels into nation-wide uniform and standard business process for all retail payment systems. The other objective was to facilitate an affordable payment mechanism to benefit the common man across the country and help financial inclusion.

### National Payments Corporation of India (NPCI)

National Payments Corporation of India (NPCI) was incorporated in December 2008 by ten core promoter banks (State Bank of India, Punjab National Bank, Canara Bank, Bank of Baroda, Union Bank of India, Bank of India, ICICI Bank, HDFC Bank, Citi Bank and HSBC). It is incorporated as a Section 25 company under Companies Act, and is operating retail settlement systems for the benefit of all the member banks and their customers. NPCI functions as a hub in all electronic retail payment systems, which is ever growing in terms of varieties of products, delivery channels, number of service providers and diverse technology solutions. At present interbank ATM card settlement for shared ATMs are looked after by it.

### Internet Banking and Payment Gateways

Internet banking has enabled bank customers to operate their accounts through internet and make payments. Customers can now transfer funds from their account to any beneficiary in his own bank or any other bank. Fund transfer through NEFT or RTGS can be effected through internet. Another important use of internet banking is in payment of utility or service bills. Customers can make payment of their electricity bills, telephone bills, mobile bills and many other bills through internet banking. These payments are made instantly. Customers can also make payment for their air, train tickets using internet. In fact, internet banking is another alternate payment instrument like credit or debit cards.

Payments through internet banking is enabled by many payment gateways created for the purposes. These payment gateways create a platform for transfer of fund from customer's bank to beneficiary's bank at the click of button. Many of the payment gateways are created and managed by banks.

In the area of utility bills payment through internet, BillDesk a platform created by M/S IndiaIdeas.com Ltd. in early 2000 has become popular with many service providers. Bank of Baroda sponsored this company. The National Venture Fund for Software and Information Technology promoted by Small Industries Development Bank of India is a partner. BillDesk enables instant payment of bills by facilitating transfer of fund from customer account to service provider's account.

# Banks and Social Lending

# 28

Public sectors banks have a responsibility cast on them for social lending. Social lending also includes priority sector lending and lending under special Govt schemes. Social lending means loans extended to mainly downtrodden for improving their lot. Our country is a democratic republic with creation of welfare society as its guiding principle. Govt has the responsibility to alleviate poverty and improve living standards of people. Govt has the responsibility to see that the progress made by the economy percolates down to poor and their lot is improved. At the time of independence, our economy was mainly a rural economy and even today, majority of people live in rural areas. Agriculture is still the mainstay of the economy.

Education level is low and employment level is also low. It is very difficult to get employment for people. In view of this, Govt put agriculture under priority sector and through RBI, advised public sector banks to lend for agriculture. In fact, a sub-target of 18% out of total 40% lending to priority sector was fixed. Until sixties banks were not lending to farmers and farm loan was not considered as bankable proposition. It was told that one bank from south when it lent to agriculture, eyebrows were raised. However, this particular bank is torchbearer and pathfinder to agriculture loans.

In a way, social lending was introduced by govt immediately after independence and initially rural credit was earmarked for Rural Coop Banks promoted to give loans to agriculture. The rural credit structure put up by the govt was:

- Primary agriculture credit societies at village levels (PACS) created in the year 1951 onwards.
- District Central Coop Banks at district levels were created by the year 1956.
- Apex Co-op Banks (State Central Coop Banks) were created by the year 1956.
- Land Mortgage Banks were created after the Land Mortgage Banks Act in 1930 was passed [later came to be known as State Cooperative Agriculture & Rural Development Banks (SCARDBs) and Primary Cooperative Agriculture & Rural Development Banks (PCARDBs)].
- Setting up of Agricultural Refinance and Development Corporation (ARDC) in the year 1963, which was subsequently taken over by NABARD.

In seventies RBI advised commercial banks to supplement the efforts of rural coop banks by providing agriculture loans.

The year 1969 was an important year from the point of view of social lending. On that year, many important decisions were taken.

First was the social control on banks. After long debate for over two years, govt introduced social control on banks with a view to further the cause of lending to the poor and to the desired sectors. As the banking was entirely in private sector, it was felt that these banks are not lending to poor. Bank credit though sparse at that time, was generally given to industries and trade at urban centres. Govt wanted the banks to lend to poor and wanted to have social control on banks.

Social control on banks was achieved in the year 1969 by passing necessary legislations. It was then prescribed that the banks shall have full time Chairman & Managing Director from career bankers instead of promoter of the bank. Banks boards were also to be reconstituted and professionals were to be inducted as directors. This was effected by amending Banking Regulation Act 1949. Approval of RBI is made mandatory for appointment of Chairman & Managing Director. The purpose is to have professional directors and career banker as Chairman so that social lending can get a fillip. This was the first attempt to exercise social control on banks in the country.

Second was the introduction of lead bank concept by RBI. Concept of lead bank for the district was introduced in the year 1969. Each district was put under a Lead District Plan (annual plan) and District Consultative Committees were formed. All the banks in the district are the members along with other govt development agencies of the district. Collector is made chairman of the committee to oversee the implementation of district development plan. One bank in the district acted as Lead Bank and in consultation with Govt depts., drew up district credit plan each year, mainly for deployment of bank credit to various schemes including priority sectors. Self-imposed targets are given to banks to achieve every year. This scheme is a success story and is continuing.

Third was bank nationalisation. Nationalisation of banks in 1969 was also to exert social control on banks so that the bank lending can be dovetailed to Govt development plans. Govt nationalised 14 major banks, which was a historical step, which changed the course of banking development in the country and proved a success story.

RBI introduced the concept of priority sector advances in the year 1974 and banks were advised to earmark 33.3%, which was then raised to 40% of total credit to this sector, comprising of agriculture, small-scale industries, and service sector.

Rural development was top of the agenda and the rural poor had to be helped to improve their lot. As the agricultural activity is seasonal and plenty of free time was available to farmers, allied activities like dairy, poultry, goat rearing, fishery, vegetable growing are supported to enable the farmers to have additional vocation and income. In order to make these schemes working, Govt formulated special schemes under which some concession, subsidies were built into the schemes. These loans were also given priority sector status.

In order to further improve rural lending, in the year 1975 Public sector banks were asked to promote Regional Rural Banks for predominantly lending to agriculture. Many regional rural banks came up and expanded their activities in rural areas.

Integrated Rural Development Programme (IRDP) was started by the Govt of India since 1980 in all the blocks of the country to help rural poor. Target group was small and medium famers, agricultural labourers and rural artisans living below the poverty line. Beneficiaries are identified from farming and other rural activities for suitable credit support depending on their vocation. Banks were asked to give loans to them. Govt supported them by giving subsidies.

Banks (rural banks and commercial banks) lending to agriculture has brought in green revolution in the country. The Green Revolution resulted in a record grain output of 131 million tons in 1978-79. This established India as one of the world's biggest agricultural producers.

Govt and RBI encouraged lending to small-scale industries as it was recognized as indispensable for the economy and can create large employment opportunities, which large industries cannot match. Service sector was also put under priority sector as these small business, professionals, small traders, small road transport operators were recognized as important segment for providing various services and also for creating self-employment.

## Banks' Approach to Social Lending

Since the banks were lending based on securities until then, banks were forced to change their views on lending and were advised to lend looking to the purpose of loan. Any loan for the purpose of developing business or trade, producing goods and services shall not be denied. All the above sectors were weak financially, mostly managed by individual entrepreneurs and needed support. In order to entice banks to lend to them some credit guarantee schemes were also introduced in the year 1971.

Though at macro level social lending was accepted by the banks, at micro level lot of problems were there. Important among them was the perception about such loans. Banks felt that the credit absorption capacity of these borrowers is very weak and default rate is high. Poor are undisciplined and mostly divert the funds or use it for consumption rather than for business. Loan recovery was a big problem. Govt advised banks to lend on a target approach basis, the sanctioning of individual loans were left to banks. During the reviews of implementation of various schemes, achievement of targets were discussed. This enabled banks to under achieve and sanction loans only under compulsion by some quarters. Willingness is still lacking. The feeling is that the schemes are political and economically non-viable and banks are going to suffer huge loss because of these loans.

It is a fact that the default rate is high and some amount of misuse of the schemes is seen. However, contrary to the general perception, the loan default in these segments does not have a major impact on bank's financial health. Moreover, Govt has provided support for recovery through various changes in recovery laws. Most of the loans are with subsidies by the govt. Even when ultimately the loan has to be written off, banks get rebate in income tax and the net loss to the banks is much less.

Social control on banking is complete with the continuous efforts of Govt and RBI. It has proved successful and had great impact on country's economy and improvement of lives of poor in the country. The progress achieved by the country in terms of green revolution and industrial revolution has no match in the world.

In a poor country, social objective to improve the lot of poor cannot be ignored. If the democracy has to survive and flourish then poor will have to be taken care of and their lot improved. Society has the responsibility to ensure that every citizen gets a fair chance to improve himself. Govt has to look after the poor and aged. The governance is for this purpose only. Poor have little capacity to absorb credit and tend to divert it to other more pressing consumption needs. We cannot grudge it and deny credits to them. It only proves that the doses administered are inadequate and need to be improved. Society and banks have to take a holistic approach and help the poor.

No doubt, banks particularly public sector banks, have done exceptionally well over the years and contributed to very large extent for social lending. Over the period, many of segments of borrowers have attained acceptability as viable banking propositions. Subsidisation in interest charges and subsidies from govt is also coming down. Recovery position is getting comfortable. Some segments of social lending that fall under priority sector definition do not require any sops now. Loans to them were earlier considered as commercially non-viable. Social lending has identified these segments. Examples are small enterprises, transport operators, small traders, professionals, etc. Lending to them are purely commercial propositions now for banks. This is a big contribution of social lending concept. It made banks to realise and identify many activities as bankable.

However, banks should continue with social lending even by losing some amount each year in larger interest of nation and the society. Bringing people above the poverty line is very important and is the key to succeed as democracy. Otherwise, gap between haves and have-nots will widen and there will be chaos.

# Banks and Financial Inclusion

# 29

In order to address the issues of financial inclusion, the Government of India constituted a "Committee on Financial Inclusion" under the Chairmanship of Dr. C. Rangarajan. The Committee submitted its final report to Hon'ble Union Finance Minister on 04 January 2008.

The Committee has defined Financial Inclusion as "the process of ensuring access to financial services and timely and adequate credit where needed by vulnerable groups such as weaker sections and low income groups at an affordable cost".

RBI has observed that nearly forty years after nationalisation of banks, 60% of the country's population does not have bank accounts and nearly 90% do not get loans. Despite heightened focus on financial inclusion, Indian banks still somewhat failed to bring the under- and un-banked into the mainstream banking fold. India has currently the second-highest number of financially excluded households in the world. Approximately, 40% of India's population has bank accounts and only about 10% have any kind of life insurance cover, while a meager 0.6% has non-life insurance cover.

Financial inclusion is the buzzword today. In this decade, this has gained momentum. Despite all the social banking and integrated rural development undertaken in the country, it is realised that majority of poor and economically weaker section are still not having bank accounts. One reason could be that the reach of the banks is not enough even now. Another reason could be that these people hardly have any requirement for banking services. Only when they are beneficiaries under some loan programme, bank accounts are opened. It is also felt that they are afraid to approach a bank even if they can have an account and have small savings.

Banks have done lot of good work in giving loans to rural populace but not everyone is covered. Banks have also started promoting self-help groups and providing micro finance to them. It is now visualised that financial inclusion is not only giving bank loans. As the economy is progressing and technology is improving, it is imperative that each citizen must have a banking account and is made part of financial system. Need is for providing them identity, and then open an account for them which may later lead to bank finance and govt support in any form. This is possible when every citizen is identified, and is part of banking system.

However, at the same time, the requirement is daunting as banks are not equipped to do it. All these accounts when opened will be sparingly operated and will have small balances making it difficult for banks economically, to maintain them. This is the big challenge for banks. Again, KYC norms are already in place, which requires some documentation for opening a bank account. This will also be difficult for this class.

In 2006, RBI issued guidelines for banks to have a special category of savings bank accounts and named it as 'no-frills accounts' or 'basic banking account'. This was meant to help poor people who have no papers and are going to receive some govt aids. Since bank account is necessary for them to collect aid, RBI permitted banks to open accounts as 'no-frill accounts' with or without introduction and without insisting for documents or proofs. Banks were advised that they need not extend all the facilities to them except for few basic facilities to enable them deposit and withdraw money from the accounts. It was also stipulated that total credits of one lakh per year can be allowed excluding govt aids and balance in the account can be up to 50,000 at any time.

Then the KYC guidelines came and a provision for such accounts were made by a simplified KYC procedure and the relaxations allowed for opening such accounts were continued. These accounts are now called as 'basic banking accounts'.

Banks have opened these accounts as social responsibility thinking that they will have to bear the cost of maintaining these accounts. Then as the accounts were opened, suddenly banks started realising that they are wrong in their thinking that these accounts are un-remunerative. They found that though the average balances are low, still it is making sense to open as many accounts as possible and the cost of maintaining is not that much. They also realised that this would be an excellent opportunity for them to expand customer base and business. Banks have now started even wooing these customers with free cheque books and even free ATM cards. Even private banks are into this now for grabbing the business opportunities.

Opening of bank accounts for everyone will create thrift for savings and whatever savings such people have will come to main economy. With technology progress in banks and in other spheres these underprivileged will be able to join the mainstream and derive the benefits like safe keeping of their savings, transfer of funds and also can find linkage to credit programmes of banks or govt. Any financial assistance or subsidies, which may come from govt and any other source, can reach them directly through the account. This also will eliminate intermediary and siphoning of funds by them.

Reserve Bank of India has also realised that with the present banking set up it will not be possible for banks to reach out and ensure total inclusion. After some study into the matter, RBI has permitted banks to have a model where they can appoint Business Facilitators and Business Correspondents. Business facilitators shall act as mere agents with no authority for financial transactions and Business Correspondents can have limited authority for doing banking transactions. Banks are now working on these models and appointing BCs and BFs. Banks have also started using technology to outreach such people. Biometric cards have been introduced and banking transactions can be done on handsets using biometric cards. Banks have also started biometric ATMs and mobile ATMs to approach the target group.

# Banks and RTI Act

30

Right to Information Act (RTI Act) was passed by the Government and implemented in the year 2005. It is trial blazing law and very progressive in nature. It empowered citizens to call for information from Government and Government sector companies. The provisions of this act cover the public sector banks being in government sector. The act required that the organisation have to part with any information it has unless it can claim exemptions under the act. Each organisation was to place on record the availability of information and the area, which is not accessible/ available. Some minimum options are there for banks like the proceedings of board meetings. Otherwise, all information is open for citizens. For public sector banks, customer information is excluded, as they are confidential and contractual in nature. It saved the banks. All other areas of bank's working are now transparent for the public to demand information.

When the act was implemented, lot of applications were received. Some were mischievous and some were from other than individuals. This issue was also discussed in a meeting of banks at Mumbai. Subsequently IBA clarified that the act gives rights to citizens only and companies and firms are not citizens for the purpose. However, a partner of the firm or a director of the company can apply in his own name for the required information.

The act gives rights to citizens of the country. Foreign nationals are not included under the act. As the right is available only to citizens, it becomes logical that the organisation has to first find out the eligibility of the applicant. Here guideline issued makes it clear that the declaration of applicant is to be accepted for this and the organisations will not pursue the matter unless it has knowledge that the applicant is not eligible.

## Information Defined

"Information" means any material in any form, including records, documents, memos, e-mails, opinions, advices, press releases, circulars, orders, logbooks, contracts, reports, papers, samples, models, data material held in any electronic form and information relating to any private body which can be accessed by a public authority under any other law for the time being in force (RTI Act).

Act defined the information as any document, record, information available in any of the records and files of the organisation. The copies of the same shall be made available. It also says that as far as possible the information sought may be furnished in the format desired by the applicant. If that is not possible then the format in which it is available shall be provided. There is a provision in the act to avoid unnecessary wastage of time and energy by the organisation in compiling with the request, refuse the same on that ground, and provide information as it is available with it.

## Providing Information

Under the provisions of the Act every organisation will have to appoint public information officer (PIO) to whom the application under the act will be addressed. When the organisation is large one with multi-locations, it can also appoint assistant public information officers (APIO) for each centre and PIO at head office. Besides, every organisation will have to name an appellate authority within, who is senior to PIO and who will deal with appeals against the decisions of PIO. Applicant may go in for second appeal against the decision of appellate authority (within the organisation) to Information Commissioner appointed under the act.

The applicant need not give the reason for his requirement and he is also free to use the information for any legitimate purpose. The organisation shall have no say in this.

The Act provides that the information shall be provided within 30 days and applicant can make an appeal against decision of information officer to higher authority in the organisation. If still not satisfied he may prefer second appeal before the Information Commissioner.

The Act provides that the information shall be given and there is no discretion to withhold information. It states that the information that cannot be denied to parliament or state legislatures shall not be denied to any person. This shows the actual seriousness of the matter and the citizen is placed at the same pedestal as that of parliament and a state legislature as far as providing information is concerned.

### Denying Information

Information can only be denied if it falls under the exemptions provided in the section 8 of the Act. While denying the information, it is necessary to inform the clause of this section under which the information is denied.

*Section 8 (1) of RTI Act*

"Notwithstanding anything contained in this Act, there shall be no obligation to give any citizen,—

(a) information, disclosure of which would prejudicially affect the sovereignty and integrity of India, the security, strategic, scientific or economic interests of the State, relation with foreign State or lead to incitement of an offence;

(b) information which has been expressly forbidden to be published by any court of law or tribunal or the disclosure of which may constitute contempt of court;

(c) information, the disclosure of which would cause a breach of privilege of Parliament or the State Legislature;

(d) information including commercial confidence, trade secrets or intellectual property, the disclosure of which would harm the competitive position of a third party, unless the competent authority is satisfied that larger public interest warrants the disclosure of such information;

(e) information available to a person in his fiduciary relationship, unless the competent authority is satisfied that the larger public interest warrants the disclosure of such information;

(f) information received in confidence from foreign Government;

(g) information, the disclosure of which would endanger the life or physical safety of any person or identify the source of information or assistance given in confidence for law enforcement or security purposes;

(h) information which would impede the process of investigation or apprehension or prosecution of offenders;

(i) cabinet papers including records of deliberations of the Council of Ministers, Secretaries and other officers:

Provided that the decisions of Council of Ministers, the reasons thereof, and the material on the basis of which the decisions were taken shall be made public after the decision has been taken, and the matter is complete, or over:

Provided further that those matters which come under the exemptions specified in this section shall not be disclosed;

(j) information which relates to personal information the disclosure of which has no relationship to any public activity or interest, or which would cause unwarranted invasion of the privacy of the individual unless the Central Public Information Officer or the State Public Information Officer or the appellate authority, as the case may be, is satisfied that the larger public interest justifies the disclosure of such information:

> Provided that the information which cannot be denied to the Parliament or a State Legislature shall not be denied to any person."

However for banks in public sector any information concerning customer accounts falls under the exemption provided in the section 8(1)(d) of the act as the same is treated as commercial confidential matters. Hence, it shall not be provided.

Of late, it is found that lot of applications are made and the purpose is to know the decisions on certain matters or reasons for not taking any particular line of action. Banks and others are dealing it in some manner. However, the issue is still debatable. The act empowers the citizen to get information. It does not empower him to pose questions and demand answers. It is not meant for question and answers. Citizen is entitled to get information. Information is defined in the act. It is something already on the record. It is to be provided by the information officers of the organisations who are duty bound and also empowered to requisition it from any authority within the organisation. Their responsibility is to locate the information and then collect it and give it to the applicant. They cannot speak for the organisation and they are not authorised as spokespersons of the organisation. They are not the very senior officers of the organization. They may have some seniority but there are other seniors and bosses in the organisation. Hence, the information officer cannot venture into making statement on behalf of the organisation.

The citizens' right is to collect whatever information is available on the subject from the organisation and then draw his own conclusion and act and use the information for the purpose they intend to use. They cannot bind the organisation to give reply to their hypothetical question or the reasons for the organisational behavior or act or inaction. Their remedies are different and they will have to approach those authorities who control the organisations for answers. That is Government of India. There are forums created by the Government to supervise and look into lapses of the organisations. Citizen can only approach them with information he has for further action. Citizen can of course go to press which is active in such matters and create pressure on the organisation. He can approach court of law for remedy or action against anyone.

The point here is that there need to be a clear distinction between information as defined under the act and a roving question for which answer in the shape of some record does not exist. For example if the information sought is why delay has taken place in deciding a matter. Then the information available with the organisation will be when the matter was referred to it. The actions taken date-wise and the final action recorded. This shall be provided but there is no need to answer the question why the delay? Because according to one view the citizen is not the controlling authority or disciplinary authority. He has no such powers. He had right to the information and he is informed. If there is delay, which is automatically admitted by the record itself by noting the dates, it can be inferred by anyone that there had been delay. If there are rules for disposal then the dates clearly shows the violation of norms. Organisation need not appease the applicant on that or give any reply to him explaining the reasons because he is not the condoning authority for such matters. There are other authorities to do it. Applicant should not mistake that the act has given him jurisdiction over the functions of the organisations. It has only empowered him to collect the information, which he can use for whatever purpose.

However, it is not to say that organisations need not worry on such things. It will make a very big difference as record proves the inefficiency and organisation has to reply to their controller. More than that, it will create bad publicity and tarnish the image of organisation. Hence, it is a serious matter. The purpose of the act is to make authorities accountable publicly for their deeds or misdeeds. Organisations have to face the press and the courts who can act based on information.

Another issue faced by banks is applications under the act by its own customers, borrowers or co-obligants and staff members. This is a contentious issue.

Customers demand information on their accounts and also borrowers and co-obligants. Here whether banks are obliged to give information is the issue. Under the act information of confidential nature cannot be given. Since the customer himself is asking for the information, as a practice, banks are giving information about their accounts. However, it appears that the right of the customer to get information about his account does not stem from RTI act. It stems from the existing laws and practices of banks. Under RTI act, only citizen is identified who can call for information from public authorities. It means that the information that has to be given under the act is same to all citizen. Either the citizen is entitled to get it or if it falls under exempted category of information, he shall not get it. Citizen claiming right under this act combined with his special status with the public authority under different existing laws is obviously not covered by RTI act. It will create anomalous situations of putting citizens under different categories based on their contractual or legal relationships with the specified public authorities. It cannot be the intention of the present act.

Individual staff/ex-staff members are at times making applications under the act to get information about their own matters.

Under Sec. 8(1)(j) information which relates to personal information the disclosure of which has no relationship to any public activity or interest, or which would cause unwarranted invasion of the privacy of the individual is exempted. In view of this personal information on staff are not given. However, while dealing with the applications of staff members for their own information, a special category is created. Again, banks are giving it as a practice but it also appears that strictly speaking such applications are not maintainable under the act.

However, the trend of decisions in such cases by appellate authorities under the act seem to be different and not accepting the above view points.

# A Peep into Future

31

What will be the future of Indian banking? May be in next ten to twenty years?

It is difficult to predict. It may be possible to forecast future level of business by juxtaposing the growth rate achieved in the past and deciding on a future growth rate. These types of forecasts are available. However, the important issues that will make the difference will be:

- Govt ownership of banks and its vision for banking.
- Extent of financial sector reforms carried forward.
- Govt decision on currency convertibility.
- Global developments in financial sector.

Govt ownership of public sector banks is a burning issue before the Govt and in view of globalisation and reforms; it was almost certain that the Govt ownership will come down gradually and may be Govt will exit from the sector in the near future. Law has already been passed for diluting Govt share to 51% and many banks have gone public. There is also thinking that ownership need not be a prerequisite for Govt control on banks, which can be achieved by other means to ensure proper direction for growth. However, the recent failure of fews international banks has put a question mark on the model adopted in developed countries, which we were trying to emulate. It is now proved that the model is not free from flaws and the nations shall have to develop a still better model for stability in the financial system.

The present Indian model of mixed economy has proved better resilient to shocks. Govt may go slow on privatisation and may not precipitate the same. Rather govt may allow things to happen in natural course as demanded by future developments. By that time social lending and priority sector lending, may become quite a bankable proposition for banks, needing no pushing by RBI or govt. Financial inclusion may also be in place by the year 2015 in which banks have a major role to play to bring in transformation. In view of these factors, public sector banks will continue in existence for next ten years may be with smaller govt holding—even below 51%.

Mergers and consolidation of banks were being talked about in the past. Many committees appointed by the govt also recommended it. Due to various reasons, and the resistance for the same, merger issues are on back burner now. Govt and RBI have indicated that this will not be forced and rather it will be left to banks' managements to decide. As things have now changed, mergers may not happen in the near future.

Financial sector reforms are on full swing now. Opening up of the economy is taking place and foreign players are allowed more freedom. This has already resulted in large number of international banks entering the country and expanding their base and activity. Generally, permitting foreign banks is on reciprocal basis. As our banks are allowed by any other countries to operate, the banks from those countries get preference to come to our country. Presence of international banks will help in improving standards and make the field competitive and will benefit the consumers.

In 1992, RBI allowed new private sector banks to come on scene and many new banks came into existence from the year 1994 onwards. Largely these banks were successful and created a niche for themselves. Their presence also helped existing banks to improve, in order to survive and retain their share of business. Second largest bank of the country is ICICI Bank that came from this breed of banks. Some more new banks are being encouraged now. This will create a healthy and strong banking system in the country. We are moving towards totally free regime where anyone with interest to start a bank can have an opportunity to do so.

Even though mergers are not forced now, still smaller banks are being merged with bigger banks due to certain compulsions. The present trend in mergers is in the interest of customers as otherwise they will lose when a small bank fails. The oversight of RBI is well developed and is now capable of identifying the weak banks and taking proactive steps to safeguard the interests of all stakeholders. This trend will continue and many smaller banks when run into trouble will opt for merger route. However, voluntary mergers are not seen, as the managements are not ready for it for many reasons.

Terrorist attacks and recent international banks failures have galvanised countries around the world to find solutions for both combating terrorist financing and bank failures. Basel accord on capital for banks is in this direction. Basel committee has already made three recommendations; I, II and III. Next 10 to 15 years will be for implementation of Basel Accords. Strengthening of banks will be top of the agenda. Risk managements and asset liability management of the banks are in place. However, in the next ten years these will be fine-tuned as at present some standard approaches are in place. This will have to be replaced by bank specific and accurate systems.

Countries have geared up to fight terrorism and many statutory changes have been made. These are being implemented. Transaction monitoring will gain importance and banks will be working for it. Coordination between banks and law agencies have become pertinent to fight the menace of terrorism for identifying the source of funding this activity.

Avowed policy of the govt is to make the currency convertible. However, govt is not hurrying the same and is waiting for opportune conditions and time for doing it. Once the capital account convertibility is allowed, it may change the investment pattern of locals, as they will have free access to foreign investments. Country may also attract more foreign investment. Ownership of businesses in the country may change with more foreign investments and corresponding changes in ownerships.

Technology is fast changing. Computerisation and telecommunication has changed the face of banking. All products and services are redefined in line with the technology progress. Things are now happening on real time basis. Internet banking is making the banking paperless. Mobile banking has just started and in next five years time this may replace other service delivery channels for the banks.

In our country, common identity document is not available at present. Identity is through many identities created for different purposes like Passport, PAN, Voter ID and Ration card, etc. Due to this, establishing identity is becoming difficult. Govt has started a unique identity document scheme (UID). This may take five years to implement. Once this is in place, identification will become easy and common. This will solve many issues on identification.

# Chronology

32

**BANKING DEVELOPMENTS IN INDIA**

Recorded history of Indian banking during 18th century and 19th century

| Year | Event | Remarks |
|---|---|---|
| | Indigenous bankers dominated the scene in earlier part of 18th century. | |
| 1720 | Bank of Bombay,—The first bank of a joint stock variety was established in 1720 in Bombay. | It collapsed subsequently. |
| 1767 | British agency houses undertook banking business in later part of the 18th century.<br>The first Agency House was Forbes & Co. started by John Forbes in the year 1767 in Bombay. | Later it was merged with Parry & Co. of Madras and Palmer & Co. of Calcutta. The first Agency House in Calcutta was opened in 1768—M/s Kelr. Reed and Cator.<br>In the year 1770, two more agency houses were opened at Calcutta: M/s Croftes and Johnson and M/s Paxton and Cockerel. These two Agency Houses undertook deposit banking and issue of paper money along with other business. |
| 1770 | Bank of Hindustan started in 1770 one of the earliest banks established in the country started by an Agency House named Alexander & Co. at Calcutta and functioned as a commercial bank. | It remained functional for more than 50 years. It was closed subsequently in 1832. This bank also issued paper money. |
| 1773 | The General Bank of Bengal and Behar in 1773 established by Warren Hastings (Governor General). | It was short-lived and closed in 1775. This bank also issued paper rupees. |

(*Contd...*)

| | | |
|---|---|---|
| 1777 | Francis Latour & Co established in 1777 in Madras. In 1810, the firm was named Arbuthnot, de Monte and Co. and in 1821 it became Arbuthnot & Co. it was a commercial bank. | It continued in business of banking for more than 100 years under the control of founder's family before it collapsed in 1906. |
| 1782 | In the year 1782, East India Company announced that the House of Gopaldas would replace Jagatseth as Govt of Bengal banker. | |
| 1784 | The Bengal bank was established in 1784 and it functioned for few years and closed in 1791. | This bank also issued paper rupees. |
| 1786 | The General Bank of India started in 1786. | It also issued paper currency. The bank was closed in the year 1791. |
| 1788 | The Carnatic Bank started. | Amalgamated to form bank of Madras in 1843. |
| 1795 | The British Bank of Madras started. | Amalgamated to form bank of Madras in 1843. |
| 1800 | By the year 1800, Calcutta had about 50 agency houses, Bombay had 17 and Madras had 10. Many of these Agency Houses acted like banks to accept deposits and give loans. | Some of them have reported to have financed the East India Company and were also issuing paper money. However, all of them perished with time. |
| 1804 | The Asiatic Bank started. | Amalgamated to form Bank of Madras in 1843. |
| 1806 | Madras Bank started. | Amalgamated to form Bank of Madras in 1843. |
| 1806 | Bank of Calcutta—The first bank in 1806 under charter. | It became Bank of Bengal in the year 1809. |
| 1819 | The Commercial Bank established. | Failed in 1828 merged with the Union Bank |
| 1824 | The Calcutta Bank established. | Failed in 1829 merged with the Union Bank. |
| 1828 | Bank of India established. | Unknown. |
| 1829 | The Union Bank was established in 1829 by Indian merchants in Calcutta. (the commercial bank and the Calcutta bank merged with it). | It failed in 1848 as a consequence of the economic crisis of 1848-49. |
| 1833 | The Agra and United Service Bank Ltd. (Earlier The Agra Bank and later The Agra and Masterman's Bank, London). | Failed in 1866. |

*(Contd...)*

| | | |
|---|---|---|
| 1833 & 1835 | Presidency Savings Banks opened at three presidency towns in 1833 and 1835. | Presidency savings banks business taken over by post offices in 1896. |
| 1835 | The Bank of Mirzapore established. | Failed in 1837. |
| 1840 | Bank of Bombay –came in 1840 under charter. | Bank of Bombay came in to problems due to speculative business and closed in 1868 and the same year the New Bank of Bombay was created which became presidency bank. |
| 1840 | North Western Bank of India established. | Failed in 1859. |
| 1842 | The Oriental Bank Corporation (Earlier, Bank of Western India) established. | In 1851, The Oriental Bank corporation, the chartered banking institution came to existence. It failed in 1884. |
| 1842 | The Agra Savings Fund established. | Failed in 1863. |
| 1843 | Bank of Madras—presidency bank came in 1843. | Later on in the year 1921 three presidency banks were merged and Imperial Bank which is the forerunner of State Bank of India (SBI) came into existence. |
| 1844 | Delhi Bank Corporation Ltd established. | Unknown. |
| 1844 | The Benares Bank established. | Failed in 1850. |
| 1844 | Simla Bank Ltd. established. | Failed in 1893. |
| 1845 | The Commercial Bank of India established. | Failed in 1866. |
| 1845 | The Cownpore Bank established. | Failed in 1851. |
| 1846 | Dacca Bank established. | Merged into Bank of Bengal in 1862. |
| 1846 | United Service Bank Ltd established. | Failed in 1894. |
| 1853 | Mercantile Bank of India is the first Exchange bank of foreign origin to arrive in 1853. | (Which is now HSBC). |
| 1858 | Chartered Bank of India, Australia and China came in 1858. | (Now Standard Chartered Bank). |
| 1860 | The Comptoire d'Escompte de Paris opened a branch in Calcutta in 1860, and another in Bombay in 1862. | Now BNP Paribas. |
| 1860 | Concept of joint stock companies with limited liability allowed by law. | |

*(Contd...)*

| | | |
|---|---|---|
| 1861 | Paper currency act passed. | Govt took over the function of issuing bank notes exclusively. |
| 1863 | National Bank of India, an exchange bank came in 1863. | |
| 1863 | The Bank of Upper India—Arrival of joint stock banks—which was established in 1863. | When it failed in 1913, some of its assets and liabilities were transferred to the Alliance Bank of Simla (opened in 1875), an exchange bank. |
| 1863 | The Punjab Bank was the first native Indian bank, formed at Rawal Pindee by Punjabi Hindus, with branches in Peshawer, Mooltan and Poona. | In 1891, the Calcutta Review noted that this bank had long been "wound up" (closed). |
| 1864 | Hongkong and Shanghai Banking Corporation came in 1864. | |
| 1865 | Allahabad Bank established in 1865. | Still functioning today, is the oldest Joint Stock Bank in India and was started by few Europeans. Nationalised in 1969. |
| 1868 | The New Bank of Bombay was established in January 1868. | After the collapse of the Bank of Bombay (Estd.:1840). |
| 1870 | District savings banks opened at selected districts in 1870. | District savings banks business taken over by post offices in 1886. |
| 1875 | Alliance Bank of Simla started as an exchange bank. | It was liquidated in 1923. |
| 1876 | Presidency banks act passed. | All three presidency banks brought under common statute. |
| 1881 | Oudh Commercial Bank, established in 1881 in Faizabad was the first entirely Indian joint stock bank. | It failed in 1958. |
| 1882 | Post Offices started opening savings bank accounts in the year 1882 and 1883. | |
| 1889 | Anyonya Co-operative Bank Limited (ACBL) located at Vadodara (formerly Baroda) in Gujarat, was the first co-operative bank in India established in 1889 with the name Anyonya Sahayakari Mandali Co-operative Bank Limited. | This bank was closed in 2008. |
| 1895 | Punjab National Bank, established in Lahore. | Inspired by swadeshi movement which has survived to the present and is now one of the largest banks in India. Nationalised in 1969. |

*(Contd...)*

| | | |
|---|---|---|
| 1899 | Nedungadi bank came into existence in the year 1899. | (Later merged with PNB in 2003.) |

**IMPORTANT EVENTS IN 20TH CENTURY AND AFTER**

| Year | Event | Remarks |
|---|---|---|
| 1902 | Citi Bank opened branch in Calcutta. | |
| 1902 | State Bank of Saurashtra established. | Made subsidiary of SBI in 1959. |
| 1904 | Co-operative credit societies act enacted. | |
| 1904 | City Union Bank established. | |
| 1906 | Canara Bank established. | Nationalised in 1969. |
| 1906 | Bank of India established. | Nationalised in 1969. |
| 1906 | Corporation Bank established. | Nationalised in 1980. |
| 1906 | Shamrao Vithal Co-op Bank established. | Urban Coop Bank. |
| 1906 | Cosmos Co-op Bank established. | Urban Coop Bank. |
| 1907 | Indian Bank established. | Nationalised in 1969. |
| 1908 | Bank of Baroda established. | Nationalised in 1969. |
| 1908 | Punjab & Sind Bank established. | Nationalised in 1980. |
| 1910 | Eastern bank—a foreign bank opened its branch. | Now Standard Chartered Bank. |
| 1911 | Central Bank of India, established. | Nationalised in 1969. |
| 1912 | Travancore National Bank established. | Merged in 1937 to form TNQ Bank. |
| 1913 | State Bank of Mysore established. | Made SBI subsidiary in 1959. |
| 1914 | Comilla Banking Corporation Limited established. | Merged with United Bank of India in 1950. |
| 1916 | Karur Vysya Bank established. | |
| 1916 | Sangli Bank established. | Merged with ICICI Bank in 2006. |
| 1917 | State Bank of Patiala established. | Made SBI subsidiary in 1959. |
| 1917 | Tata industrial Bank—a exchange bank established. | Was amalgamated with Central Bank of India in 1923. |
| 1918 | Bengal Central Bank Limited established in 1918 as Bengal Central Loan Company Limited. | Name changed to United Bank of India Limited and three other banks were amalgamated with it on December 18, 1950. |
| 1918 | Saraswat Co-op Bank established. | Urban Coop Bank. |
| 1919 | Quilon Bank established. | Merged in 1937 to form TNQ Bank. |

*(Contd...)*

| | | |
|---|---|---|
| 1920 | Catholic Syrian Bank, established. | |
| 1920 | State Bank of Indore established. | Made SBI subsidiary in 1959, later merged with SBI. |
| 1920 | Prudential Coop Bank established. | Urban Coop bank in Andhra Pradesh—failed and licence cancelled in 2004. |
| 1920 | The first Land Development Bank was started at Jhang in Punjab. | |
| 1921 | Tamilnadu Mercantile Bank established. | |
| 1921 | Imperial bank of India was formed by merging three presidency Banks. | Became SBI in 1955. |
| 1921 | American Express Bank opened its branch. | |
| 1922 | The Comilla Union Bank Limited established. | Merged with United Bank of India in 1950. |
| 1922 | Union Bank of India established. | Nationalised in 1969. |
| 1922 | Nainital Bank established. | |
| 1923 | Andhra Bank established. | Nationalised in 1980. |
| 1924 | Karnataka Bank established. | |
| 1925 | Syndicate Bank established. | Nationalised in 1969. |
| 1926 | Laxmi Vilas Bank established. | |
| 1927 | Dhanalaxmi Bank established. | |
| 1927 | Palai Central Bank was founded in 1927 as a commercial bank with its headquarters in Palai, Kerala. | It was ordered to be liquidated in 1960 by Kerala High Court on a petition moved by the Reserve Bank of India. |
| 1929 | South Indian Bank established. | |
| 1930 | Land mortgage banks act enacted. | |
| 1930 | Vysya Bank established. | (Later became ING Vysya Bank in 2002). |
| 1931 | Vijaya Bank established. | Nationalised in 1980. |
| 1932 | The Hooghly Bank established. | Merged with United Bank of India in 1950. |
| 1933 | UCPDC was first published in 1933. The Banking Commission of the ICC approved the latest revision in October 2006. | This latest version, UCPDC 600, formally commenced on 1 July 2007. |
| 1935 | RBI was established under RBI Act 1934. | |
| 1936 | Bank of Maharashtra established. | Nationalised in 1969. |

*(Contd...)*

| | | |
|---|---|---|
| 1936 | United Western Bank established. | Merged with IDBI bank in 2006. |
| 1936 | Central Exchange Bank of India promoted by Central Bank of India in 1936. | London branch of Central Exchange Bank of India was taken over by Barclays Bank in 1938. |
| 1936 | Bank of Dewas, established in 1936. | Merged with State Bank of Indore in1965. |
| 1937 | Indian Overseas Bank established. | Nationalised in 1969. |
| 1937 | TNQ bank formed by merger of two banks. | the Travancore National and Quilon Bank (TNQ Bank) failed in 1938. |
| 1938 | Dena Bank established. | Nationalised in 1969. |
| 1938 | Jammu & Kashmir Bank established. | |
| 1940 | Federal Bank established. | |
| 1940 | Lord Krishna Bank established. | Merged with Centurion Bank of Punjab in 2007. CBOP merged with HDFC Bank in 2008. |
| 1941 | Dewas Senior Bank established. | Merged with State Bank of Indore in 1965. |
| 1941 | State Bank of Hyderabad established. | Made SBI subsidiary in 1959. |
| 1941 | Bombay Mercantile Co-op Bank established. | Urban Coop Bank. |
| 1943 | Oriental Bank of Commerce established. | Nationalised in 1980. |
| 1943 | UCO Bank established. | Nationalised in 1969. |
| 1943 | Bank of Rajasthan established. | (Merged with ICICI Bank in 2010). |
| 1943 | Hindustan Commercial Bank established. | (Merged with PNB in 1986). |
| 1943 | Ratnakar Bank established. | |
| 1943 | State Bank of Jaipur established. | Made SBI subsidiary in 1959, Merged to form State Bank of Bikaner & Jaipur in 1963. |
| 1944 | State Bank of Bikaner established. | Made SBI subsidiary in 1959, Merged to form State Bank of Bikaner & Jaipur in 1963. |
| 1945 | State Bank of Travancore established. | Made SBI subsidiary in 1959. |
| 1947 | FERA enacted (foreign exchange regulation act). | |

*(Contd...)*

| | | |
|---|---|---|
| 1948 | IFCI established. | IFCI was changed in 1993 from a statutory corporation to a company under the Indian Companies Act, 1956. Subsequently, the name of the company was also changed to "IFCI Limited" with effect from October 1999. |
| 1949 | RBI was nationalized. | |
| 1949 | Banking companies act enacted. | Later changed to Banking Regulation Act, 1949 as per amending Act of 1965 (Act No. 23 of 1965) and this act gave vast powers to RBI over banking sector. |
| 1950 | United Bank of India was formed. | Nationalised in 1969. |
| 1951 | Primary Agriculture Credit societies<br>District central coop banks<br>State central Coop Banks established. | |
| 1955 | State Bank of India was created by an act of parliament. | Took over Imperial Bank. |
| 1955 | ICICI formed | Merged in 2002 with ICICI Bank |
| 1956 | RBI introduced selective credit control. | Selective credit control on all the commodities were withdrawn by RBI in the year 1996 except stipulation of margin on stocks of sugar.<br>Requirement of prior approval was discontinued in the year 2000. |
| 1957 | Export Credit Guarantee Corporation was set up to provide insurance cover for export business for banks and exporters. | |
| 1959 | SBI subsidiaries banks act was passed. | 8 Darbar banks made subsidiaries of State Bank. |
| 1960 | RBI was given powers to enforce merger and amalgamations of banks. | |
| 1960 | Credit guarantee scheme for SSI, started by RBI. | |
| 1962 | Deposit Insurance Corporation formed. | |
| 1963 | State Bank of Bikaner and State Bank of Jaipur merged. | SBBJ formed. |

*(Contd...)*

| | | |
|---|---|---|
| 1963 | Agricultural Refinance Corporation was established by an Act of Parliament. | it was renamed as Agricultural Refinance and Development Corporation (ARDC) by amending the original Act in 1975.<br>Merged with NABARD in 1982. |
| 1963 | Act passed for creation of APMCs. | Agricultural produce market committees. |
| 1963 | Limitation Act 1963. | Revised act. |
| 1964 | Bank of America opened branch in Mumbai. | |
| 1964 | Minimum support price for agri. produces introduced. | |
| 1964 | Food Corporation of India created by an act. | |
| 1964 | IDBI formed under an act. | Later merged with IDBI Bank. |
| 1965 | RBI started Credit Authorisation Scheme (CAS). | RBI withdrew the credit authorization scheme in the year 1988 and in its place; another scheme called Credit Monitoring Arrangement (CMA) ' was introduced. |
| 1967 | UAPA 1967 [Unlawful Activities (Prevention) Act, 1967] enacted. | 1967 (UAPA) has been amended by the Unlawful Activities (Prevention) Amendment Act, 2008. Government issued an Order dated August 27, 2009 detailing the procedure for implementation of Section 51A of the Unlawful Activities (Prevention) Act, 1967 relating to the purposes of prevention of, and for coping with terrorist activities. |
| 1968 | Madhavpura Mercantile Coop Bank established. | Urban Coop Bank in Gujarat failed in 2001. |
| 1969 | Social control on banks brought in. | |
| 1969 | Lead Bank Scheme introduced by RBI. | Later service area approach introduced. |
| 1969 | 14 major banks were nationalized. | |
| 1969 | Repco bank established. | |
| 1970 | HUDCO established. | |
| 1970 | non-resident external accounts (NRE) scheme introduced. | |

*(Contd...)*

| | | |
|---|---|---|
| 1971 | Industrial Reconstruction Corporation Limited was set up. | It was renamed as Industrial Reconstruction Bank of India w.e.f. Mar. 20, 1985 under IRBI Act, 1984 to take over the function of IRC. During 1997 the bank was converted to a joint stock company by naming it Industrial Investment Bank of India. |
| 1971 | Credit Guarantee Corporation formed. | Later became DICGC in 1978. |
| 1972 | The Differential Rate of Interest (DRI) Scheme was instituted in 1972. | To cater to the needs of the weaker sections of the society and for their upliftment. |
| 1973 | A minimum lending rate was prescribed on all loans, except for the priority sector. | |
| 1974 | Priority Sector concept introduced by RBI. | |
| 1974 | Reserve Bank issued detailed guidelines on consortium advances based on a committee report. | Revised guidelines were again issued in 1987. |
| 1975 | Foreign currency non-resident deposit (FCNR) scheme introduced. | In the year 1993, RBI discontinued FCNR deposit scheme and in its place allowed FCNR-bank scheme on similar line. |
| 1975 | Regional Rural Banks established. | Subsequently Consolidation of RRBs was done by amalgamating RRBs sponsored by the same bank within a State as per the recommendations of the Vyas Committee (2004). |
| 1975 | R.K. Talwar Committee formed to look into customer service area and give recommendations. | Goiporia Committee in 1986, again to look into customer service area and give recommendations. |
| 1975 | Tandon Committee report on working capital—<br>Inventory norms introduced. | Later Chore Committee (1979) went into these recommendations and it agreed to continue. |
| 1977 | Housing Development Finance Corporation (HDFC) came into existence as premier housing finance company. | |

*(Contd…)*

| | | |
|---|---|---|
| 1978 | DICGC formed by merger of Credit Guarantee Corporation and Deposit Insurance Corporation. | |
| 1978/79 | Green revolution achieved. | Record grain output of 131 million tons in 1978-79. This established India as one of the world's biggest agricultural producers. |
| 1980 | Integrated Rural Development Programme (IRDP) started. | |
| 1980 | 6 more banks nationalised. | |
| 1982 | NABARD established. | Took over ARDC. |
| 1982 | EXIM Bank established. | |
| 1984 | Banks were permitted to undertake merchant banking activities through subsidiaries. | Many banks accordingly set up subsidiaries for undertaking merchant banking and securities market related activities, equipment leasing, hire purchase, mutual funds, housing finance, and venture capital. |
| 1984 | MICR technology for clearing introduced in Bombay. | |
| 1985 | Partial computerisation of banks started—AELPMs introduced. | |
| 1985 | Govt approved nomination rules for bank deposits and bank lockers. | |
| 1985 | Health Code system introduced by RBI for asset classification. | Subsequently replaced by NPA norms. |
| 1986 | Consumer Protection Act, 1986, was passed by GOI. | Bank customers are covered under the act. |
| 1987 | National Housing Bank established | |
| 1987 | Legal Services Authorities Act 1987. | Made rules and provisions for promoting Lok Adalats at various courts. |
| 1987 | Board for Industrial & Financial Reconstruction—(BIFR) established. | |
| 1988 | New chapter—chapter VII, for dishonour of cheques added to NI Act, 1891. | Made effective from the year 1989. |
| 1988 | Basel accord I on bank capital issued. | |
| 1989 | Certificate of deposits introduced. | |
| 1990 | SIDBI established. | |

*(Contd...)*

| | | |
|---|---|---|
| 1990 | Commercial paper introduced by RBI. | |
| 1991 | The Bank of Credit and Commerce International (BCCI) business in India is liquidated. | SBI took over the business in 1994 through its subsidiary. |
| 1991 | Balance of payment crisis faced by the country. | |
| 1991 | Financial sector reforms started—<br>Prudential norms introduced to banks introduced—income recognition, asset classification, and provisioning norms.<br>Other reforms started. | Narasimham Committee Report-I in 1991.<br>Narasimham Committee-II in 1998. |
| 1991 | Nayak committee went into assessment of working capital limits for small scale industries and turnover method introduced. | |
| 1991 | SWIFT communication system made available to banks for international transactions. | |
| 1992 | Prudential norms for banks introduced by RBI. | IRAC norms, provisioning requirement prescribed. |
| 1992 | NRNR deposit scheme for NRIs introduced. | Scheme withdrawn w.e.f. 1-4-2002. |
| 1992 | RBI introduced dual exchange rate system and allowed partial convertibility of rupee. | Under this 40% of remittance received was to be exchanged at official rate of RBI and 60% was allowed to be converted at market rate. |
| 1993 | RBI scraped the dual exchange rate system and introduced uniformly market determined rates. | |
| 1993 | Debt Recovery Tribunals Act passed. | DRTs created. |
| 1993 | Government embarked on a recapitalisation programme of nationalised banks beginning from the financial year 1993-94. | The total capital contribution by the Government to nationalised banks up to March 1998 aggregated ₹ 20,046 crores. |
| 1993 | New Bank of India was merged with PNB. | |
| 1993 | Obtaining photographs of account holders was prescribed for banks. | |
| 1993 | FCNR-B scheme introduced. | |
| 1994 | Public sector banks entered capital market for public issue. | SBI and OBC were the first to do it. |

*(Contd...)*

| | | |
|---|---|---|
| 1994 | Country achieved current account convertibility. | Official exchange rate was abolished. |
| 1994 | HDFC Bank established. | New generation private sector bank. |
| 1994 | UTI Bank established. | Later became Axis Bank New generation private sector bank. |
| 1994 | Indusind Bank established. | New generation private sector bank. |
| 1994 | Times Bank established. | Times Bank merged with HDFC Bank in the year 2000. |
| 1994 | Global Trust Bank established. | Merged with Oriental Bank of Commerce in 2004. |
| 1994 | Centurion Bank established. | Merged with Bank of Punjab in 2005 to form CBOP which merged with HDFC in 2008. |
| 1994 | IDBI Bank established—public sector bank. | IDBI merged with the bank in 2005. |
| 1994 | Defaulters list called by RBI for circulation. | In 1999 willful default defined and guidelines for reporting issued. |
| 1995 | Bank of Punjab established. | Merged with Centurion Bank in 2005 to form CBOP which merged with HDFC in 2008. |
| 1995 | Development Credit Bank established. | Originally started in 1930 as a co-operative bank and converted into a commercial bank in the year 1995. New generation private sector bank. |
| 1995 | Reserve Bank of India started Banking Ombudsman Scheme. | The Banking Ombudsman Scheme was revised during the years 2002 and 2006. Covers all Commercial Banks, Regional Rural Banks and Scheduled Primary Co-operative Banks under its scope. |
| 1995 | Loan system for credit delivery started. | In 2001 fresh guidelines issued. |
| 1995 | Bridge loans barred by RBI. | RBI allowed banks to sanction bridge loans in 1997 and issued guidelines. |
| 1995 | The first RIDF was established with NABARD in 1995-96 to provide loans to the State Governments for financing rural infrastructure projects. | Banks were asked to deposit the shortfall in priority sector lending with NABARD. |

*(Contd…)*

| | | |
|---|---|---|
| 1996 | ICICI Bank established. | New generation private sector bank. ICICI merged in 2002. |
| 1996 | Local area banks were allowed. | First bank Coastal Local Area Bank Ltd., Vijayawada, Andhra Pradesh in 1999. |
| 1996 | ATMs started by PSU banks. | |
| 1996 | Multiple banking arrangements and loan syndication started. | RBI allowed discretion to banks. |
| 1997 | Deposit interest rates freed by RBI. | |
| 1997 | Credit Monitoring Arrangement was finally withdrawn. | |
| 1997 | RBI permitted banks to decide on the methods of working capital finance. Third method of lending called as cash budget method was introduced. | |
| 1997 | S.S. Tarapore Committee report to "lay the road map" to capital account convertibility submitted. | |
| 1997 | A new approach to on-site inspection of banks was adopted from the cycle of inspections commencing from July 1997. | The focus shifted to the evaluation of total operations and performance of the banks under the CAMELS system (Capital Adequacy, Asset Quality, Management, Earnings, Liquidity System and Controls) for domestic commercial banks. |
| 1997 | Banks started issuing citizen's charters to public. | |
| 1998 | Kisan credit cards launched. | Innovative credit delivery to farmers started by NABARD. |
| 1999 | Asset Liability Management system for banks introduced. | Guidelines issued in 1998. |
| 1999 | Provisioning for standard assets introduced. | At 0.25%. |
| 1999 | Banks were allowed to undertake Forward Rate Agreements/Interest Rate Swaps (FRAs/IRS) as a product. | |
| 1999 | NRSR scheme for NRIs introduced. | Scheme withdrawn w.e.f. 1-4-2002. |
| 1999 | Coastal Local Area Bank Ltd., Vijayawada, Andhra Pradesh established. | First local area bank. |

*(Contd...)*

| | | |
|---|---|---|
| 1999 | Foreign Exchange Management Act enacted. | Replaced FERA. |
| 2000 | Capital Local Area Bank Ltd, Nakodar, Punjab established. | |
| 2000 | South Gujarat Local Area Bank Ltd, Gujarat established. | Merged with Bank of Baroda in 2004. |
| 2000 | Vinayak Local Area Bank Ltd, Sikar, Rajasthan established. | In 2002, RBI cancelled the licence issued to Vinayak local Area Bank Ltd. |
| 2000 | Banks started their exposure to retail credit from the year 2000 onwards and Home loans became very popular. | Education loan was started by banks. It started with a Supreme Court order to all public sector banks in the year 1999 to extend loans to students getting admitted in private technical colleges. |
| 2000 | Core banking solution introduced in PSU banks. | |
| 2000 | CGTMSE scheme started for SSI. | Guarantee scheme. |
| 2000 | Liquidity Adjustment Facility (LAF). started by RBI. | Used this as a monetary tool to suck excess liquidity in the system through repo auctions and injects liquidity to the system through reverse repo auctions. |
| 2001 | Krishna Bhima Samruddhji Local Area Bank (Karnataka and Andhra Pradesh) established. | |
| 2001 | Online tax accounting system (OLTAS) scheme introduced in banks. | |
| 2001 | Corporate debt restructuring mechanism-CDR, introduced by RBI for large corporate borrowers. | |
| 2001 | Union Budget 2000-01 announced the establishment of a Credit Information Bureau (India) Ltd. (CIBIL). | With a view to strengthening the legal mechanism and facilitating credit information bureaus to collect, process and share credit information on borrowers of bank/FIs, |
| 2001 | Terrorist attack on USA. | 9/11 attack. |
| 2002 | Securitisation Act, 2002 passed. | |
| 2002 | First asset reconstruction company, ARCIL was formed. | |

*(Contd...)*

| | | |
|---|---|---|
| 2002 | NI Act sec. 131 amended. | Collecting bank responsibility enlarged. |
| 2002 | PMLA-2002 (Prevention of Money Laundering Act) passed. | |
| 2002 | Bancassurance was allowed. | Tie up for marketing insurance products by banks allowed. |
| 2003 | Kotak Mahindra Bank established. | By converting a NBFC established in 1985. New generation private sector bank. |
| 2003 | Interest on SB @ 3.5% prescribed by RBI. | |
| 2003 | Loan interest rates freed, BPLR introduced. | |
| 2003 | CBLO introduced. | |
| 2003 | Exchange traded Interest Rate Derivatives (IRDs) allowed for banks. | In the first phase, banks can transact only in interest rate futures on notional bonds and T-Bills for the limited purpose of hedging the risk in their underlying investment portfolio. |
| 2004 | Basel II, the second of the Basel Accords, published in June 2004. | Recommendations on banking laws and regulations issued by the Basel Committee on Banking Supervision. |
| 2004 | ATM sharing introduced—NFS started. | By RBI. |
| 2004 | RTGS introduced by RBI. | |
| 2004 | KYC detailed guidelines issued by RBI. | Originally issued in 2002. |
| 2004 | Yes Bank established. | New generation private sector bank. |
| 2005 | SME concept brought in by GOI. | |
| 2005 | NEFT introduced by RBI. | |
| 2005 | Reporting by banks to FIU-IND started. | |
| 2005 | RTI Act passed. | |
| 2005 | The Credit Information Act was enacted in May 2005, and rules and regulations thereunder were also notified. | The Act empowered the Credit Information Companies to collect information relating to all borrowers and conferred upon the Reserve Bank the power to determine policy in relation to the functioning of credit information companies and also give directions to such companies. |

*(Contd...)*

| | | |
|---|---|---|
| 2005 | Banking cash transaction tax (BCTT) introduced by GOI. | BCTT withdrawn in the year 2009. |
| 2006 | Banking Codes & Standards Board of India (BCSBI) formed as a voluntary organisation of banks. The board brought out standard code for banks, for implementation in July 2006. | Issued revised code in August 2009 and the copies of these standards were supplied to every customer of the bank. |
| 2006 | RBI appointed S.S. Tarapore Committee again to set out the framework for fuller Capital Account Convertibility. | Report submitted. |
| 2006 | No frills accounts/basic banking accounts introduced. | Simplified KYC procedure prescribed. |
| 2008 | Major bank crisis in USA. | The collapse of Lehmann Brothers Inc. |
| 2008 | State Bank of Saurashtra merged with SBI. | |
| 2008 | Electronic clearing services—credits, debits started by RBI. | |
| 2008 | Cheque truncation introduced in Delhi NCR. | |
| 2008 | Speed clearing introduced by RBI. | |
| 2008 | ASBA facility started by banks. | |
| 2008 | "Committee on Financial Inclusion" under the Chairmanship of Dr. C. Rangarajan. | The Committee submitted its final report to Hon'ble Union Finance Minister on 04 January 2008. |
| 2010 | State Bank of Indore merged with SBI.<br>Bank of Rajasthan merged with ICICI Bank. | |
| 2010 | Savings interest increased to 4%—RBI. | |
| 2010 | Base Rate concept introduced. | |
| 2010 | Basel III framework published. | The G20 leaders officially endorsed the Basel III framework on 11-12th of November 2010. |
| 2010 | Provisioning Coverage Ratio prescribed by RBI. | At 70%. |
| 2011 | IFRS introduced for Banks. | International Financial Reporting Standards. |

# Bibliography

*The Cambridge Economic History of India*, Volume 2 (by Dharma Kumar, Tapan Raychaudhuri, Meghnad Desai).

*The History of British India—A Chronology* (by John F. Riddick).

*An Economic History of India—From Pre-Colonial Times to 1991* (by Dietmar Rothermund).

Wiki/Main Page.

"Banking on the page of history: Asiatic Society seminar: focuses on how the sector went from strength to strength" by Sajjadur Rahman published on February 19, 2010.

"Workings of a Nineteenth Century Indigenous Banking System: A Case in Support of Free Banking" by Malavika Nair.

*The Fall of Arbuthnot & Co* by Rangaswamy Srinivasan.

rbi.org.in/home.aspx

*Indian Finance, Currency and Banking* (1914) by Doraiswami S.V.

RBI—Evolution of banking in India.

Speech by Deepak Mohanty, Executive Director, Reserve Bank of India—"Perspectives on Lending Rates in India"—delivered at the Bankers' Club, Kolkata on 11th June 2010.

The Address at (FIMMDA) by Dr. Y.V. Reddy, Deputy Governor, Reserve Bank of India, on June 3, 1998 at Mumbai on—Interest Rates in India : Status and Issues.

*The Story of Madras* by Glyn Barlow.

*Modern Banking in India* by S.K. Muranjan—Sydenham College, 1st August 1940.

The Divergence of the Economic Fortunes of Hindus and Muslims in British India: A Comparative Institutional Analysis by Anantdeep Singh.

*Financial Chapter in the History of Bombay city* 1910 by D.E. Wacha.

Report of Bengal Provincial Banking Enquiry Committee-1929-30.

Maharashtra State Gazetteers of Greater Bombay District.

Fiery Dragons: Banks, Moneylenders and Microfinance in Burma by Sean Turnell, Nordic Institute of Asian Studies.

*A Handbook of London Bankers* (1890) by Price, Frederick George Hilton.